On Cultural Rights

On Cultural Rights

The Equality of Nations and the Minority Legal Tradition

William Kurt Barth

MARTINUS
NIJHOFF
PUBLISHERS

LEIDEN • BOSTON
2008

This book is printed on acid-free paper.

Library of Congress Cataloging-in-Publication Data

Barth, William Kurt.
On cultural rights : the equality of nations and the minority legal tradition / William Kurt Barth.
p. cm. Includes bibliographical references.
ISBN 978-90-04-16842-8 (hardback: alk. paper) 1. Minorities--Legal status, laws, etc. 2. Multiculturalism -- Law and legislation. 3. Minorities -- Legal status, laws, etc. -- Canada. 4. Multiculturalism -- Law and legislation -- Canada. 5. Minorities -- Legal status, laws, etc. -- Europe. 6. Multiculturalism -- Law and legislation -- Europe. I. Title.
K3242.B37 2008
346.01'3--dc22

2008018962

ISBN 978 90 04 168428

Koninklijke Brill NV incorporates the imprints Brill, Hotei Publishing, IDC Publishers, Martinus Nijhoff Publishers and VSP.

PRINTED IN THE NETHERLANDS

For my darling Linda

Contents

List of Charts

Acknowledgements

It is said that success has a thousand fathers while failure is an orphan. If this book proves successful, it is only because of the help offered me by so many colleagues, friends, and family members.

My enduring gratitude goes to Dr. Desmond King, my academic supervisor in Oxford, where I researched my thesis which served as the basis for this book. Dr. King's own writings have served as much an inspiration as an education for me. His numerous books and articles, and his contributions to the field of political scholarship, are so extensive and so revered throughout the world, that it was difficult for me to come to terms with the fact that I was to be his student. His work on social citizenship gave me the idea to continue his analysis by researching how the cultural, as much as the social aspect of the right, is an important component to citizenship. His highly respected works on the struggles of African-Americans inspired me to determine how international law might provide hope of some relief for the plight of minority groups. He gave unselfishly of his time and expertise from the very beginning. If my research makes any contribution to the field, it is primarily because of him.

My wife Linda has displayed nothing but courage in helping me from the beginning; she has provided inspiration and faced many challenges during the progress of this work. She patiently listened to my readings of each chapter, and assisted me with editing. I dedicate this book to her. Candice, our daughter, has been supportive throughout my research and both Linda and I are grateful to and proud of her.

I am thankful that my mother, Geneva 'Jean' Victoria Barth, is here to see this research through to its completion. If this work is a source of pride to my mother, it is only because of the values she instilled into me from an early age. I offer a special dedication of this work to her, as well as to honour the memory of my father, the late Philip F. Barth. He would have placed great value on my Oxford experience. Not only would he have enjoyed visiting me in Oxford, he would also have offered extensive comments about my research findings.

While living as a student in Oxford and researching the materials for this book, I was honoured to be associated with the Department of Politics, the Rothermere American Institute, and St Antony's College. My sincere gratitude goes to Andrew Baldwin and Gillian Rathbone for their invaluable proof-reading of my manuscript. Marc Stears served as my principal examiner in Oxford, and helped me to improve my thesis. For their guidance in my research, special thanks to Guy-Goodwin Gill, David Miller, Alan Ryan, Ann Wawso, Elisabeth Fraiser, Rosemary Foot, Sandra Freedman, Christopher McCrudden, Sir Marrick Goulding, Gillian Cooke, Mrs. Jill Flitter, Pauley Friedhoff, Daisuke Ikemoto, and Cecile Reboul. From outside the Oxford community, my heartfelt thanks for the assistance provided by Francisco Francioni, Martin Scheinin, Patrick Thornberry, and J.R. Miller.

For lending me needed support during my research, my endearing gratitude, as always, goes to my sisters and brothers, Harilyn and Adam Fast, Rochelle and Gary Garmona, Rochelle Gerstein (for her valuable comments) and Jack Barth. I also pay special tribute to Linda's parents, Aida and the late Alfredo Bonifacio, and all my in-laws, especially Brenda and Lamar Lafave. My sincere admiration goes to my cousins Dr. Bena Fisher (who visited and helped through my academic challenges in Oxford), Sarah and Ricardo Yanez, as well as to all my nieces or nephews, for their support with this project. And I record my heartfelt appreciation for the assistance given to me by my dear friends on both sides of the Atlantic; I ask for their understanding in that they are too numerous to mention each of them by name.

Special thanks to Robert B. Reich, Barbara Sziraki, Nelson Diaz and Sara Manzano, the Revd Cecil Murray, Steven Brown, Tom Flesch and Amy Kafton, Wayne Mason, David and Diane Romero, Terry Dolan, the late John Kuhn and his mother Madeleline Kuhn, David and Debbi Pill, and Robert Devon Jones for their unwavering support.

To you, the reader, thank you for spending time with this book which spans subjects in international law, history and politics. It is my hope that an understanding of the subjects covered herein may help bring about a better world.

William K. Barth

Table of Abbreviations

Declaration on the Rights of Minorities	UN Declaration of the Rights of Persons Belonging to National or Ethnic, Religious and Linguistic Minorities, 1992
ECJ	European Court of Justice
The European Convention for Human Rights	The European Convention for the Protection of Human Rights and Fundamental Freedoms
Framework Convention	European Framework Convention for the Protection of National Minorities, 1994
Genocide Convention	Convention on the Prevention and and Punishment of the Crime of Genocide, 1948
HRC	United Nations' Human Rights Committee
ICCPR	International Covenant on Civil and Political Rights, 1966
Lovelace	Sandra Lovelace v. Canada
Minority Schools Opinion	Minority Schools in Albania, Advisory Opinion of April 6, 1935
Royal Commission	Report of the Royal Commission on Aboriginal Peoples

Section I

The Minority Legal Tradition

Chapter 1

On Cultural Rights: Introduction, Research Methodology, and Literature Review

1.1. *Introduction*

Theorists, academics, policy makers, and citizens have intense discussions about whether government should provide legal rights and exemptions as well as government-sponsored programmes for minority groups. The topic has important empirical implications for states because of the variety and complexity of questions raised by the existence of minority groups. Some minority groups suffer from invidious forms of discrimination resulting in poverty, social injustice, and inequality. Other minority groups aspire to autonomy, independence or secession from the state, which can lead to ethnic conflict and civil war. While not all minorities suffer these circumstances, questions about how minority groups should be recognised and treated have challenged states for over a century.

The normative discussion of political theorists on multiculturalism, a topic which incorporates the issue of minority rights, does not appear to analyse all the literature available that addresses the history of the minorities question. The normative literature on the subject neither provides a clear definition of multiculturalism nor does it adequately address the question of what exactly constitutes a multicultural policy. Political theorists engage in discussions about whether minorities should receive rights, privileges or exemptions from the state. They rarely incorporate the historical and legal background which bears upon the research question. A lengthy history within international law addresses the question of state obligations to minorities. Starting with the League of Nations' minority protection treaty system (1920) and continuing through the United Nations' conventions, declarations and treaties affecting minority groups, the international community has established a substantial body of legal standards that encourages recognition of minority groups. In addition, regional institutions such as the Council of Europe have also established a regime for minority protections. I describe the international evolution of this regime as the *minority legal tradition*. And, I refer to the various international treaties, conventions, and declarations that establish standards for the recognition of minority groups as an inclusive *minority regime*.[1]

My research reduces the distance between the political theory on multiculturalism and the large body of literature in the fields of history and international law that recognise the existence of minority groups. Through a qualitative examination of empirical research on the minority regime, I endeavour to address the normative question of whether minority groups actually receive differential or special treatment.

I accomplish the task in four sections. In my first, I provide an introduction to the minority legal tradition. Chapter 1 includes an extensive literature review on the history of minority rights law as well as on the political theory of multiculturalism. It also contains a discussion of the various methodologies I employ to answer the research question. In section two I examine the history and theoretical implications of minority rights within international law. This section covers two chapters which analyse the minority legal tradition beginning with the establishment of the League of Nations' minority protection treaty system through to the passage of the United Nations' human rights treaty system. Chapter 2 is a historical chapter that traces the early legal history of the minority regime after the formation of the League of Nations. Chapter 3 researches the development of the minority regime as an aspect of the United Nations' human rights treaty system and focuses particular attention on two international treaties, namely, the *Convention on the Punishment and Prevention of Genocide, 1948*, and the *International Covenant on Civil and Political Rights, 1966*.[2]

Section three incorporates Chapters four and five which deal with my two case studies that are used as empirical research models for the recognition of minority groups. Chapter 4 is my case study about how the minority regime influences Canada's recognition of Aboriginal peoples. This chapter discusses implications of the increasing political and legal recognition by international institutions of indigenous peoples such as Aboriginal Canadians. Specifically, it examines proceedings

[1] I refer mainly to the *ICCPR*, 999UNTS 171, Article 27 (minority rights), *Declaration on the Rights of Persons Belonging to National or Ethnic, Religious and Linguistic Minorities, 1992*, Resolution Adopted By The General Assembly, Forty- Seventh Session, UN Document A/RES/47/135, 3 February 1993, *Convention on the Prevention and Punishment of the Crime of Genocide, 1948*, 78 UNTS 277, *Framework Convention for the Protection of National Minorities, 1994*, Entry into force, 1/2/98, ETS No. 157, and the *European Charter for Regional or Minority Languages*, Strasbourg, 5.XI.1992. However, I also incorporate by reference all UN instruments that protect the rights of minority groups.

[2] *Convention on the Prevention and Punishment of the Crime of Genocide, 1948*, 78 UNTS 277, HMSO, Misc. No. 2 (1966), Cmnd. 2904; *ICCPR*, 999 UNTS 171; UK Treaty Series No. 6 (1977); Cmnd. 6702.

and cases before the United Nations' Human Rights Committee that affect the rights of Aboriginal Canadians.

My second case study dealt with in Chapter 5, considers how the minority regime affects groups that defy what Will Kymlicka identifies as standard minority group categories such as immigrants, indigenous peoples, or so-called national minorities. This chapter researches the Roma peoples of Europe and determines how minority rights influence state recognition of the Roma minority group. Specifically, I examine legal cases filed by the Roma before the European Court on Human Rights (ECHR). The cases involve police torture and summary execution of the Roma by various states, as well as the eviction of Roma caravan-trailers by Great Britain. This second case study provides a particular challenge because the Roma are identified, in part, by a cultural practice of *nomadism* or travelling. The Roma do not establish permanent residence (sedentarism) in a particular European nation-state and, instead, must be recognised by international political institutions operating at the transnational or supra-national level. The Romas' nomadism has also been the focus of persecution by European powers against the Roma peoples (Gypsies) that includes not only expulsion from most European states, but also slavery in Romania (19th century) and genocide of an estimated 600,000 Roma in Germany (20th century).

Chapter 6 summarises the general principles we gain by researching the minority legal tradition. Specifically, I discuss the implications of the minority regime for domestic recognition of minority groups. That is, how the jurisprudence of minority rights cases decided by the United Nations' Human Rights Committee and the European Court of Human Rights becomes diffused into the domestic legal and political order. Further, what are implications of this international jurisprudence for normative discussions on multiculturalism? From my empirical research on the minority legal tradition, I aspire to close a rarely discussed gap between the disciplines of history, law, political theory and international relations about the subject of multiculturalism. It is important that researchers close this gap because of the group poverty, ethnic violence, and civil war, as well as the coercive state practices that frequently arise concerning the treatment of minority groups.

1.1a. *What is a Cultural Right?*

Extensive literatures (section 1.3) cover the subject of multiculturalism. I use the terms cultural rights and minority rights interchangeably. However, clarification is necessary for distinguishing the context for these two different terminologies. Cultural rights comprise an aspect of human rights in that they are universal in character and guarantee all persons the right to access their culture. The United Nations' minority regime only grants cultural protection to qualified classes of persons, that is, national, ethnic (inclusive of race), linguistic, and religious minority groups. The UN's human rights covenant, namely, the *International Covenant on Civil and Political Rights, 1966 (ICCPR)*[3] identifies these particular minority group classifications as a response to state structures, themselves controlled by a dominant national group. Because most states maintain a national, in contrast to a civic character, sub-dominant groups require treaty protection.

The world's states started two world wars (20th century) that resulted in human death tolls in excess of fifty million people, as well as repeated forcible assimilation, de-nationalisation, and genocidal campaigns. This record of state practices provides the UN with justification for establishment of a corrective, namely, the minority regime. So, while cultural rights are universal in character, they are applied by treaty to four sub-dominant classes, that is, national, ethnic, religious, and linguistic minorities. The classifications are related to that aspect of state practices responsible for creating minority groups, namely, control of the state's apparatus by a dominating national group.

Several writers conclude that political thinkers should not accept the structure or existence of the nation-state and reformulate their ideas of statecraft in terms of sub-national and super-national structures to develop a type of liberal nationalism.[4] For example, Margaret Canovan writes that theorists "should acknowledge their reliance upon their idea of the nation-state and not take the nation-state for granted" because nation-states are not established by liberal democratic means.[5] Asbjorn Eide, Chair of the United Nation's Working Group on Minorities, writes that the purpose for a minority regime is to liberalise the nation-state

> [into] a civic nation which allows for double identity and loyalty: to the civic nation as a whole, respecting the common legal code with particular emphasis on equality and non-discrimination in the common domain, and at the same time to maintain one's identity to separate ethnic, religious or linguistic groups.[6]

Protecting an individual's access to culture describes the essence of a cultural right because it goes to the interiority of personhood. There is no disagreement

---

[3] *International Covenant on Civil and Political Rights, 1966* 999UNTS 171.

[4] Canovan, Margaret. *Nationalism and Political Theory* (Cheltenham, Edward Elgar, 1996), 115.
Tamir, Yael. *Liberal Nationalism* (New Jersey, Princeton University Press, 1993), 75, 77: "...state powers should devolve to smaller, autonomous national entities on the one hand, and to larger, regional frameworks on the other."

[5] Canovan, Margaret. *Nationalism and Political Theory* (Cheltenham, Edward Elgar, 1996), 107, 115.

[6] Eide, Asbjorn. "Minority Protection and World Order: Towards a Framework for Law and Policy." Phillips, Alan and Rosas, Allan eds. *Universal Minority Rights* (Turko/Abo and London, Abo Akademi University Institute for Human Rights Minority Rights Group International, 1995), 99. The Working Group on Minorities was established in 1995 as a subsidiary organ of the UN Sub-Commission on the Promotion and Protection of Human Rights (previously called the Sub-Commission on Prevention on Discrimination and Protection of Minorities).

amongst political theorists that access to culture is necessary to develop the individual capacity for autonomy. Joseph Raz, for example, explains that only through being socialised in a culture can one tap the options which give human life meaning. Individual freedom depends on options that rely on rules which constitute those options. Culture is fundamental to individual autonomy because it provides a conglomeration of interlocking practices which constitute the range of life options open to one who is socialised in them.[7] Will Kymlicka defines cultural practices as foundational to personal autonomy. Understanding cultural narratives – language, education, religion, custom, myth, symbols, morals, ethics, history, and manners – is a necessary precondition to making intelligent judgments about how to live our lives. Culture provides options through which we identify experiences as valuable. Without culture, individuals would be left to invent everything [including language] in their own lives and all aspects of conduct.[8]

While some authors disagree about whether culture, a broad and ambiguous idea, is properly recognised as part of international treaty or domestic law, the HRC has provided clarification for the administration of cultural protection.[9] When combined with similarly concerned international treaties, conventions and declarations, the protection of minority cultural identity is ensconced as an internationally recognised aspect of the UN's human rights' treaty system.[10] Taken together, UN authorities[11]

---

[7] Raz, Joseph. "Multiculturalism: A Liberal Perspective" from *Ethics in the Public Domain: Essays in the Morality of Law and Politics* (Oxford, Clarendon Press, 1995), 175–177. Raz explains that culture is indispensable to charting the life course of successive choices.

[8] Kymlicka, Will. *Multicultural Citizenship* (Oxford, Oxford University Press, 1995), 83.

Also *see*, Capotorti, Francesco. Study on the Rights of Persons belonging to Ethnic, Religious and Linguistic Minorities (Geneva, United Nations, Centre for Human Rights, 1991), 37. Capotorti cites Leiris, Michel. *Race and Culture* (Paris, UNESCO, 1951), 20–21.

[9] Barry, Brian. *Culture and Equality An Egalitarian Critique of Multiculturalism* (Cambridge, Polity Press, Blackwell Publishers Ltd., 2001), 67.

Metcalfe, Eric William. "Are Cultural Rights Human Rights? A Cosmopolitan Conception of Cultural Rights." diss., University of Oxford, 2000, 2.

[10] Niemi, Heli. National Implementation of Findings by United Nations Human Rights Treaty Bodies A Comparative Study. (Finland, Institute for Human Rights, Abo Akademi University, 2003), 1. The UN human rights' treaty system encompasses seven treaties: *International Convention on the Elimination of All Forms of Racial Discrimination, 1966, International Covenant on Civil and Political Rights, 1966, International Covenant on Economic, Social and Cultural Rights, 1966, Convention on the Elimination of All Forms of Discrimination against Women, 1979, Convention against Torture and Other Cruel, Inhuman or Degrading Treatment or Punishment, 1984, Convention on the Rights of the Child, 1989, International Convention on the Protection of the Rights of All Migrant Workers and Members of Their Families, 1990.*

[11] *Convention on the Prevention and Punishment of the Crime of Genocide, 1946* Articles 1 and II 78 UNTS 277 (existence), *ICCPR,* Articles 1 and 2 999UNTS 171 (self-determination and cultural development), *International Covenant on Economic and Social and Cultural Rights, 1966,* Articles 13

for the protection of culture provide a broad scope of protection re-quiring states to take positive steps to guarantee individual access to culture.

A graph corpus of cultural protections arranged in six categories that include education, religion, language, economy, arts, and autonomy is incorporated in this section to provide an example of the various categories intended by minority rights, broadly defined. The common theme contained in UN's cultural rights instruments is their protection and propagation of minority identity. In contrast to mere anti-discrimination laws, cultural rights require positive action by states. They provide a remedy distinguishable from traditional civil rights in that the harm committed by state violations of the protection goes, as we discussed earlier, to an individual's personal development. Eric Metcalfe explains that the word culture derives from the Latin *cultura* meaning cultivation or the tending of natural growth. The focus of culture is upon education as the development of mental capacities and the cultivation of moral virtues.[12] Education is particularly important since it is prerequisite to minority achievement of adequate living standards as well as having the ability to access culture. "Cultural rights are closely attached to the concept of rehabilitation,"[13] particularly in under-developed countries, so that minority group members can learn basic skills enabling individuals to master conditions of poverty as a pre-requisite to accessing culture. Cultural rights mandate nation-states to accommodate minorities by subsidising minority language education and minority schools with the goal of preservation of minority identity within the states' regulatory public education framework.[14]

The religious aspect of cultural rights protects religious groups against the states' long history of religious intolerance. Because cultural rights are integrated

and 15, 993 UNTS 3 (education and access to cultural life), *International Convention on the Elimination of All Forms of Racial Discrimination,* Article 2(2), *1966,* 660 UNTS 195 (social and cultural development), *Declaration On the Elimination of All Forms of Intolerance and of Discrimination Based on Religion or Belief, 1981,* Article 5 UN doc. A/36/684 (1981) (religious education). This article is frequently applied in conjunction with Article 18 of the *ICCPR* (religious practice and belief), *International Convention on the Suppression and Punishment of the Crime of Apartheid, 1973,* Article II., Gen. Assembly Resolution 2068 (life and liberty), *Convention on the Rights of the Child, 1989* Articles 4, 8, 20, 23, 29, 30, 31 UN Doc. A/44/49 (1989) (child cultural development, identity, and nationality), *Convention Against Discrimination In Education, 1960* Articles 1,3,4,5 429 UNTS 93 (non-discrimination, minority schools and cultural education), *International Convention on the Protection of the Rights of All Migrant Workers and Members of their Families, 1990* Articles 12,16,17,18, 31 UN General Assembly Resolution 45/158 (the migrant worker's cultural rights and identity), UNESCO *Declaration of the Principles of International Cultural Co-operation, 1966* (cultural life, value and development).

12 Metcalfe, Eric William, *supra,* note 9, at 7. Pp. 14, 17.

13 Capotorti, Francesco. *Study on the Rights of Persons belonging to Ethnic, Religious and Linguistic Minorities* (Geneva, United Nations, Centre for Human Rights, 1991), 60, 100.

14 *Ibid.*

into the UN's human rights treaty system, they must comply with all other human rights' requirements and may not, by definition, permit minority groups to engage in illiberal practices and human rights' violations justified by self-interested claims that invoke a defence of cultural necessity. In contrast to the arguments raised by normative critics that minority rights sanction illiberal conduct by fundamentalist religious groups, the historical record demonstrates that states hold primary responsibility for intolerant, discriminatory and sometimes genocidal conduct against religious groups. Today, 2.2 billion people enjoy only limited freedom of thought, conscience, religion and belief. UN Special Rapporteur Elizabeth Odio Benito concludes that less than 20% of UN state members have in effect constitutional or legal provisions implementing human rights' standards on religious freedom. Further, a minority group's abuse or violation of any individual human right is clearly proscribed, as are states, under the UN's minority regime. The ICCPR's Article 27 as well as the UN's Declaration on the Rights of Minorities are required to be consistent and compliant with the UN human rights treaty system.[15] Cultural rights encourage states to take

[15] Barry 36, 40, 131, 135, 141, 157, 165, 324. Barry, Brian. "Second Thoughts – and Some First Thoughts Revisited" in Kelly, Paul ed. *Multiculturalism Reconsidered* (Oxford, Blackwell Publishers Ltd., 2002), 231. Barry argues that multicultural policy sanctions illiberal practices by religious groups such as genital mutilation (clitoridectomy) of young girls, children being denied blood transfusions in life-threatening circumstances, ritual scarring, smallpox, forced marriage, illiteracy, elimination of right to divorce, sex discrimination, ritual animal slaughter, use of mind- altering drugs, dagger-carrying, and honour killings of young women for sexual transgressions. *See also* Carens, Joseph. *Culture, Citizenship, and Community* (New York, Oxford University Press, 2000), 40, 146, 149, 154, 155. Carens adds male circumcision, wife-beating, polygamy, and widow-suicide by burning (Hindu practice of Sati), noting on page 146 that, "In the 1980s, 75–80 million females in Africa underwent some form of excision."

Eide, Asbjorn. "Final text of the Commentary to the Declaration on the Rights of Persons Belonging to National or Ethnic, Religious and Linguistic Minorities, 1992." (Geneva. United Nations, Centre for Human Rights, 2001), 12. Relying on Declaration Article 4, Eide clarifies that cultural rights are not contrary to international human rights standards and that compliance with such standards must apply to the practices of majority and minority alike. "Cultural or religious practices which violate human rights law should be outlawed for everyone, not only for minorities."

Article 5.1 of the *International Covenant on Civil and Political Rights, 1996* expressly prevents any [minority] group or person from violating a right or freedom guaranteed by the covenant.

Scheinin, Martin. "How To Resolve Conflicts Between Individual and Collective Rights." eds. Scheinin, Martin and Toivanen, Reeta. Rethinking Non-Discrimination and Minority Rights (Abo, Finland, Institute For Human Rights, Abo Akademi Univesity, 2004), 222–236. Scheinin argues that states as well as religious groups should be regulated under the same minority regime. He proposes a so-called *one-way street* approach for religious groups: this would prevent religious groups from enacting new discriminations as well as encouraging the elimination of old religious discriminations that are not fundamental to theology.

positive steps to promote material equality of religious groups as well as tolerate and recognise minority religious practice.[16]

Some commentators maintain that language, because it is so meaningful and widespread a format of transmission for a peoples' culture, is the most important of all cultural rights. In section 2.6, I review the *Minority Schools in Albania, Advisory Opinion of April 6, 1935 (Minority Schools Opinion)*[17] advising that states must permit minority language schools as a condition for minority equality. A full expression of linguistic rights mandates states to establish minority schools as well as provide for mother-tongue education within schools. Cultural rights intend for states to recognise the use of minority language in the public, judicial and private sectors as well as prevent the death of cultural languages due to lack of recognition, use, and transmission failure.[18] The category of economy also represents a critical aspect of the right, especially for groups that suffer poverty in under-developed countries or live in unequal circumstances resulting from harmful conduct by states. State action that results in social, economic, and psychological harm against groups stems from wrongful practices such as segregation, coercive assimilation, and forced migration.

The strengthening of national identity through cultural development is a prerequisite for social and economic progress in post-colonial conditions. The HRC encourages states to implement affirmative action programs to return these groups to positions equal with those of the state's majority. It also recognises that cultural rights protect traditional indigenous economic activities.[19]

Pentassuglia, Gaetano. *Minority Issues Handbook, Minorities in International Law* (London, Council of Europe Publishing, 2002), 99. The right to minority identity is not the *museumification* of cultures which are subject to inevitable processes of historical change. Instead, international law seeks to locate the processes of cultural change in the protective framework of human rights.

[16] Benito, Elizabeth Odio. "Elimination of All Forms of Intolerance and Discrimination Based on Religion or Belief" (Geneva, United Nations Publication, 1989), 33, 38.
Capotorti 68.

[17] *Minority Schools in Albania, Advisory Opinion of April 6, 1935*, Series E.-No. 11, Eleventh Annual Report of the Permanent Court of International Justice (June 15, 1934-June 15, 1935), Leyden, A.W. Sijthoff's Publishing Co.

[18] Thornberry, Patrick. *International Law and the Rights of Minorities* (Oxford, Clarendon Press, 1991), 126.
Kymlicka, Will and Patten, Alan eds. *Language Rights and Political Theory* (Oxford, Oxford University Press, 2003), 42. Recall Kymlicka's warning that half of the world's languages have disappeared in the past 500 years and that "...of the world's 6,000–7,000 languages, a couple go out of business each week."

[19] Capotorti 59.
Thornberry, Patrick. *Indigenous Peoples and Human Rights* (Manchester, Manchester University Press, 2002) 161. For example, the United States was questioned by the HRC about its withdrawal of affirmative action programmes.

Examples of Cultural Protection[21]

Education	Language	Religion	Arts	Autonomy	Economy
adaptive public education system; bi-lingual programs and courses; courses in multiculturalism and inter-cultural interaction ****	preserve linguistic identity; recognise local dialects; recognition for indigenous languages *, ****	establish and maintain religious institutions and schools; *, **, **** protect access to religious education in accordance with parental wishes	support ministries of culture or arts councils; *, ****, *****, preserve indigenous funeral objects and human remains; protect indigenous art	permit minority inter-state, intra-state, and trans-frontier contacts with national, ethnic, religious or linguistic members in host and kin states*	material equality for minority groups in law and fact through the use of affirmative action *, **, ****
minority schools (primary through to university level); financial assistance for the training of competent staff, maintenance of buildings, and grants to children attending minority schools; Preserve indigenous scientific knowledge of the natural world *, **, ****	use minority language in public services, public authorities, public administration, the courts, and organs of the state; translation services in judicial administration and court proceedings involving minority parties; guarantee use of minority language in court proceedings with minority parties *, ****	protect religious sites and holy places; protect property of religious communities; protect indigenous holy sites ****, *****,	implement long-term state plan for minority cultural development based on individual access to and freedom to participate in the cultural life of the community[22]*	insure minority group participation in national economic, education, health, nutrition, housing and settlement policy; national trade investment policy as well as development assistance; minority participation in policy decisions affecting minority at local, regional, and Federal level*	guarantee minimum subsistence level permitting individual enjoyment of culture **, *******
mother tongue education courses in public school system; pre and primary school education in child's mother tongue. **, ****, ******	support minority language books and newspapers; encourage minority language television and radio programming; public subsidy for publication of minority language press. *, ****, *****	public financing for religious activities; respect religious freedom to publish religious matter ****	support cultural associations, artist unions and minority language newspapers and press; *, ****, *****	protect right to nationality; leave and return to the country, freedom of movement and residence within the borders of the state, own property alone as well as in association with others. *, *******	preserve land, water, fish and hunting resources of indigenous peoples; protect traditional cultural economic traditional practices such as Roma "travelling" Sami reindeer husbandry, and Lapp handicrafts *,****, ********

Some are recommendations without authority and all subject to consistency with modern goals, economic progress, national unity, state sovereignty, human rights, concentration and numbers of minority populations, tenure of minority population and availability of state resources. *, **, ****, *****, ******, *******, ******** symbols reflect authorities in footnote 21.

Minority group autonomy lies at the foundation of cultural rights because it provides for maximum political and cultural development without resort to internal violence or civil war. Autonomy is distinguishable from self-determination in that the latter is associated with secession that interferes with the territorial integrity of states. Under the UN's minority regime, self-determination lies beyond the scope of protecting minority identity. Secession, partition, and independent statehood are prohibited by the minority regime. In the alternative, cultural rights provide arrangements for autonomy in regard to religious, linguistic or broader cultural matters.[20] The UN's minority regime encourages tolerance by the nation-state in that it provides a corrective to its radical excesses. As states accept broader applications of the equality principle underlying minority rights, lines separating minority rights, autonomy, and self-determination may become increasingly undistinguishable.

1.1b. *State Responsibility for the Implementation of Minority Rights*

The development of the UN's human rights treaty system inclusive of a minority regime has resulted in elevating state responsibility for the implementation of human rights obligations, as well as increasing the erosion of national sovereignty. In addition to the *ICCPR*[23], other human rights treaty bodies and treaty implementation mechanisms increase the human rights responsibilities of states. Formerly, state claims of sovereignty to remain above the rule of international

---

[20] Eide, Asbjorn. *Final text of the Commentary to the Declaration on the Rights of Minorities* (Geneva. United Nations, Centre for Human Rights, 2001), 5, 18. *See* the Declaration's Article 8.4. Capotorti 35.

[21] Cultural rights are qualified in the following authorities: *International Covenant on Civil and Political Rights, 1966*, International Covenant on Economic, Social and Cultural Rights, 1966 (ICESCR).**, Convention on the Prevention and Punishment of the Crime of Genocide, 1948, International Convention on the Elimination of All Forms of Racial Discrimination, 1966, International Convention on the Suppression and Punishment of the Crime of Apartheid, 1973, Internatinal Labour Organisation Convention No. 169 concerning Indigenous and Trial Peoples in Independent Countries, 27 June 1989 ********, Convention on the Rights of the Child,1989, International Convention on the Protection of the Rights of All Migrant Workers and Members of Their Families, 1990, Convention Against Discrimination in Education, 1960 ******, UNESCO Declaration of the Principles of International Cultural Cooperation (1966), Declaration on the Rights of Persons Belonging to National or Ethnic, Religious and Linguistic Minorities, 1992****, UNESCO Recommendation on Participation by the People at Large in Cultural Life and their Contribution to it, 1976, UNESCO Declaration on Cultural Diversity (2001). *****, Universal Declaration of Human Rights, 1948* *******

[22] Capotorti 36.

[23] *ICCPR*, 999 UNTS 171.

legal obligation was achieved by the state's use of treaty reservations as well as refusal by a state to consent to bi-lateral treaty agreements. However, the successful conclusion between states at the 23 May 1969 *Vienna Convention on the Law of Treaties*[24] that entered into force on 27 January 1980 established a new era of international obligation for states. As a result of the Vienna Convention, every international treaty must now follow the doctrine of *pacta sunt seruanda*,[25] namely, every treaty in force is binding upon the parties to it and must be performed by them in good faith. By virtue of *pacta sunt seruanda*, parties give up the right of non-performance and acquire the right to call any party to account.[26] The Vienna Convention restricts the state's ability to make treaty reservations as well as withdraw, suspend, renounce, terminate, and sever international treaty obligations.[27] The Vienna Convention is one example of the proliferation of international treaties, treaty bodies, declarations, specialised agencies, regional organisations, international tribunals, and international courts that not only increase the state's international obligations but also transform the state's purpose to include the implementation of international norms inclusive of human rights. Increasingly, states find themselves compelled by international legal obligations.

Numerous regional organisations created to enhance state strategic concerns, security interests, economic and social development also serve to erode sovereignty and the state's ability to withdraw from international human rights obligations. Lured by the economic and social incentives provided through accession to regional organisation membership, states are enticed to give up aspects of sovereignty as a condition of gaining the benefits of regional membership. These bodies have created regional mechanisms necessary to achieve state compliance with human rights that include the Organisation of American States (OAS), the Inter-American system of human rights and the Inter-American Commission and Court of Human Rights interpreting the American Declaration of the Rights and Duties of Man, 1948 and the American Convention on Human Rights, 1969[28]; the African Union's (formally Organisation of African Unity/OAU) inauguration

[24] *Vienna Convention on the Law of Treaties* 8 I.L.M. 679.
United Nations, *Treaty Series*, vol.1155, p.331.
Orlin, Theodore S., Rosas, Allan, and Scheinin, Martin, eds. *The Jurisprudence of Human Rights Law: A Comparative Interpretive Approach* (Turku/Abo, Institute for Human Rights, Abo Akademi University, 2000), 6.

[25] Meaning that treaties must be observed.
Ibid. See Vienna Convention on the Law of Treaties Article 26.

[26] Henkin, Louis. *The International Bill of Rights/The Covenant on Civil and Political Rights* (New York, Columbia University Press, 1981).

[27] *Ibid. See Vienna Convention on the Law of Treaties* Articles 19–23, 45–47, 53–58, 60, 63, 71–73.

[28] *American Convention on Human Rights*, 1969 1144 UNTS 123.

of The African Charter on Human and Peoples' Rights[29] implemented by the OAU's creation of the African Commission on Human and Peoples' Rights; The Council of Europe's sponsoring of the European Convention for the Protection of Human Rights and Fundamental Freedoms (1950)[30]establishing the European Court of Human Rights.[31]

Further erosion of the idea that states can remain above the rule of international legal norms is illustrated by the proliferation of new international judicial and quasi-judicial bodies, as well as permanent and compulsory arbitration bodies - some offering compulsory jurisdiction over state conduct and action. Since the establishment of the League of Nations' Permanent Court of International Justice[32] (section 2.6), the emergence of these new bodies works to weaken claims that the state's consent is a pre-condition to the introduction of international obligation. Though still lacking the elements of what H.L.A. Hart described in his *rule of recognition*, namely, "the absence of an international legislature, courts with compulsory jurisdiction and centrally organised sanctions....",[33] the proliferation of these new judicial bodies makes it increasingly difficult for states to evade international jurisdiction.

Since the establishment by the United Nations of the International Court of Justice (ICJ),[34] over a dozen additional international judicial bodies have been created.[35] The proliferation of new UN treaty bodies and conventions, regional organisations, and international judicial institutions create new obligations, including responsibilities for the maintenance of human rights inclusive of

---

[29] *African (Benjul) Charter on Human and Peoples' Rights*, adopted June 27, 1981, OAU Doc. CAB/LEG/67/3 rev.5, 21 I.L.M. 58 (1982), entered into force on 21 October 1986.

[30] *The European Convention for the Protection of Human Rights and Fundamental Freedoms* Rome, 4.XI.1950, ETS No. 5.

[31] Orlin, Theodore S., Rosas, Allan, and Scheinin, Martin, eds. *The Jurisprudence of Human Rights Law: A Comparative Interpretive Approach* (Turku/Abo, Institute for Human Rights, Abo Akademi University, 2000), 12 – citing Council of Europe Information Sheet no. 35 (July – December, 1994) report that ASEAN Ministers of Foreign Affairs are considering a draft *Asian Human Rights Charter*, proposed by the non-governmental Asian Human Rights Commission.

[32] *Statute of the Permanent Court of International Justice*, 19 December 1920 6 LNTS 390.

[33] Hart, H.L.A. *The Concept of Law, 2nd Edition* (New York, OUP, 1961), 214, 230, 233.

[34] *Statute of the International Court of Justice*, 26 June 1945, Annex to the Charter of the United Nations XV UNCIO Doc. 355.

[35] Shany, Yuval. *The Competing Jurisdictions of International Courts and Tribunals* (Oxford, OUP, 2003), 3–7. These include the International Criminal Court (ICC), the European Court of Human Rights (ECHR), the Court of Justice of the European Communities (ECJ), the Court of Justice of the Economic Community of West Africa (ECOWAS Court), the Caribbean Court of Justice (Caricom Court), the MERCOSUR Permanent Court of Review, and the African Court on Human and People Rights, as well as a number of bodies adjudicating both international economic and political disputes.

minority protection in the conduct of domestic affairs. Some jurists describe state obligations flowing from the new international legal environment as constituting a global covenant[36] or global constitution[37] representing *binding legal norms above states and not subject to their consent.* Of course, it has also been a principle of long standing that general international law has a tendency to become universal international law.[38]

The new international legal environment curbs the potential for such human rights abuses through an intricate, multidimensional system that, though not reliant on a centralised legislature and court system with sanction power, does successfully extend jurisdiction for a rule of law over domestic sovereignty. Jurisdiction is achieved often through indirect mechanisms similar to a one-way trap door with the state having no or few opportunities to exit. Once states enter the realm of international conduct and institutions, an action that is hard to avoid in a global economy, it becomes difficult for a state to extricate itself from international legal obligation. The phenomenon might be described as a sort of international glue that, once attached to a state party, adheres as a permanent aspect of the states' obligations to meet human rights standards inclusive of minority protection.

1.2. *Research Methodologies: The Jurisprudential Context*

My research employs legal analysis, which in this and the following section I describe as the jurisprudential context. The sub-disciplines within law provide us with an important method of assessing how the international minority regime influences the domestic order on the recognition of minority groups. Furthermore, it also influences the normative discussions on multiculturalism in several respects. In the following section, I discuss these two questions as a means of explaining the reason for my research about the minority legal tradition.

Most theoretical discussions on multiculturalism do not incorporate the minority legal tradition into their analyses. Nor does the literature clearly define what is meant by a multicultural policy. Normative discussions on multiculturalism tend to focus on extracted and isolated hypothetical examples about the domestic treatment of minority groups, namely, debates about the justification for the various exemptions, exceptions, or privileges extended by the state to minority groups.

---

36 Jackson, Robert. *The Global Covenant, Human Conduct in a World of States* (Oxford, OUP, 2000), 13–19.

37 Martin Scheinin, "When Culture Clashes with Individual Rights," European University Institute/Nordic colloquium on Cultural Rights, European University, Florence, Italy, July 2005.

38 Robinson, Nehemiah. *The Genocide Convention. Its Origins and Interpretation.* (New York, Institute of Jewish Affairs, World Jewish Congress, 1949), 13.

Nor does political theory examine multiculturalism as a question within international law. Rather, theorists tend to analyse the subject as a question of whether the domestic polity should grant recognition to the diverse interests of minority groups. Many political theorists either presume or disregard implications of the national basis imbedded into the structure of world states, as well as the substantial jurisprudence of international case law on the subject.

By contrast, treaty instruments as much as jurisprudence produced by international bodies, provide a clear definition of terms, as well as clarifying the obligation of states to their minority groups. For example, Article 27 in the *International Covenant of Civil and Political Rights, 1966*,[39] as well as the *UN Declaration on the Rights of Persons Belonging to National or Ethnic, Religious and Linguistic Minorities, 1992 (Declaration on the Rights of Minorities)*,[40] provides guidance about the obligations of states to minority groups. The HRC's legal decisions in cases brought by minority groups, as well as General Comments promulgated by the HRC, provide explanatory justification regarding state recognition of minority groups. In addition, these instruments also clarify the responsibilities of minority groups to their respective states. In my research, I use the following types of materials dealing with the international law on minorities: case law decisions including decisions of the HRC and the ECHR as well as decisions of domestic supreme courts; international legal instruments such as UN treaties, declarations, and conventions; documents and memoranda, as well as secondary source material about international organisations such as the United Nations and League of Nations from books and law review articles authored by legal scholars.

Researching the jurisprudence of minority case law decisions also illuminates the relationship between the international minority regime and the domestic legal order. Alec Stone Sweet describes the process of diffusion by international case decisions into the domestic legal order as 'constitutionalisation.'[41] As an example, Stone maintains that the European Court of Justice (ECJ)'s *supremacy doctrine* provides the opportunity for judges to enhance authority to control domestic legal and policy outcomes.[42] Further he argues that ECJ decisions have not only replaced the traditional, state-centric international system but have also judicially federalised Europe, and that the ECJ is thus "the most effective supranational judicial body in the history of the world."[43]

---

[39] *ICCPR*, 999 UNTS 171.

[40] United Nations, General Assembly, *Declaration on the Rights of Persons Belonging to National or Ethnic, Religious and Linguistic Minorities, 1992* (New York, United Nations, 18 Dec 1992) Doc. No. A/Res/47/135.

[41] Sweet, Alec Stone. *The Judicial Construction of Europe* (Oxford, OUP, 2004), 14.

[42] *Ibid.*, 20.

[43] *Ibid.*, 1.

My case studies examine the jurisprudence of international minority cases before the United Nations' Human Rights Committee, as well as the European Court of Human Rights. The minority case decisions, and the subsequent incorporation of these decisions into the domestic political and legal order, demonstrate how the process of diffusion takes place. I have selected the Aboriginal minority groups in Canada, as well as the experience of the Roma peoples in Europe, as my two case studies, in part, because of the availability of jurisprudence about these groups. To clarify, there are only a limited number of case decisions affecting states that are heard by the HRC, as well as the ECHR. As I discuss in section 3.6, individual minority complaints may only be made against states that have ratified the *First Optional Protocol (OP) to the ICCPR.*[44] While 105 different world states have ratified the OP, the United States and China are among those refusing to do so and have thus denied this forum for individual complaints to members of their own states' respective minority groups. So, as a hypothetical example, an individual complaint from an African-American against the USA, is not permitted by the HRC. African-Americans, like other US minority groups, are prevented from bringing complaints before the HRC because of the USA's failure to sign or ratify the OP. However other states, such as Canada, have signed and ratified the OP, permitting their minority groups to author individual complaints before the HRC. Several HRC decisions are available concerning Canada's indigenous minority groups. Other countries such as Sweden, Finland, and New Zealand, and Namibia, are also parties to the OP, and have participated as defendants in individual complaints requesting clarification about the state' treaty obligations to domestic minority groups.

To guard against selection bias,[45] I do not attempt to provide a broad causal reference from the HRC's Canadian case decisions. Rather, I aim to demonstrate how the process of diffusion takes place only within Canada's domestic legal-political order. Additional to case decisions by the HRC, my Roma case study discusses cases decided by the European Court of Human Rights. In analysing these decisions, I also examine how the diffusion process works in the Council of Europe. The Roma case decisions involve several different European states. In this case study, I highlight only how the legal diffusion process operates with regard to the protection of Roma within several states. Finally, in my conclusion, I discuss my findings as to how the process influences domestic recognition of minority groups as well as normative questions on multiculturalism.

---

44 *Optional Protocol to the International Covenant on Civil and Political Rights*, adopted and opened for signature, ratification and accession by General Assembly Resolution 2200A (XXI) of 16 December 1966, entry into force 23 March 1976, in accordance with Article 9, 99 UNTS 171.

45 Keohane, Robert and King, Gary and Verba, Sydney. *Designing Social Inquiry, Scientific Inference in Qualitative Research* (New Jersey, Princeton University Press, 1994), 63, 99, 105, 128.

International jurisprudence provides us with empirical applications of abstract theoretical principles. It can assist normative assessment by illustrating how liberal values such as equality are applied to empirical situations of actual conflict between groups claiming unequal or disadvantaged positions within the state's structure. For example, I use this method of analysis in sections 1.3b and 2.6 by demonstrating how the equality principle embedded in liberal theory is assessed by the Permanent Court of International Justice's *Minority Schools Opinion*.[46] The Opinion concerns a claim brought on behalf of the Greek minority group residing in Albania.

My aim is to demonstrate how the minority regime provides a new framework for states to recognise minority groups. Normative discussions on multiculturalism do not generally review the relationship between the minority regime and international organisations, nor analyse how the minority regime influences the internal structure of world states. This presents an important starting point for analysis because much of the debate about multiculturalism focuses on whether minority groups are entitled to special or differential treatment. The internationalisation of the minority regime tends to universalise or flatten the concept of differential treatment. This is because the minority regime transfers jurisdiction for minority protection – and, by implication, the subject of multiculturalism - from the domestic sphere into the international domain. Decisions about minority groups are increasingly internationalised, that is, they are transformed into a human rights obligation for all states.

The normative justification for this process recognises that states themselves are imperfect structures that promote the identity of a particular national-cultural group. The minority regime provides a corrective so that the enjoyment of culture is guaranteed for all minority groups, not just the dominant group that controls the states apparatus. That is, if the liberal objection to multiculturalism is that any particular minority group should not receive differential treatment or protection by state authority, then the character of states must somehow be corrected since they are themselves group-controlled nation-states, and generally propagate, under state authority, the culture of the state's dominant national group.

Legal analysis can also enhance theoretical understanding and advance research on the subject by examining how minority rights influence international relationships between states. The minority regime is not only international in character, but also, was established, in part, to resolve violent conflict between states. As a consequence, I assess why ratification and administration of the minority

---

[46] *Minority Schools in Albania, Advisory Opinion of April 6, 1935*, Permanent Court of International Justice, Leyden, A.W. Sijithoff's Publishing Company, Series E. – No. 11, June 15, 1934 – June 15, 1935.

regime is necessary to improve the social condition of minority groups, as well as help nations peacefully co-exist. My case studies also demonstrate why purely domestic legislative approaches to minority rights, as evidenced by the establishment of civil rights or anti-discrimination laws, do not resolve claims raised by minority groups.

With the exception of indigenous groups who were incorporated into the state's territory, as well as some religious minority groups, members of minority groups usually migrated (forced and voluntary) from different states and, for various historical reasons, co-mingle with and reside in a state different from the one of their own or ancestral birth. The host state's responsibility toward minority groups owes as much to the need for harmony within inter-state relations as to the normative concerns about minority claims. Such relationships provide a different paradigm for analysis, which can lead to fresh approaches for recognition of minority groups. Minority rights are motivated by several important objectives that differ from those usually raised by normative inquiry on multiculturalism, such as what recognition should be accorded state sovereignty, the necessity for a world system of nation-states, the preservation of peace between states, and the human rights obligations of states. These new objectives provide a different starting point for analysis that I hope produces a fresh research contribution. We may discover that, by changing the paradigm of the discussion from the domestic state into the international sphere, as well as incorporating the minority legal tradition, the intensity of the normative discussion on multiculturalism is reduced, or, even eliminated as a largely unfounded controversy.[47]

1.2a. *The Contextual Approach*

In addition to legal methods, I use case studies to provide empirical illustrations for the implementation of minority rights in different states. My case studies illustrate how international treaties influence state recognition of minority groups. These case studies provide an example of the remedies available to a minority group in a minority-state conflict as well as how minority rights differ from existing anti-discrimination laws. Finally, because minority regimes encompass a number of varied topics such as genocide protection, linguistic rights, and political autonomy, my case studies increase our understanding of how minority regimes operate in different state contexts.

Case studies help us to resolve a growing tension between the fields of political theory and international law on the issue of what is required by states to provide

[47] Gary King, Robert O. Keohane, and Sidney Verba. *Designing Social Inquiry, Scientific Inference in Qualitative Research* (New Jersey, PUP, 1994), 17.

ethno-cultural justice for minority groups. Some political theorists argue that the question be addressed on a case-by-case basis with different programmatic and policy remedies offered to various categories of minority groups. Will Kymlicka maintains that the more cases about minorities that political theorists study, the stronger is the claim that ethno-cultural justice cannot be secured by a regime of common rights.[48] Other authors have come to similar conclusions. Joseph Carens provides several case studies involving state treatment of minority groups.[49] Carens recommends that states follow a doctrine he describes as evenhandedness with regard to the treatment of minorities, which necessarily requires that each minority claim "be given appropriate weight under the circumstances within the framework of a commitment to equal respect for all."[50] Kymlicka's and Carens' view that the extent to which states accommodate minority claims is contextually or category-dependent, contrasts with that of jurists such as Patrick Thornberry who use legal methods to illustrate that international protections for minority groups operate as part of an integrated system of universal human rights.[51] Using case study methodology provides an empirical basis to determine if a common regime is applicable to minority groups who make different claims against the state. Since categories and conditions of minority groups differ in each state context, case studies assist us to discover if universal rights apply to members of minority groups, irrespective of state context or minority group category. This resolves the tension between the fields of political theory and international law by providing answers to the question of whether the minority regime is properly integrated into the system of universal human rights.

---

[48] Kymlicka, Will. *Contemporary Political Philosophy: An introduction, 2nd Edition* (Oxford, Oxford University Press, 2002), 47.

Kymlicka, Will. *Multicultural Odysseys, Navigating the New International Politics of Diversity* (New York, Oxford University Press, 2007). 53, 59, & 199–231. In his latest book, Kymlicka describes the minority regime as 'liberal multiculturalism', and argues for 'targeted' minority rights that provide increased protections to national minority groups.

[49] Carens, Joseph. *Culture, Citizenship, and Community. A Contextual Exploration of Justice as Evenhandedness* (Oxford, Oxford University Press, 2000), 107, 140, 180, 200.

[50] *Ibid.*, 12.

[51] Thornberry, Patrick. *Indigenous Peoples and Human Rights.* Thornberry, however, does recommend a different legal approach and distinguishes the problems of indigenous peoples from those of other minority groups.

Kymlicka, Will and Opalski, Majda eds., *Can Liberal Pluralism Be Exported? Western Political Theory and Ethnic Relations in Eastern Europe* (New York, Oxford University Press, 2001), 6. Kymlicka lists six types of ethno-cultural [minority] groups, each of which may require different programmatic responses by states as opposed to the application of a regime of common legal rights: national minorities; indigenous peoples; legal immigrants with the right to become citizens; illegal immigrant or guest workers without the right to become citizens; racial caste groups; and isolationist ethno-religious sects.

Case study methodology is described by Joseph Carens as the contextual approach.[52] This method, in essence, places theoretical accounts and normative insights about minority group rights into an empirical context of case studies involving the relationship between states and minority groups. Carens writes:

> A contextual approach offers three interrelated advantages. First, it can clarify the meaning of abstract formulations. Secondly, it can provide access to normative insights that may be obscured by theoretical accounts that remain at the level of general principle. Thirdly, it can make us more conscious of the blinkers that constrain our theoretical visions when they are informed only by what is familiar.[53]

The contextual method is used to research how international law on minorities is applied to actual cases of specific examples of conflict between states and minority groups. My case studies illuminate how cultural rights are distinguishable from anti-discrimination laws. The cases also demonstrate how minority rights can be used by states to recognise the existence of minority groups as well as improve their social conditions.

Marc Stears explains the advantages of the contextual approach in his published research.[54] Stears argues that it is significantly wrong to contend that normative theoretical and empirical enquiry can be meaningfully separated.[55] He maintains that, while empirical inquiry must take a form of careful principled consideration, normative inquiry does not "exist in a non-empirical realm where questions of fact do not impinge on questions of principle."[56]

The jurisprudential context provides us with a similar, careful approach that can correct distortions to analyse empirical reality. By this, I do not mean to suggest that judicial proceedings are exempted from the whims, prejudices, and mores of the time. However, the essential method in a judicial proceeding is to test the reliability of empirical facts and evidence. Courts of law engage in a fact-finding process whereby evidence is rigorously tested, questioned and cross-examined by a judicially supervised adversarial process. Once discovered, facts are applied by the courts to laws based, in part, on theoretical doctrines to produce a determination of breach (civil or criminal) or innocence.

Though the jurisprudential context does not guarantee a complete objectivity, it provides a form of investigation based on an adversarial process that accounts for the self-interested considerations Stears requires from empirical inquiry. I use

---

[52] Carens, Joseph H. *Culture, Citizenship, and Community, A Contextual Exploration of Justice as Evenhandedness* (Oxford, Oxford University Press, 2000), 2.

[53] *Ibid.*, 3.

[54] Stears, Marc, *The Vocation of Political Theory: Principles, Empirical Inquiry and the Politics of Opportunity*, European Journal of Political Theory 4 (4) (2005): 325–350.

[55] *Ibid.*, 327.

[56] *Ibid.*, 329, 339, 342.

this method not only to distinguish minority rights, but also to determine the theory used by courts to justify the claims made by minority groups. Normative concerns can be assessed through such a juridical inquiry. They are revealed by the process of how courts guarantee principles of justice such as equal treatment. I use this method of empirical assessment combined with normative reflection in my discussions of cases decided by the United Nations' Human Rights Committee, as well as the European Court of Human Rights.

1.3. *Literature Review: Multiculturalism*

1.3a. *Introduction*

There exist three primary literature groups on the subject of multiculturalism; I discuss how they uncover the minority legal tradition in my next three sub-sections. Also, I explain how the literatures influence normative discussions on multiculturalism. Finally, I review how my selection of minority group case studies is determined by the literature.

These literature groups cover different aspects of multiculturalism and include the disciplines of law (human rights and international law), history, and political theory. As discussed in my research methodology (sections 1.2, 1.2a), legal scholarship analyses a jurisprudence that dates back over half a century. The first group is authored primarily by jurists. Minority rights are not only contained under the general subject area of human rights, but also fall under the subject area of international law. The jurists employ legal methodologies to discuss minority rights jurisprudence. This legal literature includes works by Patrick Thornberry, Manfred Nowak, Asbjorn Eide, Alan Rosas, Athanasia Spiliopoulou Akermark, Hurst Hannum, Martin Schenin, and James Analaya. The methods used by this literature group differ substantially to those of political theorists. These works tend to have a positivist quality since they analyse the UN's minority regime and review issues that arise from its jurisprudence, procedure, and implementation. That is, the works use empirical methodology in the study of minority rights.

The second group involves an historical literature that analyses the conflict between nation-states and minority groups. The historical literature includes works by seminal writers such as Rafael Lemkin (1944), a Jewish-Polish lawyer whose career-long campaign against the practice by states of de-nationalisation resulted in the United Nations' passage of the *Convention for the Prevention of the Crime of Genocide, 1948*;[57] also, Inis Claude (1955), a Harvard professor of government,

[57] Namely, the crimes of genocide committed against the Armenian and the Jewish peoples; *Convention on the Prevention and Punishment of the Crime of Genocide*, 1948 78 UNTS 277.

who concludes that the subject of minorities is essentially that of a conflict between nation-states and minority groups;[58] and finally, C.A. Macartney (1934), a historian who similarly defines the subject as an internal contradiction within the nation-state. For these writers, multiculturalism is not necessarily a question for political theory. Rather, for historians, jurists and social scientists, it is one about statecraft. For example, in contrast to political theory, legal and historical literature places the question of nationalism and creation of the nation-state as the starting point for discussion about minority rights. C.A. Macartney writes:[59]

> the synthesis of state and nation brings with it a problem which is full of difficulty and dangers: the problem of national minorities…The majority in a state which seeks to impose its own national culture upon a national minority is misusing the machinery set up for the regulation of their common affairs to those affairs, which by definition, are not common…A national state and national minorities are incompatibles.

As explained by jurist Hurst Hannum, the justification for minority rights as conceived under the League of Nations' Minority Protection Treaty System was to "protect minorities against the raw power of nationalism."[60] For jurists, the justification for human rights inclusive of minority protection stems from the creation of the nation-state and the ideology of nationalism. If minority rights can be simply defined, these are explained by jurists as the protection of minority identity against the states' coercive assimilation of minority groups.[61] For human rights scholars, minority protection is an over one-half-century-old jurisprudence

---

Lemkin, Raphael. *Axis Rule In Occupied Europe Laws of Occupation, Analysis of Government Proposals for Redress* (Washington D.C., Carnegie Endowment for International Peace, Division of International Law, 1944), 91. Lemkin writes his book as a part of his campaign to assign genocide to the annals of international criminal law. He illustrates the process of de-nationalisation, explaining that "the idea of nation should not be confused with the idea of nationalism. To do so would be to make the same mistake as confusing the idea of individual liberty with that of egoism."

58 Claude, Inis L. *National Minorities An International Problem* (Cambridge, Harvard University Press, 1955), Preface. Claude writes that the rise of the [minorities] problem was the logical consequence of the doctrinal ascendancy of nationalism in Western Europe.

59 Macartney, C.A. *National States and National Minorities* (London, OUP, 1934), 16, 422.

60 Hannum, Hurst. *Autonomy, Sovereignty and Self Determination, The Accommodation of Conflicting Rights* (Philadelphia, University of Pennsylvania Press, 1990), 54.

61 Henrard, Kristan. *Devising an Adequate System of Minority Protection, Individual Human Rights, Minority Rights and the Right to Self-Determination* (London, Martinus Nijhoff Publishers, 2000), 165. Henrard writes that the *ICCPR* Article 27 (rights of minorities) is "intended to protect minorities against forced assimilation."

Eide, Asbjorn. *Commentary by Asbjorn Eide, Chairperson of the Working Group on Minorities* UN Doc. E/CN/Sub.2/Ac.5/2001/2, p. 5. Eide writes that "forced assimilation of minorities is unacceptable" under international law.

intrinsic to a world states' system whose existence conflicts with human-centric principles. That is, the nation-state requires, as a condition for its perpetuation, the corrective of human rights inclusive of minority protection.

The third literature group consists of political theorists. These writers discuss the minorities question as an aspect of normative discussions on multiculturalism. They are best represented by Will Kymlicka, but also include a large number of political theorists such as Iris Marion Young, Joe Carens, Brian Barry, and Chandran Kukathas. The literature by political theorists, in contrast to legal and historical scholarship, is not bounded by the empirical existence of the minority regime. These works discuss normative questions about the subject of multiculturalism that assume the minority legal tradition is either irrelevant or inadequate.[62] As we will discover from my case studies, such laws, however inadequate, provide, in many instances, the only remedy available to minority groups.

1.3b. *Minority Rights and Liberal Theory*

In this section I discuss the political theory literature on multiculturalism and how the minority regime analyses challenges to minority protections.

My research examines the implications of the minority rights legal tradition for debates on multiculturalism amongst political theorists. Normative critics of minority rights maintain that, to insure that all people are treated equally, laws covering members of minority groups must adhere to liberal values based on at least three fundamental principles. The first is that law must provide equality of treatment (equality principle) for all individuals. It should not provide special benefits, programmes or exemptions from the law for some individuals while denying these to other people. Second, legal rights can only attach to an individual and should not recognise the idea of group or collective rights as such. Individual rights guarantee that law maintains a universal character and applies equally to all persons irrespective of any group affiliation. Third, that the law maintains strict neutrality (neutrality principle) between different groups and individuals. Neutrality guarantees that the state will have no preference between competing individuals and groups about what constitutes a good life.[63] In the section below, I review literature covering the first of these objections to illustrate

---

Also, *see* Thornberry, Patrick. *International Law and Minorities*, 141, 185, 186. Phillips, Alan and Rosas, Allan. *Universal Minority Rights* (Turku, Abo, Abo Akademi University Institute for Human Rights, 1995), 20, 374; Pentassuglia 99.

[62] Kymlicka, Will. *Politics In The Vernacular*, 80. Kymlicka concludes that human rights are insufficient, that is, too weak, to achieve ethno-cultural justice.

[63] Raz, Joseph. *The Morality of Freedom* (Oxford, Clarendon Press, 1986), 113. Raz describes neutrality as a doctrine of restraint to ensure that the state takes no action to help or hinder competing notions of the good life.

how the jurisprudential context furthers research on the subject, as well as provides theoretical support based on liberal theory for the establishment of minority rights.

Some proponents of egalitarian liberalism such as Brian Barry maintain that providing special programmes, rights, or exemptions for members of minority groups is contrary to the idea of basic equality established by the historical principle in Western thought that "likes should be treated alike."[64] In *Culture and Equality,* Barry illustrates how multiculturalism is inconsistent with his interpretation of liberal political theory. Barry maintains that, by providing special rights or legal exemptions to minority groups, a state violates the liberal commitment to civic equality and egalitarian justice:

> Laws must provide equal treatment for those who belong to different religious faiths and different cultures...The whole point of egalitarian liberalism is to ensure that people who are different are treated equally.[65]

Not only do legal exemptions (negative policies) or special rights (positive policies) for minority groups provide a retreat from liberty and equality according to Barry, but they also place state power behind practices that violate freedom and equality.[66] Critics of multiculturalism, such as Barry, argue that providing special rights based on culture to minority groups can result in the state's sanctioning of illiberal acts by minority groups in the name of protecting their cultural distinctiveness. Some religious practices that violate fundamental human rights such as female genital mutilation, withholding life-saving medical treatment from children, ritual scarring, parentally coerced marriage, and unfair religious divorce will, they argue, be protected by states which give special protection or exemptions to religious minority groups. In contrast to Barry's view, a minority group's abuse or violation of any individual human right is clearly proscribed, as are states, under the minority regime. The ICCPR, Article 27 as well as the *UN's Declaration on the Rights of Minorities* as examples, are required to be consistent and compliant with the UN human rights treaty system.[67] In contrast to Barry's claim about

[64] Westeen, Peter. *The Empty Idea of Equality*, Helm, Mark ed., Harvard Law Review, Vol. 95 (Cambridge, Harvard Law Review Association, 1981–1982), 537–596, and *see* 537.

[65] Barry 24, 76.

[66] *Ibid.*, 12, 17, 128.

[67] Eide, Asbjorn. "Final text of the Commentary to the Declaration on the Rights of Minorities." (Geneva. United Nations, Centre for Human Rights, 2001), 12. Relying on Declaration Article 4, Eide clarifies that cultural rights are not contrary to international human rights standards and that compliance with such standards must apply to the practices of majority and minority alike. "Cultural or religious practices which violate human rights law should be outlawed for everyone, not only for minorities."

Article 5.1 of the *International Covenant on Civil and Political Rights, 1996* expressly prevents any [minority] group or person from violating a right or freedom guaranteed by the Covenant.

religious fundamentalism, UN studies demonstrate that it is usually states that engage in illiberal, intolerant, discriminatory and sometimes genocidal conduct (section 1.1a).

In response to critics of minority rights, Will Kymlicka views minority rights as a method of eliminating inequality as opposed to Barry's view that differential treatment creates inequality.[68] In *Politics in the Vernacular, Nationalism, Multiculturalism, and Citizenship,*[69] Kymlicka explains that all societies, as they embark on the project of nation-building, develop a set of common institutions which he describes as:[70]

> A societal culture - that is a set of institutions, covering both public and private life, with a common language, which has historically developed over time on a given territory, which provides people with a wide range of choices about how to lead their lives... [and] requires standardization and diffusion of a common language and the creation and diffusion of common educational, political, and legal institutions - is a feature of modernization.

According to Kymlicka, states enact policies of naturalisation that promote the integration of certain minority groups (immigrants) into societal culture. The liberal principle of equality is satisfied when members of minority groups have equal opportunity to participate in common societal institutions such as schools, courts, and government services as well as economic enterprises. In order to achieve equality of treatment for these minorities, terms and conditions for integrating minority group members into societal culture must be fair. Kymlicka recommends a two-fold process, first, promoting linguistic and institutional integration so the minority group has equal opportunity in basic educational, political and economic institutions and, second, of reforming common institutions so as to accommodate the distinctive ethno-cultural practices so that integration does not require denial of ethno-cultural identity. Kymlicka refers to protection for ethno-cultural identity in earlier writings as *polyethnic rights*[71] and later, in *Politics in the Vernacular,* as *accommodation rights.*[72] Accommodation to aspects of a minority's identity is necessary, according to Kymlicka,

---

[68] Kymlicka, Will. *Multicultural Citizenship*, 109.

[69] Kymlicka, Will. *Politics in The Vernacular.*

[70] Kymlicka, Will. *Politics In The Vernacular*, 26,27,53. Kymlicka defines nation-building as the process by which a state, "...diffuse[s] a single societal culture throughout all of its territory... promoting a common language, and a sense of common membership in, and equal access to, the social institutions based on that language." *See also*, Kymlicak, Will. *Contemporary Political Philosophy*, 364. Will Kymlicka provides a diagram listing the tools employed by states for nation-building which are: citizenship policy, public service employment, language laws, education policy, centralizing power, national media, symbol holidays and military service.

[71] Kymlicka, Will. *Multicultural Citizenship*, 30.

[72] Kymlicka, Will. *Politics In The Vernacular*, 51.

because liberal democratic states are not ethno-culturally neutral as is the case between different religion, language, and cultural groups. Rather, states endorse a common [dominant] societal culture and use a process of nation-building in which minority identity may require protection. Contrary to impeding integration of minorities into societal culture, providing accommodation for minority identity, according to this view, enhances the integration of minority groups into a common societal culture by respecting minority identity as it simultaneously encourages minority integration.

Kymlicka distinguishes the case of immigrant minorities from that of national minorities who he defines as groups that have formed functioning societies on their historical homelands prior to being incorporated into a larger state.[73] He maintains national minorities already possess a common societal culture when they are incorporated into a larger state and are accorded a higher degree of protection; he considers it would be costly and unreasonable to integrate these groups into a new societal culture. In contrast with immigrant minority groups, national minorities did not voluntarily migrate to the state. To secure fair treatment for national minorities, Kymlicka suggests that the state must enable national minorities to live and work in their own societal culture and maintain themselves as distinct societies.

Kymlicka's views have the same grounding in liberal theory as do those of critics of minority rights such as Barry. Barry and Kymlicka converge on the ideal of liberal equality and place importance on the goal of achieving equality of treatment under law for all individuals. They differ on the question of whether special rights should be accorded to minority groups to attain equal treatment for minorities. Kymlicka maintains that special rights for minorities are necessary so that citizens are treated with genuine equality and that such rights compensate for unequal circumstances in which many minority groups find themselves.[74] For Kymlicka, group-differentiated rights designed to protect minority societal cultures are seen as a way of promoting equality by compensating for unequal circumstances. Liberal critics of his view maintain that universal individual rights already accommodate the cultural differences of minority groups by protecting individual rights to association and religion without interference from the state. Special or group-differentiated rights for minorities violate the principle of equality of treatment by providing benefits and protections to some groups that are denied others and are not necessary since universal individual rights against discrimination exist to insure all individuals receive equal treatment under law.

[73] *Ibid.*, 54, 54.

[74] *Ibid.*, 146–147.

Legal analysis enhances our understanding of the Barry-Kymlicka debate by illustrating how liberal values are interpreted by courts and international organisations. A review of minority rights case laws results in the application of a version of the equality principle that is closer to the Kymlickian view, namely, that the accommodation of differences is the essence of true equality.[75] An example of this type of case law analysis is illustrated by the *Minority Schools Opinion*, a 1935 case heard by the Permanent Court of International Justice (PCIJ).[76] The case is precedent setting for minority jurisprudence. It establishes the principle that the differential or special treatment of minority groups is a pre-requisite to providing minorities with equality of treatment (perfect equality) under the law. The idea, that the so-called differential or special treatment of minority groups is a prerequisite necessary to achieve the equal treatment of minorities, has since become the standard of minority jurisprudence through to the current day. The case involves the issue of whether the Greek minority group living in the state Albania was entitled to establish a minority Greek language school under Albanian law.[77] I discuss the decision in section 2.6.

The *Minority Schools Opinion* provided a new legal precedent for how international law interprets the obligations states have to guarantee equality of treatment for minority groups. Legal literature which develops the equality principle set forth by *Minority Schools Opinion* illustrates actions required by states to insure equal treatment for minority groups. Jurist Giorgio Sacerdoti writes on the importance of minority rights to the development of self-identity and explains the concept that differential treatment for minorities is required by courts in order to preserve basic features of the minority group – protect the minority right to identity as well as the right not to be assimilated – which distinguishes a minority from the majority in the population.[78] Sacerdoti maintains that the League of Nations' minority protection system provided minorities with a status in international law that included minority rights to religious practice and language as well as control of social institutions and primary schools.[79] Sacerdoti's view is similar to the view expressed in the *Minority Schools Opinion*, that equal treatment for minority groups requires the preservation of minority identity so that minority

---

75 *Ibid.*, 146.

76 *Minority Schools Opinion*, *supra*, note 17 at 10. Also, *Minority Schools in Albania, Effects of the Advisory Opinion of April 6, 1935*, Permanent Court of International Justice, Leyden, A.W. Sijithoff's Publishing Company, Series E.- No. 12, June 15, 1935 – June 15, 1936.

77 *Ibid.*

78 Sacerdoti, Giorgio, "New Developments In Group Consciousness and the International Protection of The Rights of Minorities" ed., Yoram Dinstein, *Israeli Yearbook on Human Rights*, vol.13 (Tel Aviv, Tel Aviv University Faculty of Law, 1983), 116, 137.

79 *Ibid.*, 116.

cultural characteristics are provided with the same treatment given by the state to dominant national group characteristics and language(s). Tore Modeen concurs with Sacerdoti's view and maintains that, for national minorities, minority privilege should not be regarded as a violation of the equality principle since special treatment is afforded only as a precaution or shield against assimilation which deprives the minority protection of national characteristics provided by the state to the dominant majority group.[80] The PCIJ protected minority characteristics and identity to achieve the type of equality described in the *Minority Schools Opinion*.[81] According to many jurists, the state must, at minimum, provide for the education of minority children in the minority native tongue as well as the home state language; ensure use of the minority language in state courts, public services and government administration; and protect the free exercise of religious worship (freedom of conscience).

Literature from international organisation source documents, international court decisions, legal treatises, law review articles and books by legal scholars is particularly helpful because court decisions for example, must apply concepts such as the equality principle to an empirical dispute between two contesting parties. As demonstrated by the *Minority Schools Opinion*, this approach forces the court to make an analysis of theoretical concepts such as equality based on the need to arrive at a decision that comports with due process. The incorporation of legal literature into the debate on multiculturalism is necessary not only to address concerns about minority rights raised by normative questions, but also to demonstrate the competing interpretations that can be given by courts to liberal values embodied in concepts such as equality of treatment.

1.3c. *Minority Rights Case Studies*

In this section, I discuss how the literature on multiculturalism influenced my selection of minority group case studies.

Minority rights as expounded in the *Minority Schools Opinion* are qualitatively different from universal civil rights and anti-discrimination laws in several aspects. First, minority rights are *positive rights* requiring states to take affirmative steps with respect to the recognition and treatment of minority groups. Second, minority rights rely upon a substantive as opposed to a formal idea of equality which permits the state to adapt ameliorative remedies to improve the disadvantaged condition of minority groups as well as provide for a *collective aspect* of rights exercised in community with other group members.

---

80 Modeen, Tore. *The International Protection of National Minorities in Europe* (Ekenas, Abo Akademi, 1969), 42.

81 *Minority Schools Opinion, supra*, note 17, at 10. P. 140.

Third, as illustrated by the states of Albania and Greece litigation before the PCIJ in the *Minority Schools Opinion*, such rights have an *international character* which requires inter-state comity with regard to the treatment of minority groups. That is, though minority rights are implemented in the domestic sphere, they are administered by the collectivity of all states by supra national regional or international bodies formerly by the League of Nations and in the present day, by the United Nations, and the European Court of Human Rights. They require states to recognise the multi and international aspect of the world states' system by respecting rights to the enjoyment of culture, including linguistic and religious practices, of residents who had migrated, or were ancestral migrants, or otherwise incorporated into the state from different nations.

Chapters 4 and 5 use case studies that provide empirical models for the implementation of minority rights in different states. These chapters illustrate whether minority claims can be secured by common legal rights. My case study about the Roma peoples of Europe uses the jurisprudential context to examine how minority rights influence state treatment of a minority group which suffers unique circumstances of historical discrimination. Kymlicka identifies three types of such minority groups that require the application of what he describes as ethno-cultural justice: immigrants, national minorities, and indigenous persons.[82] While numerous case studies are found in the literature on how these groups are confronted by nation-building policies of the state,[83] Kymlicka identifies examples of three minority groups that, due to unique historical circumstances, do not fall into a standard minority group category and therefore provide a new avenue for research: African-Americans, Roma guest workers in Germany, and Russian settlers in the Baltics.[84]

As I explained in section 1.2, my selections as case studies are influenced, in part, by the limited availability of minority jurisprudence. For example, despite the efforts by African-Americans to author a formal complaint against USA segregation policies in the United Nations,[85] there are no HRC case decisions regarding African-Americans. Power[86] and Hannum[87] also illustrate how African-Americans

[82] Kymlicka, Will. *Politics In The Vernacular*, 31–32. Kymlicka, Will and Opalski, Maida eds., *Can Liberal Pluralism Be Exported?*, 6.

[83] Kymlicka, Will. *Contemporary Political Philosophy*, 364; Kymlicka, Will. *Politics In The Vernacular*, 26–27.

[84] *Ibid.*, 32.

[85] Dudziak, Mary. *Cold War Civil Rights, Race and the Image of American Democracy* (Princeton, Princeton University Press, 2000), 63. Dudziak provides a dramatic account of the unsuccessful effort by William Patterson, Chair of the Civil Rights Congress, to bring a complaint against the USA for crimes committed against African Americans before the UN Human Rights Committee in Geneva.

[86] Power, Samantha. *A Problem From Hell, America and the Age of Genocide* (New York, Basic Books, 2002).

[87] Hannum 52.

engaged in a lengthy and unsuccessful effort to end segregation in the USA by gaining international assistance in the League of Nations as well as in the United Nations. African-American leaders from Marcus Garvey to Malcolm X sought international assistance to improve social conditions for African-Americans. Recall, however, that the USA is not a state party to the First Optional Protocol, ICCPR. If the USA decides to ratify the OP, it will permit individual complaints authored by USA minority groups, including African Americans, to be heard by the HRC.

Using the contextual method, I research another of the three groups identified by Kymlicka that I will describe as special minorities because they defy a standard minority group category, namely, the Roma peoples of Europe. In contrast to African-Americans, the Roma have generated minority jurisprudence within an international judicial forum, namely, the European Court of Human Rights.[88] The purpose of the case study is not to write a comprehensive history of the group experience as there is already a sufficient body of literature dealing with the tragic history and condition of the Roma. Instead, the case study provides an empirical basis from which to examine the validity of Kymlicka's argument, which I previously discussed in the methodology section above, that the application of a common regime of rights fails to secure ethno-cultural justice for minority groups.[89] The case study will review the international minority regime that covers the Roma including Article 27 of the *ICCPR* and the *Declaration on the Rights of Minorities*, as well as regional protections such as *European Framework Convention for the Protection of National Minorities* and the *European Convention for the Protection of Human Rights and Fundamental Freedoms*.[90] Next, it will determine whether the minority regime differs from existing domestic anti-discrimination and civil rights laws. Finally, I will discuss why the application of cultural rights is important to protect the existence of the Roma.

As explained by Jean-Pierre Liegois, Director of the Gypsy Research Centre in Paris, for the Roma, "the problem is not poverty but persecution."[91] Cultural rights protect the Roma's nomadic cultural and economic trading practice that

[88] Fleishman, Jeffrey, "New Gypsy Vision for the Future, The Roma use tactics from the US civil rights struggle to seek equal access to education and new opportunities for their children," Los Angeles Times, 23 June 2006. Recent press reports explain how the Roma litigation is inspired by the African-American experience of using the judicial system to pursue de-segregation.

[89] Kymlicka, Will. *Contemporary Political Philosophy*, 47.

[90] *Convention for the Protection of Human Rights and Fundamental Freedoms*, Rome, 4.XI.1950, entered into force on 21 September 1970; *Framework Convention for the Protection of National Minorities*, ETS, 157, 1995, entered into force on 1 February 1999. It has been signed by 37 states, of which 24 have ratified it.

[91] Liegois, Jean-Pierre. *School Provision for Ethnic Minorities: The Gypsy Paradigm* (Hertfordshire, University of Hertfordshire Press, 1987), 70.

has been the source of Roma persecution in Europe. As discussed in my introduction, this included a period of brutal slavery through the mid-nineteenth century in Romania. Isabel Fonseca explains that the Roma were recognised and treated as criminals[92] during their slavery experience. This also includes the Roma genocide at the hands of the Nazis during WWII. However, Europe's nearly one-thousand-year-old persecution against the Roma is grounded in the criminalisation of *vagrancy*. Europe's prosecution regime objective is to eliminate the nomadic cultural and economic trading practices of the Roma peoples.

Nomadism is essential to the Roma's cultural identity. As explained by Jean-Pierre Liegeois, travel provides the Roma with:

> adaptability, flexibility, and social cohesion...Travel (*kumpanja*) is a symbol and honour...their living space is experience itself, never shut or bounded territory, but a flexible identity unattached to any piece of earth: the land of the Gypsies lies within themselves...providing skill and earning (as well as) clan links...for marriages.[93]

The Roma's nomadic ways provide an opportunity to research how minority protection works to encourage the cultural practices of minority groups. The case also provides us with an opportunity to understand why cultural rights, by contrast to the conventional rule against discrimination, are necessary to protect minority groups and assist in their groups' development. Civil rights do not adequately protect the Roma's nomadism since these rights are concerned primarily with protecting the ethnicity of the group against discrimination, and not travelling practices of the Roma. By contrast, cultural rights are primarily concerned with protecting the Roma enjoyment of culture (travelling).

My other case study about the Aboriginal peoples responds to research challenges posed in the political theory literature, such as those of David Miller who suggests that multicultural societies need to develop state forms in which minority group and national identity can co-exist.[94] Miller maintains that minority rights may damage the ability of a state to establish common citizenship and national cohesion in a multicultural society. In *On Nationality*, he maintains that special group rights may lead to a form of politics that is fragmented along group lines.[95] National cohesion and active citizenship between different minority groups require a common identification which Miller maintains that nationality alone can provide.[96] In *Citizenship and National Identity*,[97] Miller explains that, to create

[92] Fonseca, Isabel. *Bury Me Standing, The Gypsies and Their Journey* (London, Vintage Books, 1996), 185.

[93] Liegeois, Jean-Pierre. *Gypsies An Illustrated History*, 54, 63–64.

[94] Miller, David. *On Nationality* (New York, Oxford University Press, 1995), 153.

[95] *Ibid.*, 154.

[96] *Ibid.*, 140.

[97] Miller, David. *Citizenship and National Identity* (Malden, Blackwell Publishers Ltd., 2000).

an active republican citizenship, individuals must set aside personal interests to achieve a democratic consensus that promotes common interests and the common good.[98] This challenge is important to the establishment of minority claims because, without new kinds of federalism, minority regimes produce a Balkanised political community of competing minority groups. Will Kymlicka agrees that additional research needs to be done to clarify as well as help produce forms of governance about how to respect diversity without eroding the bonds and virtues of citizenship.[99]

I use the jurisprudential context to examine theoretical issues raised by Miller and Kymlicka to illustrate how minority rights influence the establishment of political autonomy for a minority group, that is, the Aboriginal peoples of Canada. The purpose of the case is not to research a comprehensive national history but rather to distinguish international law about minority group autonomy with domestic anti-discrimination and civil rights laws. In the case, I analyse the history and development of Canada's *Indian Act*[100] and discuss why discriminatory, colonial-era legislation survived through to the current day. The case will also illustrate how the minority regime balances the state's interest in common citizenship with minority rights to political autonomy. A growing number of states have already implemented political autonomy for minority groups; these are Catalonia in Spain, Nunavik, as well as Quebec in Canada, Scotland in the United Kingdom, and the Palestinian Authority in Occupied Palestinian Territories.

The Aboriginal peoples of Canada provide us with an opportunity to examine how international laws such as the International Labour Organisation Convention No. 169 entitled, *The Convention Concerning Indigenous and Tribal Peoples in Independent Countries,*[101] and the *United Nations' Declaration on the Rights of Indigenous Peoples, 1994*[102] influences state recognition and treatment of indigenous minority groups. Further, it provides an opportunity to examine if the minority regime fosters the Balkanisation and territorial break-up of states.

---

[98] *Ibid.*, 82–83, 85–86.

[99] Kymlicka, Will and Norman, Wayne *Citizenship In Culturally Diverse Societies: Issues, Contexts, Concepts* (Oxford, Oxford University Press, 2000), 17, 37. Joseph Carens, *Culture, Citizenship, and Community. A Contextual Exploration of Justice as Evenhandedness* (Oxford, Oxford University Press, 2000), 10, 26, and 213. Illiberal requirements for citizenship are also maintained by liberal states as explained by author Joseph Carens in his discussion of the ethnic blood descendant requirements for German citizenship, which discriminate against third-generation Turkish guest workers.

[100] *Indian Act* R.S. 1985, c.1–6, s.1.

[101] *The Convention Concerning Indigenous and Tribal Peoples in Independent Countries* (1989) 28 ILM 1382.

[102] *United Nations' Declaration on the Rights of Indigenous Peoples, 1994*, Resolution 1994/5, 26 Aug 1994. *See also*, UN Doc. E/CN.4/Sub.2/1992/33.

Also whether the minority regime, as well as the Aboriginal groups who claim its protection, interferes with a singular national identity.

In Chapter 6 (conclusion), I provide a qualitative narrative to survey theoretical principles and practical lessons gained by my examination of the relationship between states and minority groups. First, I summarise how the minority regime jurisprudence influences the process of diffusion within the domestic legal-political order. Next, I discuss how the process influences the multiculturalism debate. Finally, I examine whether the minority regime has achieved public recognition of minority groups and explain how international standards enable domestic approval of minority group autonomy.

Section II

History of the Minority Regime

Chapter 2

History of the Minority Question

Nothing, I venture to say, is more likely to disturb the peace of the world than the treatment which might, in certain circumstances, be meted out to minorities.

Woodrow Wilson[1]

2.1. *Definitions*

The problem of minorities has troubled world peace and international good-will for centuries.[2] The literature on the subject of minority rights covers a range of polarising contemporary issues such as affirmative action, de-segregation, bi-lingual education, immigration reform, and multiculturalism. The debate evokes great passion from those who support or oppose the idea of special rights for individuals who are members of minority groups. However, treatment of the minority question as a subject in history differs from the modern literature, portraying the topic instead as an international question that involves the relationship between different states. The minority problem has a distinctly international character since the subject involves the relationship between different national groups who generally emigrate from different countries.[3] Disputes between states and internal state conflicts about minorities have served as a justification for war as well as other forms of violence between national groups, including WWI.[4] The minorities question is a subject that also lends itself to

---

1 Wilson's address to the eighth plenary session of the European peace conference in Versailles on 31 May 1919. *See* Thornberry, Patrick, *International Law and Minorities*, 40–41. Thornberry cites J. Robinson *et al.*, *Were The Minorities Treaties a Failure?* (New York, Institute of Jewish Affairs, 1943), 21.

2 Capotorti 6.

3 Thornberry, Patrick, *International Law and Minorities*, 3. A minority may also have formerly constituted an independent nation (tribal organisation).; been part of a nation living under its own state, which was segregated from this jurisdiction and annexed to another state; or be a regional or scattered group that has not reached a minimum degree of assimilation with the predominant group.

4 Macartney, C.A. *National States and National Minorities* (London, OUP,1934), 181. A presenting cause of WWI was the Sarajevo murder of Archduke Franz Ferdinand as well as the ethnic group conflict in the Balkan states.

international law exercised through the treaty-making power of states, since treaty law is the vehicle by which different states govern their formal relationships.

The modern nation, an abstract concept, makes it difficult to produce a clear definition for the term minority. Definitions for the nation as well as for minority groups must be researched as two aspects of the same topic, because so-called minority groups are produced by the grant of sovereignty to the nation-state itself controlled by different national groups. Therefore, to define a minority we must also find a definition for the nation. Some scholars maintain attempts to define a minority group are futile, since the idea of a minority is an inherently ambiguous concept lacking definitive characteristics. Some states unsuccessfully argue that they have no minorities.[5] Legal scholars maintain that a state's failure to recognise the existence of its minority groups does not exempt it from fulfilling treaty obligations requiring the state's recognition for the existence and identity of minority groups.[6]

Any group or association of individuals that is linked by a common interest and does not comprise a majority of the population can potentially be defined as a minority group. Social classes, families, speakers of dialects might claim benefits and protections of international law under an expansive definition of the minority group. Giving all such groups recognition and protection in law, however, would create an absurdity that demeans larger historical questions. International law bases the definition of minorities squarely upon problems and conflicts between ethnic, religious, national and linguistic groups that result from the creation of the nation-state. United Nations Special Rapporteur Francesco Capotorti's 1991 study on the rights of minorities explains that, in recommending international minority rights standards, the HRC "did not consider it necessary to define the term minority…[because] the only point at issue…is whether an indisputable objective

[5] Castan, Melissa, Joseph, Sarah, and Schultz, Jenny. *The International Covenant on Civil and Political Rights, Cases, Materials, and Commentary* (Oxford, OUP, 2000), 574.

Anderson, Carol. *Eyes Off The Prize, The United Nations And The African American Struggle For Human Rights, 1944–1955* (Cambridge, Cambridge University Press, 2003), 75. Anderson illustrates the American position against recognition of minority existence: "there are probably no national minorities in the U.S." quoting a US State Department statement in support of formation of the UN Sub-Commission on the Protection of Minorities during the 1950s.

Thornberry, Patrick. *International Law and Minorities*, 116. "In the kind of world for which we fight, there must cease to exist any need for the use of that accursed term, racial or religious minority." The quote is a statement made by the Roosevelt Administration's Secretary of State during the UN Genocide Convention.

Adarand Constructors, Inc. v Pena, 515 U.S. 200 (1995). US Chief Justice Antony Scalia recently found that "in the eyes of the [US] government, we are just one race here. It is American."

Claude 82. Claude describes how Hawaii statehood was delayed until its racial groups had been Americanised.

[6] *See* Articles 1 and 27, *ICCPR*. 999 UNTS 171.

core (religious, linguistic, ethnic, national) can be widened or restricted."[7] Instead, the United Nations identifies four groups - national, ethnic (inclusive of race), linguistic, and religious – as entitled to legal protection. Although the UN has not formalised a definition for the term minority, Capotorti has produced what Patrick Thornberry concludes is the most accepted definition.[8]

Because the type of protection accorded minorities is qualitatively different from that claimed, for example, by persons who are disabled or gay, these two groups are not incorporated into categories used to define a minority group by the United Nations. Although women have successfully achieved protections under international human rights instruments, they also are not defined as a class in the definition of a minority group. Thus far, international recognition has been limited to groups identifiable by a desire to propagate national culture in such forms as political autonomy, religious expression, educational administration, and linguistic communication. However, Will Kymlicka maintains that other groups have characteristics similar to those of national groups and may also require formal recognition. For example, persons who are deaf have a distinctive language – signing – similar to other linguistic groups, while persons who are gay may seek recognition from governmental authority to sustain social relations of same-sex desire such as gay marriage.[9] The United Nations' *Draft Comprehensive and Integral International Convention on the Protection and Promotion of the Rights and Dignity of Persons with Disabilities* proposed on 7 October 2005 in the document's Article 4 that "Persons with disabilities shall be entitled, on an equal basis with others, to recognition and support of their specific cultural and linguistic identity, including sign languages and deaf culture." Despite arguable similarities with internationally recognised national, ethnic, linguistic, and religious categories, these other groups have not yet been recognised as minority groups under the minority regime. However, at least in the case of women, they are provided with special protections by international treaties and conventions in other UN instruments.[10]

International descriptions of minority groups are not exhaustive and illustrate the dynamic tension contained in the minority question. Although my research explores the question from the perspective of conflicts resulting from establishment

---

[7] Capotorti 6, 8, 95.

[8] *Ibid.* 5–6. Capotorti warns, however, that there is still no generally accepted definition of the term "minority."

[9] Kymlicka, Will. *Finding Our Way, Rethinking Ethno-cultural Relationships in Canada* (Ontario, OUP, 1998), 91, 93, 98, 101.

[10] *Convention On The Elimination Of All Forms Of Discrimination Against Women, 1979.* 1249 UNTS 13.

International Covenant on Political and Civil Rights, 1966 999 UNTS 171.

of the nation-state, it is conceivable that movements for expansion of minority group categories to incorporate other groups will continue. The prospect of expanding categories of minority classifications ad infinitum results in criticism of special rights for minorities. Some authors favour the alternative remedy of equal opportunity and universalised protection from invidious forms of discrimination for members of groups who suffer inequality.[11] As we shall discover, anti-discrimination and equal opportunity guarantee only the protection of individuals, and do not protect minorities as groups. Illustrating the failure of anti-discrimination laws to protect African-Americans, for example, Sandra Freedman explains:[12]

> As surely as the law has outlawed racial discrimination, it has affirmed that Black Americans can be without jobs, have their children in all black, poorly funded schools, have no opportunities for decent housing and have very little political power, without any violation of anti-discrimination law.

International protections for religious belief were the earliest forms of minority rights adopted by nations. The desire to protect religious minorities often served as a pretext for war between nations. Prior to WWI, a large number of treaties dating back to 1606 were concluded to protect religious group freedom of conscience and worship. Many governments also provided religious group forms of political autonomy. The Ottoman Empire, for example, had established a *millet system* which granted religious freedoms to minorities throughout the empire from the end of the fifteenth century to the 1920's. Each millet or religious community had a degree of autonomy in civil and religious matters controlling education, taxation (subject to Turkish Sultan tribute), marriage and wills. Until the eighteenth century, the Jewish population of Europe secured autonomy in the management of their own affairs forming, for example, Jewish Kahals or autonomous communities in Poland responsible for religious and secular matters. The Congress of Vienna, conducted by the Holy Alliance of Sovereigns of Austria, Prussia and Russia on 26 September 1815 as a result of the defeat of Napoleon, also became the custodians of Europe responsible for the protection of minority groups during the era of the Concert of Europe.[13]

---

[11] Miller, David. *On Nationality* (New York, OUP, 1995), 154. Miller writes "[the] principle of nationality is resistant to special rights for groups, over…what equal treatment requires…".

[12] Freedman, Sandra, "Discrimination", *Oxford Handbook of Legal Studies,* eds. Cane, Peter, and Tushnet, Mark (Oxford, Oxford University Press, July, 2003), 220.

Makkonen, LLM. Timo, "Multiple Compound and Intersectional Discrimination: Bringing the Experiences of the Most Marginalised to the Fore" (Abo, Institute of Human Rights, April 2002), 1. Makkonen argues that individuals are sometimes located in multiple categories of minority groups.

[13] Capotorti 1.

Capotorti finds that protection of religious minorities was the pretext for the following foreign interventions: invasion of France in 1655 by England to protect the Waldensians; invasions by

2.2. *Minority Groups and the Nation-State*

> *"The greatest adversary of the rights of nationality is the modern theory of nationality. By making the state and nation commensurate with each other in theory, it reduces practically to a subject condition all other nationalities that may be within the boundary. ... The co-existence of several nations under the same state... indicates a state of greater*

Holland to protect French Calvinists; invasion of Poland by Sweden and Prussia in 1707 to protect Protestants.

Ibid., 1–2. Capotorti identifies numerous treaties protecting religious minorities, including the Treaty of Vienna of 1606 between Hungary and Transylvania protecting the Protestant minority; Treaty of Westphalia of 1648 between France and the Holy Roman Empire protecting Protestants in Germany; the Treaty of Oliva of 1660 between Sweden and Poland protecting Roman Catholics in Sweden; the Treaty of Nijmegen concluded in 1678 between France and Holland protecting Roman Catholics in Holland; the Treaty of Ryswick of 1697 between the same parties; the Treaty of Paris of 1763 between France, Spain and Great Britain protecting Roman Catholics in Canadian Territories; the Treaty of Vienna of 31 May 1815 between Austria and the Netherlands protecting the Belgian Catholic minority; the Final Act of Congress of Vienna, signed on 9 June 1815 by Austria, France, Great Britain, Portugal, Prussia, Russia and Sweden protecting national minorities; the Protocol of 3 February 1830 between France, Great Britain and Russia guaranteeing freedom of worship for Muslims; the Treaty of Paris of 30 March 1856 between Austria, France, Great Britain, Prussia, Sardinia and Turkey protecting Christians in Turkey; the Treaty of Berlin of 13 July 1878 between Germany, Austria, Hungary, France, Great Britain, Italy, Russia and Turkey protecting religious freedom in the Balkan States; the International Convention of Constantinople of 24 May 1881 between Germany, Austria, Hungary, France, Great Britain, Italy, Russia and Turkey protecting religious freedom for Muslims in Greece.

Also, Mair, L.P. *The Protection of Minorities, the Working and Scope of the Minorities Treaties Under the League of Nations* (London, Christophers, 1928), 30, includes a reference to the Conference of Constantinople of 1856 that established Moldavia and Wallachia as independent principalities.

Thornberry, Patrick. *International Law and Minorities*, 29.

Claude 8–10. On p. 8, Claude notes that in "...the Final Act of the Congress of Vienna... Russia, Prussia, and Austria committed themselves to respect the nationality of their Polish subjects." On p. 9, writing about the 1900–1909 campaign by Prince Von Bulow, German Chancellor to make Prussia a specifically German state, Claude highlights how minority issues became the subject of international dispute and unwanted intervention against national sovereignty.

Robinson, Jacob. *Were The Minorities Treaties a Failure?* (New York, Antin Press Inc., 1943), 28.

De Tocqueville, Alexis. *Democracy in America* (trans. Harvey C. Mansfield and Delba Winthrop; Chicago: University of Chicago Press, 2000), 243; Mill, John Stuart. *On Liberty and Other Essays* (Oxford, OUP, 1998), xiv, 82; *International Covenant of Civil and Political Rights* 999 UNTS 171; *Universal Declaration of Human Rights, 1948* UN doc. A/811; Benito, Elizabeth Odio. *"Elimination of All Forms of Intolerance and Discrimination Based on Religion or Belief"* (Geneva, UN Publication, 1989), 2, 3; *Declaration On The Elimination Of All Forms Of Intolerance And Of Discrimination Based On Religion Or Belief, 1981*, UN doc. A/36/684. Also *see* the *Declaration on the Rights of Minorities* UN Dco.A/RES/47/135,3 February 1993. Seminal thinkers such as Alexis de Tocqueville and John Stuart Mill provide yet another category for the term minority, based upon defending the opinions of individuals whose conscience, belief or thought differsfrom the majority view. They do not argue for the protection of a particular group, albeit religious,

advancement than the national unity which is the ideal of modern liberalism." John Emerich Edward Dalberg-Acton, First Baron, 1907.[14]

The evolution of the nation-state is important to the subject of cultural rights because it helps us to understand the origination for the modern concept of a minority. For example, E.J. Hobsbawm concludes that the term minority belongs exclusively to a "particular, and historically recent period...[and] a certain kind of modern territorial state"[15] namely, the nation-state. For Hobsbawm, the terms *nation-state, nation, nationality, and minority* are all "intertwined and sides of the same coin."[16]

After the fall of the Roman Empire, *Christendom* replaced Europe and the Roman Empire as the name for the area. Christendom was governed by a sovereign authority. From the eleventh century onwards, the Pope alone was free to decree what was right or in the public interest.[17] *De Systematibus Civitatum* is Martin Wight's seminal writing that traces the evolution of the modern nation-states system as evolving from the *Treaty of Westphalia* in 1648. The peace established by the Congress of Westphalia became the legal basis of the modern state system and marks the transition from religious to secular politics, that is, from Christendom back to Europe.[18] More than three hundred part-sovereign states were recognised by the Peace of Westphalia.[19] Wight explains how Western Christendom or *Res publica Christiana* was a system of universal jurisdiction *in temporalibus* based on unity and hierarchy that ruled through a bureaucratic distribution of power among multiple government units. Some of these units became *civitates et reginae* or a 'perfect community' that gives birth to the idea of sovereign states.[20] The states emerged out of the schism that divided Latin Christendom between two to three rival popes. The medieval

national, ethnic, or linguistic, but rather for a political and social structure that fosters human autonomy and protects the individual against what de Tocqueville describes as "tyranny of majority." Aspects of their ideas are woven into the fabric of these cited international standards protecting individual thought, conscience and belief. International conventions give protection to individual conscience and thought as well as to religious belief and worship. In addition, religious minorities are defined as a minority group under the current UN Human Rights Treaty System that specifically identifies religious groups as a protected minority.

14 Dalberg-Acton, John Emerich Edward. *The History of Freedom and Other Essays*, Eds. Figgis, John Neville; Laurence, Reginald Vere (New York, Books for Libraries Press, 1907), 290, 297.

15 Hobsbawm, E.J. *Nations and Nationalism since 1780* (Cambridge, Cambridge University Press, 1990), 9.

16 *Ibid.*

17 Hinsley, F. H. *Sovereignty* (Cambridge, Cambridge University Press, 1986), 54.

18 Wight, Martin. *Systems of States*, Ed. Bull, Hedley (New Jersey, Leicester University Press, 1977), 113.

19 Baker, P. J. *The Doctrine of Legal Equality*, The British Year Book of International Law, 1923–1924 (London, Frwode, Hodder & Stoughton, 1924), 9;

20 Bodin, Jean. *On Sovereignty* (Cambridge, Cambridge University Press, 1992). Bodin (1576) was the first man to state the theory behind the word sovereignty.

international papal monarchy was replaced by a system of secular powers as well as kings and churches organised according to nation-states that included Italy, France, Germany, England and Spain. The Holy Roman Empire was transformed into an Italian great power. Each state had its own national sentiment based upon a common religion, *cuius regio, eius religio*.[21] Later, the doctrine evolves into the more contemporary idea of the national identity derived from its particular ruler, *cuius regio eius natio*.[22]

Wight concludes that most state systems end up in a universal empire with jurisdiction over all the states of the system. This is because sovereign state systems, in contrast to universal empires, must rely upon a balance of power between them that leads to a monopoly of power.[23] Inevitably, the sovereign states of Europe formulated into the Central Power and Allied Powers (Triple Alliance) balance of power alliances that degenerated into WWI resulting, by some estimates, in fifteen million deaths. The death toll from the states-system battles in WWI was higher than that from all wars fought between the years 1793–1914.[24] The resulting carnage motivated United States President Woodrow Wilson to support the creation of a League of Nations to serve as a universal organisation for the collective peace and security of states and peoples. His objective was to prevent another great war that had ravaged not only the states of Europe but also the peoples of the world.

National culture, like that of the nation, is also a vague concept. Authors who write about the subject of culture and national identity maintain that characteristics of culture are broken down into two different aspects. Firstly, higher order culture represented by artistic, literary, scientific, and intellectual work that tends to be the preserve of the elite. And second, an anthropological type of culture reflected in a people's characteristics, the main components being not only language, religion, and education but also myth, symbols, icons, dress, customs, habits, and morals.[25] Anthony Smith explains that the basis of prejudice in the twentieth century is not physical (racial) – rather it is cultural. Smith postulates

---

[21] *Cuius regio, eius religio* means that the faith of the ruler becomes the religion of the state; literally, like king, like religion.
Wight 26–28, 44, 131, 151.

[22] *Cuius regio eius natio* means that the nation has the same identity as the ruler or that national identity derives from the ruler; literally, like king, like nation.
Claude 90.

[23] Wight 43, 44, 149.

[24] *The Messages and Papers of Woodrow Wilson*, Vol. 1, Ed. Shaw, Albert (New York, The Review of Reviews Corporation, 1924), 926–927.

[25] Eagleton, Terry. *The Idea of Culture* (Oxford, Blackwell Publishers Ltd., 2000), 118.
Akermark, Athanasia Spiliopoulou. *Justifications of Minority Protection In International Law* (The Hague, Kluwer Law International, 1997), 81.

that the problem of nationalism is found in its ethnocentrism or belief of the centrality, rightness and superiority of one's own community and a corresponding denial of value of other communities. Throughout the twentieth century, stronger nations often attacked subordinate and weaker national groups and their cultures, often by war, population transfer, de-nationalisation and genocide.

Totalitarian states resulted from nationalist-inspired campaigns throughout Europe as well as Asia, such as: Germany's National Socialism and the Third Reich under Adolf Hitler 1933–45; Greece's Third Hellenic Civilisation under Greek General Joannes Metexas 1936–41; Spain's Great Spanish Empire of the Golden Century under Francisco Franco Falangists 1939; Italy's Fascists under Benito Mussolini 1932; Japan's Land of The Rising Sun under Emperor Hirohito, 1936; Russian Pan-Slavism, from the 1867 Pan-Slav Congress to the Bolshevik revolution and continuing through the defeat of Hitler's Pan-Germanism campaign in 1949; The Young Turks of the Committee of Union Progress (CUP), and Pan-Turkism under the Ottoman Empire, 1908–18.[26]

My research does not attempt to provide a comprehensive analysis of nationalism. However, as I discuss in chapters 2 and 3, the record of state practices inspired by the ideology of nationalism is bound to the justification for the minority regime. That is, the minority regime is established as a corrective to the record of atrocity caused by state coercive assimilation campaigns inspired by the ideology of nationalism. The historical record of coercive assimilation campaigns used against minority groups is not incidental. Rather, state-sponsored violence used against minority groups in the twentieth century simply overwhelms to shock the moral conscience.

De-nationalisation campaigns that took place against subordinate national groups and weak national states resulted in such large humanitarian disasters that it is difficult to understand how nationalism survived as a legitimate ideology upon which to base the existence of a state. The Young Turks' movement to transform Turkey into a homogenised, Islamic nation under Ottoman rule (Ottomanisation), for example, began in 1894–1896 with a series of organised massacres on the Caucasus border against ethnic Christian-Armenians suspected of disloyalty. The Turkish government began a systematic murder campaign against Armenians

---

[26] Smith, Anthony D.S. *Nationalism In The Twentieth Century* (Oxford, Martin Robertson and Co., 1979), 88, 90–91. Smith maintains that physical anthropologists divide the human species into the following broad racial categories: Mongoloid, Negroid, Caucasian, Australoid, American Indian or Hottentot.

Kymlicka, Will. *Politics In The Vernacular*, 230. Kymlicka notes French Government coercion of Breton and Basque groups, Slovak government actions against ethnic Hungarians, and Latvian government activity against ethnic Russians.

Kohn, Hans. *Nationalism, Its Meaning and History* (Princeton, D.Van Nostrand Co., Inc., 1955), 80.

Kayali, Hasan. *Arabs and Young Turks: The Ottoman Empire 1908–1918* (Berkeley, University of California Press, 1997).

lasting through WWI and resulting in over 1.4 million Armenian deaths, in the first contemporary genocide by a nation-state against one of its subordinate national groups.[27]

In addition to de-nationalisation efforts, other techniques such as the transfer of entire populations out of the country were implemented as an instrument to eliminate ethnically different subordinate national groups and purge nation-states of minorities. These actions resulted in no less than seventeen migratory movements in Macedonia alone from 1912–1925. The Turko-Bulgarian Convention of 1913, for example, mandated the reciprocal exchange of 48,570 Moslem Bulgarians to Turkey for 46,764 Bulgars from Turkish Thrace. Ironically, population transfer of subordinate national groups was used by nation-states to not only rid the state of different national minority groups but also as a perverse type of protection for minorities because it resulted in the total elimination of national minorities, transforming minorities into refugees.[28]

The League of Nation's Minority Protection Treaty System, intended by the new-world body as a form of protection by treaty for minority groups, contained provisions agreeing to the exchange of minority populations. The Treaty of Peace between The Allied Powers and Bulgaria, signed at Neuilly-sur-Seine on 27 November 1919, agreed to the reciprocal population migration exchanges between Greece, Bulgaria, and Turkey; and the Lausanne Convention Concerning the Exchange of Greek and Turkish Populations of 30 January 1923 as part of Greece's peace settlement with Turkey agreed to the forcible expulsion of 2 million Greek-Orthodox Catholics from Turkey to Greece and 500 thousand Moslem residents in Greece to Turkey.[29] The Lausanne treaty had devastating effects on Greece and Turkey's respective migrating populations for generations to come. Turkey suffered economic paralysis as a result of losing its skilled and entrepreneurial, ethnic Greek residents. From 1922 through to 1928, seventy-five thousand Greek refugees from Turkey died in Greece. The fate of the remaining 1.25–1.4 million Asia Minor Greek refugees expelled from Turkey is well documented by Rene Hirchon, who uncovers the failure of these cosmopolitan Greek-Turks to assimilate back into traditional Greek society.[30]

---

27 Mair, L.P. *The Protection of Minorities, The Working and Scope of the Minorities, Treaties Under the League of Nations* (London, Christophers, 1928), 217.
Dadrian, Vahakn N. *The History of Armenian Genocide, Ethnic Conflict from the Balkans to Anatoli to Causasus* (Providence, Berghan Books, 1997), Introduction.

28 Ladis, Stephen. *The Exchange of Minorities, Bulgaria, Greece and Turkey* (New York, The MacMillan Co., 1932), 16–17, 728.

29 *Ibid.*, 728.

30 Hirschon, Renee. *Heirs of the Greek Catastrophe, The Social Life of Asia Minor Refugees in Priaeus* (New York, OUP, 1999), 36.

Germany's de-nationalisation campaign in the twentieth century resulted in the genocide of over six million Jews and one-half million Roma. The Nazis used de-nationalisation not only to kill, but also as a process to eradicate the national culture of a subordinate national group. The process was directed against national groups as an entity and the actions involved were directed against individuals – not in their individual capacity, but as members of the national group. National groups viewed states as a means to reproduce culture, often through violent means of destruction.[31] Population transfer, de-nationalisation, and genocide did not end with the defeat of the Axis Powers in WWII. Population transfers of so-called minorities or national groups continued after the war and included the exchange of twelve million Hindus and Moslems between India and Pakistan after the 1949 partition of India, as well as the migration of four hundred and twenty-five thousand Jews to Israel by 1952. Genocide of national minority groups after WWII continued to be used by nation-states as a tool to annihilate weaker national groups. In one study of genocide, Ted Gurr and Barbara Harff estimate there have been seven to sixteen million human victims of genocide since 1945. A more recent example is the murder of eight hundred thousand Tutsi tribe members by Hutu nationalist troops in Rwanda.[32]

2.3. *To End All Wars*

The League of Nations recognises the inalienable rights of nationality, the rights of minorities and the sanctity of religious belief and practice. Woodrow Wilson, 1919[33]

Religious group membership, not nationality, is the only criterion for compulsory population transfer in *The Lausanne Convention Concerning the Exchange of Greek and Turkish Populations of January 30, 1923.* Convention Article 1 identifies persons subject to compulsory exchange as Turkish nationals of the Greek Orthodox religion established in Turkish Territory and Greek nationals of the Moslem religion in the Greek Territory.

Ladis, Stephen P. *The Exchange of Minorities, Bulgaria, Greece and Turkey* (New York, The MacMillan Co., 1932), 3.

Ibid., 77. Ladis identifies three criteria, race, religion or language used to qualify persons as national minorities eligible to benefit from the several Conventions on reciprocal migration.

31 Hitler, Adolf, *Mein Kampf (My Struggle)* (London, Radius Books/Hutchinson and Co. Ltd., 1936), 356–357. Hitler exploits German culture to promote totalitarianism writing "the state…is the necessary basis for the formation of a higher culture.…The highest end of the national (Volkish) state is to *see* the preservation of those social elements which give out culture, and create the beauty and dignity of a higher humanity."

32 Power 91.

Barbara Harff and Ted Robert Gurr. *"Toward Empirical Theory of Genocides and Politicides: Identification and Measurement of Cases Since 1945,"* International Studies Quarterly 32:3 (Sept.1988) 370.

33 *The Messages and Papers of Woodrow Wilson,* Vol. 1 Ed. Albert Shaw (New York, The Review of Reviews Corp., 1924), 692. Woodrow Wilson extols the Versailles Peace Treaty 28/06/19.

Normative questions about whether minority regimes constitute special rights in contrast to an international corrective for biased state structures are discovered throughout discussions during the Paris Peace conference at the conclusion of WWI. Domestic debates focus on the desire to protect national sovereignty against interference from the League of Nations. Wight's theory about the tendency of the state system to reduce into a unity of universal jurisdiction[34] is also evident throughout these debates. The United Nations' human rights treaty system (section 1.1 a), inclusive of the minority regime, may be viewed as an example of universal jurisdiction incorporated into the sovereign obligations of states.

Lieutenant General J.C. Smuts (British Empire) proposed an article at the Paris Peace Conference for the League of Nations' Covenant to place the subjugated nations living in the German, Ottoman (Turkish), and Austro-Hungarian empires under a mandatory or trusteeship of the League of Nations. Smuts' proposal for a system of mandates or "the heir of empires" called for all new independent, self-governing nation-states arising out of conquered Central Power (Triple Alliance) states' territories.[35] Smuts justified his plan as a response to the empires placing multiple nations under state control that resulted in miniature leagues of nations (national units) in themselves held together by political repression:[36]

> Usually one dominant nation in the group overcame, coerced, and kept the rest under. The principle of nationality became overstrained and over-developed, and nourished itself by exploiting other weaker nationalities. Nationality overgrown became imperialism, and the empire led a troubled existence on the ruin of the freedom of its constituent nations.

---

[34] Wight 42.

[35] Lansing, Robert. *The Peace Negotiations, A Personal Narrative* (Port Washington, Kennikat Press, 1921), 82.

Simpson, A.W. Brian. *Human Rights and the End of Empire* (Oxford, OUP, 2001), 145–146. The League eventually passed a revised form of the plan as Article XXII. Simpson discusses League of Nations Covenant Article XXII citing seminal works describing the League's mandates system that would now administer the Central Power controlled colonies. Article XXII provided for mandates of three different types. "Class A Mandates were for…certain communities formerly belonging to the Turkish Empire [which] have reached a state of development where their existence as independent nations can be provisionally recognised…Class B mandates were for territories in Central Africa and elsewhere, which were thought to be still incapable of self-government and…inhabited by peoples not yet able to stand by themselves under the strenuous conditions of the modern world (neurasthenia)…Class C mandates were for territories, such as those in the South-west Africa and the Pacific which, because of their character or isolation, would forever have to be administered as dependencies…".

[36] Smuts, J.C. *The League of Nations, A Practical Suggestion*, Ed. Miller, David Hunter. *The Drafting of the Covenant, Vol. II* (New York, London, G.P. Putnam's Sons, 1928), 25.

Smuts' plan echoed the justifications US President Woodrow Wilson provided to support America's entry into WWI during his Fourteen Points[37] address to Congress. Wilson's justification was to not only stop Germany's expansionism[38] but also to implement an international principle of national self-governance, namely, *self-determination* for the nations living in Central Power states' controlled territories. Woodrow Wilson maintained that "the war had its roots in the disregard of the rights of small nations and of nationalities which lacked the union and the force to make good their claim to determine their own allegiances and their forms of life."[39]

Wilson proposed *the first official international recognition of minority groups* living within Central Power territories including Germany's colonies in Asia and Africa. At the conference, Wilson unsuccessfully lobbied for including minority protection in the League of Nations' Covenant preamble:[40]

> The League of Nations shall require of all new states to accord to all racial or national minorities within their several jurisdictions exactly the same treatment and security, both in law and fact, that is accorded the racial or national majority of their people.

However, Wilson's idea was opposed not only by his political opponents but also by his Secretary of State, Robert Lansing, who maintained that the phrase (self-determination) "is simply loaded with dynamite. In the end, it is bound to be discredited."[41] Lansing was concerned that the phrase would encourage movements for independent statehood by the Irish, the Indians, the Boers, the Mohammedans of Syria, Palestine, Morroco, and Tripoli as well as Jewish Zionists.[42] Wilson's Republican political opponents attacked his plans on the grounds that such a plan would interfere with American sovereignty.

---

[37] Clements, Kendrick A. and Cheezum, Eric A. *Woodrow Wilson* (Washington D.C., CQ Press, 2003), 211–214: The Fourteen Points, Woodrow Wilson address to a joint session of Congress, January 8, 1918.

[38] *The Messages and Papers of Woodrow Wilson*, Vol. I, Ed. Albert Shaw (New York, The Review of Reviews, 1924), 758. The Formula of Pan-Germanism included control of Poland, Bohemia (Czech and Slovak Republics or Czecho-Slovakia) Hungary, Romania, Jugo-Slavia, Turkey, Persia, and Baghdad.

Ibid., 912. The German Empires' formula was known as Breman to Baghdad and included control from the North Sea to Persia, crushing little Serbia and all Balkan states, taking Turkey and Arabian lands, penetrating Persia, and opening the gates of India to dominate the world.

[39] *Ibid.*, 476.

[40] Miller, David Hunter. Vol. II, 91. However, this provision was not accepted into the League Covenant.

[41] Lansing, Robert. *The Peace Negotiations, A Personal Narrative* (Port Washington, Kennikat Press, 1921), 97.

[42] *Ibid.*

Senator Henry Cabot Lodge (R-Ma) (1925) wrote that "no American soldiers or sailors must be sent to fight in other lands at the bidding of a League of Nations. American lives must not be sacrificed except by the will and command of the American people."[43] He maintained that the United States must have the exclusive right to decide all questions of domestic jurisdiction and that such questions should never be submitted to the League of Nations.[44] Theodore Roosevelt Jr. (US President 1901–1909) was more blunt, explaining that the US was fighting to beat Germany and not for a new international order.[45] Republican opposition led by William Howard Taft (U.S. President 1909–1913) to the proposed League of Nations' Covenant centred on four main points: reservation for American control of domestic questions; reservation for the Monroe Doctrine;[46] treaty withdrawal guarantees; and optional acceptance of mandatory territories.[47]

The minority regime (section 2.5) created by the League of Nations' members is based upon the Wilsonian doctrine supporting the self-determination of nations. Practical and strategic considerations frequently trumped the doctrine. Wilson was said to fear that self-determination would lead Europe to have "spots all over it"[48] and claim little islands of nationals. Also, as soon as a national group was granted self-determination in the form of statehood, new sub-national minority groups living within the territory of the new state emerged. The re-productive character[49] of the doctrine became apparent to Wilson himself who recognised that new self-governing states could not be created for every national-minority group that desired it. The drawing of state boundaries according to the ethnical character of territories became unfeasible such that protection of minority rights emerged as the new basis for ensuring peace.[50] Despite the practical limitations of Wilson's self-determination doctrine, Winston Churchill noted that as a result of the Versailles Peace Treaty, fewer than three percent of Europeans were condemned

---

43 Lodge, Henry Cabot. *The Senate and The League of Nations* (New York, Charles Scribner Sons, 1925), 174.

44 *Ibid.*

45 Bailey, Thomas A. *Woodrow Wilson and the Lost Peace* (Chicago, Quadrangle Paperbacks, 1944), 17.

46 Miller, David Hunter. *The Drafting of the Covenant*, Vol. I (New York, G.P. Putnam's Sons, 1928) 295. US President Monroe's doctrine establishes that "The American continents by the free and independent condition which they have assumed and maintain, are henceforth not to be considered as subjects for future colonisation by any European powers."

Ibid., 373. The Monroe Doctrine prohibits American intervention in European affairs.

47 *Ibid.*, 276.

48 Bailey 258.

49 Musgrave, Thomas. D. *Self-Determination and National Minorities* (Oxford, Clarendon Press, 1977), 259. Musgrave discovered that the implementation of the doctrine of self-determination usually creates further claims to self-determination from other minority groups.

50 Miller, David Hunter. Vol. II, 71.

to live under governments whose nationality they repudiated.[51] The Versailles Peace Treaty resulted in the closest to an ethnographic map coinciding with a political map that could have been created, and was considered a victory for national self-determination as many more millions of minority groups were released from alien domination than were consigned to alien domination.[52]

Political spoils resulting from the competition for power sometimes determined which minority groups would be granted statehood after WWI. Central Power states decried the unequal and, at times, hypocritical application for minority rights exclusively applied against the defeated Central Power states. The doctrine's lack of universality was one of the aspects that played a role in the demise of the League's minority regime (section 2.5). The Allied and Associated Powers, including the United States, the British Empire, France, Russia, and Japan had no obligation to provide any minority protection under the Versailles Peace Treaty. It also distinguishes the League of Nations' minority rights treaty system, from the United Nations' minority regime.

For example, Wilson had to violate his own principles of self-determination by giving Estonia, Latvia, Lithuania, the Ukraine, Georgia, and Azerbaijan over to Russian control (Great Russia);[53] France was permitted to occupy German-populated Rhine territory as well as draft indigenous populations residing in Germany's African colonies into the French army; Austrian South Tyrol inhabited by Germans was incorporated into Italy; Shantung Province in China inhabited by thirty million Chinese was awarded to Japan; and the African Congo to Belgium.[54] Also, popular views influenced by the emergence of racist pseudo-eugenics science (Chapters 4 and 5) as well as nativist movements opposing immigration were evident throughout the Conference.

---

[51] Bailey 316.

Hoover, Herbert. *The Ordeal of Woodrow Wilson* (London, Museum Press Ltd., 1958), 263. US President Herbert Hoover notes that, as a result of the Allied and Associated Powers victory in WWI, the following new nation-states emerged out of the empires established by the Central Power states: Estonia declared independence on 28/11/17; Finland on 6/12/17; Latvia on 12/1/18; Lithuania on 26/2/18; Georgia, Azerbaijan, and Russian Armenia on 26/5/18; Chechoslovakia on 25/10/18; Croatia, Slovenia, Montenegro and the Banat, joined with Serbia under a constitutional monarchy on 29/10/18; Poland on 5/11/18; Hejaz (Saudi Arabia) on 20/05/27; Hungary on 16/05/18; Austria on 10/09/19; and Turkey on 29/10/23.

[52] Bailey 315–316.

[53] Lansing, Robert. *The Peace Negotiations, A Personal Narrative* (Port Washington, Kennikat Press, 1921), 100.

[54] Bailey 169–171, 173, 218, 252, 277. German residents in the Saar Basin were granted autonomy through plebiscite.

Ibid. 282. The US press described the Allies' transfer of the Shantung Province as the Crime of Shantung (also described as the 'Rape of Shantung') and played a critical role in the US refusal to ratify the Versailles Peace Treaty and enter the League of Nations.

David Hunter Miller was the legal counsel to President Wilson during the Conference, as well as being considered one of the drafting architects for the League of Nations' Covenant. Miller's two-volume work on the drafting of the League of Nations' Covenant[55] explains that Wilson was angered by a delegation of Irish-Americans who visited him in the United States lobbying him to seek independence for Ireland at the Peace Conference.[56] He was only half joking when he said "Italians might claim hundreds of thousands of their compatriots in New York City."[57] Wilson's refusals enhanced domestic US opposition to the Treaty from Irish-American and Italian-American groups. Japan's equality of nations (section 2.4) amendment was defeated at the Conference because of American fears that recognising the equality of all nations would weaken US restrictions against Japanese, Chinese, and Hindu immigration. Wilson also was concerned that the proposal would arouse so-called coloured people all over the world as well as inflame Japanese immigrants living on the west coast. Lord Robert Cecil (British Empire) opposed the Japanese proposal, fearing it would make for "millions of uneasy coloured subjects."[58] General Smuts (British Empire) considered the German colonies in the Pacific and Africa as "inhabited by barbarians",[59] and he excluded them from his original mandates proposal. In one conversation recorded at the peace conference between Colonel Edward M. House (USA) and Arthur James Balfour (British Prime Minister 1902–1905), Balfour said that the theory written in the US Declaration of Independence that all men are created equal was "an eighteenth century proposition which he did not believe was true."[60] He did not believe that "a man in Central Africa was created equal to a European."[61] According to Lloyd George (British Empire), the only restriction on France taking the German-African colonies in Togo and the Cameroons was "not to train big nigger armies"[62] for offensive operations. However, despite these obnoxiously racist positions taken by the Allies, the inter-relationship between principles inherent in Wilson's doctrine of self-determination such as autonomy and minority protection survived to become an aspect of the modern-day minority regime.

Much of the normative discussion on multiculturalism concerns the Wilsonian dilemma of how to provide self-determination for the world's numerous

[55] Miller, David Hunter. Vol.s I &II.
[56] *Ibid.*, Vol. II, 294.
[57] Bailey 258.
[58] *Ibid.*, 274–275.
[59] Miller, David Hunter. Vol. I, 36.
[60] *Ibid.*, 183.
[61] *Ibid.*
[62] Miller, David Hunter. Vol. II, 116.

ethnographic minority groups. Many political theorists maintain that state sovereignty be accepted as a baseline and oppose equal recognition for nations on practical grounds. For example, Will Kymlicka maintains that there are too many national groups to permit each group to have its own state; Jacob Levy writes "a nationalism of all nations is simply not possible"[63]; Chandran Kukathus argues that "[group] equality is, in principle, unattainable."[64]

Brian Barry opposes the equal recognition of national groups. For example, Barry protests against Belgium's devolution initiatives that provide recognition for Dutch-speaking Flanders, French speaking Wallonia, and bi-lingual Brussels: "the endless process of haggling that is Belgian politics is so nauseating to all concerned that it is widely thought the country would have already broken up…".[65] In contrast to Barry's view that Belgium suffers "a democratic deficit"[66], the *Freedom in the World*[67] survey gives Belgium its highest rating for political rights and civil liberties. Critics of multiculturalism view cultural rights as fragmenting citizenship along group lines. For David Miller, nationality is resistant to the concept of minority rights which he describes as special rights. Miller views nationality, and by implication the nation-state, as an idea that incorporates common citizenship.[68]

By contrast, critics of a state that is based upon national in contrast to civic values, the idea of common citizenship is parasitic upon a pre-existing political community.[69] That is, by virtue of the control of a state's administrative apparatus by a majority, or even a powerful minority national group, the state's structure prevents common citizenship between its constituent heterogeneous cultural groups. The minority regime is the corrective for a national group's monopoly control of the state apparatus.

---

[63] Levy, Jacob. *The Multiculturalism of Fear* (Oxford, OUP, 2000), 69.

[64] Kukathas, Chandran. *The Liberal Archipelago, A Theory of Diversity and Freedom* (Oxford, OUP, 2003), 243.

[65] Barry 312.

[66] *Ibid.*, 226.

[67] *Freedom in the World, The Annual Survey of Political Rights & Civil Liberties 2003*, eds. Adrian Karatnycky, Aili Piano, and Arch Puddington (New York and Washington DC, Rowman & Littlefield Publishers, Inc. 2003), 88. Also, the 2005 Freedom House survey gives Belgium its highest rating for political rights and civil liberties.

[68] Miller, David. *On Nationality* (New York, OUP, 1995), 140, 154. On p. 140 Miller writes that "Trust requires solidarity…and this in turn depends upon a common identification of the kind that nationality alone can provide."

[69] Canovan, Margaret. *Nationalism and Political Theory* (Edward Elgar, Cheltenham, Edward Elgar, 1996), 41, 21, 23, 31.

2.4. *The Equality of Nations*

> *"It cannot be expected that seven hundred million white people will be able to rule one billion colored people forever." Viscount Kikujiro Ishii, Japanese Ambassador to the Versailles Peace Conference.*[70]

The initial effort to pass an article recognising that all national groups are entitled to equal treatment took place during the post-WWI, Paris Peace Conference. In this section, I discuss the unsuccessful efforts by Japan to incorporate an equality of nations' article into the League of Nations' Covenant. The equality of nations' doctrine is important because it reduced the necessity for specific laws that required the differential treatment of minority groups. Provided states accepted the doctrine's proposition that all nations are entitled to equal recognition, narrower instruments such as minority rights' treaties that protect the ethnical characteristics of particular minority groups become less necessary. I also examine the equality of nations' doctrine as well as why the Paris Peace Conference rejected the egalitarian principle that all nations, and the respective members that comprise them, are inherently equal.

The Treaty of Versailles, signed at the end of WWI on 28 June 1919 with Germany by the Allied and Associated Powers of the United States, Great Britain, France, Italy and Japan, not only established a new international order but also recognised that treatment of minority groups was indispensable to maintaining international peace. The post-WWI new state boundaries established by the victorious Allied and Associated Powers at the Conference detached almost 100 million people from their pre-war empires of Central and Eastern Europe. After the post-war frontiers had been re-drawn, 25–30 million people in Central and Eastern Europe were transformed into national minorities living within different nation-states.[71]

The establishment of minority rights treaties at the conclusion of WWI uncovers an approach to the subject rarely discussed in political theory. The agreement by post-WWI nation-states in favour of treaties protecting minorities illustrates the international as opposed to the domestic nature of the minority question.

---

[70] Ishii, Viscount Kikujiro. *Diplomatic Commentaries*, Trans. William R. Langdon (Baltimore, The John Hopkins Press, 1936), 316.

[71] Robinson, Jacob. *Were The Minority Treaties a Failure?* (New York, Institute of Jewish Affairs of the American Jewish Congress and World Jewish Congress, 1943), 35; Claude 11. Robinson puts the total population of post-WWI national minorities at between 20–25 million, while Claude writes that 25–30 million national minorities were created by the post-WWI settlement.

The establishment of a minority treaty system after WWI, however, demonstrates that the minorities question was more a political competition than a normative question. The minority treaty system showed that minority rights is not so much an issue about group versus individual rights but rather a contest for sovereignty between strong and weak nations. The evolution of the international law on minority rights reflects the tension between the interests of existing states to preserve their sovereignty with those of national groups that lack statehood.[72] Legal historians explain that minority rights were awarded by the League of Nations' minority protection treaty system as a consolation prize to national groups who failed to obtain statehood after WWI.

The drafting by the Allied and Associated Powers of the League of Nations' Covenant was considered the most important work of the Paris Peace Conference. The League of Nations' charter represented the first serious attempt by an international body to pass an article recognising the equality of nations. During the drafting of the League Covenant, the Japanese government proposed that a clause be added to the League of Nations' Covenant Preamble, stating that the Members of the League endorsed the principle of the equality of all nations and the fair treatment of their nationals (peoples). The proposal would have established the precedent that all national groups should have rights to equal treatment under domestic law:[73]

> The equality of nations being a basic principle of the League of Nations, the high contracting parties agree to accord, as soon as possible, to all alien nationals of states members of the League equal and just treatment in every respect, making no distinction, either in law or in fact, on account of race or nationality.

Acceptance of the doctrine could have served as international equal protection for minority groups and have reduced the necessity for additional international instruments and treaties protecting classifications of minority groups. The legal *Doctrine of the Equality of Nations* is clarified by L. Oppenheim as an international doctrine having three important consequences: "...every nation has the right to vote, and to one vote only; ...the vote of the weakest and smallest State has quite as much

---

[72] Stallybrass, N.T.S. *A Society of States or Sovereignty, Independence, and Equality in A League of Nations* (London, George Routledge and Sons, Ltd., 1918), 40. Stallybrass lists the following as rights of sovereignty: right to self-preservation; right to national dominion by lawful means; right to trade; right to self-government and internal constitution; right to prohibit foreigners; right to territorial inviolability; right to make treaties and alliances.

[73] Miller, David Hunter. Vol. I, 183. The equality of nations' amendment was first proposed for inclusion in the League Covenant at the fifth meeting of the Commission on the League of Nations drafting the League's Covenant during its meeting at the Hotel de Crillon in Paris.

Ibid., 461. A revised equality of nations' proposal intended for insertion into the Covenant's pre-amble was submitted by Japan's Baron Makino at the last meeting of the Commission.

weight as the vote of the largest and most powerful...; according to the rule *par in parem non habet imperium* – no State can claim jurisdiction over another full-Sovereign State (sovereign states must voluntarily accept the jurisdiction of an international Court)."[74]

Similar to concepts such as self-determination, the equality of nations' doctrine idea contained ambiguity beyond the three principles established by Oppenheim. Baron Makino (Japan) explained that the purpose of the amendment was to:

> address the grievances of the oppressed nationalities....[and] the wrongs of racial discrimination which was, and is, the subject of deep resentment on the part of a large portion of the human race. The feeling of being slighted has long been a standing grievance with certain peoples...My amendment is to lay down a general principle as regards the relations between at least nationalities forming the League.[75]

The Japanese amendment was a reaction, in part, to the eugenics pseudo-science of the time containing racist theories of genetic inferiority that served to justify racist immigration restrictions as well as colonial practices against Asian and African nationalities. At the last Commission meeting, Japan's equality amendment was revised to insert into the League of Nations' Covenant pre-amble the phrase: "by the endorsement of the principle of equality of nations and just treatment of their nationals."[76]

Viscount Kikujiro Ishii, Japan's representative at the Paris Peace Conference subsequent to Makino, maintained that America had turned against Japanese immigrant labour because Americans are "more race conscious than any other people"[77] and their racialist theories had spread to the British dominions. Ishii decried American, British, Canadian, Australian, South African, and New Zealand immigration restrictions against Japanese, Chinese, Hindoos, and Malay labourers, as well as domestic programs of segregation and sterialisation for heredity (genetic) disease based upon eugenic pseudo-science. He protested against US laws permitting the immigration of "white races only",[78] specifically Anglo-Saxon, Germanic, and Scandanavian and for their enacting the quota system of 1924 excluding immigration of so-called coloured races. Ishii accused Great Britain, France, Russia, Holland, Belgium, Italy, and the USA of subjugating

---

[74] Barker, P. J. *The Doctrine of the Legal Equality of States*, British Year Book Of International Law, 1923–1924 (London, Henry Frowde and Hodder & Stoughton, 1924), 11–12. Barker limits the doctrine to one concerning the states' right to sovereign equality, that is, equal only to the degree that all states are sovereign.

[75] Miller, David Hunter. Vol. II, 388–389.

[76] *Ibid.*, 461.

[77] Ishii, Viscount Kikujiro. *Diplomatic Commentaries*, Trans. William R. Langdon (Baltimore, The John Hopkins Press, 1936), 304, 306. Specifically, the U.S. Federal Chinese Exclusion Law, 1880.

[78] *Ibid.*, 307.

races. He noted that over four hundred million people lived under overseas British rule and that the rise in nationalism among subject peoples would lead to independence movements throughout Asia and Africa. Finally, Ishii predicted that war between Japan (representing subjugated nations in African and Asian colonies) and the USA-led white colonial powers was inevitable if the race problem was not solved.

The equality amendment had potentially far-reaching consequences for minorities, even though the Japanese intended it primarily as a vehicle to weaken immigration restrictions. The USA, as well as other 'white' powers such as Australia and Canada, had enacted severe restrictions against Japanese immigration. The equality principle could be applied to not only protect the national and cultural characteristics of minorities in League states, but also would eliminate the racially based approach to limit Japanese and Asian immigration that was enacted by the USA and other 'white' nations.

Ishii explained that it is "impossible to extinguish the language, sentiments or faith of a racial minority"[79] in any single individual nation-state. State obligation to provide for equality as well as just treatment of minority groups implies a commitment to substantive equality for members of minority groups. Minority rights jurisprudence established by the League of Nations' Permanent Court of International Justice (PCIJ) (section 2.6) defined equal treatment for minorities to include the right to access and reproduce their culture, including linguistic and religious practices, in community with other members of their group. If passed, the amendment would have increased state obligations to provide for the official recognition of minority groups within League member states.

Wilson supported the amendment in principle but opposed its inclusion in the League of Nations' Covenant. He maintained that passage of an equality of nations' amendment was unnecessary since establishing the League of Nations as well as its Covenant was the first serious and systemic attempt in the world to put nations on a footing of equality with each other in their international relations.[80] At the final Commission meeting, Wilson intended "…to quiet discussion that raises national differences and racial prejudices…this and similar suggestions have set burning flames of prejudice, which it would be very unwise to allow to flare out in the public view…"[81]. Colonel House, in a letter to Wilson, warned that the amendment "would surely raise the race issue throughout the world."[82] Wilson was particularly concerned about domestic political opposition

[79] *Ibid.*, 315.

[80] Miller, David Hunter. Vol. I, 463.

[81] *Ibid.*, 462–463.

[82] *Ibid.*, 462.

on the Japanese-conscious Pacific Coast.[83] Passage of the amendment would aggravate nativist fears about increased immigration from Asia as well as domestic opposition to America's joining the League. US Secretary of State Robert Lansing considered it international anarchy to say that the state of Liberia comprised of a "few civilised Negroes has the same right as Germany."[84]

William Morris Hughes (Australian Prime Minister, 1915–1923) put up an impassioned fight against the equality amendment, explaining that White Australia would not tolerate even the faintest suggestion of a wedge that might be used to pry open her anti-Oriental barriers.[85] Lord Robert Cecil (British Empire) fought the amendment on sovereignty grounds, explaining that it opened the door to interference in the domestic affairs of League state members. However, Cecil's position concealed the British Empire's main concern about the amendment's potential to aggravate the nationalistic passions of millions of subjects living within the empire's colonised dominions containing persons of colour, including India and South Africa.[86] Wilson manipulated the requirement for an affirmative unanimous vote at the final commission meeting as necessary to gain passage of the equality amendment. This provided him, as well as Lord Cecil and other opponents, with the cover to oppose the passage of the equality amendment without having to record their formal opposition. The equality of nations' amendment was defeated for lack of American and British support. Wilson rationalised his conduct, explaining that, "I do not think that anybody will ever interpret the result...as a rejection on our part of the principle of equality of nations."[87]

2.5. *The League of Nations' Minority Protection Treaty System*

"The crisis of the classic formula, 'every nation a state and every state a nation' is now perceptible." P. De Azcarate, Director, Minorities Section, League of Nations.[88]

Though the equality of nations' proposal was defeated, Baron Makino, heading the Japanese delegation at the Conference, did accept a declaration on equality made at the plenary session of the Conference at which the Covenant was finally

[83] Bailey 275.

[84] Lansing, Robert. *The Peace Negotiations, A Personal Narrative* (Port Washington, Kennikat Press, 1921), 24.

[85] *Ibid.*, 274.

[86] Miller, David Hunter. Vol. I, 389.

[87] *Ibid.*, 465.

[88] Azcarate, P. De. *League of Nations and National Minorities, An Experiment*, Trans. Eileen E. Brooke (Washington D.C., Carnegie Endowment of International Peace, 1945) 1.

adopted. The failure of the Japanese proposal illustrates how nation-states refused to compromise their sovereignty by providing formal recognition of weaker national (minority) groups. Denied international recognition of full equality by the Peace Conference, minority groups made the more difficult claim for special minority rights (special protection, benefits and exceptions of law) within alien states.[89]

US President Woodrow Wilson's administration made several attempts to introduce into the League charter something less than full national equality in the form of minority protections. This included a failed effort at passing the religious liberty clause to protect the free exercise of any religious belief so long as this did not conflict with the public order or morals, and to protect any person from prosecution on account of his religious beliefs. Adopted and incorporated by the Japanese delegation into its equality of nations' proposal, this proposal was also defeated, in part, by French opposition. Wilson believed that permanent peace in Europe would be impossible to maintain "unless every race should have justice."[90] Wilson warned against the dangers of placing peoples under ever-changing national borders by requiring nation-states to act in a positive manner toward racial and national minorities through the provision of more than rules against mere discrimination. Wilson's second draft covenant proposed:

> The League shall require…autonomous states to accord all racial or national minorities within their several jurisdictions exactly the same treatment and security both in law and fact, that is accorded the racial or national majority of their people.[91]

However, even this weakened proposal for special rights in contrast to a stronger right of self-determination for national groups was rebuffed for incorporation in the charter by League states, because it posed a threat to League state sovereignty.

Rather than incorporate a universal proposal for minority protection into the League of Nations' charter, the Paris Peace Conference decided instead to protect only those minorities who resided in defeated Central Power states through the administration of a minority protection treaty system targeting the defeated powers. Victorious Allied and Associated Powers states were not parties to the

---

[89] Robinson, Jacob 7.

Walters, I.P. *A History Of The League of Nations* (London, Oxford University Press, 1952), 63.

Shoichi, Watanabe. *Looking at Japanese in Japanese History: Showa Era* (Tokyo: Shodensha, 1989), 128–176.

Nakamura, Akira. *Path to the Great East Asian War* (Tokyo, Tentensha, 1990), 174–175.

[90] Robinson, Jacob 7.

[91] Janowsky, Oscar I. *The Jews and Minority Rights 1898–1919* (New York, Columbia University Press, 1933), 321.

Hannum 28. Wilson believed that peoples and provinces, "must not be battered about from sovereignty to sovereignty as if they were chattels or pawns in a game."

minority treaties. A.W. Brian Simpson's work reviewing the history of human rights regimes reveals that "the treaties caused extreme resentment"[92] from states obligated to comply. "Why for example should Poland be bound by special rules when New Zealand, for example, or the United Kingdom, was not?"[93] An attempt in 1925 by Lithuania to promote the drafting of a general convention on minority rights, universally applying the minority regime to all states, failed to secure support from the League's assembly.[94]

In response to threats upon sovereignty posed by the treaties, the League's treaty system consciously deprived minority groups of *locus standi* or legal standing. This denied minority groups the same legal personality or corporate identity provided to nation-states. Minorities had no legal standing to file petitions, bring formal complaints, litigate disputes, or compel resolution of treaty disputes. Petitions from minority groups or individual members thereof were permitted by the League for informational purposes only and had no legal effect or requirements attached to them. Only the League's state members with an interest in the dispute had the right to compel a hearing about minority complaints. Despite the decision to deny *locus standi* to minority groups, supporters of the League system such as Inis Claude maintain that the League's system of treaties, declarations, and agreements concerning minorities as well as granting minorities rights of petition to the League as informational agents, could well be interpreted as granting indirect or implicit recognition to minority groups *per se*. Minorities wished to be recognised in the League system as collective entities with the ability to petition and participate in League affairs, in a manner comparable to that of states. The fundamental inconsistency of the League's attempt to guarantee collective rights to minority groups without full recognition of the concept of collective existence was a source of on-going confusion for the treaty system.[95] P. De Azcarate, Director of the League's Minority Section, concluded that persuasion and moral pressure were not enough and that, to protect minority groups, it was necessary to impose methods of coercion organised under the international rule of law.[96]

Walters, I.P. *A History Of The League of Nations* (London, Oxford University Press, 1952), 63–4. Walters discusses French opposition to Wilson's religious liberty clause.

92 Simpson 128.

93 *Ibid.*

94 *Ibid.*

95 Mair, L.P. *The Protection of Minorities The Working and Scope of the Minorities Treaties Under the League of Nations* (London, Christophers, 1928), 230. Minority groups were formally organised into a Congress of National Minorities advocating forms of political autonomy that included language use and electoral representation.

Robinson, Jacob 319–325. A Jewish delegation arguing for similar goals was also formally represented at the Peace Conference in Versailles.

96 Azcarate 135.

The League's minority protection treaty system included the establishment of a Permanent Court of International Justice (PCIJ) to resolve disputes between states party to the minority treaties, as well as other state conflicts. This had the positive effect of ameliorating violent inter-state conflict and preventing war by transferring jurisdiction for resolution of disputes between individual states over to the League of Nation's Council or the PCIJ. The League's Council contained a Minorities Section of the League Secretariat sponsored by the Minorities Committees (comprised of three state members of the League), which also acted as the League's civil administration for minorities issues. The League system worked to prevent the abuse of intervention by individual states over the treatment of minorities. It also represented major progress toward the peaceful settlement of violent conflict between states through the establishment of international judicial and administrative procedures.

Fifteen minority treaty instruments were administered by the League minority protection treaty system by treaty conventions, agreements and declarations.[97] While not included in the League's Covenant, reference to the treaties was incorporated into Article 93 of the Versailles Peace Treaty requiring Poland, Czechoslovakia, Romania, Yugoslavia, and Greece to protect inhabitants differing from the majority in race, language, or religion.[98] Also, the League agreed to incorporate a "guarantee clause" into the Covenant accepting jurisdiction for

[97] Thornberry, Patrick. *International Law and Minorities*, 41–42. Thornberry describes the League minority protection treaty system. Treaties included in Thornberry's list are: *Minorities in Poland: Treaty between the Principle Allied and Associated Powers and Poland, Versailles, June 1919; Minorities in Austria: Treaty of Peace between the Allied and Associated Powers and Austria, Saint-German-en-Laye, September 1919; Minorities in the Serb-Croat-Slovene State: Treaty between the aforementioned Powers and the Serb-Croat-Slovene State, Saint-Germain-en-Laye, September 1919;Minorities in Czechoslovakia: Treaty between the Powers and Czechoslovakia, Saint Germain-en-Laye, September 1919; Minorities in Bulgaria: Treaty between the Powers and Bulgaria, Neuilly-sur-Seine, November 1919; Minorities in Romania: Treaty between the Powers and Romania, Paris, December 1919; Minorities in Hungary: Treaty of Peace between the Powers and Hungary, Trianon, June 1920; Minorities in Greece: Treaty concerning the Protection of Minorities in Greece, Sevres, August 1920; Minorities in the Free City of Danzig: Convention between Poland and Danzig, Paris, November 1920; Preservation of Swedish Traditions in the Aaland Islands: Agreement between Sweden and Finland placed on record and approved by a resolution of the Council of the League of Nations, June 1921; Minorities in Albania, Lithuania, Latvia, Estonia and Iraq: Declarations made to the League of Nations in October 1921 (Albania), May 1922(Lithuania), July 1923 (Latvia), September 1923 (Estonia), and May 1932 (Iraq); Upper Silesia: German-Polish Convention relating to Upper Silesia, Geneva, May 1922; Minorities in Turkey and Greece: Treaty of Peace between the British Empire, France, Italy, Japan, Greece, Romania, the Serb-Croat Slovene State, and Turkey regarding the protection of minorities in Turkey and Greece, Lausanne, July 1923; Minorities in the Territory of Memel: Convention concerning the Territory of Memel, Paris, May 1934.*

[98] Azcarate 92.

the treaties over the objection of Lord Balfour (British Empire) who maintained that the League should have the legal right to refuse guarantee of minority protection.[99]

The treaties contained general principles included in virtually all the agreements as well as specific agreements inserted in only some. The general principles incorporated nationality provisions which provided minorities with the right to regain citizenship in the state to which they formerly belonged. A second general principle of the treaties was the incorporation of provisions guaranteeing minorities equal treatment, civil and political rights, and religious freedom. The treaties also provided protection in specific categories dealing with minority group identity. These included the ability of minority groups to maintain unique characteristics which guarded them against the loss of nationality resulting from post-war territorial settlement. Minority treaty provisions gave rights to minorities which included the use of their own language in private relations; the use of their own language before the Courts; adequate facilities for primary education in their own language, whenever there was a "considerable proportion" of the minority group; the establishment of religious and welfare institutions, schools and other educational facilities under their own control and with their own language; and the right to an equitable proportion of state and communal expenditures for educational, religious and welfare purposes.[100] P. De Azcarate, explains the rights as a form of effective equality that provides minorities with "juridical, social, economic, and cultural institutions which allow them to preserve their own national consciousness."[101]

The primary purpose of the minority treaty petition system was to avoid the outbreak of war between states by removing the protection of minorities from the jurisdiction of individual states to the collectivity of all states. Minority rights took a second position to the central League mission: prevent the abuse of the right of intervention that escalates into war. The minority treaty system was designed to provide a judicial resolution to minority questions and thereby prevent violent conflict between host and kin states. Although League-sponsored rights to self-determination became *ius cogens* or a principle of customary international law and preemptory norm of universal application, the principle was not extended to include internal self-determination for national groups who comprised

---

99 *Ibid.*, 94.

100 Robinson, Jacob 36–38.

Ibid., 36. Exceptions to the Equality of Rights provisions are found in Article 2 of the Albanian Declaration which authorises change of religion, and the Turkish Treaty which grants equality before the law…to Turkish nationals belonging to non-Moslem minorities only.

Thornberry, Patrick. *International Law and Minorities*, 42.

101 Azcarate 24.

part of a state. Rather, the League's minority system was a compromise providing minorities with a form of limited autonomy short of self-determination in the form of statehood.[102]

Jurist Hannum Hurst concludes that League states feared that the minority rights would result in national self-determination for minorities and force the Peace Conference to admit claims for self-determination from desperate minority groups with long-standing complaints such as African-Americans, Southern Irish, Flemings, or Catalans. In contradiction to the League's mission for self-determination, the Allied and Associated Powers states refused to recognise such rights for different groups who comprised a section of a state. The League's administration of the minority rights treaty system provided a minority's cultural self-determination *sensu stricto*[103] to compensate for the lack of actual self-determination in the form of independent statehood.[104] The treaties protected minority identity and characteristics as distinguished from dominant national groups and provided a way for sub-dominant national minorities to participate within the state's framework without the need for secession or migration. The treaties' aim was to provide minority groups equality in fact; this would be done by treating a minority's identity and characteristics in a way similar to that accorded to the dominant national characteristics.

---

102 Stone, Julius. *International Guarantees of Minority Rights, Procedure of the Council of The League of Nations in Theory and Practice* (London, Oxford University Press, 1932), 37–39, 42, 136, 247.

Stone, Julius. *Regional Guarantees of Minority Rights, A Study of Minorities Procedure in Upper Silesia*, 54.

Eide, Asborn, Chairperson United Nations Working Group on Minorities. "Final Text of the Commentary to the Declaration on the Rights of Persons Belonging to National or Ethnic, Religious and Linguistic Minorities, 1992" (Geneva UN Document: E/CN.4/Sub2/AC.5/2001/2).

Claude 5. States containing minority groups are described as home or host states. States that have an ethnic affinity or special relationship with another state's minority groups are kin or co-national states.

Anaya, S. James, "Self-Determination As A Collective Human Right Under Contemporary International Law" Aiko, Pekka and Scheinin, Martin, eds. *Organizing The Right Of Indigenous Peoples To Self Determination* (Saarijarvo, Gummerus Printing, 2000), 3.

103 Meaning in a narrow or strict sense. That is, cultural self-determination implies a more limited form of autonomy in contrast to independent statehood.

104 Sacerdoti, Giorgio. "New Developments In Group Consciousness and the International Protection of The Rights of Minorities" ed., Yoram Dinstein, *Israel Yearbook on Human Rights*, Vol.13 (Tel Aviv, Tel Aviv University Faculty of Law, 1983), 134.

Claude 11. Woodrow Wilson viewed national self-determination as an essential corollary of democracy.

Hannum 52.

Ibid., 476. Hannum explains that, "Recognition of the right to personal autonomy and group identity is essential to ensure that the principles of self-determination, participation, and tolerance are allowed to flourish."

2.6. *The Permanent Court of International Justice and the Minority Schools in Albania Opinion*

In this section, I discuss the *Minority Schools in Albania, Advisory Opinion of April 6, 1935*[105] (*Minority Schools Opinion*), a precedent-setting case which required Albania to protect its Greek minorities' cultural characteristics. Also, how the Greek-Albanian conflict served as a pretext for this decision.

The Permanent Court of International Justice (PCIJ) was the League of Nations' judicial mechanism to further the peaceful resolution of disputes over interpretation of minority treaties as well as other contentious issues between its member states. Article 14 of the League charter established the right of the PCIJ to preside over petitions brought before the court by League-state members or by the Assembly or Council of the League. The purpose of the minority petition was to transfer the resolution of treaty disputes between states over to the jurisdiction of the League Council or to the League's international court. This process helped transform what would formerly have been considered disputes between two independent states into a sphere in which the League had exclusive jurisdiction. The treaty's petition system was the League's remedy for preventing an abuse of the right of intervention leading to violent conflict between sovereign states over treaty disputes. This was intended to prevent another deterioration of the international order like that which had contributed to the start of WWI.

The PCIJ served as a judicial mechanism not only for the resolution of treaty disputes but also as a means to clarify the nature of minority rights. Petitions brought before the Court gave it the opportunity to translate treaty obligations into definitions and enunciations of minority rights. While the PCIJ did not serve to end disputes between states over minority conflicts it did, nevertheless, establish a degree of legal protection for the maintenance and preservation of cultural characteristics for national, linguistic, ethnic, and religious groups who resided within foreign nation-states after WWI. The precedent-setting explanation for the rights to nationality and culture provided by the court provides, at the very least, advisory authority for present-day recognition of minority rights.[106]

The *Minority Schools Opinion*, issued by the League of Nations' Permanent Court of International Justice, 6 April 1935, created an important precedent for

[105] *Minority Schools Opinion*, *supra*, note 17, at 10.

[106] *Question of the Greco-Bulgarian Communities, Advisory Opinion No. 17 of July 31st, 1930*, Series E.-No.7, Seventh Annual Report of the Permanent Court of International Justice, Series E.-No.7, Leyden, A.W. Sijihoff's Publishing Co. P. 248. The Greco-Bulgarian Advisory Opinion is an example of how the PCIJ provided legal character and definition to minority rights. The PCIJ Opinion defines the term community in a manner consistent with contemporary international definitions for minority groups:

League states' treatment of minority groups. The Opinion illustrates not only how the new international court intended to enforce minority treaties, but also its interpretation of the equality principle as applied to minority groups. One must recall that the equality principle requires that all individuals receive equal treatment under law, regardless of group identification, and is a basic tenent of liberal theory. This case involved a dispute between Albania and Greece over access to religious and language education for the Greek minority living in Albania. The dispute between the two nations was not merely a technical disagreement over treaty interpretation, but rather part of a long-standing hostility between the two states that continues to the present day.

The dispute involved Greek nationals who had resided in the Northern Epirus area of Albania since early antiquity. When the Albanian state was established in 1912, it incorporated the Greek communities of Northern Epirus. Prior to the establishment of the Albanian state, Greek communities in the region lived under Ottoman-Turkish rule, enjoying a relatively generous degree of autonomy thanks to the Millet-i Rum system (section 2.1) which afforded protection to non-Islamic minorities. Hellenic (Greek) religious and cultural education thus flourished in Northern Epirus under Ottoman rule. Hellenic culture is strongly identified with Greek-Christian Orthodox religious practice, while Albania, in contrast, is Muslim (Mohammedans).

From the 1920s onwards, Albania embarked on a campaign to de-Hellenise the southern part of the country, focusing on two primary targets: the Greek Church, and Greek schools operating in the area, two pillars of Hellenism.[107] The dispute over Greek education, religious practice, and language use within the Albanian state, continued through to the end of WWII, as well as during the period of Communist Party rule. The Opinion, issued by the PCIJ, considered whether the Albanian Government was in compliance with its October 1921 Declaration, in which it agreed to the League's minority treaties, which covered the protection of Greek minorities in Albania. The Albanian Declaration was part of the Assembly's conditions for Albanian membership of the League. Lithuania, Latvia, Estonia and

...a group of persons living in a given country or locality having a race, religion, language and traditions of their own, and united by this identity of race, religion, language and traditions in a sentiment of solidarity with a view to preserving their traditions, maintaining their form of worship, ensuring the instruction and up-bringing of their children in accordance with the spirit and traditions of their race and mutually assisting each other.

Also *see*, Ladis, Stephen P. *The Exchange of Minorities, Bulgaria, Greece and Turkey* (New York, The MacMillan Co., 1932), 3, 171.

For background to the conflict also *see*, Barros, James. *The League of Nations and the Great Powers, The Greek-Bulgarian Incident, 1925* (Oxford, Clarendon Press, 1970).

[107] Kondis, Basil and Manda, Elefiheria eds. *The Greek Minority In Albania, A Documentary Record 1921–1993* (Thessaloniki, Institute for Balkan Studies, 1994), 15.

Iraq also joined the League having offered similar declarations supporting the League's minority treaties. The Opinion was issued pursuant to a referral by the Council of the League. Petitions had been filed on behalf of Greek Orthodox Christian minorities residing in Albania, concerning the passage of a 1933 amendment to the Albanian Constitution requiring the secularisation of education and the abolition of Greek Orthodox Christian private schools.[108]

In its decision, the court set forth two principles necessary to achieve compliance with the equal treatment of minorities requirement contained in the League's minority treaties. Firstly, a juridical concept the court described as *perfect equality*. The court defined perfect equality as one that is particular to relations between majority and minority groups. The opinion distinguishes equality in law or formal equality, which precludes mere discrimination against minorities, from what the court describes as equality in fact. Equality in fact recognises the necessity of different treatment for minorities necessary to *attain a result which establishes an equilibrium between different situations.*[109] The court explained that perfect equality means that nationals belonging to the minority group should enjoy the same treatment from the state as those belonging to the majority. That is, that the Greek minority should have equal access to Greek language and religious education as the Albanian majority had to an Albanian secular education.

Second, that the minority group is provided a right to their identity, namely, the ability to not only access but also to cultivate their unique characteristics and peculiarities, namely, the Greek language and religious education. According to the PCIJ, differential treatment of minority groups is necessary to preserve minority identity and to promote equality for minorities. The opinion establishes the basic principle that, unless minority identity is protected by the state, the minority cannot attain full and complete equality guaranteed by the League's minority treaties. By depriving a minority of the essence of its identity, namely, language, education, and religion, etc. equality in law becomes a mere fiction which legitimates forced assimilation and prevents state recognition of minority group existence.

The court explained that these two principles were interdependent and that there would be no true equality if minorities were deprived of their own institutions and compelled to renounce the essence of being a minority.[110] The court opinion

Kondis, Basil ed. *"The Greeks of Northern Epirus and Greek-Albanian Relations"* Historical Review From the Greek Edition (Hestia Publishers and Booksellers), Vol I: 1897–1918, Vol. II: 1919–1921. Note: No date or place of publication provided.

Clogg, Richard. *The Greek Diaspora In The Twentieth Century* (New York, St. Martin's Press, Inc., 1999), 16, 19, 161, 171.

108 *Minority Schools Opinion, supra*, note 17, at 10. P. 138.

109 *Ibid.*

110 *Ibid.*, 140.

ruled against the Albanian government, clarifying that the Greek minority had the right to maintain religious, charitable, and social institutions, schools and other educational establishments as well as the right to use their own language and to freely exercise their religion.[111]

While it was unsuccessful in resolving all disputes between Greece and Albania, the Opinion is important for establishing the precedent that preservation of minority national or cultural characteristics is fundamental to the guarantee of equality for minorities. According to the court's reasoning, unless minority groups are protected in the factors that comprise minority identity such as religious practice, language use, educational instruction, and social services, a state may be in breach of the principle of equal treatment for minorities. The court did not regard special treatment of minorities as a violation of the equality principle that provides differential privilege favouring minorities (special rights), but rather as a shield protecting minority characteristics against assimilation in order to guarantee equal treatment (equality in fact) for minorities. The holding also provides a foundation for contemporary standards established by the United Nations necessary to ensure the equal treatment of minorities in UN member states. It illustrates how the concept of internal self-determination for groups residing in foreign states is implemented through the application of a so-called minority regime. The Opinion permitted greater equality for minority groups within the states where they resided.[112]

2.7. *Decline of the Minority Protection Treaty System*

The reasons for the downfall of the minority protection treaty system do not differ significantly from the challenges encountered by all international laws. H.L.A. Hart notes that all international rules include "the absence of an international legislature, courts with compulsory jurisdiction and centrally organised sanctions, a unifying rule of recognition specifying sources of law and providing general criteria for the identification of its rules."[113] However, given the risks and stakes of war, Hart maintains that the lack of an evolved, international compliance structure does not lessen the moral obligation for states to follow what he describes as a rule of recognition to follow international treaties. Further, during the time of the drafting of the League of Nations' Covenant in 1919, no one would have believed it possible that the United States would have refused to recognise and

[111] *Ibid.*, 140–141.
[112] Modeen 24–27, 36, 42.
[113] Hart, H.L.A. *The Concept of Law*, 2nd Edition (New York, O.U.P., 1961), 214, 230, 233.

join the League of Nations, weakening the viability of the modern world's first effort at international organisation.[114]

From 1939 through to 1947, the League's minority protection treaty system did not function.[115] Perhaps the most compelling reason for its demise was the failure of the League of Nations itself to survive as a form of international governance. The League's minority protection treaty system was always subservient to the League's central mission of preventing the outbreak of war. League-state compliance with minority treaties was compromised in favour of the peaceful resolution of inter-state conflict. Other factors were the treaties' lack of a universal standard for minority protection; the failure to apply standards for minority protection equally and fairly to all League state members;[116] and the lack of a treaty enforcement procedure. This last weakness involved the absence of a set time period within which interested states would have to submit observations in response to petitions (complaints) and the consequent long delays; the use of ambiguous language and the lack of specific minority protections contained within the treaties; failure to make treaty violation findings public and thus make use of public opinion; the exemption of major powers from the system, including the United States, which failed to join the League; the inability of individual minorities, minority groups, and disinterested states to obtain *locus standi*; the rise of totalitarianism and Hitler's exploitation of the German minorities issue, using them as a fifth column for offensive military operations; failure to adequately protect minorities against coercive state assimilation campaigns; the failure of minorities to support the system and the tendency of some minorities to encourage group separateness and disloyalty to their states; failure by the international Congress of Minorities to gain official recognition as an authorised representative of national minorities;[117] and the rudimentary nature of the League's organisation.[118]

Regardless of the reasons for its decline, the League of Nations' minority protection treaty system provides a meaningful precedent within international

---

[114] Miller, David Hunter, Vol. I, 550.

[115] Thornberry, Patrick. *International Law and Minorities*, 54;
Modeen 72. The Treaty of Lausanne however is still binding.

[116] Will Kymlicka's and Joseph Carens' recommendations conflict with these explanations of decline for the minority protection treaty system. Kymlica concludes that cultural justice cannot be secured by a universal regime of common rights, while Carens maintains that the minority complaints must be examined using a [case by case] circumstance dependent method (evenhandedness). *See*, Kymlicka, Will. *Contemporary Political Philosophy*, 47; Joseph Carens, *Culture, Citizenship, and Community. A Contextual Exploration of Justice as Evenhandedness* (Oxford, Oxford University Press, 2000), 12.

[117] Azcarate 131.

[118] Hannum 54.
Claude 27, 32, 47–48.

law being the first comprehensive effort to create a formal international system designed to assist, protect, and benefit minority groups. Further, the United Nations' Study on the Legal Validity of the Undertakings Concerning Minorities[119] concluded that Greece and Turkey may still be bound by the *Treaty of Lausanne* as may Sweden and Finland by the *Preservation of Swedish Traditions in the Aaland Islands Agreement*. For all its shortcomings, the League's minority system was successful in enjoining governments against repressive policies targeting minority groups. It also had the effect of providing recognition that the international system must be concerned with rights of minorities. The League sought to achieve equality by respecting the ethnical character of minorities and authorising minority groups with the right to practice religion, cultivate language, educate children, access government services, and control social institutions. Contrary to breaching the equality principle, the treaty system of *special treatment* provided minorities with material as opposed to formal equality by shielding minority characteristics from assimilation. Tore Modeen's legal treatise on Europe's national minorities explains that cultural rights serve to protect against the psychological harm of being deprived of and forced to abandon the use of a minority's tongue and culture while those of the majority culture are preserved. Without these protections, the minority suffers materially and psychologically, being deprived of public use of their language, education, and culture, and compelled to migrate or forcibly assimilate themselves. Rights to their own language and culture provide members of a minority group with valuable physical and spiritual freedom which the state should guarantee as necessary to comply with the principle of equal treatment for all its residents. The League's minority system made what Inis Claude describes as a significant contribution to the *Rechtsbewusstsein* or moral consciousness of mankind.[120]

On p. 47, Claude explains how Hitler's use of German minorities as a *fifth column* or human dynamite ready to be detonated at the command of the Fuhrer further eroded confidence in, and indeed proved fatal to, the idea of the international protection of minorities. Other kin states encouraged disloyalty by nationals residing in host states. Hungary used its co-nationals to stir up trouble in Romania and Bulgaria. Italy incited co-nationals in Yugoslavia.

Robinson, Jacob 85, 263.

119 United Nations Economic and Social Council, Commission on Human Rights. *Study on the Legal Validity of the Undertakings Concerning Minorities, Memorandum by the Secretary General* United Nations Document E/CN.4/367/Add.1, 27 March 1951, p.2, para. 3,5.

120 Stone, Julius. *Regional Guarantees of Minority Rights, A Study of Minorities Procedure in Upper Silesia* (New York, The MacMillan Co., 1933), 52.

Modeen 24–27, 36, 42.

Sacerdoti, Giorgio, "New Developments In Group Consciousness and The International Protection of The Rights of Minorities," Israel Yearbook on Human Rights 13 (1983): 119

Claude 29.

Chapter 3

Minority Protection in the Era of Human Rights

WWII transformed the principles of national self-determination and minority protection that figured prominently in the establishment of the League of Nation's minority protection treaty system. Instead, a new approach described as universal human rights was implemented to protect the concerns of minority groups. The main reasons for this change were the successful exploitation of the minorities question by Hitler's Nazi-regime, United States' policy for the assimilation of minority groups, the cold war between the Soviet Union and the United States, preservation of the British colonial empire, and the emergence of the new doctrine of human rights. As I illustrate in the chapter that follows, human rights were promoted by the Allies as an alternative to the League of Nations' minority regime. That is, legal protections against discrimination applied universally to all individuals in contrast to protections that promote the identity of distinct ethnical groups. However, the big three Allies' objective was to prevent United Nations' interference in domestic affairs in contrast to the promotion of human rights. The Allied interest was in preserving security and ending the scourge of another world war. In this chapter, I discuss how the doctrine of human rights incorporated a new UN minority regime for the promotion of cultural rights.

3.1. *Minorities as the Nazis Human Dynamite*

A *United Nations Conference on International Organisations* was convened by the victorious Allies in San Francisco on 25 April 1945 to provide a framework charter for a United Nations international administration after WWII.[1] In contrast to the birth and functioning of the League of Nations', the United Nations was established before any peace treaty and was in no way involved in the settlement of European territorial constructions. The League of Nations had been bound up with European balances of power and the solution of territorial problems arising from the peace treaties of 1919–1920.[2] Therefore, the problem that confronted

[1] Claude 111.

[2] Capotorti 26, para. 135.

the League of Nations to satisfy the national aspirations of minorities in Europe for self-determination was not present during the Conference. Also, Hitler's use of German minority groups as a military tactic transformed Allied sentiment against minority protection. German minority groups were developed by Hitler as a 'fifth column' to disrupt, sabotage, and weaken national unity prior to his military offensives. As a result, the Conference refused to incorporate a minority protection article into the United Nations Charter.

Germany exploited opposition to the League of Nations' minority protection treaty system as being punitively applied to protect only certain groups in weaker states defeated by the Allies. Certain groups among the protected minorities were unwilling to accept minority status under any terms, notably, Germans of various minority states, the Hungarians of Rumania, and the Macedonians of Yugoslavia, all of whom "strove relentlessly to embarrass and undermine their host states."[3] Inis Claude explains that for these groups, a national minority could owe no allegiance to an alien state, since nationality was the only legitimate basis of political obligation. Hungary utilised its co-nationals to stir up trouble in Rumania, and Bulgaria and Italy undermined the authority of Yugoslavia by supporting Macedonian unrest.[4]

Hitler's 'fifth column' was developed with the assistance of Nazi psychologists to weaken the enemy from within or "conquer him through himself"[5] by cultivation of potentially disloyal groups within a country, namely, German minority groups as well as other groups sympathetic to the Nazi cause. Hitler succeeded in turning large numbers of these minority groups into "human dynamite" ready to be detonated at the command of the Fuhrer.[6] As examples, three million Sudeten-Germans were effectively used by the Nazis to fight for "hiem in Reich"[7] permitting Germany to annex Sudetenland, as well as Bohemia and Moravia, from Czechoslovakia. Stories of Czechoslovakian atrocities against ethnic Germans were spread by Nazi propaganda to encourage irredentist German minorities. Seven hundred and sixty-five thousand ethnic Germans living in Danzig, Posnania, Pomorze, and Silesia, Poland were used by Hitler to annex the ethnically German populated corridor along Danzig, Poland.[8] Nazi propaganda was used to spread stories of Poles murdering ethnic Germans. Poland's German minority was used by the Nazis to promote espionage, sabotage, and "putsches".[9]

---

[3] Claude 44.

[4] *Ibid.*, 45, 47.

[5] Davies, John Lang-Don. *Fifth Column* (London, John Murray, 1941), 9.

[6] Claude 47.

[7] Vaughan, David. *Hitler's Fifth Column*, 6 May 2006 < http://design.radio.cz/en/article/25511>

[8] Claude 52.

[9] The Polish Ministry of Information. *The German Fifth Column In Poland* (London, Hutchinson and Co. Ltd., 1942), 34, 98.

Hitler made similar use of ethnic German minorities, as well as other sympathetic groups such as the Breton in France, the IRA against Britain, the Magyars residing in Rumania, and the Mexicans adjacent to the United States,[10] to promote his expansionist campaign against the states of Europe.[11]

From 1938–1942, fear of subversive activities by minority groups was reflected in resolutions presented to Allied conferences urging precautionary measures against disloyal activities by minority groups with foreign political connections. Czechoslovakian and Polish leaders committed themselves to never taking the risks of conceding protection for minority groups. President Benes of Czechoslovakia declared:[12]

> Minorities in individual states must never again be given the character of internationally recognised political and legal units, with the possibility of again becoming sources of disturbance.

Hitler's exploitation of German minorities turned the Allies against the establishment of a minority regime during the establishment of the United Nations. On 20 November 1945, the *Allied Control Council for Germany* implemented the *Triparite Conference of Berlin*, 17 July to 2 August 1945[13] (Postdam conference), between the United States, the United Kingdom, and the Soviet Union agreement to resolve the minorities issue through a program of mandatory population transfer for minority groups that forcibly relocated them back to their ethnically-kin states. In contrast to Woodrow Wilson's approach, the Allies abandoned the principle of self-determination to consolidate ethnic minority groups in their own nation-states after WWII and instead committed themselves to frontier revisions in Europe based on security interests.[14] To resolve the minorities question, the Council approved a schedule for the forced transfer of six and a half million German minorities in Czechoslovakia, Poland, and Hungary, and an additional one hundred and fifty-thousand Germans in Austria back to Germany. Patrick Thornberry[15] uncovers various other minority group transfer treaties that were concluded by the end of WWII including: compulsory transfer of two hundred thousand Magyars out of Czechoslovakia into Hungary (February 1946); two hundred thousand Slovaks out of Hungary into Czechoslovakia; Hungary and Yugoslavia (September 1946), exchanging forty thousand Magyars for an equal number of Serbs and Croats; Poland and the Soviet Union (July 1945); and Czechoslovakia and the Soviet Union (1946).

---

10 Davies, John Lang-Don. *Fifth Column* (London, John Murray, 1941), 18.

11 *Ibid.*, 1, 141–142.

12 Claude 56–57, 74, 81, 141. At the 29 July 1946 Paris Peace Conference, Czechoslovakia also demanded the transfer of the Magyar minority group back to Hungary.

13 *Ibid.*, 114.

14 *Ibid.*, 115;

Simpson 235. Stalin's main anxiety was to protect Russia from revived German aggression.

15 Thornberry, Patrick. *International Law and Mniorities*, 114.

He reports that some fifteen million Germans were expelled from various parts of Europe (1944–1949). The estimated number of deaths that resulted from the mandatory relocation transfers varies from between tens of thousands through to over two million. Josef L. Kunz describes the relocation of ethnic Germans as "a crime against humanity."[16] The Allies had retreated to a solution used prior to WWI (chapter 2), that of preserving sovereignty by the forced relocation of minority groups.

The *Paris Peace Conference*, 29 July 1946, had only an advisory role in how to frame a new post-war European settlement. The Conference consisted of a United Nations coalition of twenty-one member states intended to examine drafts and submit recommendations for new peace treaties to the Council of Foreign Ministers.[17] Numerous proposals for positive minority rights, including protections of linguistic, educational, cultural and other rights relevant to the perpetuation of ethnic distinctiveness, were submitted by parties attending the Conference.

The big three Allies' rejection of minority protection shared a common interest, namely, human rights did not permit interference in domestic affairs (sovereignty). American and British opposition prevented the United Nations from reconstituting the League of Nations' minority regime. *The United Nations Conferences on International Organisations* (UN founding conference), 25 April 1945[18] at San Francisco's Fairmont Hotel, as well as at Harvard University's Dumbarton Oaks Hotel, 1944, failed to pass or incorporate an article, declaration or statement in support of positive minority protection into the United Nations Charter.

3.2. *One People Nationalism*

> *In the kind of world for which we fight, there must cease to exist any need for the use of that accursed term 'racial or religious minority.'*
>
> Summer Welles, American Undersecretary of State, 31 May 1943[19]

American opposition to minority regimes was based on its failure to understand the desire to protect the ethnic identity of minority groups. General Walter Bedell Smith, an American delegate to the Paris Peace Conference, remarked

---

[16] Claude 117;

Josef L. Kunz. *The Present Status of the International Law for the Protection of Minorities*. The American Journal of International Law, Vol.48, No.2 (April, 1954), 285. Kunz cites Max Rheinstein's description of the forced relocation of German minorities;

Vaughan, David. *Hitler's Fifth Column*, 6 May 2006 < http://design.radio.cz/en/article/25511> p.4.

[17] Claude 125.

[18] Sellars, Kristen. *The Rise and Rise of Human Rights* (Thrupp, Stroud, Gloucestershire, Sutton Publishing Ltd., 2000), 1.

[19] Claude 74.

"It is difficult for a citizen of the United States to understand the desire to perpetuate racial minorities rather than absorb them."[20] The American position was that minority groups should undergo a process of assimilation that suppressed their ethnical identity in favour of a dominant Anglo-American identity. Desmond King describes America's ethnically biased immigration and assimilation policies as *one-people nationalism.*[21] King explains how US Americanisation policies regarding immigration, education, and the military, as examples, used coercive assimilation and ethnic discrimination against African, Latino, Aboriginal and Asian groups. Eleanor Roosevelt, appointed chair of the United Nations' Human Rights Commission in 1947, explained:[22]

> ...the aim of states was to assimilate and absorb large foreign groups and to make them part of the nation...Minority questions did not exist in the American Continent....the United States experience with foreign groups residing within its borders had been happy, assimilation having been emphasised throughout... Provisions relating to minorities had no place in a declaration of human rights.

Serving as the US UN Representative, Eleanor Roosevelt distinguished the new US position from that previously held by Woodrow Wilson. Recall that Wilson unsuccessfully attempted to incorporate a proposed draft into the League covenant that recognised minority group identity by providing equal treatment in law and fact for national minorities. The failed Wilson proposal would have granted protection to minority identity and provided support for minority schools as well as minority linguistic and religious practice. When the proposal failed, protection was instead granted only to a limited number of minority groups identified by the League's minority protection treaty system.[23] By contrast, Roosevelt favoured an individualist approach that refused to recognise minority groups, arguing instead that there could be no support for any right that was not universal in significance, and that the "best solution of the problem of minorities was to encourage respect for human rights."[24] A.W. Brian Simpson described as "perverse"[25] Roosevelt's position refusing to include the protection of minorities into the *Universal Declaration of Human Rights.*[26] One jurist maintained that Roosevelt's position

---

20 *Ibid.*, 141.

21 King, Desmond. *The Liberty of Strangers* (Oxford, OUP, 2005), 168.

22 Claude 81, 166. Woodrow Wilson concurred with Roosevelt's view explaining, that "America does not consist of groups. A man who thinks of himself as belonging to a particular national group in America has not yet become an American."

23 Janowsky, Oscar I. *The Jews and Minority Rights 1898–1919* (New York, Columbia University Press, 1933), 321.

24 Thornberry, Patrick. *International Law and Minorities*, 135–136.

25 Simpson 442.

26 *Ibid.*

was a clear expression of the view that, somehow, minority rights are different from human rights in general and represent a historically limited conception which would have no validity in the modern era.[27] Mexico, echoing the American view, took the position that the American continent did not have the same problem of minorities as was the case in Europe or other parts of the world. Foreigners entering America were not affected by discriminatory measures and had the advantage of generously conceived naturalisation.[28]

The USA consistently took the line that they had no minorities.[29] William White, Executive Secretary of the National Association for the Advancement of Colored People (NAACP), unsuccessfully sought Roosevelt's assistance in obtaining UN intervention to eliminate US Jim Crow laws as well as practices of lynching and other forms of discrimination used against African-Americans.[30] The US also feared that permitting the UN to domestically intervene for the protection of minority groups would have implications for its reservations system that provided for the forced relocation of Aboriginal American groups (Native Americans).[31]

The United Kingdom shared the US view that the national assimilation of minority groups was preferable to a system that cultivates a minority identity. Lord Hood declared that: "Our aim should be to assimilate racial minorities in the countries where they live rather than to perpetuate them."[32] Great Britain's view was influenced by the consequences of human rights and minority protection for the British colonial empire. In 1945, Britain's colonial office presided over a colonial empire that governed sixty million human beings living in approximately thirty-eight colonial territories and dependencies.[33] A brief prepared in March 1946 for Sir Alexander Cadogan, the former Permanent Under-Secretary at the British Foreign Office, reported that enthusiasm for human rights might fuel an anti-colonial crusade by anti-colonial powers. A January 1947 memorandum by J.S. Bennett of the Colonial Office's International Relations Department raised the fear that international human rights protection could be a vehicle for introducing

[27] Thornberry, Patrick. *International Law and Minorities*, 136.

[28] *Ibid.*, 721.

[29] Simpson 332, 442.

[30] Sellars 20.

[31] Claude 170.

[32] *Ibid.*, 141.

[33] Simpson 277. British colonial territories included: Aden, the Bahamas, Barbados, Bermuda, British Somaliland, British Honduras, British Guiana, the British Solomon Islands, Brunei, Cyprus, the Falkland Islands, Fiji, the Gambia, Gibraltar, the Gilbert and Ellice Islands, the Gold Coast, Hong Kong, Jamaica, Kenya, the Leeward Islands, the Malayan Federation, Malta, Mauritius, the New Hebrides, Nigeria, Northern Rhodesia, North Borneo, Sarawak, the Seychelles, Sierra Leone, Singapore, St Helena and Ascension, Tanganyika, Tonga, Trinidad and Tabago, Uganda, the Windward Islands, and Zanzibar.

United Nations' supervision of colonial government.[34] Human rights first surfaced in the British Cabinet over the question of settling policy on the prohibition of compulsory labour in colonies.[35] British officials in the Colonial Office were aware of the consequences of human rights for British colonies. For example, J.Buist wrote: "Colonial governments are not 'democratic', as that word is usually understood …nor do 'democratic societies' exist under colonial rule."[36]

The American view during the post WWII conferences was that the League of Nations' minority protection treaty system be eliminated and subsumed under a broader foundation providing universal civil and political rights, or *human rights*, for all individuals. US Judge John J. Parker describes the approach: "If every citizen is given equal justice under law, governmental oppression of minorities cannot arise."[37] Providing a foundation for the American view, Winston Churchill defined WWII as an effort, "to establish, on impregnable rocks, the rights of the individual…"[38] The concept provided that individual civil and political rights that protect association, speech, and religion, as examples, were sufficient to safeguard the cultural interests of minority groups against a state's coercive assimilation practices. The *rule of non-discrimination*[39] is distinguishable from minority protection. In contrast to minority protection, non-discrimination does not recognise the validity of diverse languages, cultures, and religions in a positive and direct way, but rather by implication from an imaginatively interpreted standard, namely, non-discrimination.[40] The rule does not permit the preservation of a separate national character. Instead, ethnic masses are "melted" in the tradition of the American "melting-pot."[41]

The United Nations' conferences in San Francisco and Dumbarton Oaks approved the *Charter of the United Nations* on 26 June 1945. Both meetings

[34] *Ibid.*, 340–341.

[35] *Ibid.*, 336.

[36] Sellars.

[37] Claude 73.

[38] *Ibid.*, 73, 65. Jewish organisations struggling to establish a strategy for the survival of Europe's Jewish minority decimated by the Nazi holocaust endorsed the concept of a universal approach that also provided for limited minority protection. The American Jewish Committee adopted a 2 September 1943 resolution for an international bill of rights that, in addition to assuring the equal enjoyment of human rights by all citizens of all nations, insures "the inalienable rights of all religious, ethnic and cultural groups to maintain and foster their respective group identities on the basis of equality."

[39] *United Nations Charter*, 26 June 1945, Article I (3) states: "To achieve international cooperation in …promoting and encouraging respect for human rights and for fundamental freedoms for all without distinction as to race, sex, language, or religion.;"

[40] Thornberry, Patrick. *International Law and Minorities*, 128.

[41] Claude 81.

ignored the minority problem and the UN Charter makes no explicit reference to minority groups or minority rights.

3.3. *The Soviet Union, Minorities, and the Cold War*

Meeting to draft the UN Charter, the Third Committee of the UN General Assembly rejected proposals made by the representative of Yugoslavia during the initial drafting of the UN Charter to protect national minorities. The Yugoslavia proposal was influenced, in part, by the Soviet Union's policy of recognising the cultural and national autonomy of peoples and providing for equality as between different national groups that comprised the ethnically diverse Soviet Republics.[42] Josef Stalin had served under Lenin as the Soviet Union's Commissar for the Collegium of the Peoples' Commissariat for Nationality Affairs (Narkomnats). The Soviet Union's minorities policy was shaped by the ideals of nineteenth century socialist thought. The early program of the Russian Social Democratic Labour Party (1903) included education in a minority groups mother tongue, establishment of minority schools, use of minority languages in administration of public services, and the right to self-determination for all nations. Lenin also viewed the Russian Empire as a "prison house of nations"[43] while Otto Bauer maintained that all nations, however small, would flourish under socialism and administer their own cultural and linguistic affairs under a federated supranational state.[44]

Lenin, in an ongoing discussion with Rosa Luxemburg about the minority (or nationalities) question debating the future of Poland, Ukraine, Baltic States, Finland, Volga, Siberia and Transcaucasia, viewed the development of minority cultural identity as a necessary step to prepare "backward"[45] minority groups for socialism. Instituting a program of territorial autonomy for minority groups to control their own schools, courts, and public administration as well as social,

---

[42] Macartney, C.A. *National States and National Minorities* (London, OUP, 1934), 451–463. Macartney describes the Communist doctrine as the equality of all nationalities and self-determination of all nations. He illustrates political autonomy and language rights granted to Soviet Republics and the use of national languages in Soviet education from primary through to university level that includes use of Russian, Ukrainian, Georgian, Armenian, White Russian, Tatars, Yiddish, Buryats, as well as Islamic languages such as Azerbaijan, Turcomams, Uzbeks and Tadzhiks. While criticising the Soviet regime as a political dictatorship, Macartney endorses the Soviet model for its dissociation of politics and nationality or, as he writes on page 463, the "…disassociation of questions of nationality from questions of the state."

[43] Smith, Jeremy. *The Bolsheviks and the National Question*, 1917–1923 (New York, St. Martin's Press, Inc., 1999), 2, 14, 22.

[44] *Ibid.*, 11.

[45] *Ibid.*, 24–25.

political, and cultural institutions was necessary to promote national characteristics and end national "backwardness", as well as being an important step for establishing a socialist country. Stalin endorsed full cultural autonomy for minority groups, permitting them not only to promote their own languages, but also to control courts, administration, economic organisations, and schools. That is, a program of national territorial autonomy so that non-Russian minority groups could evolve to the higher stage of socialism.[46]

At the initiative of the Soviet Union, the UN's Economic and Social Council that administered the UN's Commission on Human Rights established the Sub-Commission on Prevention of Discrimination and Protection of Minorities (Sub-Commission) on 28 March 1947. The Sub-Commission's First Session requested the Economic and Social Council to ask the Secretary-General to provide a legal opinion in an effort to resurrect the League of Nations' minority protection treaty system. The opinion titled, *Study of the Legal Validity of the Undertakings Concerning Minorities*, released on 7 April 1950, found that the League's minority regime had been supplanted by UN's endorsement for universal human rights and no longer had legal standing:[47]

> Between 1937 and 1947 circumstances as a whole changed to such an extent that, generally speaking, the League of Nations system of international protection of minorities should be considered as having ceased to exist."[48]

The UN's San Francisco Fairmont Hotel conference enabled formation of the Drafting Committee of the Commission on Human Rights (1947). The Committee's role was to draft a UN Declaration of Human Rights. Its meetings were characterised by the Soviet Union's efforts to include an article in the Declaration protecting minority rights, as well as to require government support of minority cultural development. At the Commission on Human Rights Third Session, from 24 May to 18 June 1948, a proposal by India, the United Kingdom and China supported by the United States was passed to omit any reference from the Declaration that would permit the rights of minorities to use their native tongues or to maintain educational and cultural institutions. Instead, the Commission accepted a suggestion from the representative of Haiti to initiate a study on behalf of minority protection. On 10 December 1948, the UN General Assembly passed the *Universal Declaration*

---

46 *Ibid.*, 28. The Jewish and Roma peoples were not included in the project because they were a non-territorial peoples.

47 Claude 153.

48 Josef L. Kunz. *The Present Status of the International Law for the Protection of Minorities*. The American Journal of International Law, Vol.48, No.2 (April, 1954) 282–287, cites: "Study of the Legal Validity of the Undertakings concerning Minorities." UN Doc. E/CN.4/367, April 7, 1944. Also, "The International Protection of Minorities under the League of Nations." UN Doc E/CN.4/Sub2/6.

of Human Rights, successfully defeating a final effort by the Soviet Union to insert a minority rights article into the Declaration.[49]

As a consolation to the supporters of minority rights (Soviet Union, Yugoslavia, and Denmark) the UN General Assembly passed Resolution 217 (III) C, 10 December 1948, entitled *Fate of Minorities*[50] stating that the "United Nations could not remain indifferent to the fate of minorities, but....decides not to deal in a specific provision with the question of minorities in the text of [the] Declaration." The resolution explained that it was difficult to adopt a uniform solution of this complex and delicate question, which had special aspects in each State in which it arose.[51] Subsequently, the Sub-Commission successfully proposed that a provision on minority rights instead be inserted into a future covenant on human rights.[52] Protections for the existence, identity and development of minority groups had become a formal point of contention in the cold war between the United States and the Soviet Union.

3.4. *Convention on the Prevention and Punishment of the Crime of Genocide, 1948*

We can best understand this when we realise how impoverished our culture would be if the peoples doomed by Germany, such as the Jews, had not been permitted to create the Bible, or to give birth to an Einstein, a Spinoze; if the Poles had not had the opportunity to give to the world a Copernicus, a Chopin, a Curie; the Czechs, a Huss, a Dvorak; the Greeks, a Plato and a Socrates; the Russians, a Tolstoy and a Shostakovich.[53] *Raphael Lemkin, a Jewish-Polish lawyer considered to be the founder of the Genocide Convention.*

The Genocide Convention is the critical basis of the minority regime because it established a foundational basis that minority groups may not be destroyed, or what Patrick Thornberry describes as the minority right to existence.[54] Recall that the UN Allies failed to incorporate a minority regime into the UN Charter as a remedy to address Hitler's Nazi campaign to make the German nation *Judenrein*.[55] Instead, the

[49] Brownlie, Ian and Goodwin-Gill, Guy S. *Basic Documents on Human Rights, Fourth Edition* (Oxford, OUP, 2002), 2. "Relevant Provisions of The Charter of the United Nations, 1945."

[50] Resolution 217(III). C, GAOR, 3rd Session, Part 1 (1948). Also, described in Thornberry, Patrick. *International Law and Minorities*, 129. Also, Claude 157–160.

[51] Capotorti 27, para. 139.

[52] Thornberry, Patrick. *International Law and Minorities*, 129.

[53] Power 53.

[54] Thornberry, Patrick. *International Law and Minorities*, 51, 57.

[55] "Holocaust Glossary: Terms, Places, Personalities," Jewish Virtual Library, 6 June 2006 <http://www.jewishvirtuallibrary.org/jsource/Holocaust/wiesenthal_glossary.html> *Judenrein* – "Cleansed of Jews" denoting areas where all Jews had been either murdered or deported.

Allies responded to Hitler's campaign of destruction against Europe's Jewish minority by creating a penalty in international criminal law, that is, the crime of *genocide.*

Just one day prior to passing the *Declaration of Human Rights,* the General Assembly adopted *the Convention on the Prevention and Punishment of the Crime of Genocide, 1948.*[56] The Genocide Convention was drafted by the UN's Ad Hoc Committee on Genocide sponsored by the Economic and Social Committee on the initiative of the First UN General Assembly. However, the United States opposed the Genocide Convention's association with the minority problem. The Sub-Commission on Prevention of Discrimination and Protection of Minorities was not permitted to participate in the development of the Genocide Convention, and the item was referred to the Sixth (Legal) Committee at the Third General Assembly rather than to the Third (Social, Humanitarian, and Cultural) Committee, which normally handled matters relating to minority questions. One commentator speculated that the Genocide Convention might not have been "adopted if it had been presented to the Assembly as a measure for the protection of minorities, rather than as an expression of disapprobation for Hitler and respect for his victims."[57]

The passage of the *Universal Declaration of Human Rights* failed to resolve normative questions about whether human rights are individualist or collective in their approach to the protection of minority groups. UN support for international conventions addressing state abuses such as genocide illustrates that, contrary to its individualist orientation, the human rights doctrine incorporated a collective dimension. Just one year after drafting the UN Charter, the General Assembly unanimously passed Resolution 96(1), defining the crime of genocide as a denial of the right of existence of entire human groups and enabling the passage of the Genocide Convention. The Genocide Convention criminalised the annihilation of human groups by states or private individuals acting under the authority of the state. In contradiction to the individualist principle of human rights espoused by its passage just prior to the *Universal Declaration of Human Rights,* the Genocide Convention established protection under international law for the existence of the whole or part of a national, ethnic, racial and religious group. International recognition of the right to existence for human groups also established a precedent for more developed group-based protections such as the right to minority identity. The Genocide Convention adds genocide to the list of *delicta juris gentium*[58] that includes trade in slaves as well as in children, white

---

[56] *Convention on the Prevention and Punishment of the Crime of Genocide, 1948* 78 UNTS 277.

[57] Claude 154, 157.

[58] Meaning, the laws of nations. A *delicta juris gentium* crime becomes subject to a system for the universal right of punishment. Jurisdiction is vested in a state to prosecute the crime, regardless of the fact that the offence was committed outside its territory. Historically, the principle was used to prosecute the crime of piracy.

slavery, piracy, narcotics, obscene publication, and the counterfeiting of currency.[59] While not creating a minority right to self-determination, The Genocide Convention was the first international convention of the post-WWII era to entrench the right of minority groups to exist within the framework of the UN's human rights treaty regime.

Article II of the Genocide Convention classified four human groups for protection: national, ethnic, racial or religious.[60] As in all minority regimes, the Genocide Convention's identification of classifications for protection was largely a political question. The UN Secretariat's initial draft Genocide Convention proposal included unsuccessful efforts to pass articles for the protection of linguistic as well as political groups.

The question of whether or not to include political groups was "very contentious and much debated"[61] during the Second and Third Sessions of the General Assembly. The Soviet Union's position mirrored that of Raphael Lemkin, a Jewish-Polish lawyer who spent his professional life working to gain passage of the Genocide Convention and who lobbied for the protection of groups targeted by states that oppress ethnic, national, and religious minorities. The Soviet Union opposed incorporation of a political groups' classification on two grounds. First, the Soviet Union placed genocide within the sphere of regimes that protect minority groups against forms of ethnic, racial, and religious hatred. At the Second Session of the General Assembly (September- December 1947) the Soviet position "had a distinctly ideological bent, insisting upon the relationship between genocide and Facism-Nazism and other similar race theories which preach racial and national hatred. The Soviets felt that repression of genocide should include prohibition of incitement to racial hatred as well as various preparatory or preliminary acts",[62] such as restriction of the national language or destruction of religious monuments. Secondly, Stalin also feared the inclusion of political groups would hamper his efforts to rid the Soviet Union of subversive political opposition, as well as expose the Soviet Union to international interference in its domestic affairs.

---

[59] Lemkin, Raphael. *Axis Rule In Occupied Europe*, 93.
Thornberry, Patrick. *International Law and Minorities*, 64, 95–96. Thornberry describes how the crime of genocide is *ius cogens* or a preemptory norm of general international law invalidating any conflicting treaty pursuant to the Vienna Convention Law of Treaties, Articles 53, 64.

[60] *Ibid.*, 67, 142–153.
The Convention on the Prevention and Punishment of the Crime of Genocide was passed on 9 December 1948.
Genocide Convention, supra, note 56, at 79, Article II states "...genocide means any of the following acts committed with intent to destroy, in whole or in part, a national, ethnical, racial or religious group, as such...".

[61] *Ibid.*

[62] Schabas, William. *Genocide in International Law, The Crime of Crimes* (Cambridge, Cambridge University Press, 2000), 63.

By contrast, the United States unsuccessfully sought the inclusion of political groups arguing that they were similar to religious groups and used Nazi identification of Communists as a group to be persecuted as a justification. A US proposal to add the words 'or political [groups]' to the preamble of the Convention was defeated by vote of the Ad Hoc Committee.[63] The UN failure to incorporate political groups as a protected class under the Genocide Convention had implications in qualifying state-sponsored mass murders as genocide, such as the case of the Khmer Rouge's mass-murder (auto-genocide)[64] of approximately two million Cambodian people[65] (1975–1979). Another jurist maintained that confusing mass killing of the members of the perpetrator's own group with genocide is inconsistent with the purpose of the Genocide Convention which is to protect national minorities from crimes based on ethnic hatred.[66]

Both the United States and Soviet Union argued that the heinous nature of the crime should distinguish it from other violations of human and minority rights. So, the Soviet Union concluded that the rights of political groups are better protected through domestic legislation implementing political aspects of human rights identified by the Universal Declaration of Human Rights. Similarly, the United States lobbied against incorporating forms of *cultural genocide* (chapter 4) as a prohibited act under the Genocide Convention. Cultural genocide was taken by the United States to emphasise the destruction of minority group property, practices and cultural artifacts. The United States maintained that the crime of genocide should only be equated with the destruction of human beings and not, for example, the destruction of museums. However, the Ad Hoc Committee adopted two forms of cultural genocide over US objections, namely, "forcibly transferring children of the group to another group"[67] and "imposing measures intended to prevent births within the group"[68] (i.e. marital restrictions, forced sterilisation, and mandatory abortion).

What distinguished the Nazi war crimes was the systematic, almost scientific, approach of the regime to the eradication of the Jewish people and their cultural identity. Similar murderous initiatives were also used by the Nazis against other state enemies such as Soviet prisoners, Roma (Gypsies), homosexuals, the handicapped (by euthanasia), and political prisoners.[69] The Nazi genocide was not only

[63] Schabas, William. *Genocide in International Law, The Crime of Crimes*, 136.

[64] *Ibid.* 118 Auto–genocide is defined as the mass killing of members of the group to which the perpetrators themselves belong.

[65] Power 124. Cambodian death statistic used by US Senator William Proxmire (D-Wis), the most vocal US Senate supporter for ratification of the Genocide Convention.

[66] Schabas, William. *Genocide in International Law, The Crime of Crimes*, 119.

[67] *Genocide Convention, supra* note 56, at 79, Article II (e).

[68] *Genocide Convention, supra* note 56, at 79, Article II (d).

[69] Some authors attribute as many as 35 million civilian and military deaths to Hitler's campaign.

an effort to destroy individuals of their group affiliation, but also a campaign to eradicate all elements of the group's existence—that is, to annihilate the group identity and culture, including its language, arts, music, religion, and history.[70] The Nazi genocide took Hitler's Germanisation and de-nationalisation campaigns to destroy other nation-states and sub-dominant national group cultures to their most grotesque extreme. Prior to the ratification of the Genocide Convention, no international code or legal standard had criminalised such acts. Raphael Lemkin defined genocide as deriving from the ancient Greek word genos (race, tribe) and the Latin word cide (killing).[71] Lemkin distinguishes genocide from other murderous acts of homicide, tyrannicide, and infanticide. Homicide is the killing of an individual with the intent to take his or her life. Genocide is the killing of groups of individuals with intent, mens rea, to destroy an entire human group. Intent is the critical element that distinguishes genocide from other forms of destruction such as politicides or mass murder for political reasons;[72] eco-cide (environmental destruction); or ethno-cide (destruction of culture).[73]

Because of the widespread, horrific and unconscionable nature of genocidal annihilation, the crime of genocide required what Thornberry describes as a higher degree of international opprobrium. To prosecute genocide criminals, the

---

[70] Lemkin, Raphael. *Axis Rule In Occupied Europe*, 75. Jews were provided with a legal status under Nazi occupation. The definition of a Jew was based mainly upon the Nuremberg Laws (Section 5 of the law of November 14, 1935, Reichsgesetzblatt, I, P. 1333). A Jew is any person who has more than two Jewish grandparents. Grandparents are to be considered as Jewish if they are, or have been, members of the Jewish faith.

Claude 84. Claude explains that Nazi anti-Semitism turned against assimilated German Jews demonstrating that an assimilation strategy will not necessarily protect the rights of minorities.

[71] Lemkin, Raphael. *Axis Rule In Occupied Europe*, 79.

Power 17. In 1923, as a Polish student studying Linguistics at the University of Lvov, Lemkin first argued that annihilation of a human group should be an international crime. The Genocide Convention formally criminalised the act on 9 December 1948.

[72] *Ibid.* 133. *See also*, The International Commission of Inquiry on Darfur. *Report of the International Commission of Inquiry on Darfur to the United Nations* (Geneva, UN Documents, 2005), 1–177. Examples of politicide include the murder of 2.5 million Cambodians by the Khmer Rouge as well as more recent war crimes committed by the Khartoum government of General Omar Hasan Ahmad al-Bashir against Darfur tribal members in the Sudan.

[73] Dinstein, Yoram ed. *International Law at a Time of Perplexity, Essays in Honour of Shabtai Rosenne* (Dordrecht, Boston, London, Martinus Nijhoff Publishers, 1989), 811.

Harff, Barbara and Gurr, Ted Robert. *Toward Empirical Theory of Genocides and Politicides: Identification and Measurement of Cases Since 1945* International Studies Quarterly 32:3 (Sept.1988) 359–371.

Genocide Convention provided something less than *forum loci delicti commune*[74] or universal jurisdiction. Instead, Articles VI and VII of the convention limited prosecuting power to the state in which the genocide was committed, or to an international penal tribunal, and provided for the extradition of genocide criminals between states. Article IX of the Genocide Convention referred genocide disputes to the interpretation of the International Court of Justice (ICJ). More recently, the Rome Statute of the International Criminal Court passed on 17 July 1998 established the International Criminal Court to prosecute crimes of genocide as well as other crimes against humanity and war crimes incorporated by the statute. Under authority of the Rome Statute, the International Criminal Tribunal for Rwanda successfully prosecuted ten thousand suspects for genocide-related offences, namely for the murder of approximately eight hundred thousand Tutsi victims (1994) by Hutu-Rwandan forces.[75]

It has taken over forty years since the passage of the Genocide Convention to successfully prosecute a defendant alleged to have committed genocide. Samantha Power attributes most of the Genocide Convention's implementation and prosecution failures to the lack of an adequate international prosecution apparatus, as well as the failure of United States' participation, including the US Congress failure to ratify the Rome Treaty.[76] The United States Congress finally ratified the Genocide Convention with the passage of *The Genocide Implementation Act of 1987*.[77]

The genocide carried out by the Nazi regime illustrates the danger posed by totalitarian states practicing radical forms of nationalism. Lemkin warned that the idea of the nation should not be confused with the idea of nationalism, any more than individual liberty should be confused with that of egoism. His view was that states must be dissociated from national group control that forcibly (violently) eliminates or subordinates diverse cultural development. Commentators view this approach as a positive enrichment of the state's internal development as opposed

[74] Meaning a forum of universal jurisdiction. *See* Thornberry, Patrick. *International Law and Minorities*, 50, 78.

[75] Schabas, William A. *The Rwandan Courts in Quest of Accountability, Genocide Trials and Gacaca Courts* Journal of International Justice 3 (2005), (Oxford, OUP, 2005), 888.
Schabas describes the Rwandan Tribunal's record as "an impressive figure by any standard."

[76] Power 167, 382–383, 480–491. The US Senate finally ratified the Genocide Convention Implementation Act in October of 1988, forty years after the passage of the Genocide Convention. In pp. 475–479 Power notes the first successful prosecution of Serbian General Radislav Krstic who was sentenced to forty-six years for war crimes by the International War Crimes Tribunal at the Hague, as well as the prosecution of former Serbian President Slobodan Milosevic.

[77] Also titled, *The Proxmire Act*, Pub. L. 100–606, 18 USC 1091.

to a compromise of the state's national interests. Lemkin notes that contributions provided by diverse minority groups are invaluable to humanity:[78]

> The world represents only so much culture and intellectual vigor as are created by its component national groups...The destruction of a nation results in the loss of its future contributions to the world.

While the Genocide Convention recognised the right of existence for minority groups, it did not provide any rights beyond this. As with prior international instruments, the Genocide Convention permitted state sovereignty to trump the ability of groups to maintain and reproduce their identity (language, religion, and education) beyond the basic group right to existence. States were free to deny individual access to their own culture and instead promote the assimilation of groups into the dominant national culture. The Genocide Convention did not give protection to minority language, religion, education or political participation within states. In fact, the intent of the Genocide Convention was to proscribe the Nazi holocaust to the annals of international criminal law, rather than create a cultural right to self-determination or identity within states. "It provided the minority [with the] right to live but not to live as a minority" explains Tore Modeen.[79]

Commentators have identified several areas to strengthen the Genocide Convention since its passage in 1948. These include revisions authorising UN treaty implementation procedures analogous to later human rights treaties such as the *International Covenant for Civil and Political Rights* (ICCPR) that requires periodic state reporting as well as the monitoring for treaty implementation. In addition, the necessity for a so-called early warning of the genocide requirement in the reporting and monitoring system. Other modifications include mandatory extradition of criminal-genocide defendants between states, as well as incorporation of incitement to genocide as a prohibited activity. Some commentators also call for expansion of the protected group classifications to incorporate political groups.

The Genocide Convention not only serves to restrain evil abuses posed by totalitarian states, but also resolves confusion surrounding the debate over whether human rights can attach to groups, as such. It has resulted in the creation of a formal, internationally recognised, group right to existence which protects human groups from the near annihilation suffered by the Jewish and Roma peoples in WWII. Passage of the Genocide Convention gave international recognition to the idea that cultural groups are indispensable to the social fabric of humankind. It also provided the foundation for the UN's minority regime.

---

[78] Modeen 143.
Lemkin, Raphael. *Axis Rule In Occupied Europe*, 91.

[79] Modeen 111.

3.5. *The International Covenant on Civil and Political Rights, 1966*

... wherever the issue is presented, it is out of place; whenever it is presented, it is premature.[80]
Inis Claude, on UN debates concerning the minority regime.

In my next two sections, I will discuss how the Cold War between the Soviet Union and the United States, as well as continuing debates in the United Nations concerning the right to self-determination, influenced the incorporation of minority protection as a part of the United Nations' human rights covenant.

It took nearly two decades after the passage of the Genocide Convention for the General Assembly to grant minority groups the right to establish their legal identity beyond that of mere survival. Article 68 of the UN's Charter authorised the Economic and Social Council, which established the UN Commission on Human Rights, to implement the provisions of the Charter relating to human rights and fundamental freedoms. At its second session in late 1947, the UN Commission on Human Rights decided that it would prepare a convention, to be called a Covenant on Human Rights.[81] At its subsequent sessions, the Commission focused on the draft Human Rights Covenant, including its measures of implementation as well as inclusion of minority protections.

During the early 1950s, debates over the inclusion of minority rights in the draft Covenant were influenced by the Cold War. The Soviet Union positioned itself as an international spokesperson for human rights instruments that included protection for minority groups. It placed numerous draft formulations for positive minority rights before UN human rights bodies. As early as 4 May 1948, Soviet spokespersons were attempting to tie together the issue of minority rights with the principle of self-determination for colonised peoples (anti-colonialism) by placing them both in the draft Human Rights Covenant. In the Fifth UN General Assembly, Soviet-bloc countries argued that positive rights for minorities and self-determination were two inter-related issues. Bolshevik nationality theory has always made this connection, and the Soviet Union believed that combining the two issues would gain support for positive minority rights from anti-colonial states previously opposed to the idea. For example, at the meeting of the Commission on Human Rights on 17 April 1952, the Polish delegate explained that "[t]he right to self-determination could not be fully ensured without guaranteeing the

[80] Claude 165.

[81] McGoldrick, Dominic. *The Human Rights Committee, Its Role in the Development of the ICCPR* (Oxford, Clarendon Press, 1991), 5. The draft covenant is known today as: *The International Covenant on Civil and PoliticalRights, 1966*, and the *International Covenant on Economic Social, and Cultural Rights, 1966.*

right of national minorities to use their native tongue and to have their own cultural and educational institutions…".[82] The Soviet Union's position was that minority rights reflected Soviet nationality policy, and scolded "opponents for claiming to worry about security risks involved in such an innocuous matter as allowing minorities to speak their own language and maintain their own schools."[83] In debates over passage of the Universal Declaration of Human Rights, a Byelorussian representative maintained "that the right to his native culture was a basic right of every human being."[84] The Soviet Union's idealism was contradicted by its policies eliminating political independence for Eastern European states, as well as in its own domestic political repression. Despite its advocacy on behalf of human rights, the Soviet Union resisted UN interference in domestic affairs.

By contrast, the United States withdrew to a position of first, apathetic support, and then, hostile opposition to the passage of either minority protection or a human rights covenant. The US position was influenced, in part, by concern about the effect that human rights treaties could have on the maintenance of territorial possessions controlled by Western colonial powers, by bias in favour of the assimilation of immigrant groups (one-people nationalism), as well as by opposition to UN interference on questions of domestic sovereignty (e.g. maintenance of the southern states' segregation laws and Aboriginal reservations policy). US opposition to action on human rights resulted in the prevailing UN attitude during the period, which was to respond to minority regime proposals as "out of place…[and]…premature."[85] Whilst, in the US Congress, the *Bricker Amendment* (1952–1953) was proposed in order to stop the human rights covenants by placing restrictions on the executive branch's treaty-making powers under the Constitution. The Bricker Amendment was narrowly defeated by a close vote of the US Senate.[86] On 6 April 1953, John Foster Dulles, Secretary of State for the Eisenhower Administration, informed the Senate Judiciary Committee that the United States would not become a party to the human rights convenants.[87] In opposing the human rights covenants, Americans "were especially agitated by the introduction of clauses which targeted South Africa (an apartheid state) or colonial powers; or which tried to compel the United Nations to give effect to economic and social rights."[88]

Eleanor Roosevelt insisted on "divorcing"[89] the principle of self-determination from minority protection. Speaking before the Human Rights Commission on

[82] Claude, 173–174.
[83] *Ibid.*, 166.
[84] *Ibid.*, 165.
[85] *Ibid.*
[86] McGoldrick 17.
[87] Sellars 83.
[88] *Ibid*,. 79.
[89] Claude, 175.

17 April 1952, she argued for deleting minority protection from a Soviet proposal on national self-determination.[90] A leading member of the US delegation to the UN "bristled at the implications of self-determination: "Are the Aleuts of our own Territory of Alaska…to be permitted to determine whether they continue to be administered by the United States or are to join their kinspeople in Asiatic Russia?"[91] Over US objections, the General Assembly requested that the Economic and Social Council prepare recommendations on the right of all peoples to self-determination. The Human Rights Commission's eighth session (1952) was taken up in drafting articles stipulating, among other things, that, "[a]ll peoples have the right to self-determination" and decided to incorporate them as Article 1 into both of the human rights covenants. The majority view of the General Assembly was that the right should not be limited to colonial territories "but should apply to the people of any territory whether independent, trust, or non-self-governing."[92]

Roosevelt succeeded, however, in separating rights to self-determination from those of minority protection. Instead, minority protections were placed into a separate article of the Covenant for the enjoyment of culture. Today's HRC has clarified that the right of self-determination is "a right belonging to peoples",[93] whilst the minority article "relates to [cognisable] rights conferred on individuals."[94] The inclusion of the self-determination principle in the human rights covenants not only supported the objectives to encourage national independence movements by peoples living in colonial territories, but also altered international law by recognising rights-bearing individuals. Prior to the covenants, states were the only recognised agents or beneficiaries of international law.

Minority protection not only overlaps with principles of self-determination but may also be considered part of a continuum or species of human rights that elevates the individual, as well as qualified groups, to having legal personality as well as standing. Self-determination was equated with secession, as well with as independent statehood for the weaker nations of Europe after WWI (chapter 2). In the human rights context, self-determination is similarly regarded as requiring national independence for peoples in dependent, colonised territories. Increasingly, self-determination principles are used as a basis for claims to political autonomy and natural resources by indigenous groups. Self-determination was also invoked by the new Eastern European states that emerged after the collapse of the Soviet Union and Yugoslavia, and is currently invoked by and for the Palestinian peoples

---

90 Sellars 79.

91 *Ibid.*, 80.

92 McGoldrick 15.

93 Compilation of General Comments and General Recommendations Adopted by Human Rights Treaty Bodies, UN Doc. HRI/Gen/1/Rev.7, 12 May 2004 p. 158, para. 3.1.

94 *Ibid.*

living in Occupied Palestinian Territories. Minority groups who seek political independence or secession may, in restricted circumstances, qualify as peoples entitled to self-determination. Some commentators maintain "there may be a right to secession for populations of well-defined territories only when the government is not representative and severely discriminates against particular segments of the population....to activate secession: a people must be persistently and egregiously denied political and social equality as well as the opportunity to retain their cultural identity".[95]

The United States and its Western allies also opposed the inclusion of economic, social and cultural rights into the human rights covenants. At its Sixth Session (1951), the General Assembly decided after a "bitter"[96] debate to request that the Human Rights Commission split the Human Rights Covenant into two separate treaties, "one to contain civil and political rights and the other to contain economic, social and cultural rights...".[97] The US maintained that only civil and

---

[95] Alexandra Xanthaki. *The Right to Self Determination: Meaning and Scope*, Eds. Ghanea, Nazila and Xanthaki, Alexandra (Leiden, Martinus Nijhoff Publishers, 2005), 17, 19, 24–25. Authorities: United Nations Charter, 1945 Article 1 (2) states that the purposes of the United Nations are: 'To develop friendly relations among nations based on respect for the principle of equal rights and self-determination of peoples, and to take other appropriate measures to strengthen universal peace',

ICCPR, 999UNTS 171, Article 1 states that, "All peoples have the right of self-determination. By virtue of that right they freely determine their political status and freely pursue their economic, social and cultural development",

International Covenant on Economic, Social and Cultural Rights, 1966 999 UNTS 3 – Article 1 states that, "All peoples have the right of self-determination. By Virtue of that right they freely determine their political status and freely pursue their economic, social and cultural development",

UN Declaration on the Granting of Independence to Colonial Countries and Peoples, GA Res. 1514, UN GAOR, 15th Session, Supp. No. 16, p.67, UN Doc. A/L.323 and Add. 1–6 (1960),

1975 Final Act of the Conference of Security and Co-operation in Europe (Helsinki Declaration),

Declaration on Principles of International Law Concerning Friendly Relations and Co-operation among States in Accordance with the Charter of the United Nations, UNGA Res. 2625 (XXV), UN GAOP, 25th Sess., Supp. No. 28, p. 121, adopted by consensus on 24 October 1970 – beneficiaries include peoples under colonial or racist regimes or other forms of alien domination, and implies extension to peoples whose government does not represent 'the whole people without distinction as to race, creed or colour.

The (1993) Vienna Declaration and Program of Action – gives self- determination to peoples whose government does not represent the whole of the people 'without discrimination of any kind',

The Committee on the Elimination of Racial Discrimination (CERD) *General Recommendation XXI (48)* – possibility of secession 'by free agreements of all parties concerned.'

[96] McGoldrick 7.

[97] *Ibid.*

political rights were justiciable as directly enforceable against coercive state interference before the courts. By contrast, economic and social rights were subjective, being dependent upon the degree of available state resources to provide them. The Eastern Bloc states protested against the division of rights into two as tantamount to creating a hierarchy between them. The US view prevailed at the session, however, and commentators note that the *International Covenant on Economic Social and Cultural Rights, 1966*[98] (ICESCR) is a weaker treaty than the *ICCPR*, in that the ICESCR requires progressive implementation and is not yet internationally justiciable.[99]

The United States finally ratified the *International Covenant on Civil Political Rights, 1966* on 8 June 1992, nearly three decades after the treaty's passage! The US has failed to ratify the *Optional Protocol to the ICCPR*,[100] denying Americans the ability to file a human rights communication before the UN. The United States has also failed to ratify the ICESCR. One hundred and fifty-three other states, however, have ratified the ICESCR.[101] In contradiction to the basic state obligations required by the ICESCR, nearly forty-four million Americans lack insurance for basic medical treatment, and approximately eight hundred and forty-two thousand Americans qualify as homeless on any given night.[102]

3.6. *Article 27 of the ICCPR: The Rights of Minorities*

UN Special Rapporteur Francesco Capotorti's seminal paper on the rights of minorities maintains that, from 1955 to 1971, the Sub-Commission on Prevention of Discrimination and Protection of Minorities concentrated its efforts entirely on questions of discrimination, in order to comply with the UN's human rights approach protecting individuals against invidious discrimination while denying official recognition or positive rights to subordinate minority groups.[103] Capotorti

---

98 *International Covenant on Economic, Social and Cultural Rights, 1966* 993 UNTS 3

99 *Ibid.*, 7–8.

100 *Optional Protocol to the ICCPR*, 999 UNTS 171. 109 states have ratified the Optional Protocol including the Russian Federation.

101 Office of the United Nations High Commissioner for Human Rights Website, International Covenant on Economic, Social and Cultural Rights, 16 December 1966, 10/5/2006 <www.ohchr.org/english/countries/ratification/3.htm>

102 The Kaiser Commission on Medicaid and the Uninsured. *Uninsured in America, Key Facts* (Washington DC, The Henry J. Kaiser Family Foundation, March 2000), 2.

The Urban Institute. *Millions Still Face Homelessness in a Booming Economy* (Washington DC, The Urban Institute, 2005), 2.

103 Capotorti.

reports that UN minority protection debates focused merely upon the extent of protection that should be afforded minorities within UN member states. At the Commission on Human Rights' Ninth Session in 1953, the Soviet Union and Yugoslavia were the strongest advocates of protection against assimilation for minorities, including minorities' rights to use their native tongue in public and private life, to possess national schools, libraries, museums and other cultural institutions, and to pursue cultural development and reproduction without being subjected to discrimination. While the Soviet and Yugoslavian proposals were rejected, Commission members did agree that it was necessary to recommend provisions providing cultural groups with the possibility of using their own language, of professing and practicing their own religion, and of enjoying their own culture as part of a draft Covenant on Civil and Political Rights. Opposition to the protections came mainly in the form of sovereignty arguments from nation-states in Latin America and Africa, who were concerned that minority protections would threaten national unity and promote separate communities, and also threaten the public health, safety and human rights of minority group members. These nation-states were concerned that minority protection should not stop the voluntary assimilation of individual minorities into the state's dominant national culture. For example, Uruguay unsuccessfully submitted a text preventing groups from forming separate communities within the territory of a state, while Chile proposed a clause limiting application of the Article to states where minorities exist, thereby creating a potential subterfuge for states to deny the existence of minority groups. The Chilean clause was adopted by the Third Committee of the General Assembly at its 1104th meeting.[104]

The arguments raised on behalf of state sovereignty resulted in the passage of a minority rights article in the Covenant identifying three groups - ethnic (inclusive of race), religious, and linguistic - that required international protection. At its 1,496th plenary meeting on 16 December 1966, the General Assembly unanimously adopted the draft ICCPR, the first universally recognised treaty in history to offer an all-round protection of minorities as part of binding international law. The ICCPR, like other international human rights covenants, establishes a *uinculum iuris* or duty on the parties not to adopt laws or practices at variance with obligations specified in the treaty. Article 27 of the final text passed

[104] *Ibid.*, 32–34 para.176 and 177. E/CN.4/SR.368–371. Arguments against minority protection were made by representatives of Latin American and African states during the Third Committee of the UN General Assembly, at its 1103rd and 1104th meetings, 1961–1962. For example, Uruguay submitted texts preventing groups from forming separate communities within the territory of a state and Chile proposed a clause permitting states to deny the existence of minority groups.

by the General Assembly guaranteed minorities the right to access their culture in community with other members of their group:[105]

> In those States in which ethnic, religious or linguistic minorities exist, persons belonging to such minorities shall not be denied the right, in community with the other members of their group, to enjoy their own culture, to profess and practice their own religion, or to use their own language.

In addition, Article 27 positively enables the identified groups to engage in associational arrangements for cultural reproduction. That is, it presupposes and protects the associative nature of minority identity. It is these aspects that distinguish Article 27 as assigning more than *status negativus libertis* or negative liberty in the form of mere protection for individual minority group members against invidious acts of discrimination. Instead, Article 27 introduces a new category of human rights, that which I previously described as cultural rights, or the right of individual(s), acting alone or in community with other group members, to access and reproduce culture, inclusive of national, ethnic, linguistic and religious identity. Just as political, civil, and social rights each imply legal protection for a collection of activities (e.g. free speech, democratic elections, fair trial, minimum wages, and health care), so also cultural rights provide an umbrella of protection for linguistic, religious, educational and other cultural practices necessary to the maintenance and perpetuation of minority identity.[106]

Article 27 has two purposes: firstly, an absolute prohibition against forced assimilation of minorities, requiring states to adopt an attitude of tolerance towards the idea of privileged and unrestricted access to the common enjoyment of culture, inclusive of language and religion.[107] Recall in Chapter 2 that we

---

105 *International Covenant on Civil and Political Rights, Article 27* UN Doc. A/6316 (1966), 993 UNTS 171.

Passage of the "Declaration on the Rights of Persons Belonging to National or Ethnic, Religious and Linguistic Minorities, 1992" A/RES/47/135 (3 February 1993) finally expanded the categories of minority groups requiring international protection to include national groups.

Henkin, Louis ed. *The International Bill of Rights/The Covenant on Civil and Political Rights* (New York, Columbia University Press, 1981), 35.

Spiliopoulou, Akermark Atthanasia. *Justification of Minority Protection in International Law* (London, Kluwer Law International, 1997), 131.

106 Phillips, Alan and Rosas, Allan eds. *Universal Minority Rights* (London, Abo Akademi University, Institute for Human Rights, 1995), 40.

Pentassuglia 100.

107 Thornberry, Patrick. *International Law and Minorities*, 4. Thornberry distinguishes between two different state approaches with respect to minority groups: *assimilation* or producing a homogenous society by getting groups to discard their culture in favour of the dominant one, and *integration*, or a process by which diverse elements are combined into a unity while retaining their basic identity.

reviewed how radical nation-states used de-nationalisation campaigns to destroy the national patterns of subordinate groups. Many states, including liberal nation-states, implement various policies to promote the forcible assimilation of minority groups into the dominant national culture as an aspect of the state's nationalisation (state-building) efforts.[108] Examples include Australia's forced assimilation of Nyungar (Mardudjara) Aboriginal children, popularised in a 2002 documentary film based on Doris Pilkington's *Rabbit-Proof Fence.*[109] Another was the US Bureau of Indian Affairs' establishment of boarding schools to Americanise Aboriginal children in the late nineteenth century.

Secondly, Article 27 mandates a positive obligation by states to take steps guaranteeing minority rights to identity.[110] The intent in passing the Article (and, more broadly speaking, cultural rights) is that minorities are entitled to protect and reproduce their culture within the territory of the state where the group resides, analogous to a form of autonomous, cultural self-determination. That is, a form of autonomy that permits the group to deliberately, in an atmosphere of tolerance and support, protected against retaliation, to practice its linguistic, religious, ethnic and national identity, consistent with state unity and the doctrine of sovereignty. This approach, also used in the League of Nations' minority treaty protection system, represents a social compact between nation-states and minority groups whereby states recognise minority rights to identity in exchange for a group's commitment of loyalty to state unity and sovereignty. That is, a form of "cultural self determination to those groups whose demands for fuller political recognition were denied."[111]

The United Nations' Human Rights Committee, authorised by the ICCPR[112] to monitor member-states' implementation of Covenant requirements, focuses on the guarantee to maintain and reproduce minority cultural identity enshrined in Article 27. The ICCPR establishes state-reporting obligations about domestic

---

108 Lemkin, Raphael. *Axis Rule In Occupied Europe*, 79–80, 86–87.

109 *Rabbit Proof Fence*, Biography of Molly Craig and Daisy Craig Kadibil, a Rumbalara Films Olsen Levy Production, Miramax Films, Hanway, and Australian Film Corp, 2002.
Pilkington, Doris. *Rabbit Proof Fence* (New York, Miramax books, Hyperion, 1996).

110 Henrard, Kristin. *Devising an Adequate System of Minority Protection, Individual Human Rights, Minority Rights and the Right to Self Determination* (London, Nijhoff Publishers, 2000), 165–167.
Thornberry, Patrick *International Law and Minorities*, 141–218.

111 Hannum 31.
See Article 8.4 of the Declaration on the Rights of Persons Belonging to National or Ethnic, Religious and Linguistic Minorities, 1992 which expressly states: "Nothing in the present Declaration may be construed as permitting any activity contrary to the purposes and principles of the United Nations, including sovereign equality, territorial integrity and political independence of States."

112 *ICCPR, Part IV, Articles 28–45* 999 UNTS 171.

implementation, given that the primary treaty enforcement mechanism demands an initial report within one year of entry into force of the Covenant, followed by periodic state reports at the HRC's request. While the HRC is not a formal judicial body, it is the pre-eminent interpreter of the ICCPR, which is a legally binding treaty, and HRC decisions are thus a strong indicator of the state's legal obligation. Individual communications (minority complaints) to the HRC follow a judicial pattern that is effectively a decision on the merits.[113]

As with the League of Nations, the issue of minority standing under the UN's ICCPR Article 27 reflects the dilemma over how to protect minority identity without recognising the legal standing of a minority group. The General Assembly also adopted the Optional Protocol, which was drafted simultaneously as a part of the ICCPR, and provides an *individual* person with the standing to bring a communication before the HRC.[114] While the Convention itself limits such actions to member-states alone under Article 41, the ICCPR's first Optional Protocol's entry into force a decade later on 23 March 1976[115] permits *individual* complaints to be directed against states that have ratified the Optional Protocol. Major powers such as the United States and Japan refused to sign the Optional Protocol, and France, by reservation, excludes application of Article 27.[116] The HRC firmly rejected the standing of communities [minority groups] or corporate entities that represent such groups to lodge a communication. The Optional Protocol places additional requirements on individual authors to exhaust domestic remedies as well as a victim requirement that they suffer actual harm as a condition of standing. Despite these qualifications, the Optional Protocol is the first international instrument, beginning with the establishment of the League of Nations' minority protection treaty system, to permit an individual member of a

---

[113] Castan, Melissa, Joseph, Sarah, and Schultz, Jenny. *The ICCPR Cases, Materials, and Commentary* (Oxford, Oxford University Press, 2000), 14, 22.

Spiliopoulou, Akermark Atthanasia. *Justification of Minority Protection in International Law* (London, Kluwer Law International, 1997), 132.

Henkin, Louis ed. *The International Bill of Rights/The Covenant on Civil and Political Rights* (New York, Columbia University Press, 1981), 148.

Schwelb, Egon, "Civil and Political Rights: The International Measures of Implementation." American Journal of International Law 62 (3) (1968): 838

[114] Formerly referred to as a petition under the League of Nations' minority protection treaty system.

[115] *Optional Protocol to the ICCPR* was adopted and opened for signature, ratification and accession by UN *General Assembly resolution 2200A (XXI) of 16 December 1966* with *entry into force on 23 March 1976.*

[116] Castan, Melissa, Joseph, Sarah, and Schultz, Jenny. *The ICCPR* (Oxford, Oxford University Press, 2000), 606. The *Vienna Conventions on Laws of Treaties of 1969 and 1986* govern the regime of reservations to determine their admissibility and work to preserve the integrity of treaty text and the universality of participation. For example, the French reservation of Article 27 has no effect on French territories.

minority group authority to bring a communication before an international tribunal. It is the first legal procedure that authorises individual minority claims against states for adjudication by an international forum in the form of the HRC.[117] The Optional Protocol permits individuals to break free of the so-called *iron cage*[118] of state sovereignty and file minority and human rights complaints directly with the outside world.

Though limiting the grant of jurisdiction to individual members of minority groups, the nature of minority claims inevitably compels HRC hearing of Article 27 communications on the basis of collective harm. While the Optional Protocol does not recognise *actio popularis* communications on behalf of all minorities in the class or group, Yale Law School Professor Egon Schwelb maintains that a group of individuals, similarly affected, can submit a communication.[119] The language of Article 27 introduces a collective dimension to the otherwise individually conscious nature of rights protected under the ICCPR as well as human rights law more generally. Although the right attaches to an individual, it is exercised in community with other members of her or his group. Access to culture, especially in cases of religious or linguistic practice, cannot take place in the purely private realm. For example, individuals cannot limit their religious prayer or linguistic communication to whispers or ceremonies that take place in the basement of a private home. State discriminations against these activities usually take place when they are engaged in public and, in these circumstances, Article 27 acts to protect such practices.

Jurists explain that human rights' laws generally reflect this dual nature of the right, describing them as individual rights with a collective dimension or a community of individuals endowed with similar rights. While minority rights are sometimes criticised as vague and unenforceable because they are group-based,

---

117 Article 1&2 *Optional Protocol to the ICCPR* Article 1&2;
Pentassuglia 101.
Scheinin, Martin. "How To Resolve Conflicts Between Individual and Collective Rights" Scheinin, Martin and Toivanen, Reeta, eds. *Rethinking Non-Discrimination and Minority Rights* (Abo, Finland, Institute for Human Rights, Abo Akademi University, 2004), 32.

118 Daes, Erica-Irene A. *Status of the Individual and Contemporary International Law: Promotion, Protection and Restoration of Human Rights at the National, Regional and International Level* (Geneva, Centre for Human Rights, United Nations, 1992), 56–57. A new trend is developing to permit the individual to assert rights and protect interests against a foreign state, not through the intervention of her own state, but directly.
Thornberry, Patrick. *Indigenous Peoples and Human Rights*, 89. Thornberry warns that the *iron cage* of sovereignty-based international law also imprisons the legal imagination with respect to the rights of indigenous [minorities] peoples.

119 Schwelb, Egon, "Civil and Political Rights: The International Measures of Implementation." American Journal of International Law 62 (3) (1968): 864.

many human rights have this characteristic. As examples, the freedom of religion or the right to strike involve activities by individuals similarly engaged in community with other members of their group. The hybrid character of human rights is not a resolution of philosophical debate about the incompatibility of group-based rights with liberal theory, but rather a political compromise between claims by national groups with nation-states that fear minority group secession. While liberal theory resists the idea of group rights, collective group actions are recognised in state jurisdictions that permit class actions and other procedures representing individuals acting jointly on the basis of shared or common interests. The customary requirement for such actions is that the complainants share actual injury or damage emanating from the same transaction or occurrence. The collective dimension of human rights' jurisprudence may also be viewed in this fashion, namely, as protection for classes of individuals from practices by states that threaten the shared or common interests of cultural groups.[120]

As in all international treaties, state compliance with the ICCPR suffers from the general weakness of the absence of an international legislature, courts with compulsory jurisdiction and centrally organised sanctions. ICCPR implementation is primarily reliant upon states to follow the so-called rule of recognition that states should behave as they customarily behave and follow a moral obligation to comply with treaty obligations.[121] Demonstrating the reluctance of states to comply with their international requirements, legal scholars complain about a depressing rate of state non-compliance with Optional Protocol decisions; inadequate HRC meeting time; delay in issue of Optional Protocol views; and long intervals between submission of state reports and subsequent examination by the HRC.

HRC decisions based on individual minority claims against states emphasise the symbiotic relationship between the author (the victim on whose behalf the communication is brought) and her interest in the maintenance of communal group membership. In *Sandra Lovelace v. Canada*[122], the Committee overturned a Canadian Supreme Court decision used by Canada to deny the author, a Maliseet Indian woman, the right to reside on the Maliseet Tobique Reserve. The case involved a dispute between the author and the state about whether Canada's

---

[120] Scheinin, Martin. "How To Resolve Conflicts Between Individual and Collective Rights" Scheinin, Martin and Toivanen, Reeta, eds. *Rethinking Non-Discrimination and Minority Rights* (Abo, Finland, Institute for Human Rights, Abo Akademi University, 2004), 222.

Thornberry, Patrick. *International Law and Minorities*, 149.

Henreard, Kristin. *Devising an Adequate System of Minority Protection, Individual Human Rights, Minority Rights and the Right to Self Determination* (London, Martinus Nijhoff Publishers, 2000), 172.

[121] Hart, H.L.A., *The Concept of Law, Second Edition* (New York, OUP, 1961), 230–275.

[122] *Sandra Lovelace v Canada*, Communication No. R.6/24 U.N. Doc. Supp. No. 40 (A/36/40) at 166 (1981).

Indian Act violates provisions of the ICCPR and the Covenant's Optional Protocol protecting the rights of minority persons to access their cultural identity. Section 14 of the Indian Act provides that an (Indian) woman who is a member of a band [tribe] ceases to be a member of that band if she marries a non-Indian man. Canada argued that under the Act, an Indian woman, through marriage to a non-Indian man, loses her right to reside on an Indian reserve. As a result of her marriage to a non-Indian man on 23 May 1970, Lovelace lost her rights and status as an Indian under Canadian Federal law and was deprived membership in the Maliseet band. Lovelace had lived on the Maliseet Tobique Reserve in the home of her parents prior to and after the marriage break-up and divorce. Subsequent to her divorce, Lovelace sought to return and live with her children in a new house on the Maliseet Tobique Reserve, as well as to receive Federal education, social assistance and housing benefits for registered Indians denied her by the Canadian Government. The HRC ruled that, by denying Lovelace her legal right to reside on the Maliseet Tobique Reserve, the Canadian Supreme Court also deprived her of the right to enjoy her own culture and to use her own language in community with other members of her group.

In a similar case involving the right of a minority person to access his culture, *Ivan Kitok v. Sweden,*[123] the HRC made a different ruling about a state-party denial of a minority person's membership of his cultural group. Holding that the Swedish state had committed no violation of the author's Article 27 rights, the HRC simultaneously questioned the compatibility of Sweden's Reindeer Husbandry Act with ICCPR Article 27 guarantees. The author of the communication, Ivan Kitok, was a Swedish citizen of Sami ethnic origin whose Sami family had been active in reindeer breeding for over one hundred years. Sweden's Regeringsratten (High Administrative Court) upheld the decision of the County Administrative Board (Lansstyrelsen) to deny Kitok's membership in the Sorkaitum Sami Village and restrict his rights to reindeer breeding, hunting and fishing, as well as requiring him to pay 4–5,000 Swedish krona annually as a membership fee in the Sorkaitum Samby Association. Sweden qualified Sami membership under the Act, establishing a rule that a Sami who engages in a profession other than reindeer husbandry for a period of three years loses his status as a Sami and has his name removed from the rolls of the Lappby.

The HRC decision agreed with Kitok that the economic activity of reindeer husbandry is an essential element in the culture of an ethnic community and falls under Article 27 protection for a minority's enjoyment of culture in community with other members of the group. The Committee decided that, because the Act enforced a rule whereby a person who is ethnically a Sami can be denied membership as

[123] *Ivan Kitok v Sweden,* Communication No. 197/1985, CCPR/C/33/D/197/1985 (1988).

a Sami, the restrictions on Kitok were disproportionate to the legitimate ends sought by the Swedish legislation. Similar to its finding in the *Lovelace* decision, the Committee identified a conflict between the Act which protected the rights of the minority as a whole and its application to a single member of that minority. Guided by the *ratio decidendi* [124] in *Lovelace*, the HRC advised that a restriction upon the right of an individual member of a minority must be shown to have a reasonable and objective justification and to be necessary for the continued viability and welfare of the minority as a whole. In contrast to its finding against Canada in the *Lovelace* case, the HRC concluded that Sweden had not committed any violation of Article 27. Instead, the HRC decided that Kitok must be granted access to his culture and permitted, "albeit not as of right, to graze and farm his reindeer, to hunt and to fish."[125]

Distinguished from the approach used by indigenous authors in *Lovelace* and *Kitok*, minority group efforts to bring an *actio popularis* action on behalf of the entire group seeking self-determination rights have been decidedly refused by the HRC. For example, in *Lubicon Lake Band v. Canada* [126], Chief Bernard Ominayak of the Lubicon Lake Band, a Cree Indian band living within the Province of Alberta, Canada, filed a communication alleging that the Province of Alberta's issuance of private company leases for oil and gas exploration violated the group's right to self-determination under Article 1 of the ICCPR. In the *Lubicon Lake Band* decision, the HRC explained that self-determination for the Lubicon Lake Band was not an issue for the Committee to address under the Optional Protocol of the ICCPR. "The Optional Protocol provides a procedure under which individuals can claim that their individual rights have been violated. There is, however, no objection to a group of individuals, who claim to be similarly affected, collectively to submit a communication about alleged breaches of their rights."[127] In the *Lubicon Lake Band* decision, the HRC, without equivocation, reduced the ability of a group to assert a collective group right, limiting communications to the joint action of similarly affected, private individuals. However, the HRC went on to find that the Province of Alberta's actions in exploiting natural resources violated the Lubicon Lake Band's Article 27 rights to enjoy their culture in the form of access to natural resources. The HRC defined economic practices such as an indigenous peoples' access to natural resources, hunting, and fishing as an aspect of cultural rights. The Province of Alberta subsequently agreed with the HRC to remedy its violation of Article 27 through a negotiated settlement acceptable to the Lubicon Lake Band Cree.

---

124 Meaning the reason for the decision.

125 *Ibid.*

126 *Lubicon Lake Band v Canada*, Communication No. 167/1984 (26 March 1990), U.N. Doc. Supp. No.40 (A/45/40) at 1 (1990).

127 *Ibid.*

The use by the Lubicon Lake Band of ICCPR Article 1's self-determination guarantee is an increasingly standard claim of indigenous populations. As discussed earlier in this chapter, despite the appealing rhetoric and universal appeal of the doctrine of self-determination, stressing the inherent equality of nations, commentators note that self-determination is noteworthy more for its persistent breach than its faithful implementation.[128] Nation-states are concerned that self-determination rights threaten national sovereignty and result in partition of state territory. Lawyers for indigenous groups are increasingly using the right to support indigenous claims, as I discussed earlier in this chapter, for greater autonomy in circumstances of de-colonialisation, apartheid opposition, and indigenous peoples. They assert the claim to achieve types of political and administrative authority short of independent statehood, primarily in decision-making and control over natural resources.[129] Indigenous claims that make use of the doctrine demonstrate that self-determination remedies are not coterminous with statehood, secession, or partition.

---

[128] Anaya, S. James. "Self-Determination As a Collective Human Right Under Contemporary International Law", Aikio, Pekka and Scheinin, Martin. *Operationalizing the Right of Indigenous Peoples to Self-Determination* (Turko/Abo, Institute for Human Rights, Abo Akademi University, 2000), 3.

Henriksen, John B. "The Right of Self-Determination: Indigenous Peoples Versus States", Aikio, Pekka and Scheinin, Martin. *Operationalizing the Right of Indigenous Peoples to Self-Determination.* (Turko/Abo, Institute for Human Rights, Abo Akademi University, 2000), 132.

[129] Anaya, S. James. "Self-Determination As a Collective Human Right Under Contemporary International Law", Aikio, Pekka and Scheinin, Martin. *Operationalizing the Right of Indigenous Peoples to Self-Determination.* (Turko/Abo, Institute for Human Rights, Abo Akademi University, 2000), 6, 12. On p. 21, Anaya lists the following examples of circumstances in which the right to self-determination can be satisfied: mandated territories, trust territories, and territories treated as non-self-governing under Chapter XI of the UN Charter; distinct political-geographical entities subject to *carence de souverainete* (gross failure of the duties of the state); other territories in which the principle of self-determination is applied by the parties; highest level constituent units of a Federal state where that state has dissolved; formerly independent entities reasserting their independence with at least the tacit consent of the established state and where their incorporation into that state was illegal or of dubious legality.

Section III

Minority Group Case Studies

Chapter 4

The Minority Regime and the Aboriginal Peoples of Canada

The following chapter is the first case study in which I examine the relationship between the United Nations' minority regime and state recognition of minority groups. In it, I discuss how the minority regime becomes diffused into Canada's domestic regime on indigenous Aboriginal groups. I also study the consequences of the minority regime for Aboriginal-Canadians.

To accomplish this task, I first review the status, including health and living standards, of Canada's Aboriginal groups, as well as the group's relationship to non- Aboriginal Canadians. I then research the history and evolution of the Canadian-Aboriginal legislative relationship to determine the terms of the Canadian regime governing Aboriginals. Next, I contrast Canada's Indian regime with UN recommendations concerning Canada's Aboriginal policies in *Lovelace v. Canada (Lovelace)*[1], as well as other comments on Canada from United Nations' Human Rights Committee reports. Finally, I summarise the extent of domestic implementation of international treaty responsibilities concerning the treatment of indigenous groups.

A primary source of my research for this chapter is taken from the *Report of the Royal Commission on Aboriginals of Canada (Royal Commission).*[2] Commissioned on 26 August 1991 by the Canadian Federal Government to study the so-called Aboriginal problem, the inquiry covers five volumes, summarising four years of research by Commission members about Aboriginal issues.[3] This federal inquiry was the first to examine the Aboriginal-Canadian relationship with a recognition of Aboriginals as distinct peoples. The Commission makes extensive recommendations for improving Canadian policies affecting almost every aspect of Aboriginal society, chiefly by emphasising the need for a return to Aboriginal self-government.

---

[1] *Lovelace, supra,* note 122, at 95. P. 166.

[2] Dussault, Rene; Erasmus, Georges, Co-Chairs; Chartrand, Paul L.A.H.; Meekison, J. Peter; Robinson, Viola; Sillett, Mary; and Wilson, Bertha, Commissioners. *Report of the Royal Commission on Aboriginal Peoples (Royal Commission)* (Ottawa, Canada, 1996).

[3] *Ibid.*, vol.1 (1)(4) [parentheses denote chapters of the report].

It also provides a model for how states can help solve the problems of indigenous and minority groups by initiating public inquiries.

This chapter also reviews a normative criticism of multiculturalism, namely, that special rights for minorities disrupt national unity and the virtues of common citizenship within the state.[4] I analyse the concern of some political theorists that minority rights result in what I previously described as Balkanisation (section 1.3c): that is, the breakup of a state into ethnic enclaves analogous to the partition of the former Yugoslavia located in the Balkans region of eastern Europe. The relationship between minority protection and indigenous persons such as Aboriginals who reside in Canada is particularly challenging, because most indigenous groups do not consider themselves to be minorities within the traditional definition provided for in treaties, conventions and declarations that qualify minority groups. Rather, indigenous groups consider themselves autonomous nations entitled to the right of self-determination within the boundaries of the states wherein they reside.

4.1. *The Aboriginal Peoples of Canada*

Today there are 200 million indigenous people in the world, totalling 4% of the global population. Patrick Thornberry maintains that 3–13 million live in North America alone.[5] The indigenous peoples of South America number approximately 3 ½ million though this statistic is deceptive. The indigenous Aztec, Maya and Inca peoples of the region numbered between 70–90 million at the point of first contact with European-Spanish explorers. So massive was the murderous campaign by the Spanish Conquistadors against the Aboriginal South Americans[6] that the current figure represents merely the survivors of an intergenerational massacre.[7] The European immigrants from France, Britain, and Spain who made first contact with the indigenous populations in North (France and Britain) and South (Spain) America were inspired, in part, by nationalism

[4] *See* Miller, David. *On Nationality* (New York, Oxford University Press, 1995), 140, 153–154. Miller, David. *Citizenship and National Identity* (Malden, Blackwell Publishers Ltd., 2000), 82–83, 85–86.

[5] Thornberry, Patrick. *Indigenous Peoples and Human Rights*, 16.

[6] *Royal Commission, supra,* footnote 2, at 101, vol.4 (1) 2. The term 'Aboriginal peoples' refers to organic, political and cultural entities that stem historically from the original peoples of North America, not from collections of individuals united by ethnical characteristics. The term Aboriginal peoples means the individuals belonging to the political and cultural entities known as Aboriginal peoples.

[7] Batston, David. *From Conquest to Struggle, Jesus of Nazareth in Latin America* (Albany State University of New York Press, 1991), 14.

and the religious fervour of their own European states. Cristobal ('Christ-bearer') Columbus was convinced, for example, that he was carrying out his mission of evangelisation with the blessings of God.[8] To the Jesuits in North America, their mission was akin to a war against satanic forces and was intended to reap a rich harvest of souls.[9]

The Aboriginal-Canadian population, according to the *Royal Commission*, is 811,400 out of a total Canadian population of 29,963,700. According to one Library of Parliament study, the estimated Aboriginal-Canadian population in 1999 was 1,337,900.[10] Canada's statistics on Aboriginals are deceptive because they fail to take account of the nearly 400,000 Aboriginal-Canadians who died in the 200–300 years after the sustained first contact with French explorers reducing the population to 102,000 in 1871.[11] It would take more than a century, until the 1980's, before the size of the Aboriginal population regained the estimated level of 500,000 population at the time of the sustained first contact. Most Aboriginals in British North America died not by massacre, as did Aboriginals in South America, but rather through diseases such as smallpox, tuberculosis, influenza, scarlet fever and measles imported by French and British explorers.

Anthropologists divide North American Aboriginals into two primary groups, Algonkian and Iroquoian, disting`uishable by different languages and economies.[12] The Algonkian nations are migratory peoples who share a common language as well as a similar fishing, hunting and gathering (nuts and berries) economy. The Algonkian group includes the Micmac, Maliseet, and Abenaki Confederacies as well as the Ottawa, Ojibwa or Chippewa, and Cree bands that reside near James Bay, Canada. By contrast, the Iroquoian group is comprised of five nation Confederacies including the Mohawk, Oneida, Onondaga, Cayuga, Seneca, Tuscarora, Wenro and Erie, Susquehannock (Pennsylvania), Neutral, Petun, and Tabacco. The biggest Iroquoian group is the Huron Confederacy that incorporates the Bear, Rock, Cord, and Deer. The Huron are the more sedentary of the groups and rely on crops as well as game and fish to maintain their existence. Iroquoians

[8] *Ibid.*, 14.

[9] *Royal Commission, supra*, note 2, at 101, vol. 1(4).

[10] *Ibid.* vol. 1 (2) 7–10; Wherrett, Jill. *Aboriginal Self-Government* (Ottawa, Library of Parliament, Parlimentary Research Branch, 1999), 1.

[11] Miller, J.R. *Skyscrapers Hide the Heavens, A History of Indian White Relations in Canada* (Toronto, University of Toronto Press, 1989), 48. Miller attributes a smaller number of indigenous deaths to European diseases, writing that half the 200–300,000 indigenous Canadians had died thereby during the 300 years since 1634–1640.

[12] Borrows, John. *Recovering Canada, the Resurgence of Indigenous Law* (Toronto, University of Toronto Press, 2002), 3. Borrows identifies fifty different Aboriginal-Canadian languages in twelve distinct language families.

also belong to a clan (Turtle) as well as a nation (Rock).[13] An Aboriginal Confederacy is comprised of different nations (bands) that form a grand council consisting of the chiefs of the different tribes who arrive at decisions by unanimous consent.

Ignoring these anthropological origins, the Canadian government divides the Aboriginal population into three primary groups, Indian (First Nations), Metis, and Inuit.[14] These three Aboriginal groups are separated by Canadian Federal law into two distinct classes comprised of registered and non-registered Indians. Registered Indians are formally recognised by the state pursuant to *The Indian Act* passed in 1876.[15] Canada's *Indian Act* is an all-inclusive law governing all aspects of Canadian relations with Aboriginal nations, including formal definition of what qualifies a Canadian-Indian as such for recognition. Unregistered Indians are deprived of full recognition by the state. A registered or *status* Indian has been defined as a "person who pursuant to the Indian Act is registered as an Indian or is entitled to be registered as an Indian."[16] An Indian registry is maintained by the Federal Government's Department of Indian Affairs (DOIA) and Northern Development. The *Royal Commission* identifies 56 different linguistic/cultural groups that comprise the Aboriginal peoples. In the chart attached to this section, I have added the Innu peoples, though Canada does not recognise the group since they are not registered under Federal Canadian law. Also, I have added the Metis and Inuit even though Canada does not recognise these Aboriginal groups as Indians.

Social and economic conditions for Aboriginals are far behind those for most other Canadians. According to the *Royal Commission*, Aboriginal peoples are more likely to face inadequate nutrition, substandard housing and sanitation, unemployment and poverty, discrimination and racism, violence, inappropriate or absent services, and subsequent high rates of physical, social and emotional illness, injury, disability and premature death.[17] A wide range of social indicators for 1991 demonstrates that Aboriginals in Canada exist at a lower socio-economic level than the general Canadian population. As examples, the Aboriginal unemployment rate was 24.6% in 1991 compared to an overall Canadian unemployment rate of 9.9%.

---

[13] Miller, J.R. *Skyscrapers*, 6–8.

[14] Pauktuutit, *The Inuit Way: A Guide to Inuit Culture* (Ottawa, Pauktuutit and National Library, 1990), 4. Formerly referred to as Eskimo, the term is no longer used because of its origin as a non-Inuit term with negative connotations. The word 'Inuit' means 'the people' (singular, Inuk) and is the term by which Inuit refer to themselves.

Royal Commission, supra, note 2, at 101, vol.1 (4.5) 1. A distinct people, the Inuit are also called the Thule people and arrived in Canada in 1000AD. Their language is Inuktitut.

[15] *Indian Act* R.S. 1985, c. 1–6, s.1.

[16] Cobo Martinez, Jose R. *Study of the Problem of Discrimination against Indigenous Populations* UN Doct E/CN.4/Sub.2/1982/2/Add.6 20 June 1982. p. 23.

[17] *Royal Commission, supra*, note 2, at 101, vol. 3(3)1.

On the whole, Aboriginal people are substantially more likely to be tenants than other Canadians, especially on reserves where 59% of households live in band-owned housing. Aboriginal houses are twice as likely to need major repairs as those of all Canadians. Aboriginal households are

Linguistic/Cultural Grouping of Aboriginal-Canadian Peoples*

Linguistic Group Name	Population Size**	Linguistic Group Name	Population Size**
Abenaki	1385	Iroquoise Confederacy	35910
Algonkians	6635	Mohawks	25175
Attikameks	3320	Cayugas	3770
Beavers	1390	Oneidas	4395
Bella-Coolas	890	Onondagas	780
Blackfoot	11845	Senecas	530
Carriers	6260	Tuscaraoras	1260
Tsilhqot'n	2060	Kaskas	1050
Coast Tsimshian	4990	Ketenais	580
Comox	1210	Kwakwa ka'wakw	4440
Cree	137680	Lillooets	3790
Dakotas	10570	Malecites	3490
Delawares	1400	Micmacs	16965
Dene Nation	20100	Montagnais/Naskapis	10530
Chipwyans	9230	Nisga'as	3705
Dogribs	2545	Nootkas	5090
Gwisch'ins	1970	Ojibwas	94350
Hares	1170	Okanagans	2605
Slaveys	5185	Potawatomis	140
Gitksan	4210	Sarcee	900
Haida	2560	Sechelt	695
Haisla	1090	Sekani	745
Halkomelem	9725	Shuswap	5500
Han	445	Squamish	2235
Heitsuk	1465	Straits	1855
Huron	2155	Tahltan	1410
Innu	1165		
Inuit	37800		
Metis	139400		

*Source: *Royal Commission*, supra, note 2, at 101, vol. 1 (2.4) 7, taken from 1991 Canadian census. I have added Innu peoples who are not recognised by the Canadian Indian Act as registered Indians. I have also added the Metis and Inuit peoples. Total populations are as of 1991 and as reported in the Royal Commission's 1996 report and taken from the 1991 Canadian Census.

Wherret, Jill, *Aboriginal Self-Government* (Ottawa, Library of Parliament, Parlimentary Research Branc, 1999) 1. In 1999, the total Aboriginal population was reported at 1,337,900.

more than 90 times as likely as other Canadian households to be living without a piped water supply and 14% of Aboriginal reserve dwellings are still without indoor plumbing. In 1991, 57% of Aboriginal youth aged 15 and over had less than a grade 9 education compared to 37% for other Canadians. Only 3% of Aboriginal people graduated from university programs compared to 12% for non-Aboriginal people. In 1990, 41.1% of Aboriginal people who lived on reserves relied on social-welfare assistance as compared to 8.1% of the general Canadian population.[18]

The impoverished socio-economic conditions of Aboriginal people have taken their toll on their overall physical health. The infant mortality rate for Aboriginal people is two to three times that for Canadians generally. Life expectancy for Aboriginal people is approximately 10% lower than for other Canadians. Aboriginal family violence rates are so high that the problem is now almost universally pervasive. The Ontario Native Women's Association found that eight out of ten Aboriginal women had experienced violence, with 87% physically injured and 57% sexually abused.[19] Revelations about an alarmingly high degree of physical and sexual abuse of Aboriginal boys and girls compelled by force of law to attend federally-sponsored religious boarding or residential schools are just beginning to emerge.[20] The Aboriginal rate of death by injury (driving under the influence of alcohol as well as death by drowning, house fire, and gunshot) is two to four times greater than that for Canadians generally. And 80% of Aboriginal people are directly or indirectly affected by alcohol or drug abuse.[21] Aboriginal suicide rates are, on average, about three to four times higher than those for non-Aboriginal Canadians. Aboriginal youth aged 10–19 years have a suicide rate five to six times greater than their non-Aboriginal peers. The Royal Commission Report on Aboriginal suicide attributes the high Aboriginal suicide rate to mental illness, family problems, socio-economic factors, and cultural stress.[22]

In Chapter 1, I described how some political theorists maintain that multiculturalism as state policy will fragment people into separate, self-interested groupings damaging the values of republican citizenship. The history of Canada's relations

---

[18] *Ibid.* vol. 3(3)1.4, vol.3 (4)1.1, vol. 3(5) 4.0, vol.3(5) 9.3.

[19] *Royal Commission, supra,* note 2, at 101, vol. 1(10).

[20] Bumstead, J.M. *A History of the Canadian Peoples, Second Edition* (Oxford, OUP, 2003), 501. By 1990, litigation was pending in Canadian courts involving eight thousand cases of child abuse against Canada's Aboriginal residential schools.

[21] *Royal Commission supra,* note 2, at 101, vol. 3(3)1.2, vol.3(2), vol. 3(3)1.3, vol. 3(3)1.3; Miller, J.R. *Skyscrapers,* 49–50. Miller writes that Aboriginal abuse of alcohol "was motivated by a desire to escape the frustrations of a society already experiencing collapse, an implosion of values and social glues." Aboriginal abuse of alcohol is also associated with demoralisation by Miller.

[22] Chenier, Nancy Miller. *Suicide Among Aboriginal People: Royal Commission Report* (Ottawa, Library of Parliament, 23 February 1995), 1–2.

with the Aboriginal peoples illustrates that the nationalist aspirations of British (and, to a lesser degree, French) immigrants in Canada were responsible for fragmenting the Aboriginal and Euro-Canadian populations. Aboriginals were legislatively identified, segregated and subjugated through barbarous forms of differential treatment by the Canadian state. For many observers, the appalling socio-economic condition of Aboriginals is a direct result of the Canadian government's Aboriginal policies. The UN's minority regime and the history of the Aboriginal-Canadian relationship is rarely described in debates about whether Aboriginals should receive differential treatment to that provided for other Canadian citizens. That Aboriginals are different from other Canadians and should be recognised as such are terms set forth in Federal law and treaty from the time of the first sustained contact between European immigrants and the Aboriginal peoples of North America and carries through to the current day.

4.2. *The Repeal of the Indian Act*

We do not want the Indian Act retained because it is a good piece of legislation. It isn't. It is discriminatory from start to finish....No just society and no society with even pretensions to being just can long tolerate such a piece of legislation, but we would rather continue to live in bondage under the inequitable Indian Act than surrender our sacred rights.

– Harold Cardinal, Cree Indian leader and Board Member, National Indian Brotherhood, 1969.[23]

"It is a white paper for white people created by the white elephant"

– Canadian Northwest Territories editorial on the Trudeau-Chretien White Paper[24]

In this chapter's subsequent sections, I discuss two aspects about the influence of the minority regime on the Canadian-Aboriginal relationship. First, I summarise the terms that comprise the Aboriginal-Canadian relationship (sections 4.3, 4.4). I aim to demonstrate that normative criticism against the minority regime based upon its grant of extraordinary or special rights to indigenous minority groups, mischaracterises the issue. Instead, I re-construct the question to incorporate the historical-legal relationship between the nation-state of Canada with that of the Aboriginal peoples.

Recall my discussion in section 1.2a, that it is necessary to correct for empirical distortions as part of our assessment of the minority regime. To prevent distortion, I incorporate historical-legal structures such as the British North American

---

[23] Cardinal, Harold. *The Unjust Society, The Tragedy of Canada's Indians* (Edmonton, M.G. Hurtig Ltd., 1969), 140.

[24] *Ibid.*, 161.

Dominion's colonisation of Aboriginal nations into my analysis. That is, when asking whether or not it is justifiable to recognise the Aboriginal peoples, I provide an objective determination of the terms as they exist between Aboriginal groups and Canada given an over two-century, textually defined, relationship. Next, I discuss how the minority regime serves to influence terms of this defined relationship between the two nations (sections 4.7, 4.8). This will help us to assess whether special or extraordinary rights actually exist for Aboriginals. However, I only briefly review a few subject areas that cover the invidious assaults committed by Canada against Aboriginal nations. The taking of Aboriginal lands as evidenced by Canadian-Aboriginal treaties, the segregation and relocation of Aboriginals onto government created reserves, and the *pass law* creating apartheid-like conditions for Aboriginals, are just a few additional examples I do not fully cover.

My analysis incorporates the historical connection to the colonial relationship between the two nations. Canada (British North American), as well as the Aboriginal-American nations, inhabit a common territory even while they are separate and unequal in law and custom, with Aboriginals living under conditions of formal subjugation resulting from gross inequality by alien rule for over two centuries. In this chapter, I attempt to bridge the divide between minority rights jurisprudence and that of multiculturalism as a political theory with grounding in the history of the Aboriginal-Canadian relationship, as well as an understanding about the legal regime that defines it.

In 1969, an attempt to implement what can be described as a difference-blind liberalism policy for Aboriginals called *The White Paper* was made by Minister of Indian Affairs and Northern Development, Jean Chretien.[25] Criticised by Aboriginal groups and quickly thereafter withdrawn by the Elliot Trudeau Administration, the new policy attempted to end discrimination against Aboriginals by eliminating all Federal laws recognising Indian status for Aboriginal peoples. The policy called for repeal of the Indian Act, elimination of the Department of Indian and Northern Development, devolution of all Indian-related matters to provincial control, and privatisation of Indian lands under individual or band ownership. Trudeau's policy failed because it refused to restore Aboriginal sovereignty from a political status of colonial subjugation and dependence. Liberal policy aspiring to end discrimination against Aboriginal nations, based on the historical-colonial relationship created in part by treaties, as well as statutes regulating relations between the two nations, requires a transition for Aboriginal nations from that of a dependent to one of an independent status. That is, if the liberal aspiration is the elimination of discriminatory treaties and special legislation regulating Indian life, such a policy necessarily

[25] Chretien, Jean. *Statement of the Government of Canada on Indian Policy* (Ottawa, Office of the Minister of Indian Affairs and Northern Development, 1969), 7–8, 21–23.

implies a process of de-colonisation and self-determination for Aboriginal nations. This is precisely the view advocated by movements supporting international recognition for indigenous peoples in the United Nations (section 4.11).

The Indian Act is Canada's colonial-era legislation (section's 4.2–4.5), the object of which is to eliminate the Aboriginal peoples through a policy of coercive assimilation. The Indian Act defined nearly every aspect of Aboriginal society under British North America's Dominion colonisation. Just as the first post-confederation *Indian Act* of 1869 had no Aboriginal participation, so too did the White Paper of 1969 not involve any meaningful Indian participation.[26] Still, many Aboriginal groups opposed the elimination of the Indian Act, though to the current day it discriminates against Aboriginal existence and confined the group to segregation on Aboriginal land reserves. Why are Aboriginals divided on this question?

Aboriginal support for the Indian Act is based upon the fact that it provides recognition of the sovereignty of Aboriginal nations and their respective land claims, despite the Act's discriminatory terms and diminished status qualifications. The Cree Nation Aboriginal leader, Harold Cardinal, explained that there could be no changes in the Indian Act until "the question of treaty rights and Aboriginal [land] claims had been settled."[27] To abolish the Indian Act would terminate an important basis for Aboriginal sovereign land claims, even though no specific mention is made in the Indian Act about the hundreds of treaties signed by the Dominion guaranteeing Aboriginal claims. The Indian Act[28], Sections 18–29, provides guarantees for Aboriginal reserve land possession, certificates of occupancy, land improvements, land transfers, land permits, as well as, a guarantee against seizure of Aboriginal land. Canadian-Aboriginal treaties continue to be the subject of a shameful litigation process (sections 4.6–4.9), albeit after centuries of Federal violations against Aboriginal territory. The Indian Act provides a minimal if discriminatory shield of protection for the continuation of the Aboriginals' sovereign existence in Canada. As importantly, it provides a legislative base to litigate for damages arising from Federal violations against Aboriginal reserve territory.

The Aboriginal groups' various positions on whether to support or eliminate the Indian Act reflects the confusion of dependent populations about how to change legal structures imposed by alien, colonial subjugation. The *Royal Commission* reported as "startling"[29] the gulf between the perspectives and philosophies of most Aboriginal testimony about the Indian Act that was presented before the Federal government's joint committee of the Senate and House of Commons (1948).

---

[26] Miller, J.R. *Skyscrapers*, 228.

[27] Cardinal 125.

[28] The *Indian Act*. R.S., c.1–6, s.1.

[29] *Royal Commission*, *supra*, note 2, at 101, vol.1 (9.13), pp. 9–10.

The report concluded that "It is nothing less than the difference between greater Indian self-government and the revitalised goal of assimilation."[30] Part of the Aboriginal confusion, as explained by Assembly of First Nations' Grand Chief Ovide Mercredi, is that the Indian Act "...served to divide our peoples. We sometimes buy into Indian Act definitions and categories in our own assessment of people and politics. This is part of the legacy of colonialism."[31]

The Indian Act divided Aboriginal groups into separate legal classifications (section 4), with some groups failing to qualify for official recognition (status) as 'Indian'. Recall that under the Indian Act, Metis Aboriginals (creolised French-Aboriginals), Inuit Aboriginals (formally known as Eskimos), as well as other identified Aboriginal groups and individuals, fail to qualify as Indian. The Indian Act's legislative classifications were exploited by Canadian officials who used colonial 'divide and conquer' tactics by turning Aboriginal groups against one another in responding to the White Paper's proposal to eliminate the Indian Act.

Compounding Aboriginal internal divisions was the vulnerable status of Aboriginal organisation. For example, efforts by Aboriginal groups to organise were opposed by Federal Department of Indian Affairs (DOIA) agents who had legal guardianship over Aboriginals. DOIA Indian agents "openly threatened to punish Aboriginals who persisted in organisational efforts....[and] used subtle weapons such as delaying relief payments or rations...[and] harassment by the police."[32] A wide range of other difficulties challenged Aboriginals in establishing political organisation. These included poor communications, inadequate transportation systems, geographic isolation, illiteracy, group fatalism, and lack of funding. Also, religious organisations such as the Roman Catholic Church interested in controlling Aboriginal education (Christianisation) established the Catholic Indian League to attract Aboriginal members away from Aboriginal-controlled organisations.[33]

The Aboriginal circumstances in Canada demonstrate the elements of political subjugation and social struggle that the normative critics of multiculturalism do not incorporate into their discussions about minority claims. To argue, for example, that Aboriginal indigenous claims or the minority regime interferes with the development of a common, unitary citizenship, or Balkanises the state, fails to consider the colonial framework established by Canada to destroy Aboriginal society. It is difficult to conceive how the implementation of human rights conventions to benefit the subjugated conditions of Canada's Aboriginal minority groups violates the tenet of equal treatment contemplated by liberal egalitarianism.

---

30 *Ibid.*

31 *Royal Commission, supra*, note 2, at 101, vol. 4 (2.3), p. 3.

32 Cardinal 98–99.

33 *Ibid.*, 98–99, 102–103.

Further, it is not clear what remedy liberal egalitarianism would implement to eliminate the legacy of colonialism, segregation or apartheid. These practices tend to become ingrained in the social and cultural fabric of states, passed down by inter-generational custom, and last long after the state has eliminated formal structures of discrimination.

To clarify the relationship between recognition for Aboriginal-Canadian treaties and Aboriginal sovereignty, Harold Cardinal explains that "once our rights are guaranteed, there will be less need for our people to emphasise their sovereignty."[34] That is, the type of sovereignty required by the Aboriginal claim has an inverse relationship to the nature of political subjugation encountered by the group. A resolution of the conflict between the state of Canada with the Aboriginal nations that results in recognition for Aboriginal-Canadian treaties fosters equality. This is because Aboriginal rights are then being treated similarly to those of any other citizen, group, or organisation that enters into agreements with the state. To the extent that the minority regime encourages such recognition, it not only promotes equality of treatment, but also strengthens national unity by ensuring it. That is, even the treaties and agreements made with Aboriginals, once considered to be less than human beings and unable to hold rights, must now be recognised by Canada.

In the sections that follow, I discuss how Canada implemented a confusing mix of policies that involved coercive assimilation while administering colonial-style segregation against the Aboriginal nations. I aim to demonstrate that, in contrast to the normative claim that minority rights Balkanise society, or create special rights for only certain groups, rather is it coercive state practices that contradict equality of treatment and common citizenship for which the minority regime serves as a corrective.

4.3. *History of Canada's Indian [Aboriginal] Laws*

The basis for Canada's assigning differential treatment identifying Aboriginal peoples (Indians) is evidenced by a long history of self-serving if not contradictory Federal laws, numbered treaties, court cases, public policy, and international instruments initiated by Spanish, later French and finally British settlers in North America for over two centuries. Twin goals of Canada's Aboriginal policy contradicted each other by seeking to coercively assimilate the Aboriginals into the state's majority Euro-British and French culture while segregating Aboriginal nations in conditions of colonial-like subjugation. These competing goals are contained within the numerous special laws passed to identify and regulate

[34] Cardinal 36.

Aboriginal life through to the current day. So voluminous were the terms established by Canada regulating almost every aspect of Aboriginal-Canadian society that, by 1906, the Federal *Indian Act* statute consisted of one hundred and ninety-five sections in two parts under thirty-eight headings and had become too cumbersome for Federal Indian agents and judicial officials to interpret.[35] From 1781–1902, European settlers were motivated to take ownership of Aboriginal lands, concluded by reaching four hundred and eighty-three different treaties, adhesions, and land surrenders with Aboriginals. Treaties signed after 1867 are referred to by Canada as numbered treaties ranging from 1–11. Treaty no. 163 signed in 1877, for example, is better known as treaty no. 7.[36]

Canadian policy identifying Aboriginals for differential treatment started with the founding of Canada. The Dominion of Canada began with Confederation on 1 July 1867 after passage of the *British North American Act of 1867* in the British Parliament. Itself a colony of Great Britain (British North America), Parliament passed the act believing that colonies like British North America would inevitably seek independence and that the costs of imperial administration were an unnecessary drain on the public purse. However, even with Confederation, Britain's Colonial Office still had responsibility and authority over Canadian-Aboriginal policy.[37] Britain's formal relationship with Aboriginal nations of North America began with *The Royal Proclamation of 7 October 1763* by King George III. This placed Aboriginal peoples (Indians) under the "Sovereignty, Protection, and Dominion" of the British Empire, protecting the territory of Aboriginal subjects by mandating strict regulations on land purchases by European immigrants seeking to take over Aboriginal territory.

During 1800–1860, the French and British, and later, the Americans, had been fighting a battle to wrest control of North America from the Aboriginals. North American Aboriginal nations, no more unified than their European counterparts, tended to ally with the less threatening French against the British. However, the Iroquois Confederacy, illustrating diplomatic savvy, sought to play the French and British off against one another to their advantage. The battle ended with the Peace of Paris in 1763 ceding most of North America to British control.[38] After the war, Mohawk, Shawnee, Six Nations Confederacy, and Praying Indians Aboriginal nations became military allies with the British against

---

[35] Leslie, John and Maguire, Ron, eds. *The Historical Development of the Indian Act* (Ottawa, Dept. of Indian Affairs and Northern Development, Treaties and Historical Research Centre, P.R.E. Group, August 1978), 105.

[36] Martinez Cobo, Jose R. *Study of the Problem of Discrimination Against Indigenous Populations.* UN Doc. E/CN.4/Sub.2/1983/21/Add.4, p. 99.

[37] Bumsted, J.M. *A History of the Canadian Peoples* (Oxford, OUP, 2003), 182, 200, 204.

[38] Miller, J.R. *Skyscrapers*, 33–35, 37, 70–71. Indians were shrewd commercial fur traders.

the Americans. In the war of 1812, Aboriginals fought gallantly to protect British North American lands against invading Americans who had insatiable demands to take over Aboriginal territory. Aboriginal nations fought alongside the British in the hope of creating an independent Indian state in the Ohio Valley. In negotiations over terms for the *Treaty of Ghent* to end the war, the British, seeking to protect their Aboriginal allies, proposed the creation of an Indian buffer state exclusively for Indians between the Ohio Valley and the south of the lower Great Lakes. Americans rejected the proposal and the British capitulated, instead agreeing to restore land boundaries between British North America and the United States to their pre-war position. In the 1920's, over a century after their failure to secure an independent Indian state, the Iroquois Confederacy continued lobbying efforts in the League of Nations on behalf of sovereignty for Aboriginal North Americans.[39]

Failing to provide the Indians with an independent state of their own, the British North American parliament decided to instead enact Federal initiatives to assert political control over the formerly sovereign Aboriginal nations. *The Indian Lands Act of 1860* began the process by transferring political control away from Aboriginal nations to a Chief Superintendent of Indian Affairs in a united Province of Canada. The Act was a precursor to section 91(24) of the *Constitution Act, 1867* which placed control of all Aboriginal peoples and their lands under the Dominion of Canada Parliament.[40] Passage of the *Gradual Civilisation Act, 1857* provides the legal basis to begin privatising communally held, Aboriginal reserve territory. Aboriginals who agreed to abandon their legal status as Indians were rewarded with a grant of fifty acres for individual possession.[41] The grant constituted only a life estate in the property with fee simple ownership taking place only after transfer to the Aboriginal's children upon his death.[42] *The Gradual Enfranchisement Act of 1869* completed parliament's attack on Aboriginal tribal self-government by empowering the Chief Superintendent and colonial Indian Affairs officials to control elected terms of office for Aboriginal chiefs and councilors, as well as dispose at will elected Aboriginal chiefs. The Act also mandated the loss of Indian status to any Aboriginal women as well as her children for marriage to a non-Indian man, resulting later in HRC efforts to prevent this loss of Indian status.[43]

---

39 *Ibid.*, 86–87;
Anaya, S. James. *Indigenous Peoples In International Law, Second Edition* (Oxford, OUP, 2004),57.

40 *Royal Commission, supra*, note 2, at 101, vol.1(4).

41 Miller, J.R. *Skyscrapers*, 191.

42 *Royal Commission, supra*, note 2, at 101, vol.1(5).

43 *Ibid.*, vol.1(7); *Lovelace, supra*, note 122, at 95. pp. 166, 181.

The Dominion of Canada's colonial rule over Aboriginal peoples was consolidated by passage of the *Indian Act 1876*, establishing parliamentary control over Aboriginal political structures, land holdings, resources, and economic development.[44] More than any other Federal initiative, the *Indian Act* captures the essence of the Canadian-Aboriginal relationship. Ironically, the *Indian Act* is supported by some Aboriginal groups, not because of its admittedly discriminatory provisions, but rather for the Act's catagorising Aboriginals as distinct peoples, entitling the group to assert their right of self-determination under international law. Establishing a protective guardianship over Aboriginals to be implemented with a system of coerced assimilation, the *Indian Act* created artificial legal categories for Aboriginals defining, for example, which Aboriginal groups could qualify for Indian status. As I discuss in section 4.9, the purpose of the *Indian Act*, among other goals, was to eliminate the Aboriginal population by tightening restrictions for Aboriginal membership. To the current day, the Act excludes two major Aboriginal groups as recognised Indians, the Inuit as well as the mixed blood Metis (offspring of French, English, and Scottish intermarriages with Aboriginal wives). The Act also mandated establishment of the Department of Indian Affairs (currently the Department of Indian and Northern Affairs), colonising all aspects of Aboriginal society. In an effort to tighten political control and undermine the Aboriginal tribal system, parliament also passed the *Indian Advancement Act of 1884* and the *1885 Enfranchisement Act* (made compulsory in 1876). The enfranchisement policy forced assimilation upon certain classes of Aboriginals and resulted in the loss of Indian legal status including the right to membership in an Indian Band (nation) or to live on an Indian reserve. In 1920, the Superintendent General of Indian affairs could order the enfranchisement of any Indian, male of female, over the age of twenty-one who was fit for enfranchisement. Amended in 1933 and again in 1951, the policy was maintained to allow the coercive enfranchisement of Indian women who married non-Indian men until the passage of C-31 in 1985.[45] Seeking to increase political control over the Aboriginal nation, Canada also passed The *Indian Advancement Act of 1884* which authorised the Superintendent General of Indian Affairs to dispose of elected Indian chiefs at will that he considered unfit, and remained part of the *Indian Act* until 1951.[46]

In 1881, an amendment to the *Indian Act* prohibited the sale of Aboriginal agricultural products without permit and under penalty of fine and imprisonment. This ban was later extended in 1941 to include a ban on the sale of furs and wild

---

[44] *Royal Commission*, *supra*, note 2, at 101, vol. 1(8).
[45] *Ibid.*, vol.1 (9).
[46] Miller, J.R. *Skyscrapers*, 190.

animals. The ban on the sale of agricultural products remains to the current day and exposes the self-interested manner in which Canada manages its relationship with Aboriginal nations. The Act was passed to protect Indian farmers from being swindled by non-Indian agricultural consumers who would, for example, purchase agricultural products from Indians for alcohol. The real purpose of the amendment was to prevent Aboriginal farmers from competing with non-Indian farmers.[47] Illustrating the duplicitous nature of Canada's Aboriginal policy, parliament restricted Aboriginal economic production and trade while simultaneously promoting the policy of coercive assimilation justified by advancing the Aboriginals' economic development. Canada's self-serving policy is litigated against by Aboriginals to the current day, for example, in *Ronald Edward Sparrow v. Her Majesty the Queen*, an unsuccessful Supreme Court appeal by Ronald Sparrow, a Musqueam Band Indian, convicted of violating a British Columbia Fishery Regulations and Fisheries Act, R.S.C. regulation limiting Indian fishing drift nets to 25 fathoms in length.[48] Also, in *Dorothy Marie Van der Peet v Her Majesty the Queen*, Appellant Dorothy Van der Peet, a member of the Sto:lo Nation, successfully reversed her conviction for selling 10 salmon fish in violation of s. 61(1) of the *Fisheries Act, R.S.C.* 1970, c. F-14 and s. 27(5) of the *British Columbia Fishery (General) Regulations* prohibiting the sale or barter of fish caught under an Indian food fish license.[49]

For all the harm it caused Aboriginal Americans, however, the British-Canadian policies succeeded in establishing a legal regime segregating the Dominion of Canada into two separate nations, one Aboriginal, and one Anglo-French European, inhabiting the same territory. In section 4.4, I uncover the terms of the relationship between Canada and Aboriginal peoples.

4.4. *The Basis for Canada's Aboriginal Legal Regime*

Similar to conduct by European powers against peoples living in colonised territories, Canada, to the current day, has failed to define a clear definition of the state's formal relationship with Aboriginals. As a result, some jurists define the relationship between a state and its indigenous peoples as *sui generis* from the Latin term meaning "of its own kind" or unique in its characteristics.[50] *Sui* – of its own, and *generis* - a genitive form of genus or kind, is the Latin term used for example by

[47] *Royal Commission supra*, note 2, at 101, vol.1 (9).

[48] *Ronald Edward Sparrow v Her Majesty the Queen* [1990] 1 S.C.R. 1075.

[49] *Dorothy Marie Van der Peet v Her Majesty the Queen* [1996] 2 S.C.R. 507.

[50] Macklem, Patrick. *Indigenous Difference and the Constitution of Canada* (Toronto, University of Toronto Press, 2001), 87.

the Canadian Supreme Court in *Delagamuukw v British Columbia*[51], to describe the Aboriginal title to land holdings in Canada as distinguished from other proprietary interests. *Delagamuukw v British Columbia* is a precedent-setting case brought by Gitsan and Wet'suwet'en heredity chiefs claiming title to fifty-eight thousand kilometres of territory in British Columbia, where the court established a new precedent that strengthened the ability of Aboriginals to bring claims for title historically refused by Canadian courts.[52] This included not only the court's strong application of *The Canadian Charter of Rights and Freedoms* recognising Aboriginal treaty rights, but also the use of Aboriginal oral histories as evidence in support of claims for title.[53] Authors invoke the *blue water doctrine* (*salt water thesis*)[54] that identifies the Aboriginal peoples of North and South America, separated by the Pacific Ocean from the European continent, as different in legal form and historical content from the question of national minorities in Europe, described in my previous chapters 1–3. Unfortunately, this definition also fails because many European states experienced conflict with their own indigenous populations. This includes the Sami peoples living in Finland, Norway, and Sweden. Also, the Inuit (Thule) peoples who had developed an extensive culture in the harsh environment of the circumpolar artic region, establishing residence not only in the contemporary states of Canada and the USA (Alaska) but also in Greenland, Newfoundland, and the Russian Federation.[55]

An extensive historical-legal literature examines the philosophy used to define the early relationship between European immigrants, primarily from Spain, and the Aboriginal peoples of the Americas.[56] Dominican cleric Francisco de Vitoria (1486–1547) and jurist Alberico Gentilis (1552–1608) provide the primary theological and jurisprudential foundation to justify placing Aboriginals

---

[51] *Delgamuukw v. British Columbia* [1997] 3 S.C.R. 1010.

[52] For example, *see St. Chatherines Milling & Lumber Co. v The Queen* (1888) 14 App. Cas. 46 (J.C.P.C.).

[53] *The Canadian Charter of Rights and Freedoms* is also known as, *The Constitution Act, 1982.* Part II, Rights of the Aboriginal Peoples, Section 35 (1) of the Act states, "The existing Aboriginal and treaty rights of the Aboriginal peoples are hereby recognised and affirmed."

[54] Anaya, S. James. *Indigenous Peoples In International Law*, 75.

Eide, Asbjorn and Daes, Erica. *Working paper on the relationship and distinction between the rights of persons belonging to minorities and those of indigenous peoples*, 19 July 2000. UN Doc. E/CN.4/Sub.2/2000/10 para. 25. Eide explains that the *blue water doctrine* hold[s] that the indigenous are those people beyond Europe who lived in the territory before European colonisation and settlement, and who now form a dominant and culturally separate group in the territories settled primarily by Europeans and their descendants, and therefore is America-centric.

[55] *Royal Commission, supra*, note 2, at 101, vol. 1 (4.5). Archaeologists date the arrival of the Thule people in Canada at approximately 1000 A.D.

[56] Anaya, S. James. *Indigenous Peoples In International Law*, 16–23. Anaya provides us with a comprehensive historical summary.

in the Americas under what was, at base, Euro-Spanish colonial administration. These authors developed a theory not based upon the discovery of the new world's vast and largely barren land but rather of just war justified by theological imperative as well as secular rationale, including the requirements of national defence and the recovery of property. Later, Swiss philosopher Emerich de Vattel (1714–1769), in his treatise, The Law of Nations, develops an additional justification by accepting the Lockean notion that 'cultivating land established a greater right to the land than did hunting and gathering.'[57] De Vattel provides the rationale for the legal doctrine of terra nullius. Derived from Roman law, the Latin terra nullius, that is, land of no one or empty land, was used to support European immigrants to settle American land as if it were owned by no one and unclaimed by a sovereign.[58] De Vattel's treatise, also titled *Principles of the Law of Nature Applied to the Conduct and Affairs of Nations and Sovereigns*,[59] argues that over-populated, more industrious European states are justified in taking possession of Indian lands in North America because "savages stood in no particular need [and] made no actual and constant use"[60] of the land. De Vattel concludes that if all nations followed the example of the North American Indians, namely, living "only by hunting, fishing, and wild fruits, our globe would not be sufficient to maintain a tenth part of its present inhabitants."[61] However, de Vattel places clear limits on his doctrine, requiring that European settlement in North America be confined within justifiable boundaries, take possession of only those parts of the land not in use, as well as purchase from the Indians lands that were intended for colonisation. It is these limitations that were largely ignored by European settlers in North America.

This philosophical reasoning was supported by popularly held ideas as well as an emerging new science of the times regarding the nature of colonised peoples residing in lands separated by vast oceans from the European continent. For example, Juan Gines de Sepulveda, a respected jurist and imperial official

---

[57] *Ibid.*, 23. Anaya cites Vitoria, Francisco de. *On the Indians Lately Discovered (De indis et de ivre belli relectiones)* (Classics of International Law ed. 1917), Gortius, Hugo. *The Law of War and Peace* (Classics of International Law ed. 1925), 40, de Vattel, Emerich. *The Law of Nations, or Principles of Natural Law* (Classics of International Law Series, 1916).

[58] *Royal Commission, supra*, note 2, at 101, vol.1 (4). The Commission reviews the doctrine of *terra nullius* in this section.

Thornberry, Patrick. *Indigenous Peoples and Human Rights*, 74.

[59] De Vattel, Monsieur; Chitty, Joseph ed. *The Law of Nations; or Principles of the Law of Nature Applied to the Conduct and Affairs of Nations and Sovereigns* (London, Law BookSellers and Publishers, 1834), Book I, Chapter VII, Section 81, Pp. 35–36, Book I, Chapter XVIII, Section 209.

[60] *Ibid.*

[61] *Ibid.*

proclaiming a popular view held during a 1550 debate before the Holy Roman Emperor at Valladoid, Spain, portrayed the Aboriginals in the Americas as:[62]

> ...by the rudeness of their nature, natural slaves... They are persons of inborn rudeness and inhuman customs. Thus one part of mankind is set aside by nature to be slaves, slaves in the service of masters who are born for a life free of manual labour. Prudent and wise men have been given dominion over them for their own welfare. If inferior beings refuse this overlordship, they may be warred against justly, as one would hunt down wild beasts.[63]

These views provided theological support from French and British missionaries called to proselytise Indians to Christianity during French, and later, British colonisation of North America. Aboriginal-advocate Harold Cardinal explains that missionaries used to teach the Aboriginals that European immigrants considered the Indian an "ungrateful little savage."[64] By the nineteenth century, these views found support from a newly acquired veneer of scientific legitimacy in emerging new fields of phrenology, cultural anthropology, and Social Darwinism. These new forms of scientific racism were used in Britain to justify expansion and domination in Africa and Asia. Great Britain, as explained by J.R. Miller, had long regarded non-White populations throughout the world as economically, socially, and politically inferior. "In the United States they were employed to defend first the institution of slavery and later the 'Jim Crow laws' that succeeded it; and in British North America they served as handy rationalisations to justify attempts to coerce [subjugate] and change [assimilate and civilise] Indian societies."[65] Explaining British North American colonial educational policy as dedicated to the purpose 'to have the Indian educated out of them' at the second annual convention of the Association of Presbyterian Workers among Indians, 27–28 July 1905, RB Heron states:[66]

> To be successful the colony must be under the school and missionary supervision. The problem of the Indian race is similar to that of Negroes in the USA, Hindoos of India or native races of Africa.

---

[62] Thinking they had discovered the West Indies, the Spanish settlers gave the title Indians to Aboriginals.

[63] Royal Commission, *supra*, note 2, at 101, vol. 1(5) cites: "On the Just Causes of War: The Debate at Valladolid" (The Canadian Broadcasting Corporation, "Ideas", 1985).

[64] Cardinal 23.

[65] Miller, J.R. *Skyscrapers*, 96–97.

[66] Miller, J.R. *Shingwauk's Vision, A History of Native Residential Schools* (Toronto, University of Toronto Press, 1996), 151, 189. Miller cites: Symington, Fraser. *The Canadian Indian: The Illustrated History of the Great Tribes of Canada* (Toronto, McClelland & Stewart 1969), 228, quoting an Indian agent or teacher who said: "These children require to have the Indian educated out of them."

By the twentieth century, scientific racism had developed the field of eugenics inspiring, among other Acts, Canadian anti-immigration laws such as the Immigration Acts of 1906 and 1910. The Acts discouraged immigration by ethnic Chinese, Black, and Jewish peoples and placed restrictions upon persons who were pimps, prostitutes, upon the insane, retarded, epileptic, deaf, and dumb, because members of these groups, according to eugenic science, lowered the standard of civilisation. In the United States, eugenics science was creating more extreme policies. In addition to immigration restrictions, US policies included marriage laws, sterialisation, and segregation to control the reproduction of the least desirable members of society.[67] By contrast to its active participation against the Nazis in WWII, astonishingly, at the 1936 Berlin Olympics, the Canadians gave Hitler a Nazi salute. From 1933–1939, as perfidy to the state's liberal values, Canada accepted only four thousand of eight hundred thousand Jews who escaped Nazi-controlled territory.[68]

4.5. *The Forced Assimilation of Aboriginal-Canadians*

"The great aim of our legislation has been to do away with the tribal system and assimilate the Indian people in all respects with the inhabitants of the dominion..."
British North American Prime Minister John A McDonald, 1887[69]

"It is inconceivable that one section of society should have a treaty with another section of society. The Indians should become Canadians as have all other Canadians."
Canadian Prime Minister Elliot Trudeau, 1969[70]

Critics of multiculturalism who oppose protection for the enjoyment of culture, argue that the disadvantaged economic and social position of some minority group members has no relationship to the right to access culture. According to Brian Barry, "culture is not the problem and culture is not the solution."[71] Using a similar conceptual analysis that stresses assimilation (civilisation), Tom Flanagan instead attributes the depressed socio-economic status of Aboriginal-Canadians to the displacement of hunter-gatherer societies by agricultural peoples and the extension of rule by organised states over

[67] King, Desmond. *In the Name of Liberalism, Illiberal Social Policy In The United States and Britain* (Oxford, OUP,1999), 53.

[68] Bumstead, J.M. *The Peoples of Canada, A Post-Confederation History, 2nd Edition* (Oxford, O.U.P, 2004), 163, 189, 244.

[69] *Ibid.*, 20.

[70] Cardinal 28.

[71] Barry 317.

stateless societies.[72] However, the legal history of Aboriginal-Canadian relations as evidenced in the passage and revisions of the *Indian Act* contradicts arguments to the effect that Federal violations of Aboriginal cultural identity have no relationship to the social condition of Aboriginal-Canadians. The history of Canadian policy toward the Aboriginal peoples has been guided by one central principle, namely, the eradication of Aboriginal culture. Though according to both the supporters and critics of cultural protection for Aboriginal peoples, this failed as a policy, if it had not been for the implementation of the ICCPR's Article 27[73] (minority rights), Canada's subjugation of Aboriginal peoples would be continuing just as it did for over a century. Canadian practices with regard to Aboriginal people constitute what jurists describe as ethnocide[74], or actions committed with intent to destroy the culture of a national, ethnical, racial or religious group.[75]

Recall that the Genocide Convention failed to incorporate cultural genocide as a separate crime into its final text because state parties sought to distinguish acts of group murder from the systematic destruction of historical, religious or artistic monuments, as well as the elimination of other cultural practices. Also, cultural genocide represented an indefinite concept that the Genocide Convention was not able to adequately define, and it instead assigned the subject to the jurisprudence on minority rights. Nevertheless, as a compromise in the debate over the inclusion of cultural genocide, the final text of the Genocide Convention did include a Greek motion in the final text dealing with the forced transfer of children.[76] Canada's residential school system activities (section 4.6) are contemplated by this section of the Genocide Convention.

Recent international instruments provide additional responsibilities for state conduct in the area of cultural protection, and more specifically cultural heritage. These instruments illustrate another new development within international law to criminalise crimes against culture, if not cultural genocide. For example, the soft law entitled the *2003 UNESCO Declaration on International Destruction of Cultural Heritage* not only recommends increasing state responsibility, but also

---

72 Flanigan, Tom. *First Nations? Second Thoughts* (Montreal and Kingston, McQuill-Queen's University Press, 2000), 28–30, 38.

73 *ICCPR* 999UNTS 171.

74 Dinstein, Yoram ed. *International Law at a Time of Perplexity, Essays in Honour of Shabtai Rosenne* (Dordrecht, Boston, London, Martinus Nijhoff Publishers, 1989).

75 Lemkin, Raphael. *Axis Rule In Occupied Europe*, 91.

76 *Genocide Convention, supra* note 56, at 79, now repealed and replaced by the International Criminal Court Act 2001. Article II(e) proscribes the act of "*forcibly transferring children of the group to another group.*"

Robinson, Nehemiah. *The Genocide Convention. Its Origins and Interpretation.* (New York, Institute of Jewish Affairs, World Jewish Congress, 1949), 18–19, 46.

advocates criminal liability to protect cultural heritage of significant importance to humanity. *The 2003 UNESCO Convention on the Safeguarding of Intangible Cultural Heritage*[77] goes beyond material and built objects to maintain oral and intangible traditions of groups that contribute and form their identity.

While the *blue water doctrine* maintained that indigenous and minority groups in the Americas were distinguishable from the so-called national minorities on the European continent, state conduct in the Americas bears a remarkable similarity to the radical nationalism practiced by European nation-states that I previously discussed in chapter 3. Canada's century-long campaign of forcible assimilation directed against Aboriginal peoples had many similarities to campaigns engaged in by European states practicing radical forms of nationalism such as Russification and Germanisation.[78] This is reflected in Canada's emphasis on targeting for brutal assimilation, Aboriginal practices in the areas of religion, language and education, three of the main categories in the reproduction of societal culture.

What distinguished the conduct toward indigenous peoples in Canada was not only its brutality but also the guardianship exercised over nearly every aspect of Aboriginal life. Defined by jurists as the *trusteeship doctrine*,[79] Canada's Federal policy assumed responsibility for Aboriginals analogous to that of guardian and minor. Refusing to recognise Aboriginals as human persons under international law, US Chief Justice John Marshall, capturing the view of the period in the case of *Johnson v M'Intosh*, describes Aboriginals as "fierce savages, whose occupation was war, and whose subsistence was drawn chiefly from the forests."[80] Viewed as childlike, savage, and uncivilised, after suffering losses in the war of 1812, Britain's Aboriginal allies no longer served any relevant purpose for the crown. Not wanting to incur the expenses or moral retribution suffered by the United States that were engaged in expensive wars of Aboriginal extermination necessary to secure new land holdings, Britain instead selected a policy to eliminate the Aboriginal population through a policy of forcible assimilation. Though different in method, the British objective was the same as that of the Americans, namely, "the extinction of Indians as Indians was the ultimate end."[81] On the whole, their view of Aboriginals as uncivilised and savage pales when compared to the practices

[77] *2003 UNESCO Declaration on International Destruction of Cultural Heritage*, 17 October 2003; *2003 UNESCO Convention on the Safeguarding of Intangible Cultural Heritage*, 17 October 2003, Misc./2003/clt/ch/14.

[78] Musgrave, Thomas D. *Self-Determination and National Minorities* (Oxford, Clarendon Press, 1997), 10.

[79] Anaya, S. James. *Indigenous Peoples In International Law*, 31.

[80] *Ibid.*, 29;
Johnson v M'Intosh, 21 U.S. 543, 5 L.ED. 681, 8 Wheat. 543 (1823).

[81] Miller, J.R. *Shingwauk's Vision*, 184.

of their European and Anglo-American counterparts. Aboriginal-North American society was more peaceful, spiritual, generous, and community-oriented, as well as less material and selfish.[82] Fighting fewer, less violent wars than their Anglo-European counterparts, the idea of Aboriginal savagery was ironic, if not surreal in quality. Still, forcible assimilation of Aboriginals remained the focus of British-Canadian Aboriginal policy up to and in the current day.

Canada's policy of forced assimilation was implemented by Federal initiatives described as the Bible and the Plough.[83] The intent of the policy was that assimilation (also referred to as civilisation) of Aboriginal peoples into Canadian society would take place by a system of missionary-subsidised education and the religious conversion of Aboriginals to Christianity. Integration of Aboriginals into the Canadian economy would proceed by forcing a transition from the communal Aboriginal economy into a privatised system of agricultural production by individual land plots. That is, under Federal administration, Aboriginals would be compelled to give up communally held territory as well as their traditional economic trades of hunting, fishing, and gathering and, instead practice European-led economic production through the cultivation and sale of agricultural products. Aboriginals' participation in the system would be limited to their legal status, namely, that of a minor or non-legal person, incapable of responsibility, morality, or civility. Instead, the Federal government, through a system of pan-Britannic administration and missionary-subsidised education, would assume guardianship for Aboriginal society. J.M. Bumstead describes the British colonisation of Aboriginal nations as an imperial federation whose mission was to create an Anglo-centric vision through assimilation to the English language and Protestant norm for the Dominion of Canada.[84]

Formal legislative efforts to eradicate Aboriginal culture began with the passage of the 1876 *Indian Act* that criminalised Aboriginal religious practices and ceremonies. In 1884, the Indian Act was amended to assign jail terms to any Indian convicted of participating in the Aboriginal Potlatch and Tamanawas dance. In an 1876 letter to Canadian Prime Minister, Sir John A. Macdonald, Indian Reserve Commissioner Gilbert M. Sproat charged that the Aboriginal customs produced indigence and thriftlessness as well as forcing women into prostitution, urging that Ottawa, "lay an iron hand upon the shoulders of the people" to eradicate the evil.[85] The Aboriginal Potlatch ceremony was a central institution of Northwest Coast Aboriginal culture and was the occasion on which traditional

---

[82] Miller, J.R. *Skyscrapers*, 10–11, 13, 15, 27, 46, 58–59, 61–62, 76.
[83] *Ibid.*, 189–207.
[84] Bumstead, J.M. *The Peoples of Canada*, 146–149.
[85] Cole, Douglas and Chaikin, Ira. *An Iron Hand Upon the People, The Law Against the Potlatch On the Northwest Coast* (Seattle, University of Washington Press, 1990), 15.

name, rank or hereditary privilege was claimed. It was held at significant points of the life cycle – e.g. the naming of a child, acquisition of a traditional family name, a girl's first menses, marriage, and death. Potlatching, that is, 'giving away', was accompanied by feasting and dancing. The practice not only kept Aboriginal patrimony including name and ancestrial honour intact, but also represented the method of Aboriginal cultural transmission from ancestors to descendents. Aboriginal prestige was enhanced not, as in the case of Europeans, by accumulation, but rather by the distribution and destruction of wealth. A true Oweekano Kwakiutl Chief, for example, always died poor. The idea of hoarding or accumulating wealth would be regarded as abnormal, unthinkable, and shameful.[86] In 1895, additional Indian Act amendments were passed criminalising other Aboriginal cultural practices such as the Blackfoot sundance as well as the Cree and Saulteaux thirst dance. A 1914 Amendment barred western Indians from participating in "Aboriginal costume in any dance, show, exhibition, stampede, or pageant."[87]

4.6. *Coercive Tutelage and the Residential School System*

> *"After a lifetime of beatings, going hungry, standing in a corridor on one leg, and walking in the snow with no shoes for speaking Inuvialuktun, and having a heavy, stinging paste rubbed on my face, which they did to stop us from expressing our Eskimo custom of raising*
>
> *our eyebrows for 'yes' and wrinkling our noses for 'no', I soon lost the ability to speak my mother tongue. When a language dies, the world it was generated from is broken down too."*
>
> Inuit woman's testimony about residential school's language policy made to members of the Royal Commission on Aboriginal People.[88]

> *"...closer scrutiny of past treatment of native children at Indian Residential schools would show 100% of children at some schools were sexually abused."*
>
> Rix Rodgers, Special Advisor to the Minister of National Health and Welfare on Sexual Abuse, 1990[89]

The primary institution used by Canada for the forcible assimilation of Aboriginals was the residential school system. This section will illustrate the danger inherent in the state's policy of coercively assimilating minority groups. In it, I incorporate secondary source research material, namely, the seminal works of J.R. Miller. The establishment of residential schools for Aboriginals took place

[86] *Ibid.*, 5–6, 10–11.
[87] *Royal Commission, supra*, note 2, at 101, vol.1 (9).
[88] *Ibid.*, vol.1(10.3).
[89] Milloy, John S. *A National Crime, The Canadian Government and the Residential School System, 1879–1986* (Winnipeg, The University of Manitoba Press, 1999), 298.

with the transfer by British Canada of responsibility for Indian affairs from military to civilian authorities in the 1830s. Viewing the United States 'euthanasia [extermination and removal campaign] for savage communities' as inimical, expensive, and politically dangerous, the British, influenced by Church groups in England, embarked instead upon a policy to assimilate Aboriginals through a programme of evangelisation, agriculture, and education.[90]

The policy was promoted by English church groups who identified indigenous populations for assimilation throughout the British colonial system. A British-Canadian colonial government inquiry, the Bagot Commission, recommended the institution of residential education as part of the new formulation for Britain's assimilation policies. The central goal of the schools was to reconstruct Aboriginals as pseudo-Caucasians by re-making them culturally through religious conversion to Christianity (Christianisation) and economic adjustment to Euro-Canadian ways.[91] In 1846, the system began with the establishment of manual labour schools whose mission was to provide "large doses of religion" for Aboriginals, while developing their agricultural farming and trade skills for eventual assimilation into British North America's agricultural farming economy. Colonial officials determined, in part thanks to lobbying by religious denominations, that the Anglican, Roman Catholic, Presbyterian, Methodist and United Churches should manage the schools and be responsible both for the students' conversion to Christianity, and for their secular education. Sharp and bitter competition for government funding took place between religious denominations throughout the existence of the school system.[92]

Under a 'half-day system', Aboriginal students would spend half the day in the classroom and half engaged in manual labour practicing their new skills. In 1869, the US Grant Administration had implemented a similar half-day system in the Industrial Schools for Indians and half-breeds as part of the US policy of aggressive civilisation. The role of so-called mixed-bloods, half-breeds, and half-castes in the United States, as well as Aboriginal boarding schools in Australia, was critical to eliminating what the new science of the times believed to be sub-human Aboriginal ethnic and cultural characteristics trapped in the earliest stages of human evolution.[93] Australian officials believed the half-caste Aboriginal to be smarter than their full-blooded Aboriginal counterpart, requiring their isolation and training as domestic servants and labourers. In contrast to the Canadian policy of assimilation, the goal of Australian policy was to breed out Aboriginal

---

[90] Miller, J.R. *Shingwauk's Vision*, 74–75, 414.

[91] *Ibid.*, 74–75, 414.

[92] Scott, Duncan Campbell. *The Administration of Indian Affairs in Canada* (Hangchow, The Canadian Institute of International Affairs, 1931), 14.

[93] Miller, J.R. *Skyscrapers*, 83, 101–102.

genetic characteristics.[94] Following similar policies of Christianisation, Canada, Australia, and the United States used varying methods of assimilation, extermination, and elimination to destroy Aboriginals as a group. The policy was accurately described by one US Bureau of Indian Affairs official as "the extinction of the Indians as Indians."[95]

As in the case in most of Canada's Aboriginal colonial policies, the residential school system was – as indicated earlier – involved the competing goals of assimilating Aboriginals into Euro-Canadian society while simultaneously keeping them in colonial subjugation. The true purpose of the half-day system, for example, was to exploit Aboriginal student labour to financially subsidise the residential school system. The half-day system ensured that students' education was limited to menial vocational, as opposed to academic development, even while being touted by government officials as a vehicle for Aboriginal skill development in the new Euro-based economy of farming or fishing. The schools were perpetually under-funded by Ottawa and considered as an expensive drain on the Canadian Treasury, as were other colonial institutions intended for the guardianship of dependent populations. By 1938, for example, the Department of Indian Affairs used a $180 per capita Aboriginal student funding mechanism for the schools. By contrast, the province of Manitoba provided grants of $642 and $550 per capita respectively to the non-Aboriginal School of the Deaf as well as the School for Boys. Other examples of distinction favouring non-Aboriginal education include the Knowles School of Boys receipt of $362 for each boy from the Community Chest, and the Catholic Church's provision of the non-Aboriginal St. Norbert's Orphanage with $294 per capita.[96]

The system of industrial and boarding schools (1883–1923) was converted to a new system of residential boarding schools that were better equipped to resolve disputes between Aboriginal groups, religious organisations, and government officials over financing, educational methods, and school conditions.[97] In 1907, seventy-seven schools were operational and had increased to eighty residential schools by 1931. I have included a chart illustrating the religious denomination managing each Canadian residential school in this section. John Burrows writes "colonisation is not a pretty thing when you look at it."[98] Student life in the

---

[94] Pilkington, Doris. *Rabbit Proof Fence* (New York, Miramax Books, Hyperion, 1996), 40.

[95] Miller, J.R. *Skyscrapers*, 163, 274.

"The only good Indian is a dead Indian." Philip Henry Shuidan, American Union Cavalry Commander, US Civil War, Fort Cobb, January 1869, explains the Federal government's Indian policy.

[96] *Royal Commission, supra*, note 2, at 101, vol.1(2.10).

[97] Miller, J.R. *Skyscrapers*, 100–127.

[98] Burrows, John. *Recovering Canada, The Resurgence of Indigenous Law* (Toronto, University of Toronto, 2002), 98.

under-funded residential school system was neither pretty nor humane. Residential school life for native children was, according to J.R. Miller, "akin to animal care on a well-run stock ranch or dairy farm."[99] The missionaries who ministered in the residential schools, which were inspired by eugenics, the new field of scientific racism, utilised these institutions for the coercive religious conversion, cultural assimilation, and economic adjustment of Aboriginal students.[100]

Enrollment and attendance of Aboriginal students were mandatory under colour of Indian Act authority. In a process called the "Fall Round Up", state Indian agents would use the Royal Canadian Mounted Police to break down the doors of Aboriginal reserve homes and pry frightened, screaming children from parents' arms, and rush them to holding areas before herding them into cattle cars for transport to boarding schools located great distances away from the Aboriginal reserves where their parents resided. The children were taken by the government with the intent that by removing them from parental influence and visits, family unity and Aboriginal identity would be destroyed. Treated as 'dirty savages' doomed to damnation for having Aboriginal religious beliefs, the school missionary teachers administered a system for the students characterised by overwork, under-funding, attacks on Aboriginal culture, harsh punishment and torture, wide-scale physical, psychological and sexual abuse, tuberculosis epidemics, starvation, cold temperatures, and death. Attendance in the residential school system resulted in a *50% death rate for enrolled students.*[101]In 1990 government experts confirmed that *100% of the children at some schools were sexually abused* including teacher to student, student to student, hetero- and homo-sexual abuse.[102] The schools' environment of abuse, intimidation, and neglect produced student on student violence, including young boys being gang-raped by older boys and girls being sexually molested by bigger girls. The Ontario College of Physicians and Surgeons investigating sexual misbehaviour by doctors uncovered that Native women had been fondled, raped, and abused mentally, physically and spiritually by doctors at residential schools.[103] The *Royal Commission* not only found sexual abuse to be pervasive but also discovered that school principals and staff saw to it that, as part of a system of administered corporal punishment, children were frequently beaten severely with whips, rods and fists, chained and shackled, bound hand and foot and locked in closets, basements, and bathrooms, and had their heads shaved.[104]

---

[99] Miller, J.R. *Shingwauk's Vision*, 290.

[100] *Ibid.*, 414.

[101] *Ibid.*, 133, 216, 289, 423.

[102] Milloy, John S. *A National Crime, The Canadian Government and the Residential School System, 1879–1986* (Winnipeg, Manitoba, University of Manitoba Press 1999), 298.

[103] *Globe and Mail*, 20 February 1991 citied in Miller, J.R. *Shingwauk's Vision*, 330, 336.

[104] *Royal Commission, supra*, note 2, at 101, vol. 1(10).

The residential schools' primary objective of suppressing Aboriginal cultural institutions through the use of coercive tutelage was the justification used by its administrators for taking disciplinary action against the children that included slaps, slurs, insults, and physical, emotional and sexual abuse. The residential schools' assault on Aboriginal culture focused on suppressing the use of Aboriginal languages by students, or 'talking Indian'. Its attack on Aboriginal culture also included punishments for engaging in Indian dances and forbidden Indian games. Schools also pursued programmes for 'adopting out' children to non-Aboriginal parents as part of the effort to destroy Aboriginal identity. In addition, residential schools implemented an 'outing system' akin to involuntary servitude that assigned students to non-Aboriginal farms and families as servants. A penalty given to one female student caught speaking Saulteaux included writing 'I will not talk Indian any more' five hundred times. Common punishments inflicted on students for engaging in Aboriginal cultural practices included being strapped, made to kneel in a corner for half an hour, one hundred blows with a strap, blows with a stick, ear pulling, head slapping, hitting knuckles, shaving, and hair cutting. Another common penalty was forcing students to kneel in a public place with arms outstretched for hours. Other penalties included whipping with five belts, being burnt with a cigarette lighter, and being brutally sodomised, as well as children having their faces smeared in their own soiled clothing. Verbal-abuse techniques used by teachers included calling children "stupid Indians", or "little savages". Missionaries also cut down Aboriginal totem poles and burnt Aboriginal regalia.[105]

The physical and structural conditions of the schools were similarly defined. Malnutrition of the students was widespread. Children were ill-fed and ill- clothed and turned out into the cold to work. As late as 1969, a Saskatchewan administrator reported that he had to serve the cheapest food on the market in the school system. Due to under-funding, the residential schools had poorly designed physical infrastructure and school buildings that contained students in unsafe structures with hazardous fire conditions, poor lighting, heating, and ventilation affording scant protection against cold weather. Combined with overcrowding, poor sanitation, lack of care and cleanliness, and malnutrition, the schools became breeding grounds or 'hotbeds' for tuberculosis disease as well as tonsillitis and typhoid. J.R. Miller describes school conditions as "sadistic" and an insult to "human dignity", with punishment being "arbitrary and cruel". Miller also reports that the children were kept in a dirty, cold, and diseased condition, with their heads and bodies full of vermin.[106]

---

105 Miller, J.R. *Shingwauk's Vision*, 204, 216, 301, 324, 327, 330, 427.

106 *Ibid.*, 304, 309, 316, 328.

The Canadian government's response to the scandalous disclosures about the residential school system is to deny responsibility for the Aboriginal group harm resulting from school practices. In 1990, efforts by Canadian Members of Parliament Rod Murphy and Reginald Belair to commission an independent inquiry into Canada's residential school system were unsuccessful. Again in 1996, the *Royal Commission* failed to convince government officials to establish a commission of inquiry with Aboriginal members to investigate remedies, compensation, funding for treatment and obtain public apologies, pursuant to the *Public Inquiries Act.* Former Conservative Minister of Indian and Northern Affairs, Tom Siddon, attempted to reverse responsibility for the state's conduct, placing the burden on individual Aboriginal victims of abuse to file complaints for Criminal Code violations. Siddon also worked to limit government remedies to satisfying Aboriginal claims for self-government and assist First Nations to design and develop their own educational programmes. The Canadian state eventually consented to funding the establishment of an Aboriginal Healing Foundation, which was to administer a $350 million fund for community healing initiatives. In 2000, eight thousand separate lawsuits filed by injured Aboriginal plaintiffs were pending in domestic courts. Displaying only limited tolerance for Aboriginal spirituality, most Canadian churches issued formal apologies: these included the United Church of Canada and the Anglican Church in 1986, the Canadian Conference of Catholic Bishops and Missionary Oblates of Mary Immaculate in 1991, and the Presbyterian Church in 1994. In 1998, Canada's Minister of Indian Affairs, Jane Stewart, also issued a statement, stating that the Department of Indian and Northern Affairs was "deeply sorry." The last residential school closed in 1996.[107]

Recall that in section 4.1, I discussed the appalling social conditions of Aboriginals in Canada. Social scientists and medical researchers confirm a direct relationship between the depressed conditions of minority groups and state practices such as Canada's residential school system. For example, researchers at the Winnipeg Children's Hospital who investigated child abuse on the Sandy Bay and other reserves in Manitoba concluded in their report it was "apparent that the destruction of traditional Indian culture has contributed greatly to the incidence of child sexual abuse and other deviant behavior."[108] Persons who attended residential schools

[107] Milloy, John S. *A National Crime, The Canadian Government and the Residential School System, 1879–1986* (Winnipeg, Manitoba, University of Manitoba Press 1999)), 299, 300;

Royal Commission, supra, note 2, at 101, vol. 1(10). *See* Recommendations1.10.1, 1.10.2, 1.10.3; Bumstead, J.M. *The Peoples of Canada*, 540–542.

Sarah Shenker, "Legacy of Canada's residential schools," BBC NEWS 11 June 2008 <http://news.bbc.co.uk/2/hi/americas/7438079.stm>. The Federal government formally apologised for forcing Aboriginal students to attend residential schools as part of a C$2bn Indian Residential Schools Settlement Agreement, which includes cash payments to former students.

[108] *Royal Commission, supra*, note 2, at 101, vol. 1(10).

struggle with their identity years after being taught to hate themselves and their culture, inflicting similar abuse on their own children and families in a vicious inter-generational cycle of learned behaviour by adults exerting power and control through abuse. Studies on the psychological consequences of discrimination illustrate an increase of symptoms bearing on psychological well being including anxiety and depression. Psychological responses such as denial and avoidance result in victims believing that the discriminatory framework was legitimate and blaming themselves for what happened. At the extreme, the victim may even completely give up the discriminated aspect of his or her identity. Long-term persecution may result in erosion of the group's culture, customs, and self-esteem, leading to health problems, family breakdown, violence, substance abuse, and child abuse. The high rates of Aboriginal suicide, alcohol abuse, and family violence are causally related to, among the many other Canadian practices concerning Aboriginals, the residential school system and its mission to eradicate Aboriginal culture.[109]

Canada's failure to take responsibility for the inter-generational injuries sustained by Aboriginals as a result of the operation of the residential schools illustrates the dangers resulting from state assimilation practices, as well as the necessity for minority rights protection against forced assimilation. As previously discussed in chapter 2, the growth of nationalism and the resulting state conduct throughout Europe and Asia, including the Ottoman and Russian empires, illustrates the necessity for increasing state responsibility to recognise and protect the identity of minority groups. Canada's inaction over residential schools also illustrates the need,

Canada's Residential Schools 1931*

Nova Scotia	**Shubenacadie (RC)**		
Ontario	Albany Mission (RC)	Cecilia Jeffrey (PR)	Chapleau (CE)
	Fort Frances(RC)	Fort Williams (RC)	Kenora (RC)
	McIntosh (RC)	Mohawk (CE)	Moose Fort (CE)
	Mount Elgin (UC)	Shingwauk Home (CE)	Sioux Lookout (CE)
	Spanish (RC)		
Manitoba	Birtie (PR)	Brandon (UC)	Cross Lake (RC)
	Eikom (CE)	Fort Alexander (RC	Mackay (CE)
	Norway House (UC)	Pine Creek (RC)	Portage la Prairie (UC)
	Sandy Bay (RC)		
Saskatchewan	Beauval (RC)	Cowessess (RC)	Duck Lake (RC)

109 Ghanea, Nazila. "Repressing Minorities and Getting Away With It: A Consideration of Economic, Social and Cultural Rights." eds. Ghanea, Nazila and Xanthaki, Alexandra. *Minorities, Peoples, and Self-Determination* (Leiden, Martinus Nijhoff Publishers, 2005), 206–208.

Canada's Residential Schools 1931* (*Cont.*)

Nova Scotia	**Shubenacadie (RC)**		
	File Hills (UC)	Gordon's (CE)	Guy (RC)
	Lac La Ronge (CE)	Muscowequan (RC)	Onion Lake (CE)
	St. Phillips (RC)	Thunderchild (RC)	
Alberta	Blood (RC)	Blue Quills (RC)	Crowfoot (RC)
	Edmonton (UC)	Ermineskins (RC)	Holy Angels (RC)
	Lesser Slave Lake (CE)	Morley (UC	Old Sun's (CE)
	St. Albert (RC)	St. Bernard (RC)	St. Bruno (RC)
	St. Cyprian (CE)	St. Paul's (CE)	Sacred Heart (RC)
	Sturgeon Lake (RC)	Vermillion (RC)	Wabasca (CE)
	Wabasca (RC)	Whitefish Lake (CE)	
Northwest Territories	Aklavik (RC)	Fort Resolution (RC)	Hay River (CE)
	Providence Mission (RC)		
British Columbia	Ahousaht (UC)	Alberni (UC)	Alert Bay (CE)
	Cariboo (RC)	Christie (RC)	Coqualeetza (UC)
	Kamloops (RC)	Kitamaat (UC)	Kootenay (RC)
	Kuper Island (RC)	Lejac (RC)	Port Simpson (UC)
	St. George's (CE)	St. Mary's Mission (RC)	Sechelt (RC)
	Squamish (RC)		
Yukon	Carcross (CE)	St. Paul's Hostel (CE)	

In 1931 there were 44 Roman Catholic (RC), 21 Church of England (CE), 13 United Church (UC) and 2 Presbyterian (PR) schools. These proportions among the denominations were constant throughout the history of the system.

In Quebec two schools, Fort George (RC) and Fort George (CE), were opened before WWII. Four more were added after the war: Amos, Pointe Bleue, Sept-Iles and La Tuque.

*Sources: Royal Commission, *supra*, note 2, at 101, vol.1(10.1); Malloy, John S., "A National Crime", The Canadian Government and the Residential School System, 1879 to 1986 (Manitoba, The University of Manitoba Press, 1999) 307.

as discussed in section 4.5, for new international standards in the area of crimes against culture. The practices of residential schools should not be limited to civil remedies provided by the international minority regime. The operation of Canada's residential schools more accurately falls within the purview of international criminal law. While Genocide Convention protections do not extend to crimes of cultural genocide or ethnocide, they do however protect against "forcibly transferring children of the group to another group."[110] Canada's mandating the residential school system's forced removal and transfer of Aboriginal children from their families, relocating them to training centres administered under the guardianship of different religious and ethnic groups who engage in torture and abuse, as well as maintaining conditions resulting in the death of Aboriginal children, may qualify for protection under Article II (e) of the Genocide Convention. The Genocide Convention lacks a mechanism that would allow an individual legal standing to bring a communication directly against the state, unlike the Optional Protocol to the ICCPR.[111] Complaints brought under the Genocide Convention are limited to those made by a state party, including the Canadian state. The restriction on standing for individual minority group members to bring complaints under the Genocide Convention renders it less accessible to minority groups seeking protection for criminal violations of human rights standards committed by either a state or individual(s). It also leaves Aboriginals injured by Canada's residential schools without an effective systemic remedy for criminal activity, other than individual claims for monetary damage in domestic courts or communications to the HRC under ICCPR Article 27. Canada's assimilation policy (Christianisation) demonstrates how state practices with regard to indigenous minority groups incorporate illiberal and, as in the case of the Aboriginal children in Canada, alleged criminal violations of human rights. This example demonstrates that the critics of multiculturalism are wrong to oppose minority regimes that prohibit the forced assimilation of minority groups.

4.7. *The Canada - HRC Relationship*

The evolution of Canada's relationship with the United Nations' Human Rights Committee and how the UN's minority regime has influenced Canadian recognition of Aboriginal peoples helped to re-define terms for the Aboriginal-Canadian relationship. The basis for UN treaty implementation is to promote greater recognition for Aboriginal equality in Canada. I could not identify any effort by the HRC, nor any article of the *ICCPR*[112] that promote either Balkanisation of Canadian society or special rights, other than those provided for by international and domestic treaty. Rather, the claims are simply to enforce promises made to formerly sovereign Aboriginal nations by Canada that domestic courts chose over the centuries to ignore or weaken. My purpose, however, is to illustrate precisely how international treaties now influence state practices with regard to the recognition and treatment of indigenous minority groups.

---

110 *Genocide Convention, supra* note 56, at 79, Article II(e).

111 *Optional Protocol to the ICCPR,* Article 2.

112 *ICCPR,* 999 UNTS 171.

Even with the UN's effort to assist Canadian treaty implementation, the terms of the Canadian-Aboriginal legal relationship is ambiguous to the current day. In this section, I review the evolution of the Canadian-HRC relationship concerning the implementation of the minority regime. Recall my earlier analysis in chapter 3 about the HRC 30/07/81 recommendation in *Lovelace*.[113] The HRC recommendation in the case initiated a two-decades-long dialogue between Canada and the HRC regarding challenges to the implementation of the HRC decision in *Lovelace*. The delays by Canada on implementation of the HRC decision make it easy to criticise and question the credibility of international human rights standards and, more specifically, the HRC for its lack of sanction authority over recalcitrant states that refuse to implement HRC recommendations. The HRC, however, is not so much a judicial organ lording over states or ruling on state conduct as an interpretative body that helps states to understand their treaty obligations and assist in the implementation of their treaty responsibility. In becoming a signatory to an international treaty, states incorporate treaty obligations into their own domestic legal framework. Whether states incorporate treaty obligations as part of one universal order with the state's domestic law (monistic) or as a part of international obligations separated from their domestic system (dualistic), international treaties are considered to be a part of all states' domestic law. Several states combine elements of monistic and dualistic systems in the implementation of treaty obligations.[114]

Earlier, I discuss how periodic state-reporting requirements (chapter 3) constitute the UN's implementation mechanism for the ICCPR.[115] These mechanisms provide a good illustration of Canada's ability to meet its treaty obligations. For example, in their early reports to the HRC, Canadian representatives attempted to excuse the states' slow implementation of treaty obligations by arguing that covenant requirements were not automatically incorporated into domestic legislation, since the Federal Executive Government, which executed the treaties, simply did not have the required law-making powers. "It was up to the Parliament", argued

---

113 *Lovelace, supra*, note 122, at 95.

114 Orlin, Theodore S., Rosas, Allan, and Scheinin, Martin, eds. *The Jurisprudence of Human Rights Law: A Comparative Interpretive Approach* (Turku/Abo, Institute for Human Rights, Abo Akademi University, 2000), 12–13.

Shaw, M.N., *International Law*, Third Edition (Cambridge: University of Cambridge, 1994), 102.

Henkin, Louis. *Constitutionalism, Democracy and Foreign Affairs* (New York, Columbia University Press, 1990).

Drzewicki, K. et al. eds. *Social Rights as Human Rights: A European Challenge*, Scheinin, Martin, "Direct Applicability of Economic, Social, and Cultural Rights: A Critique of the Doctrine of Self-Executing Treaties" (Turku/Abo, Institute for Human Rights, Abo Akademi, 1994), 73–87.

115 *ICCPR*, 999 UNTS 171, *See* Article 40 (1) through 40(5).

Canadian government officials, to pass any necessary legislation as far as federal law was concerned and, where provincial jurisdiction was involved, the provincial legislatures had to act; failing which, Canada was not in a position to apply treaty provisions that involved the need to change existing laws.[116] In later reports to the HRC, Canadian government representatives changed their rationale and attributed Canada's slow implementation of HRC reporting requirements, in part, to the difficulty of integrating treaty reporting obligations into its domestic relationship between the Federal government and provinces in the Canadian Federal system.[117]

Canada uses vertical and horizontal mechanisms within the Canadian government itself to implement its Covenant obligations under the ICCPR. The vertical mechanisms are within a ministry or department, whether at federal or provincial level, and the horizontal mechanisms exist between ministries or departments between the federal and the provincial governments. Each minister is responsible for administrating his or her mandated area, subject to general administrative policy guidelines established by the government. Coordination for implementation of the Covenant is also exercised through the Commissions on Human Rights as well as the Federal Interdepartmental Human Rights Committee and Federal-Provincial Committee of Officials responsible for Human Rights.[118]

Canada's implementation of international obligations is similar to that of other UN member-states, not always dictated by horizontal, top-down rulings from an international treaty body such as the HRC. Rather, international obligations are already incorporated into many domestic constitutional civil and political protections, so they are frequently the subject of vertical decision by state-domestic courts that interpret the state's international treaty responsibility. For example, Canada's Fourth periodic report to the HRC notes that the Supreme Court of Canada was persuaded by or relied upon ICCPR Article 27 protecting minority rights in numerous domestic court cases such as those ruling on freedom of religion (*R v Gruenke*), freedom of expression (*R v Keegstra*), (*R v Zundel*), the right to an interpreter (*R v Tran*), and minority language educational rights *(In Reference re Public Schools Act [Man])*.[119] The legitimacy of these domestic

---

[116] CCPR A/40/40 (1985). para. 220.

[117] Canada uses a circular argument or excuse since all governments, irrespective of their Federal character, are responsible for a high degree of bureaucratic coordination.

[118] CCPR A/35/40 (1980) para. 178, also CCPR A/40/40 (1985) para. 217.

[119] *R. v Keegstra* [1995] 2 S.C.R. 381, *R. v Zundel* 381 [1992] 2 S.C.R. 731; *R. v Tran* [1994] 2 S.C.R. 951, *In Reference re Public Schools Act (Man)*, s. 79(3), (4) and (7) [1993] 1 S.C.R. 839.

Canada's Addendum to the Fourth periodic reports of States parties due in 1995 CCPR/C/103/Add.5 (15 October 1997) para. 284.

Jurists sometimes refer to the domestic implementation of international obligations as *self-executing* treaties.

judicial decisions is recognised as a source of international law in the *Statute of the International Court of Justice,* Article 38(d).[120] Further examples are found in the common practice for courts in many countries via the doctrine of *comity* to consider the decisions of cases emanating from judicial systems other than their own. Finally, some domestic systems rely on quasi-judicial bodies such as Ombudsman offices, administrative human rights commissions, government-organised non-governmental organisations (CONGOs) and legislative human rights committees adding additional layers of vertical protection that expand international human rights norms.[121] For example, Canada obligated itself to expand its Office of Ombudsman to review and report on Canadian compliance with international human rights in its 1999 report to the HRC.[122]

4.8. *Canadian Implementation of the Lovelace Decision*

> It is necessary to begin by recalling that for a century, as a result of the enactment of the *Indian Act,* which purely and simply legalized discrimination, an Aboriginal women who married a non-Aboriginal man was driven out of her community, cut off from her family and deprived of her status and...the rights pertaining thereto.[123]
>
> -Philo Desterres, Quebec Native Women's Association
> Montreal, Quebec 21 May 1993

In this section, I review two issues. Firstly, how an international quasi-judicial body reconciles a state's domestic obligations with its international treaty obligations and secondly, how Canada implemented the HRC decision in the Sandra Lovelace[124] communication.[125] In *Lovelace,* the HRC decided that Canada had obligations to the domestic Indian Act[126] as well as to the ICCPR.[127] The HRC found that, since the ICCPR did not come into force for Canada until 19 August 1976, there

---

120 *Statute of the International Court of Justice,* Article 38 (d) states: "subject to the provisions of Article 59, judicial decisions and the teachings of the most highly qualified publicists of the various nations, as subsidiary means for the determination of rules of law."

121 Orlin, Theodore S., Rosas, Allan, and Scheinin, Martin, eds. *The Jurisprudence of Human Rights Law: A Comparative Interpretive Approach* (Turku/Abo, Institute for Human Rights, Abo Akademi University, 2000), 14–15.

122 "*Fourth Periodic Report of Canada*" CCPR/C/SR.1738 (7 March 1999) para. 74.

123 *Royal Commission, supra,* note 2, at 101, vol.4 (2.3).

124 Ms. Sandra M. Lovelace Nicholas represents the province of New Brunswick in the Senate of Canada as a member of the Liberal Party. She received the Order of Canada, 1990 and the Governor General's Award in Commemoration of the Persons Case in 1992.

125 *Lovelace, supra,* note 122, at 95.

126 *Indian Act.* R.S., c.1–6, s.1.

127 *ICCPR,* 999 UNTS 171.

was a jurisdictional issue as to whether ICCPR protections applied to Lovelace whose marriage to a non-Indian man - causing the loss of her Indian status – had taken place on 23 May 1970, nearly six years prior to the establishment of Canada's ICCPR treaty obligations. The Committee, however, decided that the lingering effects (loss of Indian status) on Lovelace required a determination as to the *Indian Act*'s compliance with articles of the ICCPR, irrespective of the marital date. Once HRC jurisdiction had been established, the Committee reconciled Canada's dual obligations explaining that protection under the domestic Indian Act and protection under Article 27 of the ICCPR must be distinguished. Examining Canadian domestic conduct and its international obligations, the HRC narrowly interpreted *Indian Act* compliance with the ICCPR, limiting the scope of its review to merely one section, 12(1)(b). Next, the HRC established a legal test for the domestic statute affecting the minority right to residence on a reserve, explaining the restriction must have a reasonable and objective justification as well as be consistent with the other provisions of the Covenant. The HRC went on to find the right of Lovelace to access to her native culture and language in community with other members of her group had been interfered with by the Indian Act's section 12(1)(b) restriction.[128]

In establishing a minimal test of reasonableness, the HRC used a lower level of review in assessing Canadian domestic law finding that the Indian Act deals primarily with a number of privileges not falling within the scope of the ICCPR.[129] In effect, the HRC gave wide latitude, or a presumption of validity, to Canadian domestic law. As discussed in section 3.6, the HRC's jurisdictional limitations require individual communications, as opposed to, for example, a group action

---

128 *Lovelace, supra*, note 122, at 95. *See* paras. 10,13.1,14–16.

129 For example, the US Supreme Court uses a similar *rational basis* test e.g. rationally related to a proper (constitutionally permissible) state interest as a form of low-level judicial review in equal protection cases that do not involve a suspect class (minority group) or fundamental liberty right. In these cases, the Court applies only minimal scrutiny to the governmental action. The government classification is *presumed valid* unless the person challenging it demonstrates it is invidious, wholly arbitrary or capricious. *Lindsley v. Natural Carbonic Gas Co.*, 220 U.S. 61 (1911), *McGowan v. Maryland*, 366 U.S. 420 (1961), *United States Railroad Retirement Board v. Fritz*, 449 U.S. 166 (1980), *New York City Transit Authority v. Beazer*, 440 U.S. 568 (1979), *Northlinger v. Hahn*, 112 S.Ct. 2326 (1992), *Johnson v. Robinson*, 415 U.S. 361 (1974).

By contrast, US cases involving racial or ethnic classifications affecting, for example, African-Americans, require a higher level of judicial scrutiny, e.g. *strict scrutiny* and are prohibited as a form of discrimination unless the government can justify the classification by demonstrating a compelling state interest. *McLaughlin v Florida*, 379 U.S. 184 (1964) [invalid prohibition of interracial cohabitation], *Loving v Virginia*, 388 U.S. 1 (1967), *Anderson v Martin*, 375 U.S. 399 (1964) [invalid racial designation disclosure requirement for political candidates].

Adarand Constructors v Pena 515 U.S. 200 (1995). The more recent US Supreme Court cases demand application of the higher level strict scrutiny test for all racial classifications, even classifications used to remedy racial and ethnic discrimination.

claiming the right to self-determination, under ICCPR Article 1. State rules governing eligibility for membership in a minority group may become an aspect of a communication for group self-determination, and thus, beyond the scope of review for an individual communication. Furthermore, the HRC found that most of the Lovelace claims relating to the Indian Act did not adversely affect the enjoyment of rights protected by the ICCPR. The HRC clarified that ICCPR Article 27 does not grant the right as such to live on a reserve and that domestic restrictions on the right to residence are not ruled out by ICCPR Article 27. Several paragraphs of the decision emphasised the need to maintain the general integrity of the Indian Act, acknowledging "the merits of the Indian Act in other respects", and thus limiting its recommendation to section 12(1)(b) of the Indian Act.[130] The HRC's recommendation in *Lovelace*, while establishing an important international precedent for the right of minorities to access their culture and language in community with other members of their group, refused to grapple with the larger historical precedent set by Canada in passing the *Indian Act.* Initially passed by Canadian authorities following the adoption of *The Constitution Act of 1867*[131] (formally *The British North American Act of 1867*), passage of *The Indian Act of 1876* brought Aboriginal peoples under the exclusive authority of the Parliament of Canada. *The Indian Act* regulated all aspects of Canadian-Aboriginal relations, from strict definitions of what constitutes an Indian, to the terms for Aboriginal existence in Canada.

The legal relationship established by the Indian Act is analogous to a form of [internal] colonialism practiced by the state over opposition to a group of otherwise self-governing peoples. Canadian policy of colonial subjugation was thought, at the time, to be morally superior to the American Indian policy of Aboriginal extermination carried out by conducting expensive Indian wars and accomplishing the destruction of the bison.[132] The HRC's decision in *Lovelace* did not review the question of whether placing Aboriginal peoples under the supervisory control of the Federal government was consistent with the UN's human and minority regime; specifically, the Indian Act's compliance with self-determination requirements in Article 1 of the ICCPR, Article 1(2) of the *UN Charter*, and general assembly resolutions prohibiting colonial and colonial-type practices (e.g. apartheid, segregation,

---

[130] *Lovelace, supra*, note 122, at 95. *See* paras. 14, 13.1, 15, 17.

[131] *The British North American Act, 1867*, 30 & 31 Victoria, c.3.; *See* also *UN Core Document, Report of States Parties: Canada* 12/01/98 UN Doc. HR1/CORE/1/Add.91 The Constitution Act 1867 did not make Canada an independent country. Canada achieved international sovereignty through a process of devolution of powers by the United Kingdom, which lasted nearly 60 years; the completion of this process was marked in 1931 by the Statute of Westminster, which formally established the federal government's jurisdiction over foreign affairs.

[132] Miller, J.R. *Skyscrapers*, 163.

forced assimilation). Though the HRC has made a finding on behalf of Aboriginal self-determination in response to later Canadian reports,[133] implementation of the *Lovelace* decision resulted in awkward delays as well as procedural difficulties with implementation despite Canadian efforts to bring the *Indian Act* into compliance with HRC recommendations. As we discover in the sections that follow, the Indian Act authorises the federal government to exercise a guardian-like control over the Aboriginal peoples of Canada. Any revisions to the Indian Act, even the positive changes made by Canada protecting the status of Indian women who inter-marry with non-Indians, fail to address the central question of whether Aboriginals will be permitted to self-determine the issue of Aboriginal membership. Instead, Canada decided to continue its centuries-old trusteeship over Aboriginals by retaining federal administration and control over pre-established terms for Aboriginal membership. Under Canada's Indian Act amendments, the Federal government would continue to maintain control over who was entitled to membership as a registered Indian, as well as the terms and conditions for such recognition.

The HRC decided the *Lovelace* case on 31 July 1981. In response to the HRC recommendation, the Canadian Parliament passed Bill C-31 on 17 June 1985, amending the Indian Act so as to provide limited protection for the status of Indian women[134] who married non-Indian men.[135] However, the Canadian amendment illustrates the difficulty of making a piecemeal revision of the Indian Act system established to govern Canadian-Aboriginal relations. As a result, the HRC continued to make findings of violations of the ICCPR Article 27 against Canada for failure to implement revisions to the Indian Act that protect the status not only of Indian women and children, but also that of subsequent

[133] *Concluding Observations of the Human Rights Committee: Canada. 07/04/99* CCPR/C/79/Add.105 7 April 1999. *See* para. 8. In this report, the HRC confirms Canadian responsibility to provide the right of self-determination to Aboriginal-Canadians under Article 1 of the ICCPR.

Compilation of General Comments and General Recommendations Adopted by Human Rights Treaty Bodies UN Doc. HR1/GEN/1/Rev. 7, 12 May 2004, para. 3.1 As discussed in Chapter 3, self-determination is not a right cognisable under the ICCPR Optional Protocol. Article 27 does not permit individual claims for self determination rights brought pursuant to ICCPR, Article 1. Aboriginal self-determination rights are also reviewed in Section 4 of this chapter.

[134] Cardinal 77–78. Cardinal explains that the Cree-Aboriginal term for woman or lady, *Squiew*, is used by non-Aboriginals in a derogatory manner. The English word *Squaw* is used by non-Aboriginals to equate the status of all Indian woman, whether wife, daughter, mother, or sweetheart, with the connotation of a *whore*.

[135] Furi, Megan and Wherrett, Jill. *Indian Status and Band Membership Issues* (Ottawa, Parliamentary Information and Research Service, February 2003), 4. The Bill was given royal assent on 28 June 1985 and then backdated to 17 April 1985 so that the *Indian Act* would conform to the equality provisions of the *Canadian Charter of Rights and Freedoms*.

generations left unprotected by the new amendments. Under Bill C-31, the progeny of inter-marriages between Indian women and non-Indian men were left unprotected, forcing future generations of Aboriginals to lose their Indian status, restricting them from practicing their cultural heritage in community with other members of their group. Findings of violations against Canada in the *Lovelace* decision were made by the HRC in follow-up activity reports under the Optional Protocol through to Canada's current fifth reporting cycle in 2004, twenty-three years after the UN's rendering of the *Lovelace* decision![136]

4.9. *Bill C-31 and the Indian Act*

Bill C-31 amendments to the Indian Act passed by the Canadian parliament in 1985 were a response, in part, to mounting political and legal pressures surrounding the Indian Act. However, even the new legislation's promotion of gender equality did not alter the essential objective of the colonial-era legislation. In this section, I demonstrate how the central purpose of the Indian Act, namely, the use of restrictive qualifications intended to destroy Aboriginals as a group, continues up to the current day.

By the 1960's and 1970's, Aboriginal women's groups had been organised in opposition to Section 12(1)(b) and other provisions of the Act that discriminated against women and their children. Influenced by the civil rights movements of 1951-1985, a prominent feature of the socio-political landscape in North America, in 1970 the Canadian Royal Commission on the Status of Women identified as a primary area of concern the particular discrimination suffered by Aboriginal women under the terms of the Indian Act's *marrying out* provisions. The Commission recommended that Indian women be permitted, upon marriage to a non-Indian man, to retain their Indian status and pass it onto their children.[137]

---

[136] Examples of HRC *findings of violation* against Canada are found at CCPR A/40/40 (1985). para. 188; CCPR A/46/40 (1991) para. 55, 93; CCPR A/51/40, vol. 1 (1996) para. 429; CCPR A/52/40 (1997) para. 524; CCPR A/53/40, vol. 1 (1998) para. 486; CCPR A/54/40, vol.1 (1999) para. 241, 461; CCPR/A/56/40, vol. 1(2001) para. 180; CCPR A/57/40, vol. 1 (2002) para. 228; CCPR A/58/40, vol. 1 (2003) para. 223; CCPR A/59/40 vol. 1 (2004) para. 230;

Concluding Observations of the Human Rights Committee: Canada. 07/04/99 CCPR/C/79/Add.105 7 April 1999, para. 19.

Pursuant to the ICCPR, the HRC established six reporting due dates for Canada as follows: Initial report due 18 August 1977, Second periodic due 8 April 1988, Third periodic due 4 April 1990, Fourth periodic due 8 April 1995, Fifth periodic due 30 April 2004, Sixth periodic due 30 April 2009. Canada failed to timely meet all of its reporting deadlines and turned in its Fourth periodic report on 4 April 1997, two years after the deadline.

[137] *Royal Commission, supra*, note 2, at 101, vol. 4 (3.1), 8–9.

However, there was political division within the Aboriginal community over whether to support such piecemeal revision of the Indian Act, or to press instead for comprehensive constitutional reform. By 1984, the controversy over 12(1)(b) had become the single most contentious issue in Canadian Indian policy.[138]

In the early 1970's, legal actions were initiated by Aboriginal women to abolish the so-called *marrying out* rule of Section 12(1)(b), whereby an Aboriginal-Canadian woman loses her legal status as an Indian upon her marriage to a non-Indian man. These legal initiatives were consolidated in a 1974 appeal heard by the Canadian Supreme Court in *Attorney-General of Canada v Lavell; Isaac v Bedard* (1973).[139] The actions were brought by Jeanette Corbiere Lavell, a member of the Wikwemikong band whose name was removed from the Indian register upon her marriage to a non-Indian, and Yvonne Bedard, a Six Nations Indian woman, who sought an injunction preventing her eviction from her home on the Six Nations Reserve following her divorce from a non-Indian man.[140] The Supreme Court upheld the *marrying out* provision in the Indian Act and struck down the actions brought by the Aboriginal women. The court held that authority for the Indian Act under s.91(24) of the *British North America Act, 1867*, to legislate in relation to "Indians, and Lands reserved for Indians",[141] pre-empted any civil rights claims for equality of treatment brought by the Aboriginals pursuant to the *Canadian Bill of Rights*.[142]

In following such a narrow or thin view of equality, the Canadian Supreme Court's ruling in *Lavell* illustrates how the liberal equality principle (equal treatment before the law) was interpreted to permit invidious discrimination against Aboriginal-Canadian women and children. Thus, it was not until the later HRC decision in *Lovelace* which struck down the marrying out provision as a breach of ICCPR Article 27, that the Canadian government finally moved to amend the sexually discriminatory provisions of the Indian Act. After the passage of the C-31 amendments, Canadian officials reported a dramatic increase of up to 133,134 in the registered Indian population.[143] Countering

---

138 Silman, J. ed., *Enough is Enough: Aboriginal Women Speak Out* (Toronto, The Women's Press, 1987).

139 *Attorney-General of Canada v Lavell; Issac v Bedard* (1973), 38 D.L.R. (3rd) 481 also reported: 23 C.R.N.S. 197, 11 R.F.L. 333, [1974] S.C.R. 1349.

140 *See Bedard v Isaac* (1971), 25 D.L.R. (3rd) 551 (also reported: [1972] 2 O.R. 391) Ontario High Court, Osler, J 15 December 1971.

141 *Attorney-General of Canada v Lavell; Issac v Bedard* (1973), 38 D.L.R. (3rd) 481 also reported: 23 C.R.N.S. 197, 11 R.F.L. 333, [1974] S.C.R. 1349.

142 *Canadian Bill of Rights* (1960, c.44).

143 *Second periodic reports of States parties due in 1988, Addendum, Canada* CCPR/C/51 Add.1, 3 November 1989. para. 146. Canada reports 33,000 newly registered Indians resulting from the amendment; HRC *Comments* CCPR A/46/40 (1991) para.55 reports 76,000 newly registered Indians;

the nationalist tendency of Canada to forcibly assimilate Aboriginal women and their children by narrowing the inter-generational restrictions on Aboriginal membership, the HRC succeeded in persuading Canada to revise the terms for what constitutes an Aboriginal-Canadian. As a result of these changes, substantial increases in the number of Aboriginal-Canadians earned recognition as status Indians due to the decision and follow-up actions taken by the HRC in *Lovelace*.

The immediate benefit of formal registration as a recognised Indian for Aboriginals is an economic one. For those living on a reserve, the federal government provides funds for housing, elementary and secondary education, health services and social assistance. Under earlier amendments to the Indian Act passed in 1951, status or registered Indians were also generally band members[144] with rights to live on a reserve, share in band moneys, and own and inherit property on the reserve. Status Indians are eligible to apply for Federal non-insured health benefits and post-secondary educational assistance. Political rights are also provided for registered Indians, in the form of being able to vote for band council and chief as well as participate in band elections including becoming a candidate for chief of the band.[145] However, in *Lovelace*, the HRC did not test the political or economic aspects of how Lovelace's rights under ICCPR[146] were breached by the *Indian Act*, nor how it affected her right to gender equality. Rather, the HRC concerned itself exclusively with the issue of how the Indian Act interfered with the communication author's ICCPR Article 27 *right to enjoy her culture...in community with other members of her group.*[147] Recall that Article 27 is not intended to address subjects of gender discrimination or family life covered under other articles of the ICCPR. Its purpose is to entrench the cultural protection of minority groups as a part of international human rights law.

Furi, Megan and Wherrett, Jill. *Indian Status and Band Membership Issues* (Ottawa, Parlimentary Information and Research Service, February 2003), 5. Megan reports 114,512 Aboriginal people gaining status as a result of C-31 amendments with some authorities claiming 120,000 new Indian registrants;

Royal Commission, supra, note 2, at 101, vol.4. 3(2). The Royal Commission reports 133,134 new Indian registrants.

144 The Canadian government's term 'band' [tribe in the United States] is also referred to as tribe, nation and clan by Aboriginal peoples.

145 Furi, Megan and Wherrett, Jill. *Indian Status and Band Membership Issues* (Ottawa, Parliamentary Information and Research Service, February 2003), 3, 8–9.

See Goodswimmer v Canada [1997] 1 S.C.R. 309, [1995] 2 F.C. 389, upholding the right of a non-status Indian to be a candidate for Chief of the Strugen Lake Indian Band.

146 *ICCPR,* 999 UNTS 171.

147 *Lovelace, supra*, note 122, at 95. *See* para. 13.2.

The primary injury suffered by Lovelace, according to the HRC decision, was the loss to a person of her ceasing to be Indian. Once Lovelace was denied her Indian-status under the law, she was deprived of the "cultural benefits of living in an Indian community, the emotional ties to home, family, friends and neighbours, and [suffered] the loss of identity."[148] The loss of cultural benefits suffered by Lovelace meant that she was barred from engaging in traditional Aboriginal ways of life in community with other members of the Tobique band, including the benefits of possessing or residing on lands on a reserve,[149] engaging in traditional hunting and fishing, cutting timber free of dues on an Indian reserve, as well as from other Aboriginal religious and linguistic practices, dances, tribal customs and traditions that have existed since time immemorial. Under the ICCPR, the enjoyment of culture has special meaning for indigenous groups such as the Aboriginals. General Comment No. 23 to the ICCPR's Article 27 explains that in the case of indigenous groups, culture manifests itself in many forms, including:[150]

> a particular way of life associated with the use of land resources....That right may include such traditional activities as fishing, hunting and the right to live in reserves protected by law. The enjoyment of those rights may require positive legal measures to ensure the effective participation of members of minority communities in decisions which affect them.

Like those of indigenous peoples, Aboriginal-Canadian cultural practices manifest themselves in a unique fashion. The Aboriginal peoples' attachment to land, natural resources, and communal practice include a spiritual-religious aspect. Their belief systems incorporate the notion of the world as a continuum where all people, animals, and fish, as well as physical aspects of nature including flora and minerals are animate. Deity resides in all aspects of the continuum and each element contains souls or spirits that require respectful treatment at all times. Humans hold no special place in the continuum on earth or in the cosmos. This contrasts with the Christian view that g-d created man in the deity's image and that the non-human world is available for human use and g-d's glorification. Further, as a result of evolving capitalism, the ethic of sharing was not as important to European immigrants as it was to North American societies.[151] The

---

148 *Ibid.*, para. 13.1.

149 *Indian Act.* R.S., c.1–6, s.1, section 20–29.

150 *Compilation of General Comments and General Recommendations Adopted by Human Rights Treaty Bodies*, UN Doc HR1/GEN/1/Rev.7, P. 160, para. 7.

151 Miller, J.R. *Skyscrapers*, 12–18.

Article 27 right to enjoy culture is not static, that is, it does not exist to promote the mummification of Aboriginal cultural practices. Rather, it is a dynamic right. As explained in cases brought by indigenous peoples in other states, indigenous cultural benefits are not determined in the abstract but have to be placed in context with competing values such as economic development (*Lansman et al.v Finland*). Further, they not only protect traditional means of livelihood for minorities, but also allow for adoption of those means to the modern way of life and ensuing technology (*Mahuika et al. v New Zealand*).[152] John Burrows captures this aspect of Aboriginal cultural rights by explaining that indigenous traditions "are not static; their strength lies in their ability to survive through the power of tribal memory…not in how closely they adhere to their original form, but in how well they are able to develop and remain relevant under changing circumstances."[153]

As I explained at the beginning of this section, and as noted by the *Royal Commission*, the public condemnation voiced in the HRC *Lovelace* decision was a tremendous embarrassment to Canada which had long prided itself as a human rights' champion.[154] However, C-31 Amendments to the status and membership provisions of the Indian Act sidestepped the question of cultural rights by focusing on the precise issue of gender discrimination that the HRC in *Lovelace* considered unnecessary to be examined under the ICCPR.[155] The HRC focused exclusively upon how the Indian Act restricted Lovelace's ability to enjoy [access] her culture by being deprived Indian status as well as residence on the Tobique Reserve. Refusing to follow the HRC recommendation, C-31 Amendments introduced only a limited revision against gender discrimination in the Indian Act, and failed to safeguard the cultural rights of future Aboriginal generations protected by ICCPR Article 27. Canada's emphasis on gender discrimination, in contrast to ICCPR Article 27 cultural rights, resulted in future generations of Aboriginal children still being denied status under the 1985 *Indian Act* revisions. Instead of amending the Indian Act to provide Aboriginal self-governance on the

---

152 *Lansman et al. v Finland*, Communication No. 511/1992, 26 October 1994, CCPR/C/52/D/511/1992, paras. 9.3–9.5; *Mahuika et al. v New Zealand*, Communication No. 547/1993, 27 October 2000, CCPR/C/70/D/547/1993, para. 9.4.

Macklem, Patrick. *Indigenous Difference and the Constitution of Canada* (Toronto, University of Toronto Press, 2001), 53–57. Summarises Aboriginal cultural rights.

153 Burrows, John. *Recovering Canada: The Resurgence of Indigenous Law* (Toronto, University of Toronto, 2002), 76.

154 *Royal Commission, supra*, note 2, at 101, vol. 1 (7.2) 10.

155 *Lovelace, supra*, note 122, at 95. *See* paras. 13.2 & 18.

questions of Indian status and membership, Canada opted to limit Indian Act changes to a smaller, narrow class of Aboriginal women deprived of status in the event of their marriage to a non-Indian man. Refusing to protect the Aboriginal people's enjoyment of culture, Canada used a convenient method to narrow and restrict future generations from Aboriginal membership in the name of fighting gender discrimination.

At least six major revisions of the *Indian Act* have been passed by the Canadian Parliament since 1869. In its latest 1985 revision, the Canadian Parliament decided to maintain control of the terms by which an Aboriginal might qualify as a recognised status Indian by establishing two legal categories of qualification, Indian Act's Section 6 (1) (a-f) and Section 6(2). Neither legal qualification has any relationship to actual Aboriginal ancestry. Section 6 (1) (a-f) is a catch-all [comprehensive] provision that seeks to qualify those Indians for status that were excluded under previous discriminatory provisions of the Act. These include not only Section 12(1) (b) but also Section 12(1)(a)(iv), the so-called *double mother rule*, which eliminated the Indian status of children born to a non-Indian mother and non-Indian grandmother who obtained status through marriage to an Aboriginal, status Indian father.[156] For Aboriginals who fail to qualify as status Indians under Section 6(1), Section 6(2) provides a further opportunity for registration if an Aboriginal-Canadian can demonstrate that at least one parent, either alive or at time of death, was also entitled to be registered under Section 6(1). Thus, if an individual has one parent covered by Section 6(2) but cannot demonstrate the parent's eligibility under Section 6(1), and a second parent who is non-Indian, the individual is not entitled to status.

Aside from the apparent complexity of the amendments, the revisions illustrate the difficulty states encounter when they attempt to reverse historic legal traditions that discriminate against indigenous groups. The Canadian revisions are not only difficult to apply, but also make it unduly burdensome for Aboriginals who may not have documentary proof or adequate records, especially in areas where Aboriginal oral traditions are used as a part of administrative or judicial procedure. Furthermore, status Indian children adopted by non-Indian parents may have a difficult time later accessing necessary records covered under Canada's *Privacy Act*[157] or difficulty obtaining provincial records.

---

[156] *Royal Commission, supra*, note 2, at 101, vol. 4 (3.1). The rationale behind the double mother rule was to further restrict Aboriginal membership based on tests of mixed culture and blood quantum.

[157] *Privacy Act* (R.S. 1985, c). 21.

The new amendments also create an artificial legal distinction between Section 6(1) and Section 6(2) status Indians. The effects of the distinction are felt most acutely in the third generation, as the particular section under which parents and grandparents achieved status will determine whether later generations of Aboriginal-Canadians will also have status. So, a status Indian brother and sister, depending upon the Indian Act qualification of their spouses, and, subsequently, their children's spouses, may produce grandchildren of whom only some qualify for status.[158] The original legislative intent of the Indian Act to eradicate the membership of Aboriginal peoples through a policy of forcible assimilation that, along with other Acts, constrict Aboriginal membership, continues with the C-31 revisions. As noted by in the *Royal Commission*, demographic trends show that, as a result of the C-31 Amendments, within a few generations, the number of status Indians is likely to decline drastically, despite the initial increase in the number of Indians with status that I described earlier in this section.[159] After passage of the C-31 Amendments, the central purpose of Canada's Aboriginal policy to destroy the Indian through marital restrictions, voluntary enfranchisement, and loss of status remained unchanged.[160] To illustrate the process, I provide a graph on page 144 of how C-31 Amendments deny status to the children and grandchildren of status Indians.

4.10. *De-Colonisation and Aboriginal Legal Status*

At its 947th Plenary meeting on 14 December 1960, the United Nations General Assembly passed *Resolution No. 1514 (XV)*. The resolution was entitled *Declaration on the granting of independence to colonial countries and peoples*, and marked a major turning point in world affairs. In passing the resolution, the United Nations General Assembly ended centuries of colonial subjugation by European powers through granting the right of self-determination to the peoples of Asia, Africa, and the Americas. The Declaration committed the United Nations to end colonialism in all its manifestations and re-affirmed the UN Charter's Article I principle

---

158 *Royal Commission*, *supra*, note 2, at 101, vol.4 (3.3).

159 Ibid., vol. 4 (3.1); vol. 1 (9.14).

160 Miller, J.R. *Canada and the Aboriginal Peoples, 1867–1927* (Ottawa, The Canada Historical Association, 1997), 11.

Effects of Indian Act revision (Bill C-31) on Indian status of Aboriginal Children[161]

Example 1

Section 6(1) Indian marries Section 6(1) Indian

Child is Section 6(1) Indian

Example 3

Section 6(1) Indian marries Section 6(2) Indian

Child is Section 6(1) Indian

Example 2

Section 6(1) Indian marries non-Indian

Child is Section 6(2) Indian.

Section 6(2) Indian Child later marries a non-Indian

Grandchild is **non-Indian**

Example 4

Section 6(2) Indian marries Section 6(2) Indian

Child is Section 6(1) Indian

Example 5

Section 6(2) Indian marries non-Indian

Child is **non-Indian**

[161] *Royal Commission*, *supra*, note 2, at 101, vol. 1 (3.3);
Indian Act R.S. 1985, c. 1–5, Section 6(1) a-f, Section 6(2).

that all peoples have the right to self-determination.[162] Using the term *dependent peoples* to refer to colonised nations, the Declaration incorporates a role for the UN Charter's International Trusteeship System, initially resisted by European colonial powers, to assist dependent peoples living in Non-Self-Governing Territories with their transition to self-determination within independent, self-governing states.[163] The Declaration refers to colonised territories as *dependent territories* that have not yet attained independence. Article 77 of the UN Charter creates a list of territories subject to the UN's International Trusteeship System.

Aboriginal-Canadian lands, as in the cases involving the territories of indigenous peoples living in other states, were not included as a dependent, Non-Self-Governing territory under the UN Declaration granting independence to European administered colonies. European colonial powers such as Belgium and France unsuccessfully attempted to have the General Assembly include enclave indigenous peoples living within the frontiers of many states into the scope of obligations and procedures created for Non-Self-Governing Territories by the UN Charter.[164] S. James Anaya writes that colonial powers invoked the *blue water* or *salt water thesis* to argue that "primitive communities living within the frontiers of many states were in relevant respects indistinguishable from peoples living in colonial territories".[165] Used by colonial powers for self-serving ends to limit the scope of de-colonisation and assist European powers to maintain control of at least some colonial territory, the argument failed and was not supported by the General Assembly. Instead, the *blue water doctrine* was incorporated into the territorial definition for the description of territories required to fulfil de-colonisation reporting obligations for Non-Self-Governing Territories.[166] Under *Principles I and IV* in *General Assembly Resolution 1541*[167], reporting obligation was limited to "territories which were then known to be of a colonial type" and which were "geographically separate and…distinct ethnically and/or culturally from the country administering [them]." Territories held by indigenous groups within state borders were not incorporated into a state's

[162] *G.A. Res. 1514 (XV),* 14 December 1960, UN Doc. A/4684 (1961). Note Declaration No. 3: Inadequacy of political, economic, social or educational preparedness should never serve as a pretext for delaying independence. One commentator (Tom Flanigan, *supra*). who opposes Aboriginal self-government stresses the Aboriginals' lack of capacity [inadequacy] for self-determination.

[163] *United Nations Charter*, 26 June 1945, *See* Chapter XI, XII.

[164] *Ibid.* Chapter XI, Article 73.

[165] Anaya, S. James. *Indigenous Peoples In International Law*, 75–76. Anaya cites: Ofuatey-Kodjoe, W. *The Principle of Self-Determination in International Law* (1977), 115–128, and Bennett, Gordon, *Aboriginal Rights in International Law* (1978), 12–13.

[166] *General Assembly Resolution 1541 (XV), Principles which should guide members in determining whether or not an obligation exists to transmit this information called for under Article 73e of the Charter*, 15 December 1960, UN Doc. A/4684.

[167] *Ibid.*

de-colonisation reporting obligations.[168] Beside the European-held colonies, only the occupied territories and those territories determined to be Non-Self-Governing Territories by a relevant organ of the United Nations are entitled to claim the right of self-determination.[169]

The restrictive interpretations placed on the geographic description for a Non-Self-Governing Territory left indigenous peoples, including the Aboriginal peoples of Canada, removed from the UN system ending colonisation. In contrast to European administered colonies now free to establish independent states, indigenous peoples were forced to remain under colonial administration within states that contained Aboriginal territory. Aboriginal peoples would continue to live with social, economic, political, and cultural conditions of domestic as opposed to more traditional types of foreign, colonial subjugation.

The colonial status of Aboriginals in North America is also reported in the jurisprudence of domestic North American courts. In *Cherokee Nations v the State of Georgia, 1831,*[170] the US Supreme Court was asked to define whether the Cherokee peoples constituted a foreign state under the US Constitution. In that case, Cherokee-Aboriginals sought injunctive relief against intrusions into their domestic affairs from the state of Georgia. In his opinion, US Chief Justice John Marshall refused to grant Cherokee nations the same status as foreign nations. Rather, Justice Marshall described the status of Cherokee nations as domestic dependent nations resembling that of "a ward to his guardian."[171] The decision is noteworthy for identifying Aboriginal-American status in the same manner used by the UN General Assembly to describe the status of former European colonies as dependent territories. In *Worcester v Georgia*[172], clarifying their dependent status, Chief Justice Marshall described Aboriginals as constituting otherwise sovereign and independent peoples. The *Worcester* case was an appeal by a Georgia resident indicted for residing in Cherokee nation territory without a state license. Reversing the indictment and declaring void the application of Georgia state law over Cherokee national territory, Justice Marshall writes:[173]

---

168 *UN Charter*, Chapter XII, Article 77(c). Note, however, that there is no prohibition against a state's voluntarily placing a territory under the UN International Trusteeship System.

169 Eide, Asbjorn and Daes, Erica. *Working paper on the relationship and distinction between the rights of persons belonging to minorities and those of indigenous peoples*, 19 July 2000. UN Doc. E/CN.4/Sub.2/2000/10 para. 21.

170 *The Cherokee Nation v. The State of Georgia* 30 U.S. 1, 5 Pet. 1, 8 L.Ed.25 (1831).

171 *Ibid.*, 2.

172 *Worcester v. Georgia*, 31 U.S. 515, 6 Pet. 515, 8 L.Ed. 483 (1832).

173 *Worcester v. Georgia*, *Ibid.* 22.

> The Indian nations had always been considered as distinct, independent political communities, retaining their original natural rights, as the undisputed possessors of the soil, from time immemorial, with the single exception of that imposed by irresistible power, which excluded them from intercourse with any other European potentate than the first discoverer of the coast of the particular region claimed... .The very term 'nation,' so generally applied to them, means 'a people distinct from others.'

After ushering the end of European colonialism over geographically separate territory, international law has provided additional support to end the use of legal doctrines that support colonial administration of Aboriginal territory. For example, in *Western Sahara, Advisory Opinion of 16 October 1975*[174], the International Court of Justice (ICJ) voided the doctrine of *terra nullius* which had been used, as described earlier in this chapter, to justify administrative control over Aboriginal lands. In ruling on Spanish claims to that of protectorate over the territories of Rio de Oro and Sakiet El Hamra, the ICJ advised that the doctrine of terra nullius did not apply if "at the time of colonisation Western Sahara was inhabited by peoples which, if nomadic, were socially and politically organised in tribes and under chiefs competent to represent them."

Though indistinguishable from dependent peoples residing in the former colonies administered by European powers, indigenous peoples may not, as yet, rely on the UN's de-colonisation regime to end domestic colonial administration of their territory within the various states where they reside. Instead, indigenous peoples are limited to the use of international legal remedies for cultural protection that are provided for in the UN's minority regime. The passing of new international legal norms governing the treatment of indigenous peoples such as the 27 June 1989 passage of the *International Labor Organisation Convention No. 169 concerning Indigenous and Tribal Peoples in Independent Countries*[175] that I discuss in section 4.11, increases the potential for qualified indigenous groups to claim the right to self-determination. Until a new status within international law is recognised for Aboriginal peoples, a state that contains an indigenous peoples is free to govern Aboriginal lands without regard to the *UN Charter*, Article 73 (b) which requires states "to develop self-government, to take due account of the political aspirations of the peoples, and to assist them in the progressive development of their free political institutions...".[176] As I discussed in sections 4.2, 4.3, and 4.4, Canada, like other states that incorporated the territory of indigenous

---

174 *Western Sahara, Advisory Opinion of 16 October 1975, International Court of Justice.*

175 *Convention (No. 169) concerning Indigenous and Tribal Peoples in Independent Countries*, Adopted on 27 June 1989 by the General Conference of the International Labour Organisation at its seventy-sixth session, entry into force 5 September 1991.

176 *United Nations Charter*, 16 June 1945, Article 73(b).

peoples into their own, takes full advantage of this international legal vacuum to maintain colonial-like administration of Aboriginal society.

4.11. *Restoring Aboriginal Sovereignty: Transition From Dependent to Independent Peoples*

In this section, I demonstrate how the question of Aboriginal equality must be satisfied through the restoration of Aboriginal sovereignty. That is, for Aboriginal-Canadians to be treated as other Canadian citizens, the group must be de-colonised by the implementation of a regime that restores Aboriginal sovereignty. It is a mistake to view the restoration of Aboriginal sovereignty as a special or extra-ordinary right since the alternative is to continue a pre-established, legally defined, colonial relationship between Canada and the Aboriginal nations.

In this chapter, we have reviewed the historical evolution of Canada's legal regime governing the Aboriginal nations. We have also discussed the horrific consequences of Canada's regime, including its practices of coercive assimilation used against Aboriginal children as demonstrated in the coercive tutelage polices of the Residential School System. The minority regime works to restore a proper balance to the Canadian-Aboriginal relationship. As I explained in sections 2.4 and 4.10, it is not that the minority regime creates a special right for Aboriginals, but rather that it recognises the group's equality as a nation. The question may be re-stated as not that of one granting special rights to Aboriginals but, that of providing recognition for the equality of Aboriginals as a nation. Namely, should Aboriginal nations be granted equality by Canada, or, should they remain as internally colonised? Recall that a process of de-colonisation inherently requires state recognition for the territorial and political sovereignty of the dependency. There is no third option as demonstrated by the failure of the Canadian White Paper that I discussed in section 4.2.

The process discussed above is a complex one, in that both the Canadian and the Aboriginal nations have an interest in maintaining Canadian sovereignty and national unity. Aboriginal nations in Canada, similar to other indigenous groups, seek a framework for integration by the implementation of agreements providing for the autonomy of Aboriginal territories within Canada.

In a resolution passed on 3 March 1995, the United Nations Commission on Human Rights established a working group dedicated to the sole purpose of elaborating a "United Nations declaration on the rights of indigenous peoples" for adoption by the General Assembly.[177] The working group brings together

[177] Resolution 1995/32 of 3 March 1995. Chavez, Luis-Enrique. *Report of the working group establishd in accordance with Commission on Human Rights resolution 1995/32 of 3 March 1995 on its tenth session*, UN doc. E/CN.4/2005/89 28 February 2005.

sixty-eight indigenous organisations as well as sixty-four governments including Canada.[178] On 29 June 2006, the UN's recently established Human Rights Council adopted the working groups' Declaration on the Rights of Indigenous Peoples.[179] However, Canada, in a coalition with other developed nations, effectively blocked passage of the Declaration by the UN's General Assembly. The failed Declaration represented the first international instrument to recognise the right of self-determination for indigenous peoples.[180]

The UN's International Labor Organisation also passed *ILO Convention No. 169 concerning Indigenous and Tribal Peoples in Independent Countries*, adopted 27 June 1989, governing state recognition for indigenous peoples.[181] *ILO Convention No. 169* contains forty-three articles requiring that states provide a broad range of protections for indigenous and tribal peoples, and regulating forms of Aboriginal political participation, self-governance, land and resources protection, employment conditions, craft and traditional skills development, language protection, cross-border contacts, social security and health schemes.

While Canada has failed to ratify *ILO Convention No. 169* and also voted against passage of the Human Rights Council's resolution supporting the *Declaration on the Rights of Indigenous Peoples*, recall in chapter 1, I cited the longstanding principal that rules of general international law have a tendency to become universal international law.[182] *ILO Convention No. 169* and the UN's *Declaration on the Rights of Indigenous Peoples* demonstrate a movement toward state recognition that indigenous peoples, as distinguished from other classes of minority groups, qualify for the right to self-determination.

Recall my earlier discussions in chapters two and three regarding definitional ambiguity affecting several terms used by minority rights laws. For example, scholars have achieved neither accuracy nor consensus about how to define the term, nation. A similar criticism can be made about the use of other terms, as well

---

178 *Ibid.*, Resolution of the Sub-Commission on Prevention of Discrimination and Protection of Minorities, 1994/45 of 26 August 1994.

179 Human Rights Council, First Session, 19–30 June 2006. Burayzat, Musa. *Report to the General Assembly on the First Session of the Human Rights Council*, UN Doc. A/HRC/1/L.10, 30 June 2006, 56–72.

180 *Ibid.*, *Declaration on the Rights of Indigenous Peoples*, Article 3 states: "Indigenous peoples have the right of self-determination. By virtue of that right they freely determine their political status and freely pursue their economic, social, and cultural development."

181 *ILO Convention No C107 Indigenous and Tribal Populations Convention, 1957* adopted 6/26/57 (outdated instrument) revised in 1989 by *ILO Convention No. 169 concerning Indigenous and Tribal Peoples in Independent Countries*, Adopted 27 June 1989, entry into force 5 September 1991.

182 Robinson, Nehemiah. *The Genocide Convention. Its Origins and Interpretation.* (New York, Institute of Jewish Affairs, World Jewish Congress, 1949), 13.

as principles of international law. Precise definitions for terms such as 'peoples', 'minority', 'culture', as well as principles such as 'self-determination', have not as yet been established. The failure to adequately define these terms raises normative concerns that the minority regime is ambiguous, illiberal or unenforceable. Furthermore, critics argue that the potential for a proliferation of minority classifications results in unlimited claims being made against, as well as internal divisions within, the polis. This includes claims of indigenous and tribal groups for self-determination.[183] Neither the classification for indigenousness, nor the principle of self-determination, are clearly defined within international law.

Article 27 of the ICCPR[184] provides for the protection of indigenous and tribal persons under existing classifications, that is, ethnic (inclusive of race), linguistic, and religious minority groups. Many of the protections provided by *ILO Convention No.169* are also implied, and claimed by indigenous groups, under ICCPR, Article 27. Examples can be found in the growing number of cases brought by indigenous groups claiming Article 27 protection such as *Lovelace*, and their results comprise HRC jurisprudence. However, in General Comments to the ICCPR, the HRC explains that "self-determination is not a right cognisable under the Optional Protocol" to the ICCPR, limiting the application of Article 27 to those "rights conferred on individuals as such."[185] Instead, the right to self-determination of peoples is recognised in Article 1 of the ICCPR, as well as several other UN instruments including Articles 1 and 55 of the *United Nations Charter*, and Article 1 of the *International Covenant on Economic, Social and Cultural Rights*.[186] Canadian indigenous groups, like those in other states, seek legal qualification as distinct peoples with a right to self-determination. ICCPR Article 27, and more broadly, minority rights, do not provide these groups with the remedy of independence to which they aspire. Despite these limitations, minority rights are not a remedy distinct from other human rights, particularly the right to self-determination guaranteed by ICCPR Article 1. Minority group rights to various forms of political participation such as autonomy, as well as internal and external forms of self-determination, are better understood as a continuum for the protection of cultural

---

183 Alfredsson, Gudmundur. "Minorities, Indigenous and Tribal Peoples and Peoples". Ghanea, Nazila and Xanthaki, Alexandra eds. *Minorities, Peoples and Self-Determination, Essays in Honour of Patrick Thornberry* (Leiden, Martinus Nijh of Publishers, 2005), 164. Alfredsson illustrates the threat of proliferation with a rough estimate for the existence of 12–14,000 different minority, indigenous and tribal groups in the world. He estimates that about 1.5 billion individuals belong to these groups or 25% of the world's population.

184 *ICCPR*, 999 UNTS 171.

185 *Compilation of General Comments and General Recommendations Adopted by Human Rights Treaty Bodies* HRI/GEN/1/Rev.7 12 May 2004, 158, para. 3.1.

186 *International Covenant on Economic, Social and Cultural Rights* 993 UNTS 3.

rights. The type of remedy provided for by international law, e.g. autonomy (ICCPR, Article 27) or self-determination (ICCPR, Article 1) are dependent upon legal and political determinations regarding a group's qualifications.

The international community of states has qualified groups under the classification of *peoples* only in a limited number of circumstances linked to major historical events. Recall, at the end of WWI, self-determination rights were granted to a limited number of identified nations (peoples) living under the rule of Axis powers, namely, the Austria-Hungarian and Ottoman Empires, as well as the states of Germany and Italy. The second qualification of groups as *peoples* took place in 1960, when the UN passed the *Declaration on the granting of independence to colonial countries and peoples.*[187] This Declaration recognised the formal end of colonialism and granted self-determination and independent statehood to formerly dependent or colonised *peoples*. As discussed in section 4.10, indigenous peoples, including Aboriginals, were consciously excluded from the process of liberation from colonialism through shrewd manipulation by state powers. Abandoned by the UN in the de-colonisation process, Canada's Aboriginal peoples aspire to qualification as *distinct peoples* in contrast to that of a minority group, because this first status provides the only remedy that will enable Aboriginals to progress from a dependent into an independent political and legal status.

Increased recognition for Aboriginals has been taking place at the domestic level even prior to the passage of new international instruments supporting indigenous populations. Recall that human rights implementation is not a top-down process, but instead a practice frequently left to the operation of domestic legal and political systems. For example, the Canadian Supreme Court issues parameters for the potential secession of Quebec in *Reference re Secession of Quebec*. In a brief passage from this decision, the Court ruled that the Aboriginal people have achieved "their right to self-determination."[188] The court's view in the *Reference re Quebec Sucession* case was supported by the HRC. In comments on Canada's fourth periodic report to the committee, the HRC advised Canada to fully implement recommendations of the *Royal Commission* and grant Aboriginal claims to a greater share of land and resources, since these were necessary to implement Aboriginal self-government, and required for realisation of their right to self-determination in accordance with ICCPR, Article 1.[189]

These rulings motivate Canada's federal-executive government into agreements for internal forms of self-determination with several Aboriginal nations.

---

[187] *General Assembly Resolution 1514 (XV)* 947th plenary meeting, 14 December 1960.

[188] *Reference re Secession of Quebec* [1998] 2 S.C.R. 217.

[189] *Concluding observations of the Human Rights Committee: Canada.* 07/04/99 CCPR/C/79/Add.105, 7 April 1999 para. 8.

In 1983, the House of Commons' *Penner Report* recommended that the federal government recognise First Nations as a distinct order of government within the Canadian federation, and pursue processes leading to self-government.[190] As early as 1975, a series of agreements between Canada's Federal and provincial governments with the different and widely scattered Aboriginal nations provided Aboriginal groups with increased forms of self-determination including arrangements for self-government, judicial administration, education, social, and public services, land rights, and cultural, environmental and resource protection. The various agreements are notable for the protection they provide of Aboriginal culture including Aboriginal languages.[191] These agreements include the James Bay and Northern Quebec Agreement (Quebec), 1975, the *Sechelt Indian Band Self-Government Act* (British Columbia), 1986, the Tungavik Federation of Nunavut land claim agreement (Northwest Territories), 1991, authorising creation of the Inuit-Aboriginal controlled Nunavut Territory, Yukon First Nation's Final Agreements (Yukon), 1993, Nisga's Final Agreement (British Columbia), 2000, and the Mamuitun and Nutashkuan Agreement (Quebec) still pending.[192]

These agreements fall short of the comprehensive recommendations made by the *Royal Commission* for the creation of a federal cabinet position of Minister for Aboriginal Relations, the establishment of a new Department of Aboriginal Relations, as well as the passage of an *Aboriginal Parliament Act* to enable the creation of a House of First Peoples as a branch of the Canadian Parliament.[193] If the status of distinct peoples is recognised for qualified indigenous groups by international consensus, the right of self-determination that accompanies the new status belongs to the holder of the right, not the state in which the right holders reside. The various political forms taken by exercise of the right to self-determination belongs to the collective will of the Aboriginal peoples.

However, thus far, Aboriginal groups have not sought secession or independence from Canada. Rather, they have established a form of limited provincial autonomy within Canada as evidenced by the creation of the Northwest Territories' Inuit Nunavut Territory. These agreements do not Balkanise Canada but rather redefine the terms of its pre-existing relationship with Aboriginal nations. The only

---

190 Wherret, Jill. *Aboriginal Self-Government* (Ottawa, Library of Parliament, Parliamentary Research Branch, 1999), 3.

191 Report of the Nunavik Commission, March 2001. *Amiqqaaluta, Let Us Share, Mapping the Road Toward a Government for Nunavik* (Nunavik, Nunavik Commission Report, 2001), i. The report recommends the creation of a Council of Elders to protect Inuit cultural institutions.

192 Hilling, Carol, Venne, Janique. *Proposal for an Agreement-In-Principle With the First Nations of Mamuitun and Nutashkuan* (Ottawa, Library of Parliament, Parlimentary Research Branch, 2003).

193 *Royal Commission, supra,* note 2, at 101, vol.2 (3) 2.3.47, 2.3.51, 2.3.52.

changes to Canadian sovereignty involve changing a pre-existing unjust and inequitable relationship into a fair one for Aboriginal nations. After centuries of suffering acknowledged subjugation, the Aboriginal peoples of Canada deserve nothing short of the full expression of self-determination through the restoration of Aboriginal sovereignty. The process illustrates how the application of human rights enables the creation of new human communities such as those currently being established in Canada by the Aboriginal peoples.

Chapter 5

Minority Rights and the Roma of Europe

Chapter 5 is my second case study and examines the influence of the international minority regime on public recognition of the Roma[1] people in European states. I review legal initiatives to improve conditions for the Roma. This question is timely, given accession of Romania and Bulgaria to the European Union on January 1, 2007.[2] Romania contains the largest concentration of Roma population in Europe.

My case study on the Roma reveals another schism between political theory and international law on the subject of differential treatment for minority groups. To demonstrate this, I distinguish the conclusions of Will Kymlicka from the international jurisprudence that protects minority groups. I analyse Kymlicka's claim that multicultural policies are contextually dependent, and not an appropriate subject for a common legal regime of international human rights treaties. To determine the implications of human rights jurisprudence for this normative claim, I also research court cases filed by the Roma under the *European Framework Convention for the Protection of National Minorities, 1994, (Framework Convention)* and the *European Convention for the Protection of Human Rights and Fundamental Freedoms (European Convention for Human Rights).*[3]

I distinguish the international treaties that protect minority groups from political theorists' accounts of multiculturalism in three areas. Firstly, my article discusses jurisdictional issues concerning whether the particular groups defined by minority rights, irrespective of their geographic location or contextual experience, are the proper subject matter of protection by a common rights regime. Next, I illustrate how cultural rights are distinguishable from traditional civil

---

1 In describing the Roma people, *Rom* is used as the singular and *Roma* as the plural.

2 *Treaty Between Member States of the European Union and The Republic of Bulgaria and Romania Concerning The Accession of the Republic of Bulgaria and Romania to the European Union*, April 25, 2005, L 157/11.

3 *Convention for the Protection of Human Rights and Fundamental Freedoms*, Rome, 4.XI.1950, entered into force on 21 September 1970; *Framework Convention for the Protection of National Minorities*, ETS, 157, 1995, entered into force on 1 February 1999. It has been signed by thirty-seven states, and ratified by twenty-four states.

rights laws. Finally, I examine how the historic persecution of the Roma violates human rights standards that protect minorities.

Determining how human rights jurisprudence governs minority protections is important because, even though Kymlicka is predisposed in favor of protection for minority cultures, he disputes the necessity for a common legal regime. Kymlicka maintains that the issue of multiculturalism is a complex international question and not properly the subject of such a regime. By contrast, the growing body of human rights' jurisprudence is developing as a common regime that shields minority groups in the light of a long record of state-initiated coercive assimilation campaigns. Human rights, by definition, focus protection primarily on the individual's right to access culture in community with other members of his or her group. The human right to the enjoyment of culture[4] is not contextually dependent, at least not in terms of the particular minority groups identified by Kymlicka; rather, it is a universal human right.

Kymlicka concludes that the Roma peoples, along with African-Americans and Russian settlers in the Baltic states, are ethno-cultural groups that do not fit into the standard minority categories of immigrant groups or so-called national minorities. I have selected the legal challenges facing the Roma as the subject for my case study. Kymlicka classifies all minority groups within six different categories, namely, national minorities, indigenous peoples, legal immigrants with the right to become citizens, illegal immigrants or guest workers without the right to become citizens, racial caste groups, and isolationist ethno-religious sects.[5] He maintains that these various categories are entitled to relative degrees of legal protection, or what he terms accommodation or polyethnic rights, against integration [assimilation] into societal culture.[6] For example, national minorities, a term placing artificial limitations upon persons and categories of minority groups qualified by Article 27 of the ICCPR,[7] deserve greater protection than immigrant groups.

---

4 The human right to the enjoyment of culture is protected in the following treaties and other international instruments: *International Covenant on Economic, Social and Cultural Rights*, 1966; Article 27, *ICCPR.*; Declaration on the Rights of Minorities, 1992. UNESCO instruments on the human right to culture include: Declaration of the Principles of International Cultural Cooperation (1966); the Recommendation on Participation by the People at Large in Cultural Life and their Contribution to it (1976); Declaration on Race and Racial Prejudice (1978); Declaration on Cultural Diversity (2001); *Draft Convention on the Protection of the Diversity of Cultural Expressions* (2005).

5 Kymlicka, Will and Opalski, Majda, eds. *Can Liberal Pluralism Be Exported?* 6.

6 Kymlicka, Will. *Politics In the Vernacular*, 51.

7 *ICCPR*, 999UNTS 171;

Kymlicka, Will. *Multicultural Odysseys, Navigating the New International Politics of Diversity*, *supra*, note 48, at 20. In his most recent book, Kymlicka argues for 'targeted' rights to benefit national minority groups.

However, the ICCPR does not make Kymlicka-type distinctions between categories of minority groups. For example, the ICCPR's Article 27 extends a common protection to all linguistic, ethnic (inclusive of race), national, and religious minority groups. By contrast, Kymlicka maintains that the greater the number of minority groups he studies, the stronger the claim that minority protection (ethno cultural justice) "cannot be secured by a regime of common rights."[8] Instead, he argues that the application of minority rights should be contextually dependent. That is, protection for minorities should be restricted to groups that qualify as a separate, distinct society, and whom it is therefore unfair to forcibly assimilate.[9]

My case study on the Roma also provides an opportunity to examine how regional transnational courts, such as the European Court of Human Rights, influence states to provide cultural protection for minority groups. In this chapter, I illustrate how the regional implementation of those human rights that are inclusive of minority protection contrast with those provided for in United Nations treaties. One must recall from Chapter 1 that the administration of international human rights[10] is frequently carried out by states, as well as by regional political bodies. For example; the Council of Europe sponsors *The European Convention for Human Rights* (1950),[11] which establishes the European Court of Human Rights. I discuss individual court cases to illustrate whether the European Court of Human Rights has influenced European states' recognition of the Roma peoples. The Roma have a long and unique relationship with European states, and this can serve to illustrate whether or not a common regime of minority rights safeguards the cultural development of the Roma.

5.1. *Summary of Europe's Minority regime*

Recall that in Chapter 1, we discussed how the sovereignty of states is eroded by the social, monetary, strategic, and trade enhancements offered by membership of regional organisations such as the Council of Europe (CE). State members of

---

[8] Kymlicka, Will. *Politics In the Vernacular*, 47.

[9] *Ibid.*, 29.

[10] This includes the *American Convention on Human Rights,* 1969 1144UNTS 123, and the *African (Benjul) Charter on Human and Peoples' Rights*, adopted June 27, 1981, OAU Doc. CAB/LEG/67/3 rev.5, 21 I.L.M. 58 (1982), entered into force on 21 October 1986. Also, Council of Europe Information Sheet No. 35 (July–December, 1994) report that ASEAN Ministers of Foreign Affairs are considering a draft *Asian Human Rights Charter*, proposed by the Asian Human Rights Commission.

[11] *The European Convention for the Protection of Human Rights and Fundamental Freedoms* Rome, 4.XI.1950, ETS No. 5.

the Council of Europe also assume obligations for the implementation of the human rights regime inclusive of minority rights as a condition of membership. The integration of states into a type of regional-federalism for the supra-national governance of trans-national society is the focus of scholarly confirmation. For example, Alec Stone Sweet concludes that the *Treaty Establishing the European Community as Amended by Subsequent Treaties*[12] (Rome Treaty) establishes a constitutionalisation of Europe.[13] This takes place under a legal and civil administration with jurisdictional powers granted to the European Court of Justice (ECJ). The ECJ's doctrines of supremacy and direct effect make it the authoritative interpreter of European Community law. The system bestows rights on the ECJ to confer judicial rights and obligations on all legal persons and entities, public and private within EC territories.[14] The ECJ maintains a degree of judicial supremacy over domestic-state legislative policy and court decisions. Additional CE conventions have been establishing institutions that diminished sovereignty while strengthening the integration of European states, as well as implementing human rights, ever since the end of WWII.

Similar to the *UN Charter* (26 June 1945), passage of *The Statute of the Council of Europe*, 5 May 1949[15] was motivated by the scourge of two world wars in Europe that had resulted in the deaths of over fifty-six million people. The statute provided a foundation to prevent a recurrence of armed conflict by means of European integration and cooperation, as well as adherence to a human rights regime. Article 3 of the *Statute of the Council of Europe* requires that CE member-states accept the rule of law, as well as the enjoyment of human rights and fundamental freedoms within their jurisdiction.[16] *The European Convention for Human Rights*[17] was also drafted within the Council of Europe. It was opened for signature in Rome on 4 November 1950 and entered into force in September 1953. Taking as their starting point the *Universal Declaration of Human Rights, 1948* the framers of the convention passed a catalogue of fundamental civil and political human rights implemented by three regional institutions: the European Commission of Human

[12] *Treaty Establishing the European Community as Amended by Subsequent Treaties*, Rome, 25 March 1957.

[13] Sweet, Alec Stone. *The Judicial Construction of Europe* (Oxford, OUP, 2004), 14; Sweet, Alec Stone and Brunell, Thomas. "Constructing a Supranational Constitution," Sweet, Alec Stone. *The Judicial Construction of Europe* (Oxford, OUP, 2004), 64.

[14] *Ibid.*, 14–15,20–21,23, 64–65.

[15] *Statute of the Council of Europe*, London, 5.V.1949, ETS No. 001.

[16] Drzewicki, Krzystof. *Human Rights and the Rights of Minorities in the OSCE and the Council of Europe* (Turku, Abo, Abo Akedemi University Institute for Human Rights, 2005), 2.

Dryzemczewski, Andrew. *The Prevention of Human Rights Violations: Monitoring Mechanisms of the Council of Europe* (Athens, Panteion University Colloquy, 1999), 113.

[17] *The European Convention for Human Rights, supra*, note 11, at 157.

Rights (1954), the European Court of Human Rights (ECHR) (1959) and the Committee of Ministers of the Council of Europe.[18] Legal standing to enable an individual to file a complaint in the ECHR against his or her own state was made compulsory by the passage of *Protocol 11,* and came into force on 1 November 1998.[19] Applications to the ECHR filed on behalf of the Roma against various states are the subject of my discussion in sections 5.3 and 5.4.

On 10 November 1994, the Committee of Ministers of the Council of Europe adopted the first comprehensive convention protecting the right to the enjoyment of culture for Europe's minority groups, namely, the *Framework Convention for the Protection of National Minortiies, 1994,*[20] with forty-two participating member states (thirty-eight have ratified the Convention). The preamble to the Council of Europe's *Framework Convention* incorporates existing United Nations' conventions and declarations protecting minority rights. However, the *Framework Convention* contains textual language more restrictive of cultural protection for minorities than other international minority rights instruments, namely, the UN's *Declaration on the Rights of Minorities.*[21] For example, Article 5 of the Framework Convention requires that states merely *promote* conditions necessary for minority cultural development.[22]

By contrast, the UN's *Declaration on the Rights of Minorities* uses stronger language assigning cultural protection to the level of the right declaring that state parties *shall protect* minority cultural identity in Articles 1 and 2. Article 19 of Europe's *Framework Convention* reconciles these differences by clarifying that the *Framework Convention* is restricted by any existing international conventions, including UN legal protections for minorities. A Roma whose application has been denied by the ECHR may have standing to file a communication with the UN's HRC under ICCPR[23], Article 27.

Recall that human rights jurisprudence inclusive of minority protection, similar to other areas of international law, is not a consistently ordered legal regime such as those found within a federal political system. Also, human rights are not a part of a legislative framework mandated by a world parliament or enforced by

---

18 *Historical Background, The European Convention on Human Rights of 1950,* Council of Europe, European Court of Human Rights, 14 February 2006, <http://www.echr.coe.int/ECHR/EN/Header/The+Court/The+Court/History+of+the+Court/>

19 Protocol No. 11, 1 November 1998, *The European Convention for Human Rights,* ETS No. 155.

20 *Framework Convention for the Protection of National Minorities, 1994,* Entry into force, 1/2/98, ETS No. 157.

21 *Declaration on the Rights of Minorities,* General Assembly Resolution 47/135, 18 December 1992.

22 *Framework Convention, supra,* note 20, at 159.

23 *ICCPR,* 999 UNTS 171.

a global-federal administration. Rather, human rights jurisprudence is created by regional and international treaties ratified by independent states which voluntarily assume human rights obligations. The relationship between regional and international human rights institutions are not vertical, rather they are horizontal. It is, in substantial part, a self-implementing regime that relies upon the legal doctrine of comity as well as the good-will of participating state-members and party signatories. Patrick Thornberry notes, for example, that overlaps between the UN's HRC and the ECHR occasionally take place.[24] However, this does not prevent the filing of a communication to the HRC by an author whose application was previously denied by the ECHR. A state that seeks to prevent such appeals can only do so by a formal reservation to the ICCPR. *The European Convention for Human Rights,* Article 35(2)b, as well as the *First Optional Protocol to the ICCPR, Article* 2(a)[25] reject an application or communication that has already been submitted to another procedure of international investigation or settlement. *The European Convention for Human Rights,* Article 35(1) and *First Optional Protocol ICCPR,* Article 2(a) also require that domestic remedies be exhausted prior to the filing of an application or communication. Standing to file a communication requires that applicant (ECHR) or author (ICCPR) make an election between the two different international forums through to the exhaustion of the remedy. *The First Optional Protocol to the ICCPR,* 5(b) and *The European Convention for Human Rights,* Article 6 (fair trial) and Article 13 (effective remedy), provide an exception to this rule in cases where a domestic judicial forum engages in an abuse of process such as an unnecessary delay of trial.

Additional minority protections were also passed by the CE as well as by other regional institutions. For example, the *European Charter for Regional or Minority Languages*[26] entered into force in March 1998 and was signed by 29 European states as of 23 September 2002. The charter includes specific protection for the Romany and Yiddish languages that have no precise territorial base within any state member.[27] Also, the Organisation for Security and Cooperation in Europe (OSCE/CSCE) established the post of OSCE High Commissioner on National Minorities (HCNM). Protection of minority groups has been the subject of OSCE interest in the prevention of war resulting from ethnic violence, primarily in the Balkans as well as in other parts of central and eastern Europe. The Copenhagen Document

---

[24] Thornberry, Patrick and Estebanez, Maria Amor Martin. *Minority Rights in Europe, A Review of the Work and Standards of the Council of Europe* (Strasbourg, Council of Europe Publishing, 2004), 14.

[25] *Optional Protocol to the ICCPR,* entry into force on 23 March 1976.

[26] *European Charter for Regional or Minority Languages,* Strasbourg, 5.XI.1992.

[27] Aarnio, Eero J. *Minority Rights in the Council of Europe.* Eds. Philips, Alan and Rosas, Allan. Universal Minority Rights (Turku, Abo, Abo Akedemi University Institute for Human Rights, 1995), 125. Aarnio cites Resolution 192 (1988) adopted by the Standing Conference of Local and Regional Auth orities of Europe and Opinion No. 142 (1988) on this Resolution by the Parliament of Europe.

of the Conference on the Human Dimension of the CSCE (June 1990) and the Report of the Geneva Meeting of Experts on National Minorities of July 1991 are also critical OSCE instruments for the international protection of Europe's national minority groups.

The statutory framework establishing the Council of Europe also instituted the Parliamentary Assembly of the Council of Europe (PACE) comprised of representatives from 46 member-states. PACE has adopted numerous Recommendations on the recognition and treatment of minorities.[28]

5.2. *The Roma Peoples*

Similar to the Jewish diaspora, the Roma have lived in what Jean-Paul Clebert terms a dispersion that dates back to the 10th century AD.[29] Like the Jewish peoples, the Roma are distinguished by a history of persecution that almost lacks credulity because of the degree and consistency of persecution against them that continues through to the current day. In contrast to the Jewish peoples, the Roma do not suffer discrimination based upon their religious beliefs. European persecution of the Roma is targeted against nomadism (crime of *vagabondage* – section 5.8a) that is practiced by the Roma peoples. This includes the Roma's nomadic economic trading within the various states of Europe. Other than the parallel dispersion and persecutions suffered by the two groups, there is no ethnical connection between the Roma and Jewish peoples. Both groups, nevertheless, suffered genocidal extermination campaigns led by the Nazis in WWII. The migration patterns of the Roma make their history a challenge for scholars as they are difficult to accurately research. Although the Roma world population numbers fifteen million persons who reside in the Americas, Australia, Africa and some parts of Asia,[30] Europe is the continent that contains the largest concentration of Roma. The Roma population in Europe is estimated at between eight to ten million people.

[28] *Statute of the Council of Europe,* London, 5.V.1949, ETS No. 001. These include Recommendation 1134 (1990) – on the rights of minorities; 1177 (1992) – language and mediation rights of minorities; 1275 (1995) – against racism, xenophobia, anti-semitism and intolerance; 1353 (1998) – minority access to higher education; and 1492 (2001) – national minorities. Specific recommendations concerning the Roma peoples include Recommendations 563 (1969) – situation of Roma and other travellers in Europe; 1203 (1993) – Roma linguistic, educational and cultural rights as well as appointment of a Roma ombudsmen; 1557 (2002) - legal situation of Roma in Europe.

[29] Clebert, Jean-Paul. *The Gypsies,* 10.

[30] Bernal, Jorge. *The Rom In the Americas* (Geneva, UN Commission on Human Rights, Sub-Commission on Promotion and Protection of Human Rights, 2003), UN Doc. E/CN.4/Sub.2/AC.5/2003/WP.17, p.2; Ghandi, Indira. *I Feel Kinship with the Roma People* Prime Minister's Address to the Second International Romani Festival, Chandigarh, India. 29 October 1983. Ghandi explains that the world Roma population totals fifteen million persons.

1987 Estimate of Numbers of Roma and Travellers in Europe*

State	Population
Albania	100,000
Austria	25,000
Belarus	15,000
Bosnia-Herzegovina	50,000
Bulgaria	800,000
Croatia	40,000
Cyprus	1,000
Czech Republic	300,000
Denmark	2,000
Estonia	1,500
Finland	9,000
France	340,000
Germany	130,000
Greece	200,000
Hungary	600,000
Ireland	28,000
Italy	110,000
Latvia	3,500
Lithuania	4,000
Luxembourg	150
Macedonia	260,000
Moldavia	25,000
The Netherlands	40,000
Norway	1,000
Poland	50,000
Portugal	50,000
Romania	2,500,000
Russia	400,000
Serbia-Montenegro	450,000
Slovak Republic	520,000
Slovenia	10,000
Spain	800,000
Sweden	20,000
Switzerland	500,000
Turkey	500,000

1987 Estimate of Numbers of Roma and Travellers in Europe*

State	Population
the Ukraine	60,000
United Kingdom	120,000
Europe (approximately)	**8,500,000**

*Liegeois, Jean-Pierre. *School Provision for Ethnic Minorities: The Gypsie Paradigm* (Hertfordshire, University of Hertfordshire Press, 1987) 35. This 1987 population estimate has increased; however, proportional percentages of the Roma population for each country is still useful.

However, the Roma cultural trait of travelling or *nomadism* makes the exact population number, like other statistics about the Roma, difficult to obtain.[31] Also, no comprehensive inquiry has been commissioned by the Council of Europe to research the history or status of the Roma. Recall that, as discussed in Chapter 4, Canada provided the *Report of the Royal Commission on Aboriginal Peoples* that served as an original source for research into the Aboriginal peoples of Canada.

As I discuss in Chapter 4's case study, Canada authorised the *Royal Commission*[32] to perform a comprehensive inquiry into the history and nature of, and the solution to, the Canadian-Aboriginal relationship. Such studies are necessary to help us understand the persecution encountered by minority groups and how best to remedy their problems within the parameters established by domestic and international minority rights. As I discuss in section 5.9, theorists such as Kymlicka and Carens are correct to argue that the amount of justice dispensed to a minority group is circumstance-dependent. However, these theorists mistakenly conclude that simple justice can be applied in the absence of a common regime of minority rights laws. For instance, my case study on Canada uncovered colonial subjugation experienced by Aboriginals in North America. By contrast, the Roma's nomadism caused states to identify them as stateless persons subject to violent assimilation practices motivated by economic forces. Roma and Aboriginal minorities, irrespective of their different social and historical contexts, are subject to a common regime of cultural protections under the jurisdiction of the ICCPR. However, unlike in the Aboriginal case, no comprehensive inquiry researching the Roma peoples has yet

[31] Yeung Sik Yuen, Y.K.J. *Prevention of discrimination against and the protection of minorities, The human rights problems and protection of the Roma* (Geneva, United Nations Economic and Social Council, Commission on Human Rights, Sub-Commission on the Promotion and Protection of Human Rights, 2000), UN Doc E/CN.4/Sub.2/2000/28, para. 13.

[32] *The Royal Commission*, *supra*, note 2, at 101.

been produced by the European Union. A trans-national inquiry concerning the history of the Roma persecution experience in Europe is necessary to obtain a comprehensive solution to their problems. The UN's Sub-Commission on the Promotion and Protection of Human Rights endorsed the need for a formal inquiry:[33]

> Considering the magnitude and complexity of Roma human rights problems there is a need to initiate a study to identify the reasons why, unlike other minorities who integrate successfully in the countries of their choice, the problems of the Roma are recurrent in spite of the fact that they have been living for several generations within the same countries.

The court cases and legal challenges involving the Roma's right to travel primarily focus on unauthorised camping, town planning, and trailer-park disputes that I will examine in my next four sections. Examples include challenges to domestic laws such as the United Kingdom's *Caravan Sites Act, 1969, Public Order Act, 1986, Town and Country Planning Act, 1990,* and *Criminal Justice and Public Order Act, 1994.*[34] These acts delegate trailer seizure, trailer eviction, and caravan-site approval powers to local authorities, as well as reducing the number of trailer encampments. One third of England's Roma population, for example, does not have a lawful place to camp and is criminalised by being forced to stop in unauthorised encampments.[35] The primary questions affecting the Roma such as illiteracy and the education of Roma children, official recognition of the Romani language, migration reforms that respect Roma cross-border travel,[36] commercial support for nomadic trades, representation in domestic and European parliaments, and statehood (Romanestan) require a formal inquiry by Europe's regional institutions.

No original source material of equivalent breadth and substance to the *Royal Commission* exists to research the Roma people. Instead, I examine primary international and regional studies from organisations such as the Organisation for Security and Co-operation in Europe (OSCE), the United Nations, and the World Bank. I also research secondary sources by scholars who use demographic material such as census data contained in official records from individual European states,

---

33 Yeung Sik Yuen,Y.K.J., *supra*, note 31, at 163.

34 *Criminal Justice and Public Order Act, 1994*, Chapter c.33; *Town and Country Planning Act, 1990* c.8; *Public Order Act, 1986*, 1986 c.64.

35 Clements, Luke *et al. The Criminal Justice and Public Order Act and Its Implications for Travelers* Ed. Acton, Thomas. *Gypsy Politics and Traveler Identity* (Hertfordshire, University of Hertfordshire Press, 1999), 61–63.

36 Office for Democratic Institutions and Human Rights (ODIHR). *OSCE Supplementary Human Dimension Meeting on Roma and Sinti Report* (Washington D.C., The International Bank for Reconstruction and Development, The World Bank, 10–11 April 2003), 11.

as well as legislative records illustrating historic laws and decrees tracing official persecution within individual European states to illustrate the status and plight of the Roma peoples. These authors frequently provide research support for organisations that provide legal defenses against new persecution efforts against the Roma by states in Europe.

An example of secondary source research about Roma migration patterns is provided by Jean-Pierre Liegeois, the Director of the Gypsy Research Centre in Paris, who finds that the homeland of the Roma people is eastern India (Hindustan) where they lived prior to the 10th century.[37] By contrast, Jean-Paul Clebert explains that the Roma formed a loose conglomeration of nomad tribes dispersed over northern India and particularly in the basin of the Indus.[38] Clebert's view is supported by the UN official Y.K.J. Yeung Sik Yuen as well as by Elena Marvshiakova and Vesselin Popove, who find that the Roma originate from north-west India.[39] The Roma comprise part of the Gond peoples known in Nepal and Burma as Gond-Sindu or Gond-Sinti, who existed within the Indian Dom *jati* or caste (Hindi-Dom).[40] Yaron Matras, editor of the Romani Project[41], discovered that in various parts of India, the Dom were known as a low-status caste of commercial nomads who worked as cleaners, sweepers, musicians, singers, jugglers, metal workers and basket-makers. The self-designation dom>rom appears to have originally been a caste-designation used by different populations with similar types of trade.

The Roma have maintained their language, Romani cib, throughout their over- one-thousand-year dispersion from India through to the current day. Romani cib is descended from Indian Sanskrit and, while similar to other northern Indian languages such as Hindi, Bengali, Punjabi, Gujerti, and Rajasthani, is closest to Hindi. While preservation of the Indian-Roma language is in itself a remarkable achievement, Romani cib also reflects the linguistic influences from the dispersion. Maintaining its Hindi and Punjabi roots, the language incorporates aspects from the languages of Asia Minor (including Kurdish), Greece, Iran, Armenia, as well as the Balkan languages from Hungary, Romania

[37] Liegeois, Jean-Pierre. *Gypsies: An Illustrated History*, 22, 36.

[38] Clebert, Jean-Paul. *The Gypsies*, 22.

[39] Marvshiakova, Elena and Popov, Vesselin. *Gypsies in the Ottoman Empire, A Contribution to the History of the Balkans*. Trans. Olga Apostolova, Ed. Donald Kenrick (Hertfordshire, Centre de recherches tsiganes, University of Hertfordshire Press, 2000), 11.

[40] Kenrick, Donald and Poxon, Grattan. *The Destiny of Europe's Gypsies* (London, Cox and Wyman Ltd., 1972), 13; Liegeois, Jean-Pierre. *Gypsies: An Illustrated History*, 22, 36.

[41] "History of the Romani Language," Romani Project, ed. Yaron Matras, 2006, University of Manchester, UK, 25 February 2006, <http://www.llc.manchester.ac.uk/Research/Projects/rmani/files/11_origins.shtml>

and Germany. On page 167 is a lexicon comparison showing the origin of the Roma language as well as borrowings made during the Roma dispersion.[42] Proudly confirming the Roma contribution not only to the Indian language but also to human culture and Indian national heritage, Indian Prime Minister Indira Ghandi proclaimed during the second International Romani Festival in Chandigarh, India:[43]

> It is apt the [Romani] Congress is being held here, for the Roma people have an affinity with the Punjab. Roma culture has imbibed and absorbed features of many lands and peoples and it retains memories of elements of Indian civilisation ....The Indian people support the effort of the Roma in enriching human culture.

The Roma comprise 70 percent of the population of groups in Europe that practice nomadism or travelling as one aspect or trait of their cultural heritage or group lifestyle.[44] Many nomadic or travelling groups (travellers) in Europe such as the Yeniches of Belgium and France, Woonwagenbewoners of the Netherlands, Landfahrer in Germany, Tattares in Sweden, and Kalderash in Eastern Europe do not share the Roma's Indian heritage. Because these groups are not qualified as Roma-Indian, they are popularly described as travellers and frequently identified, not by their cultural heritage but rather by one aspect or trait of their culture, that is, nomadism or travelling. In the European context, the term traveller describes indigenous groups not generally considered to be of Indian origin. Nomadism (travelling) as a practice has been associated with a wide range of other groups that do not fall into categories of protection offered by the minority regime as such, namely, vagabonds, tramps, hobos, itinerant smiths and wanderers.[45] However, these groups, as well as members of the Roma, do fall under the scope of protection offered by other international and regional instruments established for the protection of social and economic rights such as the *International Convention on the Protection of the Rights of All Migrant Workers and Members of Their Families*, 1990, as well as the *European Convention on the Legal Status of Migrant Workers.*[46]

---

[42] Liegeois, Jean-Pierre. *Gypsies, An Illustrated History*, 33–36, chart on p. 167.

[43] Ghandi, Indira. *I Feel Kinship with the Roma People.* Prime Minister Indira Ghandi's Inaugural Address to the Second International Romani Festival. Chandigarh, India. October 29, 1983; 12 December 2005, <http://www.romani.org/rigadr.html>.

[44] Liegeois, Jean Pierre and Gheorghe, Nicolae. *Roma/Gypsies: A European Minority* (London, Minority Rights Group, 1995), 8.

[45] Okely, Judith. *The Traveler-Gypsies* (Cambridge, Cambridge University Press, 1983), 10; Liegeois, Jean-Pierre. *Roma Gypsies, Travelers* (Strasbourg, Council of Europe, Publishing and Documentation Service, 1994), 37; Clebert, Jean-Paul. *The Gypsies*, 24.

[46] *International Convention of the Protection of the Rights of All Migrant Workers and Members of Their Families, 1990*, UNGA 45/158 of 18 December 1990, *European Convention on the Legal Status of*

Lexical Comparisons Showing the Origin of Romani and Borrowings Made In Dispersion*

Romani (Kalderas)	**Hindi**	**Punjabi**	**English**
av-	a-	Au	to come
de-	de-	de-	to give
dikh-	dekh-	dekh-	to see
ker-	kar-	kar-	to do
khel-	khel-	khel-	to play
phir-	phir-	phir-	to walk
cor	cor	cor	thief
kan	kan	kann	ear
nakh	naqk	nakk	nose
andre	andar	andar	inside
kalo	kala	kala	black
kolo	lal	lal	red
jekh	ek	lkk	one
duj	do	do	two
Romani (Kalderas)	**Persian**	**Kurdish**	**English**
baxt	baxt	bext	luck
kez	kaz	kez	raw silk
koro	kur	kor	blind
tang	tang	teng	narrow
zor	zur	zor	strength
Romani (Kalderas)	**Greek**		**English**
drom	dromos		road
kakavi	kakkabe		kettle
kokalo	kokkalon		bone
staidi	skiadi		hat
xoli	khole		anger
zumi	zoumi		soup
Romani	**Hindi**		**English**
yakh	akh		eye
yag	ag		fire

Migrant Workers, 1977 ETSW No. 193. Other international conventions applicable to nomadic or travelling groups include the *Convention on the Reduction of Statelessness*, 1961 989 UNTS 175, and the *Convention Relating to the Status of Refugees*, 1951 189 UNTS 137.

Lexical Comparisons Showing the Origin of Romani and Borrowings Made In Dispersion*(*Cont.*)

Romani	**Hindi**	**English**
kalo	aala	black
ker	kar	to do, make
khil	ghi	butter
kin	kin	to buy
amaro	amara	our

*Clebert, Jean-Paul. *The Gypsies*, 37.

Europe's legal persecution regime segregated the Roma into deplorable and inhumane social and economic conditions that exist to the current day. A number of organisations such as the Organisation for Security and Co-operation in Europe (OSCE) as well as multi-state studies disclose the plight of the Roma, even though the Council of Europe has failed to commission a continental inquiry to recommend comprehensive solutions for this minority group's degraded legal, social, and political status. For example, a World Bank study[47] on the Roma uncovered the fact that 80 percent of Roma households in Bulgaria, 70 percent in Romania, and 40 percent in Hungary qualify as poor.[48] In 1993, unemployment levels for Roma rose to 74 percent in Hungary and 70 percent in the Czech Republic (1999).[49] Another important study by the Organisation for Security and Co-operation in Europe's High Commissioner on National Minorities, Max van der Stoel, reported that, in the Slovak Republic, unemployment rates for the Roma which are close to 100 percent in some areas.[50] The Housing statistics for the central and eastern European Roma are similarly bleak. Only 9 percent of Roma houses in Bulgaria and 10 percent in Romania have hot water. Over half

[47] Office for Democratic Institutions and Human Rights (ODIHR) *OSCE Supplementary Human Dimension Meeting on Roma and Sinti Report* (Washington D.C., The International Bank for Reconstruction and Development, The World Bank, 10–11 April 2003), 26. This World Bank study reports that "data on social welfare in Central and Eastern Europe are plagued with problems due to weak and sometimes biased statistical systems inherited from the socialist era and the use of definitions and methodologies that are often outdated, inconsistent with international standards, or not comparable across countries." Also, seemingly straightforward questions, such as how many Roma live in a particular country, prove extremely challenging.

[48] *Ibid.*, 28. Describe the numbers of Roma living on less than $4.30 PPP per capita and per day.

[49] *Ibid.*, 35.

[50] van der Stoel, Max. *Report on the situation of Roma and Sinti in the OSCE Area* (The Hague, Organisation for Security and Co-operation in Europe, High Commissioner on National Minorities, 2000).

of Roma households in Bulgaria have wet walls and leaky roofs. Jean-Pierre Liégeois reported that, in Bulgaria (1980), 68 percent of Roma dwellings had no toilets and 85 percent had no drainage. It is common for two to three generations of Roma to live in a single room four by four metres, while two or three rooms are a rarity and kitchens are set up in the hall.[51] The percentage of Roma households with their own telephone is 12 percent in Bulgaria, 26 percent in Romania, and 41 percent in Hungary.[52] Roma illiteracy is 50–100 percent, depending on the country, and half of the Roma children never attend school. For the Roma children who do attend school, 80 percent are in classes for the socially handicapped.[53] In Bulgaria, only 10 percent of Roma children have secondary education, and less than 1 percent of Roma students in Bulgaria, Romania, and Hungary continue past secondary education. In the Czech Republic, it is estimated that less than 2 percent of the Roma receive a regular academic education, while some 75 percent of Romany children attend special schools for the mentally retarded.[54] In Czech and Slovak Republics infant mortality for Roma is double the number for that of non-Roma. There remains a 10–15-year life-expectancy gap between Roma and non-Roma in Czech and Slovak Republics, as well as in Hungary.[55]

Poverty Rates among Roma and Non-Roma Households, 2000[56]

	50 % of median*		**$2.15****	**$4.30****
Country	**Per equiv. adult**	**Per capita**	**Per Capita**	**Per Capita**
Bulgaria				
Roma	36.1	37.2	41.4	80.1
Non-Roma	3.8	3.4	4.1	36.8

[51] Liegoise, Jean-Pierre. *Roma, Gypsies, Travelers* (Strasbourg, Council of Europe, Publishing and Documentation Service, 1994), 187.

[52] Office for Democratic Institutions and Human Rights (ODIHR). *OSCE Supplementary Human Dimension Meeting on Roma and Sinti Report* (Washington D.C., The International Bank for Reconstruction and Development, The World Bank, 10–11 April 2003), 31.

[53] Liegoise, Jean-Pierre. *Roma, Gypsies, Travelers*, 203–204, 210.

[54] Institute for Jewish Policy Research Report (Jewish Policy Research, 2002). 5. 27 February 2006 , < http://www.jpr.org.uk/>

[55] Office for Democratic Institutions and Human Rights (ODIHR). *OSCE Supplementary Human Dimension Meeting on Roma and Sinti Report* (Washington D.C., The International Bank for Reconstruction and Development, The World Bank, 10–11 April 2003), 37, 41.

[56] Dean Ringold, Mitchell A. Orenstein, and Erika Wilkens. *Roma in an Expanding Europe: Breaking the Poverty Cycle* (Washington D.C., The World Bank, 2003), 28. The chart illustrates per capita income levels comparing Roma and non-Roma in three countries from the Comparative Research undertaken in the Sociology Department of Yale University, 2000 report.

Poverty Rates among Roma and Non-Roma Households, 2000 (*Cont.*)

	50 % of median*		$2.15**	$4.30**
Country	**Per equiv. adult**	**Per capita**	**Per Capita**	**Per Capita**
Hungary				
Roma	24.5	26.3	6.6	40.3
Non-Roma	4.5	3.6	0.5	6.9
Romania				
Roma	39.5	43.1	37.6	68.8
Non-Roma	10.9	11.1	7.3	29.5

*Relative line amounting to half of median per capita and per equivalent adult expenditures.
**Two International Poverty Lines, $2.15 and $4.30 per person, per day, adjusted for purchasing power parity.

Household Characteristics by Ethnicity, 2000 (% of households)[57]

	Bulgaria		**Hungary**		**Romania**	
	Non-Roma	**Roma**	**Non-Roma**	**Roma**	**Non-Roma**	**Roma**
Households with:						
Electricity	99.6	94.5	99.0	98.1	99.1	94.5
Central or gas heating	16.	4.1	78.6	35.3	51.2	25.6
Cold running water	96.8	67.6	92.0	65.3	67.4	41.4
Hot running water	39.1	9.4	83.2	45.1	35.3	10.7
Telephone	80.6	12.1	76.0	41.4	58.2	26.4
Bathroom/shower	82.5	23.5	88.8	50.2	54.3	18.9
Indoor toilet	65.2	15.0	86.4	49.9	52.6	18.3
Wet walls	20.6	50.4	16.6	40.1	21.0	44.9
Leaky roofs	19.2	54.2	9.6	33.0	4.8	40.2
Earthen floor (sleeping)	7.4	36.7	5.8	13.2	19.3	39.0

[57] Dean Ringold, Mitchell A. Orenstein, and Erika Wilkens. *Roma in an Expanding Europe: Breaking the Poverty Cycle* (Washington D.C., The World Bank, 2003), 34, citing Yale Dataset; Revenga *et al.* 2002.

5.3. *Extra-judicial Execution of the Roma*

In the modern day, the deplorable socio-economic status of the Roma, as well as human rights violations committed against them, have become the subject of scrutiny by regional courts as well as international organisations. The OSCE High Commissioner on National Minorities report notes that widespread civilian violence against the Roma has been documented in recent years, with the largest number of skinhead attacks recorded in the Czech Republic, Bulgaria and the Slovak Republic.[58] The High Commissioner also reported skinhead attacks and violence against the Roma in Albania, Austria, Bosnia, Croatia, Hungary, Poland, Romania, Russia, Ukraine and Yugoslavia. In addition, the Roma have suffered physical assaults by police who are frequently implicated as a part of the civilian violence taken against them.[59] As reported by the OSCE High Commissioner on National Minorities:[60]

> Roma in most countries of the Central and Eastern European region encounter police violence in almost any…everyday life situation. Information about police ill-treatment of Roma or of use of excessive force…against Roma comes from almost all countries of Central and Eastern Europe, and occasionally from Western Europe as well. Few of these cases have been investigated or prosecuted.

Further, the OCCE report disclosed that Romani communities have been targets of pogroms, as well as civilian violence, in Italy, Spain, Kosovo, and Romania. In several OSCE countries, victims face obstacles to secure legal redress for these attacks.[61] The Roma increasingly seek protection from the European Court of Human Rights (section 5.4) as well as the United Nations. Several ECHR cases successfully penalised central and eastern European states for human rights violations committed against Roma applicants. For example, in the *Case of Moldovan and Others v. Romania*[62], the ECHR ordered Romania to pay 262,000 Euros as damages to Roma applicants. In the *Case of Moldovan*, the ECHR case ruled that the Romanian police acting with the co-operation of the state's judicial administration had participated in the commission of a

---

[58] van der Stoel, Max. *Report on the situation of Roma and Sinti in the OSCE Area* (The Hague, Organisation for Security and Co-operation in Europe, High Commissioner on National Minorities, 2000), 41–45.

[59] *Ibid.*, 41–45.

[60] *Ibid.* 45; Dimitrinia Petrova. *The Human Rights Situation of Roma in Europe* (Warsaw, OSCE Implementation Meeting on Human Dimension Issues, 26 October – 6 November 1998), 11.

[61] van der Stoel, Max. *Report on the situation of Roma and Sinti in the OSCE Area* (The Hague, Organisation for Security and Co-operation in Europe, High Commissioner on National Minorities, 2000), 36.

[62] *Case of Moldovan and Others v. Romania* (ECHR, 30 November 2005, No. 41138/98 and 64320/01).

pogrom, as well as acts of torture, against Roma living in the village of Hadaeni (Mures district), Romania that resulted in the death of three Roma and the destruction of Roma homes and property. In other cases, the ECHR issued judgments against Bulgaria and Greece for the beatings and torture as well as the extra-judicial or arbitrary executions of Roma while in police custody.[63] A 1996 United Nations Special Rapporteur's report on extrajudicial, summary or arbitrary executions issued allegations against Bulgaria, the Czech Republic, and Romania for the summary executions of Roma prisoners while under police arrest or custody.[64]

I describe these ECHR cases involving Roma applicants as traditional minority rights cases in contrast to the cases I discuss in section 5.4. The positive outcome for the Roma in the traditional cases demonstrates that the ECHR is willing to act positively on applications from Roma for redress against state acts of torture and murder committed by police. That is, in the police abuse cases, the state activity complained of was targeting individual Roma for special (discriminatory) treatment. By contrast, the more recent caravan-settlement cases target the Roma group's cultural practice of nomadism. The ECHR decisions, that I discuss in section 5.4 about the Roma's nomadic-caravan settlements, illustrates that the court is less inclined to protect the cultural practices of the Roma. Patrick Thornberry cautions however that, even in the traditional minority rights cases of police abuse, the Roma applicants were expected to meet a burdensome standard of proof in order to demonstrate that the

---

[63] *Case of Bekos and Koutropoulos v. Greece* (ECHR, 13 December 2005, No. 15250/02) Decision (Award of 20,000 Euros) against the Greek government for the beatings of two Roma while in police custody.

Case of Nachova and Others v. Bulgaria (ECHR, 26 February 2004, No. 43577/98 and 43579/98) Decision (Award of 50,740 Euros) against the Bulgarian government for the murder of two Roma- army conscripts while under military police arrest.

Case of Anguelova v. Bulgaria (ECHR, 13 September 2002, No. 38361/97) Decision (Award of 22,550 Euros) against the Bulgarian government for the death of a 17-year- old Roma boy while in police custody in Razgrad.

Case of Assenov and Others v. Bulgaria (ECHR, 28 October 1998, No. 90/1997/874/1086) Decision (Award of 6,000,000 Bulgarian levs or 14860 British pounds sterling) against the Bulgarian government for the beating and torture of a Roma father and son while in police custody.

Case of Velikova v. Bulgaria (ECHR, 18 May 2000, No. 41488/98) – Decision (Award of FRF 139,047.55) against the Bulgarian government for the murder of a Roma man while in police custody.

Case of Balogh v. Hungary (ECHR, 20 October 2004, No. 20 July 2004) Decision (Award of 14,000 Euros) against the Hungarian government for the torture of a Roma man while in police custody.

[64] Ndiaye, Bacre Waly. *Extrajudicial, summary or arbitrary executions* UN Doc. E/CN.4/1996/4, 25 January 1996, paras. 81,161, 406.

wrongful police conduct also constituted an act of discrimination under the *European Convention for Human Rights* Article 14 (prohibition of discrimination).[65]

For example, in the case of *Anguelova v. Bulgaria*[66], a 17-year-old Roma boy, Anguel Zabchekov, died while in police custody from an accumulated epidural cerebral hamatoma on the left-hand side of his forehead. Mr. Zabchecov's death took place in the Razgrad police station after his arrest for an alleged theft of a used car battery for which he was taken into police custody. The ECHR found that the Bulgarian police officers, as well as police records, referred to the deceased applicant as "the Gypsy".[67] The ECHR made findings that Bulgaria had violated Zabchekov's *European Convention for Human Rights* Articles 2 (right to life), 5 (right to liberty), and 13 (right to effective remedy). However, Bulgaria prevailed in its argument that the state complied with the Convention's Article 14 (prohibition of discrimination). In the Anguelova case, the ECHR applied a burdensome "beyond reasonable doubt" standard that required a difficult evidentiary test to be met by the Roma as a pre-requisite to prove that Bulgaria's actions were racially motivated. Judge Bonello's dissenting opinion argued that the ECHR had mistakenly applied a standard of proof equivalent to that required of a state for a criminal conviction. Further, that Bulgaria had been cited by numerous international monitoring organisations for racially prejudiced ill-treatment of the Roma by police.[68] Judge Bonello concluded that the standard used by the court was legally untenable to demonstrate a case of ethnic prejudice.[69] The ECHR's application of the standard also made it difficult for Roma applicants to prove ethnic discrimination in other cases of police torture and abuse. As examples, Roma applicants failed to prove the state violated Article 14 (prohibition of discrimination) in the case of *Velikova v. Bulgaria*[70] which involved the death of a 49- year-old Roma man while in police custody. Similarly, the Roma failed to prove discrimination in the case of

---

[65] Thornberry, Patrick and Estebanez, Maria Amor Martin. *Minority Rights in Europe, A Review of the Work and Standards of the Council of Europe*, 69. Thornberry cites the dissenting opinion of Judge Bonello in the *Case of Anguelova v. Bulgaria* (ECHR, 13 September 2002, No. 38361/97).

[66] *Ibid.*, paras. 106, 116, 119.

[67] *Ibid.*, para. 164.

[68] *Ibid.*, Dissenting Opinion of Judge Bonello para. 5, 6, 7: Judge Bonello cites Amnesty International. *Bulgaria, Shooting, Death in Custody, Torture and Ill Treatment* (AI Index: EUR 15/07/96), a second report issued by Amnesty International on the same topic as AI Index EUR 01/06/97, *Bulgaria: Concerns about Ill Treatment of Roma by Bulgarian Police* (AI Index: EUR 15/05/95), European Roma Rights Centre. *Profession: prisoner, Roma in detention in Bulgaria* (Country Reports Series no. 6, December 1997). Judge Bonello also cites general works by the Human Rights Project, the Bulgarian Helsinki Committee, and Human Rights Watch.

[69] *Ibid.*, Dissenting Opinion of Judge Bonello, paras. 9–12.

[70] *Case of Velikova v. Bulgaria* (ECHR, 18 May 2000, No. 41488/98) para. 94.

Balogh v. Hungary[71] in which a Roma man was tortured by Hungarian police while in police custody at the Oroshaza Police station.

In more recent cases, however, the ECHR altered its application of the "beyond a reasonable doubt" standard demonstrating a willingness to shift the legal burden against state activity that offend the human rights of Roma. For example, the *Case of Nachchova and Others v. Bulgaria*[72] involves the killing of two, 21-year-old Roma-Bulgarian Construction Force military conscripts. The unarmed transcripts were shot by Bulgarian military police in the village of Lesura after their escape from an apartment construction site where they were arrested for being absent without approved leave. The ECHR decided that the shooting violated the applicants' recourse to Article 2 (right to life). The decision also established a rule that Article 2.2 prohibits the use of "[police] firearms to arrest a person suspected of a non-violent offence who is known not to pose a threat to life or limb, even where a failure to do so may result in the opportunity to arrest the fugitive being lost."[73]

In the *Case of Nachchova and Others,* the ECHR made a decision to revise the "beyond a reasonable doubt" standard in qualified Article 14 (prohibition of discrimination) cases. During the military police killing of the Roma, a Bulgarian Army Major was reported as saying, "you damn Gypsies."[74] The ECHR qualified the "beyond a reasonable doubt" standard explaining that it should not be interpreted as requiring such a high degree of probability as the standard used in criminal trials. Rather, "sufficiently strong, clear and concordant inferences or similar unrebutted presumptions of fact"[75] was enough to prove discrimination. The ECHR went on to establish a principle used in American court de-segregation (sections 5.6, 5.7) cases that acts may be considered discriminatory on the basis of disproportional prejudicial effects or impact on a particular group, notwithstanding that the measure is not specifically aimed or directed at that group. As important, in cases involving acts of violence (killing and torture) by state agents against a minority group, the court may presume a negative interference with Article 14 and reverse the burden of proof to the respondent government.[76] In the *Case of Nachchova and Others*, the ECHR shifted the burden of proof against Bulgaria and required the state to prove by a convincing explanation that the killings were not shaped by a "prohibited discriminatory attitude."[77] The ECHR decision

[71] *Case of Balogh v. Hungary* (ECHR, 20 October 2004, No. 20 July 2004) para. 77.

[72] *Case of Nachova and Others v. Bulgaria* (ECHR, 26 February 2004, No. 43577/98 and 43579/98).

[73] *Ibid.*, para. 105.

[74] *Ibid.*, para. 31.

[75] *Ibid.*, para. 166.

[76] *Ibid.*, para. 169.

[77] *Ibid.*, para. 171.

restricted the burden of proof test to cases of violent acts motivated by prejudice that are tied to substantive convention articles such as Article 2 (right to life) or Article 3 (prohibition against torture). That is, the court considers Article 14 (prohibition of discrimination) as a procedural right to be implemented in conjunction with the other substantive convention articles, for example, such as those prohibiting torture or killing. In his dissenting opinion, Judge Bonello argued that the ECHR instead make a separate finding of Article 2 (right to life) against Bulgaria that was not connected to other convention articles.[78] Additional ECHR civil rights cases qualifying the burden of proof standard include the *Case of Balogh v. Hungary*.[79] In the *Case of Balogh*, the ECHR required that the Roma produce sufficient necessary evidence to make a finding of discrimination by the state. A police officer's statement to "Tell the Miskolc gypsies that they had better not set foot in Oroshaza",[80] was held as insufficient evidence to prove discrimination in the case of police torture of a Roma man who was arrested for selling coal.

5.4. *The Roma-British Challenge to Persecution for Vagrancy*

> *An individual who breaks a law that conscience tells him is unjust, and who willingly accepts the penalty of imprisonment in order to arouse the conscience of the community over its injustice, is in reality expressing the highest respect for the law.*
>
> Rev. Martin Luther King Jr.[81]

From 1996–2001 the European Court of Human Rights issued decisions in seven cases filed by Roma applicants seeking protection against restrictive domestic caravan-settlement laws. The cases are *In the Case of Buckley v. The United Kingdom* (1996), *In the Case of Lee v. The United Kingdom* (2000), *Case of Varey v. The United Kingdom* (2000), *Case of Chapman v. the United Kingdom* (2001), *Case of Coster v. The United Kingdom* (2001), *Case of Beard v. The United Kingdom* (2001), *Case of Jane Smith v. The United Kingdom* (2001).[82] Each of

---

[78] *Ibid.*, Dissenting Opinion of Judge Bonello, para. 1–5.

[79] Case of Balogh v. Hungary (ECHR. No. 47940/99, 20 October 2004) paras. 75, 79.

[80] *Ibid.*, para. 75.

[81] Reverend Martin Luther King, Jr. "Letter from a Birmingham Jail", 16 April 1963, letter to Bishop C. C. J. Carpenter, Bishop Joseph A. Durick, Rabbi Milton L. Grafman, Bishop Paul Hardin, Bishop Holan B. Harmon, the Reverend George M. Murray, the Reverend Edward V. Ramage and the Reverend Earl Stallings.

[82] *In the Case of Buckley v. The United Kingdom* (ECHR, 26 August 1996, No. 23/1995/529/615); *Case of Varey v. The United Kingdom* (ECHR, 21 December 2000, No. 26662/95); *In the Case of Lee v. The United Kingdom* (ECHR, 29 November 2000, No. 25289/94); *Case of Chapman v. The United Kingdom* (ECHR, 18 Januray 2001, No. 27238/95); *Case of Coster v. The United Kingdom*

the applications was brought by Roma-British citizens who challenged the United Kingdom's domestic legislative regime limiting nomadic-caravan settlements. Each decision incorporates dissenting opinions written by ECHR judges who decry the failure of Europe's human rights court to protect the Roma in modern times. In reaching their decision, a majority of ECHR judges were persuaded that the *Framework Convention*[83], the PACE and the OSCE, as well as the other regional instruments protecting minority cultural practices, failed to provide sufficient authority to influence either stricter judicial scrutiny or a presumption to shift the legal burden against the United Kingdom's domestic restrictions on Roma caravan settlements. The legal eviction of all seven Roma applicants from their lands was upheld in the ECHR's decisions. There is no alternative international remedy for the Roma applicants. Because the United Kingdom refused to join the 105 state-members to the First Optional Protocol to the ICCPR[84], individual communications authored by Roma-British residents may not be filed with the HRC.

The factual circumstances and ECHR decisions are similar in all seven of the Roma caravan-settlement cases. The cases also demonstrate how historic persecution against the Roma is continued today by legal procedures that criminalise the Roma for parking their trailer-caravans on their own, privately held lands. *In the case of Buckley v. the United Kingdom* (1996), Mrs. June Buckley, a Roma-British citizen, resided in a caravan with her three children on land she owned located in South Cambridgeshire, England. Mrs. Buckley had lived in trailer caravans all of her life and as a child had travelled with her parents in South Cambridgeshire. In her application, Mrs. Buckley stated that she intended to maintain a travelling life and pass this tradition on to her children. Mrs. Buckley was denied permission to park her trailer caravans on her land by order of the South Cambridgeshire District Council. In refusing Mrs. Buckley's application, the council explained that South Cambridgeshire had reached a saturation point for Gypsy accommodation and ordered Mrs. Buckley to remove her caravans from her land. As in the other seven cases, Mrs. Buckley failed to comply with the Council eviction order and was subsequently prosecuted several times by local authorities as well as fined. She unsuccessfully sought protection against eviction from her land from the ECHR under several articles of *The European Convention for Human Rights*, including Article 8 (right to respect private and family life) and Article 14 (prohibition of discrimination).

(ECHR, 18 January 2001, No. 24876/94); *Case of Beard v. The United Kingdom* (ECHR, 18 January 2001, No. 24882/94); *Case of Jane Smith v. The United Kingdom* (ECHR, 18 January 2001, No. 25154/94).

[83] *Framework Convention, supra*, note 20, at 159.

[84] *Optional Protocol to the International Covenant on Civil and Political Rights*, 1996 999UNTS171 – as of 26 January 2006, there are 105 parties to the Convention.

All of the Roma case applicants went through similar evictions and prosecutions as a part of the domestic planning administration. Each of these Roma applications was also similarly denied relief against eviction from their lands by the European Court of Human Rights. Local magistrates fined or awarded jail sentences to the Roma for their failure to comply with their respective local authority's eviction orders. As examples, in the *Case of Varey v. The United Kingdom*, Roma applicants Mr. Joseph and Mrs. Mary Varey were evicted from their land by the South Stafford District Council. They suffered three prosecutions and were fined over 2,000 British Pounds Sterling (BPS). Mr. Varey was also sentenced to 14 days' imprisonment (suspended) for his non-compliance with the expulsion order. In the *Case of Chapman v. The United Kingdom*, the Three Rivers District Council in Hertfordshire evicted Mrs. Sally Chapman and her husband from her land in Hertfordshire, also fining them over 1200 BPS. Both Mrs. Chapman's daughters were forced to abandon enrolment in their schooling as a result of the council's expulsion order. In the *Case of Coster v. the United Kingdom*, Mr. Thomas and Mrs. Jessica Coster were evicted and fined over 1250 BPS. The education of their four children was continually disrupted as a result of eviction orders issued by the Borough of Maidstone in Kent. In the *Case of Beard v. the United Kingdom*, Mr. John and Mrs. Catherine Beard were evicted from their land by the Lancaster City Council. They were also prosecuted by Lancaster Magistrates who sentenced Mr. Beard to three months' imprisonment (suspended). In the case of *Lee v. the United Kingdom*, Mr. Thomas Lee was evicted from his Stour Valley land in the village of Chartham by the Canterbury City Council. The case decision reports Mr. Lee remains under the constant threat of civil and criminal prosecution and has been evicted from forty different Roma sites.[85]

In the case of Buckley v. The United Kingdom, the ECHR was asked to decide whether Britain's caravan-settlement regime complied with *The European Convention for Human Rights*. The existence of the United Kingdom's caravan-settlement laws illustrates the challenge faced by a human rights court in judging ancient legal regimes that expel the Roma. International human rights courts are mindful of the treaty relationship they have with the state whose laws are being reviewed. The relationship is not analogous to that of a supreme court in a federal system ordering a subordinate province's compliance. Rather is it a relationship that provides a reasonable degree of latitude to the domestic law of the state member. Recall in the *Lovelace* case[86] (Chapter 4), the HRC was reluctant to criticise Canada's Indian Act as colonial-era legislation the purpose of which was the eradication of Aboriginal culture. Rather, the HRC

---

[85] *In the Case of Lee v. The United Kingdom* (ECHR, 29 November 2000, No. 25289/94) paras. 11&20.

[86] *Lovelace, supra*, note 122, at 95.

restricted their review, challenging only those provisions of the Indian Act that prevented Mrs. Lovelace from returning to her home on the Tobique Indian Reserve. Similarly, the ECHR refused to analyse the United Kingdom's caravan-settlement laws as an aspect of Europe's ancient Roma persecution regime. Instead, the ECHR gave substantial latitude to the United Kingdom's caravan-settlement and town-planning laws by finding them neutral in character, as well as sensitive to the special needs of the Roma. The ECHR's majority view in Buckley held, "In so far as it was necessary [for the United Kingdom] to afford Gypsies special protection, this need had been taken into account."[87]

The ECHR did not give legal categories identifying Gypsies [Roma] strict or increased judicial scrutiny. While classifications targeting the Roma were discovered by the ECHR, laws impacting the Roma are distinguishable from traditional discrimination based, for example, on race, sex, religion or nationality (section 5.7). The Roma cases involve planning and environmental laws that appear to be acts that are neutral in content. However, these laws result in a disproportionate impact that interferes with the Roma's nomadic (travel) practices. Neutral planning and caravan-settlement laws are the modern-day component of Europe's ancient persecution regime that coerces expulsion of the Roma (section 5.8a). The motives that underlie these laws are suspect and deserve increased judicial scrutiny that considers legal classifications for the Roma as part of a suspect class (presumption of invalidity).[88] Under the rule established by the ECHR in the *Case of Nachchova and Others*, the burden for proving discrimination under Article 14 (prohibition of discrimination) must shift to the respondent state, when the discriminatory activity is combined with other substantive convention rights. The Roma's nomadic-substantive convention rights are protected under Article 8 (right to family and private life). The United Kingdom's environmental and planning regime identifies Roma private and family life for special (discriminatory) treatment under Article 14.

Examples of classifications used by the United Kingdom to target the Roma include, *The Caravan Sites Act, 1968*[89]section 16, excluding trades associated with the Roma such as "...travelling showmen, or persons engaged in travelling circuses...". Also, *The Caravan Sites Act, 1968*, sections 9 and 10[90] enables

[87] *In the Case of Buckley v. The United Kingdom* (ECHR, 26 August 1996, No. 23/1995/529/615) para. 69.

[88] The US Supreme Court uses a similar standard of review for cases involving minority groups. *See Yick Wo v. Hapkins*, 118 U.S. 356 (1886); *Mayor of Philadelphia v. Educational Equality League*, 415 U.S. 605 (1974).

[89] *The Caravan Sites Act, 1968*, c.52.

[90] *In the Case of Buckley v. The United Kingdom* (ECHR, 26 August 1996, No. 23/1995/529/615) para. 37.

qualified local authorities to make it an offence for any Gypsy [Roma] to station a caravan within a designated area with the intention of living in it for any period of time. *The Criminal Justice and Public Order Act, 1994*[91] defines circumstances permitting local authorities to evict, as well as make it a criminal offence to park an unauthorised [Roma] camper. *In the case of Buckley v. the United Kingdom*, the South Cambridgeshire District Council sought to limit the Roma by depriving Mrs. Buckley of residence in the area because, "Gypsy caravans…in the South Cambridgeshire area had…reached saturation point."[92] That is, the Council's action expressly deprived Mrs. Buckley of residence in South Cambridgeshire because of her membership of the Roma. Also, in *the case of Buckley v. the United Kingdom*, the Secretary of State for the Environment's inspector's report cited the necessity to limit the Roma population stating:[93]

> I consider it important to keep concentrations of sites for Gypsies [Roma] small, because in this way they [Roma] are more readily accepted by the local community.

The state inspector's administrative decision subordinated the human right of Mrs. Buckley to purchase land and reside with her family in the community of her choice in favour of the majority unwillingness to accept residence by a member of the Roma minority group.[94] In the *Case of Chapman v. the United Kingdom,* the Department of Environment inspector noted that the United Kingdom Secretary of State, *Circular 1/94* (5 January 1994), Paragraph 13 states that "…gypsy sites are not regarded as being amongst those uses of land which are normally appropriate to green belts."[95] Judge Pettiti's dissenting opinion in the Buckley case objected to the classifications explaining that if the United Kingdom's laws and procedures targeting the Roma "were transposed to a family of ecologists or adherents of a religion instead of Gypsies, the harassment to which Mrs. Buckley [and the Roma are] subjected would not have occurred".[96]

---

[91] *The Criminal Justice and Public Order Act 1994*, c.33.

[92] *In the Case of Buckley v. The United Kingdom* (ECHR, 26 August 1996, No. 23/1995/529/615) para. 14 (1).

[93] *Ibid.*, para. 16.

[94] *Ibid.*, Judge Pettiti Dissent P.26 - "It is not in keeping with the spirit of Article 8 [*The European Convention for Human Rights*, Article 8- Right to respect for private and family life] to subordinate respect for the applicant's right to family life…to the greater convenience of the greater local community and its willingness to accept others…".

[95] *Case of Chapman v. The United Kingdom* (ECHR, 18 January 2001, No. 27238/95) para. 17(26).

[96] *In the Case of Buckley v. The United Kingdom* (ECHR, 26 August 1996, No. 23/1995/529/615) Judge Pettiti Dissent - P. 24.

5.5. *Great Britain's Margin of Appreciation*

The margin of appreciation is the term used by the European Court of Human Rights (ECHR) to describe the scope of discretion that is accorded state domestic laws that are the subject to review under the European Convention on Human Rights. It is also the legal standard used by the ECHR's scope of review for the UK's caravan-settlement laws that target the Roma. The standard was introduced in *Handyside v. the United Kingdom*,[97] and provides a practical illustration of how Alec Stone Sweet's theory of constitutionalisation is judicially implemented by the ECHR. In the *Handyside* case, the ECHR decided whether the United Kingdom's prosecution of a London book publisher under the *Obscene Publications Act*, 1959/1964 violated Article 10's (freedom of expression) protection guaranteed by the European Convention on Human Rights. The ECHR held that the convention:[98]

> ...leaves to contracting states a margin of appreciation. This margin is given both to the domestic legislator...and to the bodies, judicial amongst others, that are called upon to interpret and apply the laws...Nevertheless...the domestic margin of appreciation goes hand in hand with a European supervision. Such supervision concerns both the aim of the measure challenged and its "necessity"...The court's supervisory function obliges it to pay the utmost attention to the principles characterising a democratic society.

Within the convention's framework, domestic law is the primary arbiter of the values and morals that provide the justification for domestic rules. The ECHR gives deference to the United Kingdom's legitimate interest in planning and environmental rules that disproportionately impact upon the Roma as necessary in a democratic society. The judicial scrutiny imposed by the ECHR is one of reasonableness, that is, it determines whether the infringement imposed by the domestic law is proportionate to the legitimate aim pursued. In the Roma cases, the ECHR found the planning rules used by the United Kingdom were proportionate to a legitimate aim and that national authorities enjoy a *wide margin of appreciation* because they are in the best position to decide local planning questions.[99]

---

[97] *Handyside v. the United Kingdom* (ECHR, 7 December 1976, No. 5493/72) para. 48–49.

[98] *Ibid.*

[99] *Case of Chapman v. The United Kingdom* (ECHR, 18 January 2001, No. 27238/95) para. 92; *In the Case of Buckley v. The United Kingdom* (ECHR, 26 August 1996, No. 23/1995/529/615) para. 75, 80, and 84.

Also, *see* my discussion in section 5.7 that contrasts the ECHR approach to that used by the US Supreme Court. The US Supreme Court applies a test of heightened or strict scrutiny in reviewing legal classifications that target or impact African-Americans as well as other US minority groups. It shifts the legal burden (presumption of invalidity) and demands that states demonstrate a compelling state interest to justify racial categories or laws that have a desperate impact on African-Americans as well as on other minorities.

In the *Case of Chapman v. the United Kingdom*, the applicant urged that the ECHR reduce the margin of appreciation granted to the United Kingdom's planning regime based on the *Framework Convention.*[100] The ECHR refused to implement the *Framework Convention*, explaining that there was no concrete consensus between states to derive any guidance about how to apply the convention or implement the convention in any particular circumstance.[101] However, an important joint-dissenting opinion co-authored by seven judges hearing the case discovered an *emerging consensus amongst "the member-States of the Council of Europe recognising the special needs of minorities and an obligation to protect their security, identity, lifestyle.* ...not only for the purpose of safeguarding the interests of the minorities themselves but also in order to preserve a cultural diversity of value to the whole community."[102] Furthermore, the dissenting judges found that the *Framework Convention* required states to refrain from practices that discriminate against the Roma and to take positive steps to improve the Roma's situation through specific legislation or programmes.[103]The ECHR's strong dissenting opinion in the *Case of Chapman v. The United Kingdom* demonstrates that the Court's interpretation of the *Framework Convention* is controversial and subject to re-examination in future cases involving the Roma. The ECHR also failed to incorporate into its opinion domestic obligations to other international minority rights instruments such as the ICCPR's Article 27 or the UN's *Declaration on the Rights of Minorities.* These UN instruments firmly entrench state-party obligations to enhance the enjoyment of culture for minorities such as the Roma's practice of nomadic-trading and travel. When considered together with regional minority protections, the ECHR will inevitably be compelled to evolve a new legal standard governing domestic-caravan settlement and planning laws that target the Roma. The ECHR is the reigning human rights institution in

---

[100] Recall that the *Framework Convention* did not enter into force until 2/1/98, approximately fourteen months after the ECHR's decision *In the Case of Buckley v. The United Kingdom.* The ECHR failed to order the UK to revise its caravan-settlement planning regime in the later Roma cases.

[101] *Case of Chapman v. The United Kingdom* (ECHR, 18 January 2001, No. 27238/95) para. 94; *Case of Coster v. The United Kingdom* (ECHR, 18 January 2001, No. 24876/94) para. 107; *Case of Beard v. The United Kingdom* (ECHR, 18 January 2001, No. 24882/94) para. 105; *In the Case of Lee v. The United Kingdom* (ECHR, 29 November 2000, No. 25289/94) para. 96.

[102] *Case of Chapman v. The United Kingdom* (ECHR, 18 January 2001, No. 27238/95) para. 3 – *See* Joint Dissenting Opinion of Judges Pastor Ridruejo, Bonello, Tulkens, Straznicka, Lorenzen, Fischbach and Casadevall.

[103] *Ibid.*, para. 3.

Thornberry, Patrick and Estebanez, Maria Amor Martin. *Minority rights in Europe. A review of the work and standards of the Council of Europe*, 115. Thornberry maintains that the *Framework Convention* is a binding treaty in international law and its language of international obligation is clear.

Europe. It is duty-bound under several international minority rights conventions to safeguard Roma travel freedom and to prevent states from engaging in ancient practices that result in the expulsion of the Roma peoples.

5.6. *The Concept of Equality in the ECHR Roma Cases*

> *"It was a wise man who said that there is no greater inequality than the equal treatment of unequals."*
>
> - U.S. Supreme Court Justice Felix Frankfurter[104]

In the Roma cases, the applicants persuaded the ECHR to apply a standard of minority rights jurisprudence according to which discrimination takes place when parties in unequal situations are treated equally. In other words, the law should, in principle, reflect the relevant differences between individuals.[105] The ECHR established the precedent for this principle in the case of *Thlimmenos v. Greece.*[106] In the *Thlimmenos* case, the applicant, Mr. Iakovos Thlimmenos, was denied government employment in Greece as a chartered accountant because of a prior criminal conviction for his refusing to undertake military service on account of his religious beliefs. The ECHR found that the Greek government had committed a violation of the *Convention for the Protection of Human Rights and Fundamental Freedom's* Article 14 (prohibition of discrimination) by failing to recognise that Thlimmenos's criminal conviction was different from convictions for other, more violent crimes:[107]

> The right not to be discriminated against in the enjoyment of the rights guaranteed under the Convention is...violated when States without an objective and reasonable justification fail to treat differently persons whose situations are significantly different.

The ECHR applied this discrimination principle established in the *Thlimmenos* case to the Roma cases, and required that the United Kingdom demonstrate an objective and reasonable justification for failing to "treat differently Roma whose situations are different."[108]

[104] *Dennis v. United States, 339 U.S. 162, 184 (1950). See also,* Shrager, David S. and Frost, Elizabeth. *The Quotable Lawyer* (New York, Facts on File Publications, 1986), 96, Section 48.20.

[105] Lawson, Rick. *Suum Cuique, or towards tailor-made rules: on new challenges of human rights to domestic legislators,* Advanced Course on the International Protection of Human Rights, Session 5, Abo Akedemi University Institute for Human Rights, 24 August 2005.

[106] *Thlimmenos v. Greece* (ECHR, 6 April 2000, No.34369/97).

[107] *Ibid.*, para. 44.

[108] *Case of Chapman v. The United Kingdom* (ECHR, 18 January 2001, No. 27238/95) para. 129.

The ECHR agreed that Roma caravan-sites may have been singled out for special treatment by the government's planning regime because, unlike house dwellers, the Roma sites did not benefit from a systematic assessment of and provision for their needs arising from their tradition of living and travelling in caravans. For a Roma, coerced eviction from a caravan-settlement site means the elimination of his or her ability to exercise the enjoyment of culture by the practice of nomadic travel. The ECHR also acknowledged that the Roma lack an adequate number of caravan-settlement sites. In 1976, a respected government-commissioned study performed by Sir John Cripps uncovered that there are no legal caravan sites available for 75 percent of the 40,000 Gypsies [Roma] living in England and Wales:[109]

> Provision exists for only one-quarter of the estimated total number of gypsy families with no sites of their own. Three-quarters of them are still without the possibility of finding a legal abode....Only when they are travelling on the road can they remain within the law: when they stop for the night they have no alternative but to break the law.

The ECHR also considered a January 2000 report by the UK Government's Department of Environment, Transport and Regions, which stated that approximately 2156 Roma trailer-caravans were settled on unauthorised and untolerated sites.[110] Finally, in 1994, a study by the Advisory Council for the Education of Romany and other Travellers (ACERT) revealed the loss of 100 Roma caravan sites per year. The ACERT study concluded that, if trends continued, the ethnic, cultural and linguistic identity of Gypsies and Travellers could not be protected.[111]

Despite the growing shortage of caravan-settlement sites, the ECHR decided that the development of minority rights law in Europe does not yet require that contracting states have a positive obligation to provide an adequate number of suitably equipped caravan-settlement sites for the Gypsy [Roma] community. The ECHR was reluctant to decide a political question that would obligate state-members to provide increases in funding for additional Roma caravan-settlement sites, as well as order changes in immigration, planning and environmental policies that firmly guaranteed protection for Roma nomadic-travel practices. Similar to US court decisions in segregation cases, American courts engaged in a century-long

---

109 *Ibid.*, para. 35; Cripps, John. Accomodation for Gypsies: A Report on the Working of the Caravan Sites Act 1968 (HMSO, London, 1977) 9 as cited in: van der Stoel, Max. *Report on the situation of Roma and Sinti in the OSCE Area* (The Hague, Organisation for Security and Co-operation in Europe, High Commissioner on National Minorities, 2000), 116.

110 *Case of Chapman v. The United Kingdom* (ECHR, 18 January 2001, No. 27238/95) para. 53. The United Kingdom, Department of Environment, Transport and Regions' figures on Gypsy caravans in England disclosed that, of the 13,134 caravans counted, 6,118 were stationed on local authority patches, 4500 on privately owned sites and 2,156 on unauthorised sites.

111 *Ibid.*, para. 50.

refusal to order the de-segregation of African-Americans prior to the US Supreme Court's decision banning segregation in the case of *Brown v. the Board of Education*.[112] The fact that a shortage of caravan-settlement sites makes them too expensive for most Roma to afford merely places the Roma "in the same unfortunate position as many others who are not able to afford to continue to reside on sites or in houses attractive to them."[113] This ECHR view is consistent with that of the HRC in *Lovelace* which maintained that Article 27 of the ICCPR did not guarantee a general right to live on a reserve.[114] These two minority group cases illustrate that human rights courts are focused not on guaranteeing a broad social right to affordable housing, but rather on protecting a limited minority right to access housing necessary for the enjoyment of culture. Nothing in the Roma decisions prevents the ECHR from making a future determination that contracting states have a greater obligation to preserve caravan-settlement sites as necessary to insure Roma cultural identity, as well as protect their enjoyment of nomadic travel.

The discrimination principle in the case of *Thlimmenos v. Greece* continues a precedent established by the League of Nations' Permanent Court of International Justice in the *Minority Schools Opinion,*[115] discussed in section 2.6. In that Opinion, the PCIJ decided that different treatment for minorities was necessary to *attain a result which establishes an equilibrium between different situations*. According to the PCIJ, differential treatment of minority groups is necessary to preserve minority identity and promote equality between minority and majority groups. The standard of *perfect equality* established by the PCIJ requires that minorities have "suitable means for the preservation of their racial peculiarities, their traditions and their characteristics."[116]

It is now a well-established principle of minority rights jurisprudence that a state's failure to provide differential treatment to members of a minority group may constitute an act of discrimination. Although the ECHR required differential treatment for the Roma cases, it found that they were "not treated worse than any non-Gypsy who wants to live in a caravan and finds it disagreeable to live in a house."[117] By this statement, the ECHR retreats from the difficult challenge of protecting

---

[112] *Brown v. Board of Education* 347 U.S. 483 (1954) – Segregation by race is a classification that appears to treat both races equally; however, evidence for the necessary finding of segregative intent may be drawn from actions having foreseeable and anticipated disparate impact [*see Columbus Board of Education v. Penick*, 443 U.S. 449 (1979)].

[113] *Case of Chapman v. The United Kingdom* (ECHR, 18 January 2001, No. 27238/95) para. 126.

[114] *Lovelace, supra*, note 122, at 95. *See* para. 15.

[115] *Minority Schools Opinion, supra*, note 17, at 10. P. 138.

[116] *Ibid.*

[117] *Case of Coster v. The United Kingdom* (ECHR, 18 January 2001, No. 24876/94) 111; *In the Case of Lee v. The United Kingdom* (ECHR, 29 November 2000, No. 25289/94) para. 99.

nomadic travel and ordering contracting states to revise legal regimes that expel the Roma. It also reflects the failure of the ECHR to consider the historic evidence of Roma persecution. The ECHR has an obligation to take judicial notice of the proven, historic, and overwhelming evidence of legal persecution conducted against the Roma people by the states of Europe. Planning and environmental laws that disproportionately impact the Roma require careful scrutiny and a restricted margin of appreciation.

As noted in Judge Pettiti's Dissent in the *Buckley* case:[118]

> The [ECHR's] difficulty…is that the deliberate superimposition and accumulation of administrative [planning] rules…result, firstly, in its being totally impossible for a Gypsy family to make suitable arrangements for its accommodations, social life and integration of its children at school … Such unreasonable combinations of measures are in fact only employed against Gypsy families to prevent them living in certain areas.

Judge Pettiti's view is supported by a report of the OSCE's High Commissioner on National Minorities, which explains how the lack of legal caravan-parking sites entails an interlocking set of social and civil problems for the Roma. The report found that the Roma become hard-pressed to keep their children in school. In France and other countries, difficulties establishing lawful residence may effectively disenfranchise nomadic groups and disqualify them from social benefits.[119]

The ECHR concluded that the United Kingdom successfully demonstrated an objective and reasonable justification for its failure to incorporate the different circumstances of the Roma into local planning and environmental decisions. In fact, the ECHR decisions found that the planning scheme incorporated the difficult circumstances of the Roma before making its determination to evict Roma caravans from the applicants' own, privately held lands. The ECHR found that any interference with the Roma's rights were proportionate to the legitimate aim of preservation of the environment.[120]

5.7. *Cultural Protection for the Roma Minority*

The case of the Roma highlights the necessity to provide cultural protection for minority groups in Europe. Civil rights legislation that protects individuals against discrimination on the basis of race, religion, gender, sexual preference,

[118] *In the Case of Buckley v. The United Kingdom* (ECHR, 26 August 1996, No. 23/1995/529/615), Dissenting Opinion of Judge Pettiti.

[119] van der Stoel, Max. *Report on the situation of Roma and Sinti in the OSCE Area* (The Hague, Organisation for Security and Co-operation in Europe, High Commissioner on National Minorities, 2000), 111.

[120] *In the Case of Lee v. The United Kingdom* (ECHR, 29 November 2000, No. 25289/94) paras. 127–129.

disability, or national origin, for example, does not contemplate protection of cultural group practices such as the Roma's association with travel. Civil rights laws are not intended to terminate legal persecution regimes that criminalise the cultural practices of groups. The primary goal of the legal persecution regime used against the Roma is the eradication of the cultural practice of nomadism. Travelling is not only central to Roma cultural identity, but it is also the foundation of the Roma commercial trade system. States continue to adopt laws that either ban or regulate nomadic practices and, though neutral on the face of it, have a disproportionate impact on the Roma. State laws regulating the right to travel for nomadic groups contain a suspect motive because of the history of legal persecution used against the Roma. From the viewpoint of the Roma, Europe's domestic laws regulating trailer-park camping, road use, and community planning, though seemingly neutral, constitute *de facto* discrimination because of the laws' disparate impact on the cultural practices of the Roma people. So-called neutral planning and camping laws require close scrutiny by state and regional courts because of the suspect and discriminatory motives underlying such laws. Traveller classifications may be considered a *suspect classification* in a manner similar to the way US Federal courts review racial classifications for African-Americans in civil rights and de-segregation cases. This is the term used by US Federal courts for laws that do not appear to impose burdens on ethnic groups but still result in a discriminatory impact.[121]

Laws incorporating suspect classifications are similar to those regulating the movements of Roma travellers. US Federal courts imply a presumption of invalidity against such classifications and impose a heavy burden to prove a compelling state interest to justify their use. The *European Court of Human Rights* may employ a similar standard of review in cases involving the use of traveller classifications by domestic laws. Remember that, in the *Case of Nachchova and Others,* the ECHR decided that in cases involving state violations of Article 14 (prohibition of discrimination), the addition of substantive convention rights shifts the legal burden against states. Domestic planning regimes that restrict the Roma caravan-settlements meet the requirement established in the *Case of Nachchova and Others.* Discriminatory planning regimes that result in the expulsion of the Roma also involve additional substantive convention protections, including Article 8 (right to private and family life). To this date, however, the ECHR is not yet willing to reverse the legal burden against states in cases involving environmental and planning restrictions that target the Roma.

---

[121] Examples in US law include *McLaughlin v. Florida,* 379 US 184 (1964) restricting inter-racial co-habitation [invalid] and *Loving v. Virginia,* 388 US 1 (1967). restricting inter-racial marriage [invalid].

The legal persecution regime used against the Roma is complicated by the regime's emphasis on travel practices in contrast to traditional kinds of discrimination based on categories of race, religion, gender, or national origin etc. Because nomadic travel is adopted by many non-Roma groups as an alternative to sedentary wage-labour employment, the application of minority rights alone does not resolve grievances of non-Roma travelling groups. Remember in Chapter 1 where I discuss an issue raised by critics of multiculturalism that minority rights will inevitably lead to a proliferation of claims from all groups who encounter acts of discrimination against them. For example, providing a minority rights remedy for the Roma may encourage additional legal challenges against such laws from other travelling groups who are not qualified minorities, such as hobos or travellers. However, remember that the international minority regime is intended as a corollary to the problem of nationalism and is not a shield for all groups who suffer discrimination. Only minority group members qualified under linguistic, ethnic (inclusive of race), religious or national categories, for example, have the standing to bring a communication before the HRC under Article 27 of the *ICCPR*.[122] Further, that travelling groups such as hobos or tramps who do not qualify as recognised minority groups derive unintended benefits from official recognition for the Roma, is a positive outcome since it serves to increase the state's tolerance, as well as responsibility for the implementation of human rights obligations. The Roma qualify for international legal protection under several categories of the minority regime, including those of being a linguistic, ethnic and national minority. As an ethnically Indian and Romani-speaking minority group, the Roma are entitled to protection of their nomadic travel, as well as commercial trading, considered an inherent part of Roma cultural identity under *ICCPR*, Article 27, and also under Europe's regional *Framework Convention*.[123]

Nomadism represents only one aspect of the Roma culture, even though the Roma are often solely identified by their travel practice. Incredibly, most aspects of the Roma culture such as their family clans, legal system, language, marital arrangements, dress, hygiene, traditions, customs, and values have survived their over one-thousand-year persecution, as well as their dispersion experience since the Roma's migration from India. Recall Raphael Lemkin's conclusion that a group's culture represents an invaluable contribution to humanity.[124] Somehow, the Roma have acquired the ability to survive as a people while preserving their cultural contribution for the betterment of the human condition. According to

---

[122] *ICCPR*, 999UNTS 171.

[123] *Framework Convention*, *supra*, note 20, at 159.

[124] Lemkin, Raphael. *Axis Rule In Occupied Europe*, 91.

the Roma's principle of descent, their offspring are raised in the 'Gypsy' way of life that includes transmission of the ideology of travelling, the value of self-employment, adherence to specific rituals of cleanliness, and knowledge of the Romani language.[125] Contrary to popular stereotypes, the Roma do not travel or wander aimlessly, but do so in a way rather based on a complex inter-relationship of politics, economics and ideological factors.[126] Roma travelling tends to be within regions for work contracts and incorporates additional factors such as the degree of official and police harassment they will encounter.[127] Their travel practices contain a rich cultural and psychological meaning that stresses the values of adaptability, flexibility, and social cohesion. The Roma view society through the social groups to which they belong. The practice of travelling permits Roma groups to engage in continuous social and commercial exchanges. Liegeois explains that travelling "separates relatives, relates the unrelated, and introduces an element of unity."[128] Also, the Roma have evolved rituals surrounding *cleanliness* based on a spiritual and religious foundation that is contrary to a popular stereotype about their lack of hygiene. For example, the Roma ban various practices from taking place inside of their trailer homes in order to preserve spiritual cleanliness. For example, clothes washing, childbirth, urinating and death are banned. Toilets and domestic rubbish are also not permitted inside a Roma trailer. The Roma inner body is also the subject of cleanliness rituals, and they exercise extreme personal hygiene. Food preparation is handled, packaged and stored using great care. They are less concerned with external tidiness, but only because they are the subject of constant evictions by state authorities.[129] Europe's legal persecution regime that criminalised the Roma as a class not only shocks the moral consciousness but also was a shameful failure. The result of the regime merely served to impoverish, segregate and marginalise the Roma from mainstream society. The legal regime's self-fulfilling objective also results in the stereotyping of Roma in the most degraded fashion as a class of professional beggars, pick-pockets and thieves.

The Roma dispersion resulted in the development of an elaborate, worldwide network of diversified family groups and clans constituting what some experts claim to be a *sui generis*[130] social entity. The Roma-clan groups exist

---

125 Okely, Judith. *Gypsies Traveling in Southern England* Ed. Farnham, Rehfisch. *Gypsies, Tinkers and Other Travelers* (London, Academic Press, 1975), 61–62.

126 Okely, Judith. *The Traveler-Gypsies*, 121.

127 *Ibid.*, 71.

128 Liegeois, Jean Pierre. *Gypsies: An Illustrated History*, 54, 56, 64.

129 *Ibid.*, 83, 86–87.

130 Meaning 'of its own kind', or unique to itself.

one for another in a perpetual cooperation as well as in a struggle for influence blending Roma economic, marital, political and familial relationships. Other aspects of Roma cultural practices include development of their own courts of justice – Kris or Kalderas Rom - that help them to maintain social order.[131] Also, Roma birth, marriage, and death customs include strict prohibitions against marriage with the Gorgio (non-Roma people), first cousins, different generation persons, and within an immediate family; and they value marriage as a permanent and monogamous ideal.[132] Death, in contrast to birth, is viewed as their life marker and the Roma destroy a dead person's property to remind themselves that accumulated property is associated with sedentarism (a kind of spiritual death for the Roma).[133]

My brief summation of Roma customs does not begin to highlight the elaborate culture evolved over the centuries by the Roma people. I intend only to illustrate why the Roma, in contrast to other travelling groups, qualify for international treaty protection. Further, how human rights courts can use heightened judicial scrutiny for cases involving cultural restrictions. I aim to demonstrate the necessity for a minority regime that protects the existence and development of minority cultures.

5.8. *The Roma and Minority Self-identification*

Records confirming the first appearance of Roma-Indians on the European continent go back to 9th century Byzantium and most scholars agree that the Roma's primary migration to Europe started between the 14th–16th centuries. To those in Europe, the Roma-Indians were identifiable by racial characteristics and, with their appearance in Europe, the term brownie was used by the French and British to identify as well as describe the Roma's matt complexion and dark skin colour. However, neither race nor religious affiliation was the primary source of discrimination used against the Roma.

---

[131] Liegoise, Jean-Pierre. *Roma, Gypsies, Travelers*, 63, 69, 74.

Ibid., 63. Older laws intended to criminalise the Roma include the *Highways Act, 1980, Caravan Sites and Control of Development Act, 1960, Law of Property Act,1925* and the *Environmental Protection Act, 1990.*

Recent British domestic court challenges to local powers used to harass the Roma include: *Mole Valley District Council v. Smith* (1992) 90 LGR 557; *Wrexham County Borough Council v. Berry, South Bucks District Council v. Porter and another, Chichester District Council v. Searle and others* [2003] UKHL 26.

[132] Okely, Judith. *The Traveler-Gypsies*, 154, 159.

[133] *Ibid.*, 229.

The Roma expressed diverse religious affiliations and were exposed to numerous religious influences as a result of their dispersion from India. For example, in Bulgaria, the Dasikane Roma became Christians while the Xoranane Roma turned Muslim. In Italy, the Roma converted to a wide variety of practices including the Catholic, Orthodox, Pentecostalist, and Muslim religions. In contrast, Roma Russians are Orthodox while Roma Latvians living in Estonia are Lutheran. English Romanichals practice Pentecostalism whilst Irish Travellers became Roman Catholic.[134] A survivalist instinct encouraged the Roma people to adopt whatever dominant religious belief was necessary in the hopes of avoiding persecution and reaping the benefits that membership might bring.[135]

The Roma did not self-identify in Europe as members of an ancient, Indian national culture. Instead, they were labelled by the states in which they travelled as Gypsies, a corruption of the word Egyptian. The actual Roma migration through Egypt from India is, at best, unclear and only the subject of hypothesis, legend or myth.[136] In English, to 'gyp' from the roots Egypt and Gypsy is pejorative slang, meaning to trick, swindle or cheat.[137] The various terms used to identify the Roma were de-linked from the Roma's Indian national and cultural heritage. By contrast, words describing the group referred to a single aspect of the group's lifestyle, namely, travelling, implicitly denying all other aspects of the group's rich cultural background. The word Gypsy is not found in the Romani cib language, nor are the other terms used to describe Roma-Indians.[138]

A series of different names in various states are used to identify Roma-Indians, many pejorative. In Germany for example, the word used to identify the Roma was *ziegeuner* which comes from the Greek root meaning "untouchable."[139] During WWII, the Nazis established a segregated section at the Auschwitz human extermination camp for the Roma known as *ziegunerlager* or Gypsy camp. The Nazis also tattooed the letter "Z" onto the arms of Roma upon their arrival in Auschwitz. Recall that historical events suffered by the Roma included the genocidal murder of up to, by one estimate, 600,000 Roma in Nazi Germany during WWII. Illustrating the lack of international opprobrium granted these crimes, Germany

---

[134] Liegeois, Jean-Pierre. *Roma, Gypsies, Travelers*, 89.

[135] Fonseca 48.

[136] Liegeois, Jean-Pierre. *Gypsies: An Illustrated History*, 23, 25; Kenrick, Donald and Poxon, Grattan. *The Destiny of Europe's Gypsies* (London, Cox and Wyman Ltd., 1972), 15.

[137] Lewy, Guenter. *The Nazi Persecution of the Gypsies* (Oxford, OUP, 2000), 10.

[138] Clebert, Jean-Paul. *The Gypsies*, 27.

[139] Fonseca 28, 128. Fonseca explains that the term *die Zeigeuner* was used to imply cannibalism (a stereotype that still remains with the Roma) or a relish for human flesh. Fonseca argues that, in German, the term *ziegeuner*, is similar to the racial insult and slander evoked by the term 'nigger'.

Lewy, Guenter. *The Nazi Persecution of the Gypsies* (Oxford, OUP, 2000), Preface. Lewy argues that "there is nothing pejorative per se about the word 'Ziegeuner' ".

refused to even acknowledge the Roma genocide until 1982. As yet, no reparations to the Roma have been authorised by Germany. Isabel Fonseca discovered that the Roma orphaned by the Nazi genocide do not even qualify for social security payments.[140]

In Bulgarian, the word used to label the Gypsies, namely Tsiganin, is considered an extreme insult. The actual translation for the term is "Gypsie", but used in a pejorative manner.[141] Other names imposed upon the Roma by non-Indian states are described by Clebert as "bizarre";[142] they include the term Luri in Baluchistan, Luli in Iraq, Karaki and Zangi in Persia [Iran], Kauli in Afghanistan, Cinghanes or Tchinganes in Turkey and Syria, Katsiveloi, Tsiganos and Atsinganio among the Greeks, Tsiganies and Cigain in France, Zingari in Italy, Ciganos in Portugal, and Sigoyner in Norway. Other host countries for the Roma labelled Roma-Indians with names that included Tsigan in Romania, Hungary and Bulgaria. In Romania, the Roma experienced a half-millennium period of enslavement slavery (14th–19th centuries) with abolition of the Roma Ursari slave caste failing to arrive until 1856.

Roma-Indians were also described as "little Egypt" upon their first appearance in Europe.[143] Roma dispersed from Wallachia and Bohemia were named Bohemians and Bohemianos. Liegeois explains that the French labelled the Roma Bohemians when they arrived in France bearing letters from the King of Bohemia in Spain.[144] Names assigned Roma creolised by inter-marriage included the North Welsh Kale, South Welsh and English Romanichals, Irish Pavees or Minceirs, as well as the Tinkers or Tynkers, and Scottish Travellers.[145]

5.8a. *The Cultural Basis for Persecution of the Roma*

Previously, I discussed the normative claim that culture is too vague a concept to be made the subject of international legal protection. Further, that culture is neither the source nor the solution to solving group inequality. My empirical analysis of the

140 Fonseca 275. The Roma genocide was acknowledged by German Chancellor Helmut Schmidt in 1982; Clements, Luke and Thomas, Philip A. and Thomas, Robert. *The Rights of Minorities: A Romany Perspective* (OSCE Office of Democratic Institutions and Human Rights Bulletin, Fall 1996), vol.4 no.4.

141 Liegeois, Jean-Pierre. *Roma, Gypsies, Travelers*, 187–190.

142 Clebert, Jean-Paul. *The Gypsies*, 27.

143 Liegeoise, Jean-Pierre and Gheorghe, Nicolae. *Roma Gypsies: A European Minority* (London, Minority Rights Group, 1995), 7.

144 Liegeois, Jean-Pierre. *Gypsies: An illustrated History*, 46; Liegeois, Jean-Pierre. *School Provision for Ethnic Minorities: The Gypsy Paradigm*, 32.

145 *Ibid.*, 32.

over-one-thousand year legal persecution regime established by states in Europe against the Roma-Indians demonstrates the opposite of this view point. Europe's persecution of the Roma has been consistent if not unrelenting in one central goal, that is, to eradicate Roma culture, especially the Roma cultural practice of travelling (nomadism). The over–one-thousand-year-assault on the Roma was not targeted against Roma racial characteristics but rather against what was historically identified by the legal persecution regime as vagabondage. The practice of vagabondage[146], namely, wandering about without recognised domicile or occupation, was first criminalised by France in 1350.[147] Attributing the crime of vagabondage (vagrancy) to the Roma people constituted a group slander that demeaned the sophisticated commercial trading system developed by the Roma. In fact, the Roma created highly specialised nomadic trades that defined various groupings of Roma. Clebert describes two such groups of Roma, that is, the Kalderash who reside in the Balkans, Turkey and Central Europe, and are smiths – tinsmiths, coppersmiths, etc. (Roumanian caldera - copper pot, boiler; Spanish caldera – cauldron, boiling pan), and a second group he describes as the Manush. The Manush, also known as Sinti because of their Indian origin from the banks of the Sind, are divided into sub-groups that include the Valsikanes or French Sinti, who work as travelling showmen and circus people. Another Roma travelling group that developed specialised trades in horse-dealing are called the Irish Tinkers. Yet another are the Ursari Roma who, known as bear trainers, innovated animal training to advanced levels which helped them develop circus trades in dancing bears and clapping monkeys.[148] Other Roma groups identified for their advanced trade skills are the Blidari, also known as makers of kitchen objects in wood, the Chivutse, women employed as painters in the building trade to whitewash or colour-wash the fronts of houses, the Ciobatori, makers of boots and cobblers, the Costorari, tinsmiths and tinners, the Ghilabari, musicians, the Lautari, musicians and makers of stringed instruments, the Lingurari, makers of wooden objects, the Meshteri Lacatuschi, locksmiths, the Rudari, makers of wooden objects, the Salahori, masons and bricklayers, the Vatraschi, agriculturalists and gardeners, and the Zlatari, gold-washers. Roma known for their skill in palmistry are described by the Greeks as Astingani.[149] Contemporary trades with

---

[146] The practice was also criminalised as vagrancy (vagrants), itineracy (itinerants). and nomadism (nomads).

[147] Clebert, Jean-Paul. *The Gypsies*, 59.

[148] Fonseca 180–182.

[149] *Ibid.*, 24–25.

Kendrick, Donald and Puxon, Grattan. *The Destiny of Europe's Gypsies* (London, Cox and Wyman Ltd., 1972), 15, 17.

which the Roma are associated include tinning, metalworking, basket-making, stuffing chairs, circus trades, music and dance, secondhand car-dealing, vine-cutting and grape-harvesting, copper making, gathering medicinal herbs and fortune-telling.

The commercial trading practices of the Roma threaten the established economic and political order of Europe. In contrast to Europe's sedentary economic system (sedentarism)[150], nomadism does not contain private land rights, exploit land ownership, nor stress capital accumulation. The nomadic practice of travelling resists proletarianisation or lumpness created by individual property relationships, and permits groups such as the Roma to escape the system of sedentary wage-labour in exchange for self-employment gained by the development of trading skills founded on the practice of travelling. The travelling economic system, also known as tramping, provides an opportunity for labourers to resist unemployment. Robbie McVeigh explains that "by their very existence, nomads bear witness to the illegitimacy of contemporary property relations."[151] Nomadic travelling also serves as an alternative economic system adopted by many non-Roma groups that do not qualify as minority groups such as tramps, hobos, itinerants, and travellers (section 5.7).

Nomadic trades were criminalised by state laws targeting the Roma (Egyptians or Gypsies) through decrees and legislation that outlawed vagrancy, vagabondage, rogues, tramps, pedlars, wanderers, beggars, and hawkers. For example, English laws (1530–1800) criminalised all people who engaged in nomadic practices, using terms such as idle, vagraunte, loyterynge, sturdy roags, masterless men, lewd and ill-disposed persons.[152] French laws (1350–1789) not only criminalised the Roma as vagabonds, but also associated the Roma with other banned groups such as wandering scholars, itinerant extractors of teeth, sellers of theriac (antidote for snake-bite), surgeons, players of the game of tourniquet (modern roulette), marionette showmen, singers of laments, and prowlers after girls.[153]

Europe's campaign to eradicate the Roma was as brutal as it was relentless. The tactics used by states in Europe were similar to the vicious campaigns of extermination and forced assimilation used against nomadic Aboriginal-North Americans

[150] McVeigh, Robbie. "Theorising Sedentarism: The Roots of Anti-Nomadism." *Gypsie Politics and Traveler Identity* Ed. Acton, Thomas (Hertfordshire, University of Hertfordshire Press, 1997), 9. McVeigh defines *sedentarism* as "that system of ideas and practices which serves to normalise and reproduce sedentary modes of existence and pathologise and repress nomadic modes of existence."

[151] *Ibid.*, 21.

[152] Mayall, David. *English Gypsies and State Policies* (Hertfordshire, University of Hertfordshire Press, 1995), 27.

[153] Clebert, Jean-Paul. *The Gypsies*, 59.

(sections 4.5, 4.6). From the 15th century through to the current day, states employed techniques to eliminate Roma that included over five hundred years of slavery in Romania (1400–1856)[154], the forced removal of Roma children in Austria, Hungary, Prussia, Spain, Finland, and Switzerland, and the genocide of Roma-Indians that took place in Nazi concentration camps such as the *zieguner-lager* human extermination camp in Auschwitz. The legal persecution regime employed three primary techniques against the Roma, namely, expulsion (deportation), banishment, and containment (assimilation). Strands of these approaches remain the primary legal approach used to eliminate Roma nomadism through to the current day.

An example of how European society viewed the Roma is provided by a Lithuanian pastor (1787) who explains that "gypsies in a well ordered state are like vermin on an animal's body."[155] As I discussed in the paragraph above, the initial legal technique used by most European states against the Roma was one of expulsion or banishment.[156] As examples, France, Spain, and England all passed legislation to prevent Roma migration as well as to force expulsion (banishment) of the Roma from their countries. For instance, the *Egyptians Act of 1530* was passed in England; this required that the Roma travelling on English roads depart voluntarily or suffer imprisonment and deportation. In 1554, England passed a second *Egyptians Act* that required payment of a fine for anyone transporting the Roma into the country. Scotland attempted to expel the Roma by passing the *Trespass Act of 1865* and the *Road and Bridges Act of 1878* that prohibited camping.[157] English authorities had great difficulty regulating migrations because the Roma's mobility made apprehension difficult and immigration controls ineffective.[158] The first official repression in France was in 1539 when the Parliament of Paris records an expulsion order against the Roma (Gypsies). In 1560, the States General of Orleans called upon 'all those impostors known by the name of Bohemians or Egyptians [Roma] to leave the Kingdom under penalty of the Galleys.' Expulsion orders against the Roma were also promulgated in France by Kings Henry IV (1607), Louis XIII, and Louis XIV (1660). However, French expulsion was also ineffective because of protection received from Gentry and Lords' Justiciaries who gave the Roma refuge in castles and houses, notwithstanding the decrees of Parliaments that expressly forbade this. Furthermore, expulsion

---

154 Liegeois, Jean-Pierre. *School Provision for Ethnic Minorities: The Gypsy Paradigm*, 39. Also Roma slavery in Spain (1500–1700).

155 Liegeois, Jean-Pierre. *Gypsies: An illustrated History*, 101.

156 *Ibid.*, 77 – The actual process of expulsion from a country is described by Liegeoise as, "a social and psychological death sentence."

157 *Ibid.*, 133.

158 Mayall, David. *English Gypsies and State Policies*, 20–21.

in practice failed as a policy because adjacent countries confronted with the same so-called Gypsy problem also sought to prevent Roma emigration.[159] Similar repressions of the Roma existed in Germany and Switzerland, whilst Spanish legislation decreed banishment of the Roma under penalty of death in 1619.[160] From 1500–1950, expulsion of the Roma was repeatedly prescribed in law after law and in state after state.[161]

Containment is the term used to describe the policy employed by European states after failing to successfully expel the Roma through banishment or expulsion. Containment is distinguishable from the policy of forcible assimilation used on Canada's Aboriginals for two reasons. First, the primary goal of containment was to eradicate the Roma practice of nomadic travel. Second, containment did not stress any religious conversion since, in contrast to the Aboriginals, the Roma adopted if not welcomed Christianity, as well as Islamic religious influences for those Roma who lived under the Ottoman Empire, as a means of avoiding persecution.

An example of containment policy is uncovered in the *Egyptians Act of 1554* that exempted from prosecution Gypsies (Roma) that "abandoned their 'naughty idel and ungodly life and company', adopted a sedentary way of life and took up a settled occupation."[162] The objective of containment was to force settlement and assimilation of the Roma into sedentary society and end the nomadic travel that characterised Roma identity. In the appendix, I provide a chart illustrating the persecution regime used by England, France and Spain against the Roma peoples.

The most hideous crime committed against the Roma by a European power was the Nazi 'final solution' promoting the use of *genocide* to solve the so-called Gypsy question. As discovered by Michael Burleigh and Wolfgang Wippermann in their research on the racial policies of the Nazis, Heinrich Himmler signed the order dispatching Germany's Roma population to the Auschwitz human extermination camp on 16 December 1942.[163] The Nazi campaign to exterminate the Roma is known in Romani as the *Porajmos* or the Devouring.[164] An Organisation for Security and Cooperation in Europe (OSCE) study finds that up to 600,000

[159] Clebert, Jean-Paul. *The Gypsies*, 61–62.

[160] *Ibid.*, 59–60.
Liegeois, Jean-Pierre. *Gypsies: An illustrated History*, 107.

[161] *Ibid.*, 88.

[162] Mayall, David. *English Gypsies and State Policies*, 21–22, 28.

[163] Burleigh, Michael and Wippermann, Wolfgang. *The Racial State, Germany 1933–1945* (Cambridge, Cambridge University Press 1991), 125.

[164] van der Stoel, Max. *Report on the Situation of Roma and Sinti in the OSCE Area* (The Hague, Organisation for Security and Co-operation in Europe, High Commissioner on National Minorities, 2000), 23.

Roma were murdered by the Nazi regime, though the exact number remains a matter of dispute among researchers.[165] The German genocide of the Roma illustrates the Nazis success at promoting eugenic (hereditary) pseudo-science. Frances Galoton (1872–1911) developed the theory based upon Charles Darwin's, *On the Origins of Species by Means of Natural Selection, or the Preservation of Favoured Races in the Struggle of Life.*[166] Galoton maintained that natural selection could be used to improve biological human health by eugenics - a programme for improving the human race by genetic means such as judicious mating, education, public health and welfare. Nazi public-health initiatives to ensure the racial-hygenic improvement of the German people were justified by eugenics.

Recall that in section 4.4, I discussed how eugenic pseudo-science provided a veneer that legitimised theories of racial supremacy, not only in Germany but also in many liberal democracies such as Great Britain, Canada, Australia, and the United States. Nazi health programmes targeted groups that threatened the biological and political health of the German nation, namely, the Jewish peoples (war on the Jews), as well as the Roma, Blacks, so-called Rhineland bastards, the asocial, the hereditarily ill, the hereditarily inferior, homosexuals, mental patients, the hereditarily blind, deaf and deformed, the workshy, and alcoholics. The Nazis implemented intiatitives against these groups that included the use of racially selective breeding, forced sterilisation, compulsory castration, compulsory abortion[167], certificates of fitness to marry, proofs of ancestry, expanded euthanasia programmes, hereditary health courts, miscegenation laws, systemic murder of persons mentally and physically handicapped, prohibition of marital

[165] Clements, Luke and Thomas, Philip A. and Thomas, Robert. *The Rights of Minorities: A Romany Perspective* (OSCE Office of Democratic Institutions and Human Rights Bulletin, Fall 1996), vol.4 no. 4.

Lewy, Guenter. *The Nazi Persecution of the Gypsies* (Oxford, OUP, 2000), 222–228. Illustrating the need for research on the subject of Roma history, Lewy quotes a lower Roma death count in Nazi Germany ranging from 196,000 to 219,000. Lewy postulates the specious argument that the Nazis did not commit the crime of genocide against the Roma.

McVeigh, Robbie. "Theorising Sedentarism: The Roots of Anti-Nomadism." *Gypsie Politics and Traveler Identity* Ed. Acton, Thomas (Hertfordshire, University of Hertfordshire Press, 1997), 19. McVeigh claims a substantially higher Roma death rate of 1.5 million.

[166] Darwin, Charles. *On the Origin of Species by Means of Natural Selection, or the Preservation of Favoured Races in the Struggle for Life* (London, 1959). Also *see* Binding, Karl and Hocke, Alfred. *Permission for the Destruction of Life Unworthy of Life* (1920) cited in Burleigh, Michael. *The Third Reich, A New History* (Oxford, Pan Books, 2000), 350.

[167] Burleigh, Michael and Wippermann, Wolfgang. *The Racial State, Germany 1933–1945* (Cambridge, Cambridge University Press 1991), 49. The *Law for the Alteration of the Law for the Prevention of Hereditarily Diseased Progeny,* 26 June 1935, sanctioned compulsory abortion up to and including the sixth month of pregnancy, for women who had been categorised as 'hereditarily ill' by Germany's health courts.

and extra-marital relations between Jews and Aryans, and compulsory divorce for inter-marriage with Jews. For example, the *Law for the Protection of German Blood and Honour*, 14 November 1935, mandated restrictions on German inter-marriage with Roma (Gypsies), as well as Blacks, bastards and Jews.[168] Nazi public health initiatives took the European assault on Roma nomadism to its radical extreme by re-defining Roma travelling practices as a criminal disease pathology that resulted from heredity defects.

The 'final solution' of the Gypsy question was initiated by Himmler's order to send the Roma to Auschwitz B II e camp (*ziegunerlager*), where the Roma and their families were subjected to torture, human medical experimentation, murder, and mass extermination. In 1953, after WWII, Germany opened a new travellers' office within the Bavarian Criminal Police and continued deportations (expulsion) of the Roma from eastern Europe through to November 1989.[169] Unfortunately, the morbid public fascination with eugenic pseudo-science did not end with Germany's genocide of the Roma and Jewish peoples in Europe. For example, in his 28 September 2005 radio show, the United States government's former Secretary of Education and Drug Czar William Bennett used a eugenics argument to make the corrupt, scientifically flawed, and pro-genocide statement that the crime problem in the United States could be lowered through a programme of mass abortion for all Black women.[170]

Eastern European states during the socialist period were similarly brutal, using similar assimilation-containment practices to eliminate Roma nomadism. A Slovakian law (1958) and a Polish law (1952) put an end to nomadic travel by authorising police to shoot horses and remove the wheels from caravans to stop people in their tracks. Roma children were enrolled in special school programs reinforced with compulsory military service that also incorporated long-term assimilation programs. The Soviet Union also refused to recognise the Roma as a national minority because they lacked the essential criteria of the Stalinist definition, notably territory. As a result, the Roma were obliged to find a place of residence, work as organised and become strictly monitored by Soviet authorities.[171]

---

[168] *Ibid.*, 29, 46, 48–49, 58–59, 69, 71, 82, 110, 130.
Burleigh, Michael. *The Third Reich, A New History* (Oxford, Pan Books, 2000), 230, 357, 383.

[169] *Ibid.*, 114, 120, 125, 127 172–173.

[170] *Bennett under fire for remarks on blacks crime*. CNN.Com 30 September 2005. 1 March 2006, < http://www.cnn.com/2005/POLITICS/09/30/bennett.comments/> . Former US President George H.W. Bush's Secretary of Education Bill Bennett said during his radio show that "if you wanted to reduce crime, you could – if that were your sole purpose – you could abort every black baby in this country and your crime rate would go down."

[171] Okely, Judith. *The Traveler-Gypsies*, 148, 150.

The Roma failure to obtain recognised status as a national minority in the Soviet Union also took place in many other states. This resulted in their inability to obtain official recognition of the Romani language, amongst other forms of cultural deprivation. Most states in Europe failed, neglected or refused to recognise the Roma as a minority group that had migrated from India, instead treating them as stateless, non-employed, and aimless so-called vagrants. In current-day eastern Europe, the Roma are barred from restaurants, swimming pools and discotheques. In 1994 the Roma were persecuted by the Serbs during the hostilities in Bosnia and, later, suffered hostilities from ethnic Albanians in Kosovo because some of them allegedly sided with ethnic Serbs. The Roma are pejoratively stereotyped in the media and physical assaults against the Roma are often condoned or ignored by the police and judiciary.[172] Jean-Pierre Leigeoise finds that, even after the defeat of the Nazis, other countries, namely, Romania, Czechoslovakia, and Bulgaria, continued the practice of forced sterilisation for Roma women.[173]

5.9. *Conclusion*

Recall that, in section 5, I discuss Kymlicka's view that minority rights are not the proper subject for a common international rights regime. It is difficult to imagine how the Roma could prosecute their right to access and develop their nomadic culture in Europe without the benefit of common minority rights such as those found in Europe's *Framework Convention.* Despite the disappointing outcome of the ECHR caravan-settlement cases for the Roma, they now have at least some basis to assert legal claims that protect their cultural development within the different states where they travel. The international minority regime guarantees that a state's treatment of its minority groups is the subject of regional and international scrutiny. Without an international minority regime, minority groups would lack a forum to appeal claims beyond the state in which they reside. The international minority regime does not permit restrictions on cultural protection in a subjective, contextually dependent manner. Otherwise, the survival of minority groups would become subordinated to the whim of majority sentiment. Kymlicka's view that minority protection is contextually dependent is correct only to the extent that protection required for the enjoyment of culture, as in the Roma cases we discussed, differs with the factual circumstances of each particular case.

In the minority rights jurisprudence that I reviewed in Chapters one to four, the extent and degree of remedy or cultural rights protection granted to a minority

[172] Yeung Sik Yeun, Y.K.J. *The Human Rights Problems and Protections of the Roma* UN Doc. E/CN.4/Sub.2/2000/28, 28 June 2000, para. 22.

[173] Liegeois, Jean-Pierre. *Gypsies: An illustrated History*, 175.

group is contextually dependent upon the facts and circumstances of any particular case or communication filed by a minority group member. However, my case study in Chapter 4 demonstrates that a common regime of minority rights does indeed exist (in fact it has evolved to include a substantial international jurisprudence), and has successfully compelled Canada to recognise as well as shield a minority culture against majority sentiment. Normative discussions on multiculturalism have not incorporated the evolution of human rights jurisprudence into their analysis. In opposing a common minority regime, Kymlicka does not argue against international law as a mechanism to regulate the conduct of states towards each other. If we accept the administration of international legal norms in complex areas of statecraft involving refugees, immigration, trade, monetary policy, environmental protection, labour standards, criminal activity, nuclear proliferation, and military security, it is inconsistent to oppose their use in the area of minority protection as a part of the human rights treaty system.

An example of the requirement for a common minority regime is the need for groups such as the Roma to not only safeguard cultural practices (including nomadic travel) against state persecution, but also to identify themselves as a cultural minority group. The need for minority self-identification is pronounced in the case of the Roma because European states have frequently exercised illiberal approaches to regulating Roma membership and cultural practices. In response to the history of European persecution against the Roma, delegates at the first World Romani Congress held in London in 1971 rejected identification terms given by European states for the Roma, such as Tsiganes, Zigeuner, Gitanos, and Gypsies, which were not theirs and did not coincide with reality anywhere, opting instead for the term Rom.[174]

Remember that earlier, in Chapter 1, I describe the importance of minority self-identification in the area of minority rights. Self-identification provides groups such as the Roma with a mechanism to re-define the stereotypes perpetrated upon them by various alien host states. Permitting members of minority groups to self-identify or define the criterion for minority group membership, however, is opposed by some political theorists. Critics of multiculturalism maintain that the process of minority group self-identification encourages arbitrary, illiberal practices against an individual who seeks entrance into a minority group or disassociation (exit) from a minority group. That is, the criterion established by a minority group for membership may be manipulated by the group and unfairly denied to an individual. Also, an individual might be denied the prospect of leaving his or her minority group once membership is assigned. For example, in my prior case study on the Aboriginal peoples of Canada, at least one Aboriginal

[174] Liegeois, Jean-Pierre. *Roma, Gypsies, Travelers*, 258.

band attempted to deny band (tribe) membership to new applicants in an effort to preserve limited budgets, resources, and housing supplies on band reserves. The international minority regime mandates due process protection to individuals at the domestic and international levels against arbitrary membership practices by a minority group because it is incorporated into broader human rights protections.[175] For example, the HRC provide in their general comments for Article 27 that minority group existence [membership] must be established by objective criteria.[176] Further, regional bodies prescribe similar protections against arbitrary and subjective actions by minority groups or state parties as evidenced in the European *Framework Convention*.[177] Article 3 of the Convention recommends:

> Every person belonging to a national minority shall have the right freely to choose to be treated or not to be treated as such and no disadvantage shall result from this choice or from the exercise of the rights which are connected to the choice.

The regime also serves as an appeal against arbitrary state conduct regulating minority group membership. For example, recall in Chapter 4, I discuss the *Lovelace* case where the HRC overruled Canadian government actions to arbitrarily deprive Lovelace, a state-registered Maliseet Indian, of her membership in the Tobique Band, including Canada's effort to deny Lovelace of her residence on the Tobique Reserve. International authority for the self-identification of Roma-Indians is recognised by European governments under Article 27 of the *ICCPR* [178] as further clarified in the *Declaration on the Rights of Minorities,* as well as Europe's regional *Framework Convention.* "The corollary of the obligation to protect minorities under international instruments is a duty to recognise them."[179]

The minority group aspirations in each of my case studies demonstrate how cultural protections belong to a common species of rights. Roma nomadic travelling practices, as well as Aboriginal natural resource management as examples, fall under the same umbrella of protection provided for by cultural rights. The diverse elements of human culture, as well as the ability of individual human

---

175 *ICCPR.* UN Doc. A/6316 (1966) 999 UNTS 171. *See* Article 2 (discrimination), 16 (standing), 17 (privacy), 22 (association), 26 (equal protection), 27 (minority rights).

176 *Compilation of General Comments and General Recommendations Adopted By Human Rights Treaty Bodies.* UN Doc. HRI/GEN/1/Rev. 7, 12 May 2004. See HRC General Comments that clarify Article 27 protections at p.159, para. 5.2. Furthermore, paragraph 6.1 requires that *positive measures* be taken by a state against private parties [including minority groups] that impede the exercise of an individual's right to enjoy his or her culture.

177 *Framework Convention, supra*, note 20, at 159.

178 *ICCPR,* 999UNTS 171.

179 Gilbert, Geoff. "Individual, Collectives and Rights." Eds. Ghanea, Nazila and Xanthaki, Alexandra. *Minorities, Peoples and Self-Determination* (Leiden, Martinus Nijhoff Publishers, 2005), 159.

beings to access it, require the formal recognition of minority groups. Cultural rights are intended to eliminate the suffering of groups such as the Roma peoples who withstood persecution to protect their nomadic ways. Before passage of the international minority regime, the Roma's only alternative to persecution was to accept their containment in sedentary society. Instead, the Roma rejected forced containment and managed to survive as a peoples. The passage of a minority regime in Europe is intended to bring the demise of the over-one-thousand-year-old persecution suffered by the Roma.

The Roma cases also demonstrate that the problem with the implementation of cultural rights is not inherent in the complexity of multi-cultural political theory or in the different cultural standards of states. That a common minority regime evokes resistance from states is no reason to withdraw such protection from the corpus of human rights laws. Rather it is a historic phenomenon common to the resistance by many states of human rights that have as a foundation the dignity of the person and the advancement of the human species. The contribution of ethnical, linguistic, religious, and national groups to the advancement of world cultures represents an important, if not critical enrichment of human society. The legal protection for this value, as in the case of all human rights, does not come without a degree of social conflict. Over the course of history, states may now evolve not only to recognise, but also benefit from the contributions of these groups as an enhancement to the quality of human life. The principle is explained by the slain African-American civil rights leader, Reverend Martin Luther King Jr:[180]

> We know through painful experience that freedom is never voluntarily given by the oppressor; it must be demanded by the oppressed.

[180] Reverend Martin Luther King, Jr. "Letter from a Birmingham Jail", 16 April 1963, letter to Bishop C. C. J. Carpenter, Bishop Joseph A. Durick, Rabbi Milton L. Grafman, Bishop Paul Hardin, Bishop Holan B. Harmon, the Reverend George M. Murray, the Reverend Edward V. Ramage and the Reverend Earl Stallings.

Section IV

Conclusions

Chapter 6

Conclusion

Fiat iustitia, ruat caelum
Let justice be done though the heavens fall
-Latin Proverb

In the preceding five chapters, I have attempted to demonstrate not only how minority rights evolved into a legal tradition, but also the political and legal challenges that confronted their formation. In my conclusion, I will discuss the two questions I raised at the beginning of my research. Firstly, how does the minority regime affect the recognition of minority groups and second, how does it influence normative discussions of political theorists on multiculturalism? I will also discuss how the minority regime creates new forms of political autonomy for minority groups.

6a. *Canada's Recognition of Aboriginal Nations*

In section 1.2, I discussed Alec Stone Sweet's methodological process of diffusion between the international and domestic legal order. The jurisprudential context of case decisions that we examined in my Aboriginal and Roma case studies demonstrated support for the contitutionalisation of the minority regime. However, the case studies also illustrate that the integration of national and supra-national legal systems with regard to minority rights is a slow and cumbersome process. I do not consider how all states operationalise their international treaty obligations but, rather, how the process takes place within the context of my case studies. Therefore, I attempt no broad causal reference about the HRC jurisprudence. Instead, I illustrate the success and difficulty of integration within Canada, as well as in the political and legal regimes of European states.

Evidence supporting incorporation of the minority regime into Canada's domestic law is revealed in its periodic reporting to the HRC.[1] Canadian reports to the HRC (section 4.7) disclosed that the Supreme Court of Canada was persuaded by, or relied

[1] *Canada's Addendum to the Fourth periodic reports of States parties due in 1995* CCPR/C/103/Add.5 (15 October 1997) para. 284;
Also, *see* section 4.7.

upon the ICCPR's Article 27 (minority rights) in making several important domestic case law decisions affecting freedom of religion, expression, rights to an interpreter, and minority language and education rights. Furthermore, Canada is now obligated to expand its domestic Office of Ombudsman to review Canadian compliance with international human rights as explained in its reports to the HRC.

In section 4.8, I discussed Canada's response to the HRC decision in the *Lovelace* case. The Canadian parliament passed Bill C-31 revising the Indian Act on 17 June 1985, nearly four years after the HRC had issued its decision supporting Lovelace's right to live on the Tobique Band Reserve. Canada's legislative Bill C-31 eliminated the so-called marrying out provision of the Indian Act. This provision had resulted in Sandra Lovelace's expulsion from her band reserve homeland, as well as a denial of her legal status as a so-called Indian (Aboriginal) because she had married a non-Aboriginal man. The *Royal Commission* reported 133,134[2] new Aboriginal member-registrants as a result of the elimination of discriminatory marriage restrictions in the Indian Act. The statistic demonstrates the dramatic impact that the HRC's ruling had upon Aboriginal membership. However, other constitutionally obnoxious provisions of the Indian Act remained unchanged. Namely, the double-mother rule continues as a part of domestic law regulating Aboriginal society. As a result, the progeny of marriages between Aboriginal and non-Aboriginals are denied official recognition as Indians (Aboriginals). The dramatic increases in Aboriginal membership witnessed in Canada will, over time, be reduced and, eventually, eliminated. Canada's colonial objectives with regard to Aboriginal minority groups have remained unchanged for over a century. That is, to destroy the Aboriginal culture by a legal regime that places strict, inter-generational qualifications upon Aboriginal membership dedicated to reducing and, ultimately, eliminating Aboriginals as a group.

The HRC continued to make findings against Canada, even after the state removed discriminatory marital provisions in the Indian Act. HRC follow-up reports under the Optional Protocol made findings against Canada for twenty-three years after its rendering the Lovelace decision (section 4.8)! However, the double mother rule denying Indian status recognition to the Aboriginal progeny of inter-marriages was not raised as an issue in the *Lovelace* case. By contrast, the HRC focused exclusively upon the issue of whether the marrying out provisions of the Act excluded Lovelace from accessing her cultural identity. The Indian Act's inter-generational restriction on Aboriginal membership was only raised in later findings made by the HRC against Canada.

Nevertheless, the effect of the Lovelace case on Canada's domestic legal and political order is undeniable. The fact that social struggles continue to take place within

[2] *Royal Commission*, *supra*, note 2, at 101, vol.4. 3(2). The Royal Commission reports 133,134 new Indian registrants.

Canada over revising other provisions of the Indian Act does not alter the effect of the HRC ruling on domestic legislative reforms to the Indian Act, such as Bill C-31. While other aspects of the Indian Act remain in need of reform as much as the Indian Act needs to be replaced by formal recognition of Aboriginal sovereignty, this does not invalidate the diffusion of the minority regime within Canada's domestic laws. As I discussed in section 6.1a, Indian Act reform merely reflects the difficulty both states and minority groups experience in reforming complex discriminatory regimes. It does not contradict the proposition that the minority regime has successfully diffused to enhance Canadian recognition of the Aboriginal peoples.

The diffusion of the minority regime into the domestic legal order is similar to that of other state human rights obligations. Recall that human rights administration is not a vertical regime and relies, in substantial part, upon domestic monitoring and implementation. Hence, Canadian Supreme Court decisions are largely self-executing in recognising the sovereignty claims of Aboriginal groups. Recall how in section 4.4, I discussed *Delgamuukw v. British Columbia*[3] in which the domestic Supreme Court upheld the rights of Aboriginal groups to bring land claims in cases historically refused by Canadian courts. The Canadian Supreme Court continues to support claims recognising Aboriginal sovereignty in *Dorothy Marie Van der Peet v. Her Majesty the Queen*[4] though not always positively as illustrated in *Ronald Edward Sparrow v. Her Majesty the Queen*[5] (section 4.3). Legal commentators find that, in *Reference re Secession of Quebec*[6] (section 4.11), the Canadian Supreme Court recognises Aboriginal rights to self-determination within Canada. The Supreme Court rulings are consistent with new arrangements for Aboriginal autonomy. This includes the Tungavik Federation of Nunavut land claim agreement that led to the creation of Canada's Nunavut Territory (section 6.1 a). These agreements illuminate the successful diffusion of the minority regime. With these agreements, Canada now recognises the inherent rights to self-determination in the form of political autonomy for the Aboriginal peoples.

6b. *State Recognition of the Roma Peoples*

My Roma case study also provided substantial support for the idea that the diffusion of the minority regime increased domestic recognition of the Roma peoples. The analysis of case decisions by the ECHR only served to confirm the diffusion of international norms into the domestic legal-political order. Recall in section 1.2 that we discussed how courts with regional jurisdiction caused the work of judicial

[3] *Delgamuukw v. British Columbia* [1997] 3 S.C.R. 1010.

[4] *Dorothy Marie Van der Peet v. Her Majesty the Queen* [1996] 2 S.C.R. 507.

[5] *Ronald Edward Sparrow v. Her Majesty the Queen* [1990] 1 S.C.R. 1075.

[6] *Reference re Secession of Quebec* [1998] 2 S.C.R.217.

and legislative authorities to become increasingly interdependent, even interchangeable, diffusing into general modes of governance, as well as bearing on integration of national and supra national legal systems throughout the European Community.[7] Case decisions by the ECHR supporting the rights of the Roma only serve to confirm a similar process.

The process is revealed in the ECHR cases I discuss regarding extra-judicial execution and police torture of the Roma (section 5.3). These include a number of actions brought by the families of tortured and murdered Roma against Romania, Bulgaria, Greece and Hungary.[8] The most important contribution of these cases to the diffusion thesis is the very existence of the cases themselves. That is, as a result of the human and minority rights regimes, the provision of a judicial remedy is now available enabling the Roma to bring a complaint against the state that is decided by a regional human rights body rather than to a domestic court. Recall that one of the primary objectives of human rights is to permit an individual to escape the iron cage (section 3.6) of state sovereignty which, prior to the establishment of human rights laws, prevented an individual complaint against her or his state.

The cases illustrated evolution within the ECHR regarding human rights protections for the Roma. In the *Case of Nachova and Others*[9], the ECHR increased the burden upon states such as Bulgaria to justify discriminatory police actions against the Roma minority group. In each of these cases, the ECHR issued decisions mandating that the states pay punitive monetary awards to the tortured or murdered Roma or their families. As a result, these cases provide a supra-national precedent that European states will pay heavy fines (section 5.3) for violent actions taken against the historically persecuted Roma minority group. Without Europe's regional human and minority rights regime, such a precedent would not have been possible. In the absence of such regimes, the Roma would be limited to seeking a remedy in the domestic courts within the very state authorities

[7] Sweet, Alec Stone. *The Judicial Construction of Europe* (Oxford, OUP, 2004), 1, 6, 12, 69;
The European Court of Justice (ECJ) was created by the *Treaty Establishing the European Community as Amended by Subsequent Treaties*, Rome, 25 March 1957. The ECJ is distinguished from the European Court of Human Rights (ECHR) which was established by the *Convention for the Protection of Human Rights and Fundamental Freedoms*, Rome, 4.XI. 1950.

[8] *Case of Moldovan and Others v. Romania* (ECHR, 30 November 2005, No. 41138/98 and 64320/01), *Case of Bekos and Koutropoulos v. Greece* (ECHR, 13 December 2005, No. 15250/02), *Case of Nachova and Others v. Bulgaria* (ECHR, 26 February 2004, No. 43577/98 and 43579/98), *Case of Anguelova v. Bulgaria* (ECHR, 13 September 2002, No. 38361/97), *Case of Assenov and Others v. Bulgaria* (ECHR, 28 October 1998, No. 90/1997/874/1086), *Case of Velikova v. Bulgaria* (ECHR, 18 May 2000, No. 41488/98), *Case of Balogh v. Hungary* (ECHR, 20 October 2004, No. 20 July 2004).

[9] *Case of Nachova and Others v. Bulgaria* (ECHR, 26 February 2004, No. 43577/98 and 43579/98).

responsible for their torture and persecution in the first instance. This is why political theorists who empathise with the plight of minority groups, such as Will Kymlicka, are wrong to conclude that minority groups cannot be helped by a regime of common rights. Without a regime of common rights, the Roma would be left with no practical remedy.

Support for the diffusion of the minority regime into the domestic sphere is also found in the Roma trailer-caravan settlement cases. The cases were disappointing because they failed to strike down Great Britain's planning regime that is part of the historic and ancient practice of expulsion of the Roma minority group. However, even these cases demonstrated that Europe's states will increasingly be required to meet a judicial burden to provide for the differential treatment of minority groups (section 5.6). The negative decisions reflected as much the uncertainty of the ECHR on how to adjudicate cases involving Europe's *Framework Convention.*[10] Recall that in the first Roma caravan settlement decision, *In the Case of Buckley v. The United Kingdom*, the *Framework Convention* had not entered into force. In the later case decisions, the ECHR decided that it lacked guidance about how to apply the *Framework Convention* in any particular circumstance. *The Case of Chapman v. The United Kingdom*[11], a case decided years after the *In the Case of Buckley*, contained a strong, joint dissenting opinion by ECHR judges urging protection for the security, identity, and lifestyle of Europe's minorities under the *Framework Convention.*[12] The cases, though disappointing to the Roma, reflect the beginning in contrast to an end of the minority regimes diffusion into the domestic sphere. The ECHR review of domestic actions involving the Roma, however negative, provided some authority in favour of domestic laws that recognise the unique characteristics and travelling culture of the Roma. Furthermore, the Roma peoples themselves are increasingly dedicated to pursuing a judicial-litigation strategy to achieve the equality of treatment guaranteed by the minority regime within domestic and regional courts.[13] State obligations to recognise the Roma have now become the purview of regional and domestic courts responsible for the implementation of human rights protection.

---

[10] *Framework Convention, supra*, note 20, at 159.

[11] *Case of Chapman v. The United Kingdom* (ECHR, 18 January 2001, No. 27238/95), para. 3. *See* Joint Dissenting Opinion of Judges Pastor Ridruejo, Bonello, Tulkens, Straznicka, Lorenzen, Fischbach and Casadevall.

[12] *Ibid.*

[13] Fleishman, Jeffrey, "New Gypsy Vision for the Future, The Roma use tactics from the US civil rights struggle to seek equal access to education and new opportunities for their children," Los Angeles Times, 23 June 2006.

6c. *Constitutionalisation of the Minority Regime*

My case studies on the Roma and Aborginal peoples demonstrated support for the constitutionalisation of the minority legal tradition by domestic regimes. Several European states were compelled by the ECHR to pay punitive awards to Roma damaged by improper police actions. Additionally, states such as Great Britain that practice expulsion of Roma caravan-trailers will now be scrutinised by Europe's regional human rights body for compliance with the *Framework Convention*. Similarly, Canadian indigenous minority groups have prevailed in overturning long-standing domestic rules harmful to their Aboriginal heritage by virtue of their successful communications adjudicated by the United Nations' Human Rights Committee. In the absence of a common regime of universal minority rights, neither of these groups would have succeeded in their claims against the domestic legal-political order. In both of my case studies, progress toward social justice and greater equality was achieved thanks to the existence of the minority regime. I make no claim that similar results may be achieved by minority groups in all domestic states. However, recall the principle that general international law has a tendency to become universal international law.[14] It is fair to conclude that such is the case with respect to the diffusion of the minority regime into the domestic legal-political order.

6.1. *Consequences of the Minority Regime*

In this section, I explain the consequences of the minority regime for normative questions on multiculturalism. In section 6.1 a, I also discuss how the regime has evolved to create new claims by minority groups for autonomy within states.

The minority legal tradition is founded in the international states' system that developed after the *Treaty of Westphalia, 1648* (section 2.2). Legal scholarship and historical literature bases the justification for the minority regime in the concept of the nation, the ideology of nationalism, and the structure of the nation-state. Normative discussions generally resist the challenge to analyse multiculturalism as a question about the structure of states. The minority regime challenges the tendency to accept the nation-state's structure as a given. It establishes an obligation that all states comply with human rights standards, irrespective of the state's national bias or majority sentiment.

It is not my intent to challenge the ideology of nationalism, or even, the framework for the nation-state. Over the past two centuries, the attraction to establish

[14] Robinson, Nehemiah. *The Genocide Convention. Its Origins and Interpretation.* (New York, Institute of Jewish Affairs, World Jewish Congress, 1949), 13.

the world's states based upon the national, cultural, or ethno-centric characteristics of peoples has proved attractive, if not, in many cases, successful. The ideology of nationalism appears to have prevailed over competing doctrines of liberalism and socialism to provide the bases for the structure of most world states; though many states combine elements taken from one or more of these principles. It is enough for me to demonstrate that, in the past century, the minority legal tradition developed in response to state practices that resulted in two world wars (with fifty-six million deaths), forced population transfers, campaigns of expulsion, coercive assimilation, formal segregation, and crimes of genocide against minority groups.

Rather, my purpose is merely to provide justification for the minority regime. Legal scholarship explains the minority regime as a corrective for a multi-national states system based upon the control exercised by powerful nations of the state's administrative apparatus. Proper understanding of the justification for the minority regime is important because, in the writer's opinion, it reduces the intensity as well as the necessity for a normative debate on multiculturalism. The minority regime creates a paradigm shift from the domestic polity into the international sphere. Within the domestic context, minority rights appear a regime that qualifies only certain groups for exemptions, as well as differential or special treatment. The international perspective changes the paradigm. The international perspective demands that all nations, as well as minority groups, be afforded equal treatment by the world's states. Human rights also require the application of equality for all minority groups, irrespective of their power relationship within any particular state. The minority regime requires that all domestic states recognise, as well as provide equality to, different national and minority groups, especially those who maintain unequal positions.

It is the international character of the minority regime that provides the most significant contribution to discussions on multiculturalism. The minority regime was established at the supra-state, regional and international levels, and encourages domestic regimes to implement the equal treatment of minority groups. The minority regime is an effort to implement a system that recognises the multi-national (and multi-cultural) nature of states; also, to prescribe guidance on how states conduct their recognition of groups emigrated, descended, or incorporated from different nations. That is, a regime of universal human rights that attempts to harmonise inter-state and intra-state relations by permitting individuals, in community with other members of her or his group, access to culture.

In section 2.4, I discussed the doctrine for the equality of nations. This doctrine is important because it dictates that all nations, as well as the individual members which comprise a nation, are entitled to equality of treatment. To qualify, the doctrine is admittedly old and contains ambiguity as to the type of equality to which the world's nations are entitled. Furthermore, the doctrine was never written into the League of Nations Covenant. However, I resurrect the equality of nations' doctrine because it maintains contemporary salience. The doctrine was drafted into the Purposes and Principles of Chapter I, Article 2 (2) in the *United Nations Charter.*[15]

As I discussed in section 2.3, many political theorists dismiss the idea that all nations are equal on practical grounds, namely, there are too many nations to give all equal recognition. Some even reject the idea on theoretical grounds, arguing that such an equality of nations is not achievable, and therefore, is not a valuable standard. However, there is a flaw in this line of reasoning. If we accept the premise that nations are neither equal nor entitled to equal treatment or recognition then, by implication, we must also accept the view that the individual members who comprise these nations are unequal. Nations, at base, are groupings of individuals who comprise the nation's membership. That individuals are inherently unequal by virtue of their national affiliation is an obnoxious conclusion.

Differential or special treatment for minority groups in the domestic sphere is now an established jurisprudential principle necessary to insure equality for minority groups. Recall that in section 2.6, I discussed the precedent established by the League of Nations' Permanent Court of International Justice *Minority Schools Opinion*[16], that perfect equality requires states to 'attain a result which establishes an equilibrium between different situations.' That is, to guarantee equality, states must grant to minorities 'suitable means for the preservation of their racial peculiarities, their traditions and their characteristics.'[17] As I discussed in section 5.6, the concept of differential treatment for persons whose situations are significantly different was reaffirmed by the European Court of Human Rights in the *Case of Thlemmenos v. Greece* (6 April 2000), over half a century after the PCIJ *Minority Schools Opinion.*[18]

6.1a. *Balkanisation and The Minority Regime*

In this section, I address the consequences of the establishment of the minority regime for three additional normative claims. First, I briefly address the claim that the minority regime constitutes an illiberal form of group rights. Next, I discuss the idea that the minority regime Balkanises states and damages common citizenship. Thirdly, there is the claim that the minority regime provides authority for the illiberal acts of religious fundamentalist groups.

---

15 *United Nations Charter*, Chapter I, Article 2(1) states: The Organisation is based on the principle of the sovereign equality of all its members.

16 *Minority Schools Opinion, supra*, note 17, at 10. P. 138.

17 *Ibid.*

18 *Thlimmenos v. Greece* (ECHR, 6 April 2000, No. 34369/97).

The controversy of whether the minority regime constitutes group-based versus individual rights is described by one commentator as a *red herring*.[19] Minority rights are both, that is, individual human rights with a collective dimension. The concept of group-based legal remedies is a well-established principle of jurisprudence within domestic and international law courts. I explained how this principle works as demonstrated by class action remedies available in the USA (section 3.6). Also, actions brought on behalf of members of religious groups and labour organisations are frequently raised on behalf of individuals, as well as their group associations. The HRC decision in *Lubicon Lake Band v. Canada*[20] found that, under the minority regime, "there is no objection to a group of individuals, who claim to be similarly affected, collectively to submit a communication about alleged breaches of their rights." The so-called group rights controversy is neither controversial or a new concept as a subject of jurisprudence.

I now address the two additional challenges posed by normative objections to minority rights: firstly, the idea that minority rights damage common citizenship and national unity, resulting in a Balkanisation of the state, and second, that minority rights inherently conflict or clash with universal human rights. In sections 4.3 and 4.4, I examine the historical regime that governs the relationship between Aboriginal nations and the state of Canada. The chapter summarises the history of the Indian Act as well as its progeny of statutes regulating almost every aspect of Aboriginal society. These included the so-called numbered treaty agreements extending benefits to Aboriginal nations entered into by Canada in an effort to appropriate Aboriginal lands. I demonstrated that the Indian Act remains the subject of criticism as discriminatory legislation, even while the numbered treaties continue to serve as a basis for Aboriginal property claims through to the current day. However, the biased aspect of Canada's regime against the Aboriginal nations does not, by itself, provide an answer to the question of whether minority rights damage common citizenship and result in a Balkanisation of the state.

My Canadian case study reveals that the Balkanisation of Canada was legislated by the Dominion in order to partition indigenous nations for subjugation. That is, Canada, similar to other states that contain Aboriginal and indigenous nations, had

---

19 The use of this term means that the subject is an attempt to distract attention from the real question or, worse still, is irrelevant. A red herring is an oily Baltic sea fish that, when smoked, assumes. a brownish-red colour and, when used for training purposes by hunters for a fox hunt, has a strong scent capable of leading hounds away from the fox trail. Martin Scheinin, "When Culture Clashes with Individual Rights," European University Institute/Nordic colloquium on Cultural Rights, European University, Florence, Italy, July 2005.

20 *Lubicon Lake Band v. Canada*, Communication No. 167/1984 (26 March 1990), UN Doc. Supp. No. 40 (A/45/40) at 1 (1990).

segregated the Aboriginal peoples in order to colonise their territories. The history of the Canadian-Aboriginal relationship conflicts with the normative claim that the minority regime Balkanises the state. Instead, my case study demonstrates the reverse, namely, that the state was Balkanised prior to the application of the minority regime. Aboriginals were segregated, colonised, and forcibly relocated onto Aboriginal band reserves, long before the establishment of a minority regime. In fact, the minority regime provided Aboriginal nations with the only effective remedy to permit their re-integration into Canada on terms based upon modern notions of equality, in contrast to those demanded under colonial subjugation.

Other examples of minority group-state relations demonstrate similar patterns. That is, legal regimes that segregated minority groups and thereby Balkanised the state, pre-existed the establishment of the minority regime. The Indian Act controversy I discuss in section 4.2 illustrates how difficult it is for states such as Canada to change a pre-existing discrimination regime. For example, regimes such as the Indian Act are complex and have multiple objectives including the regulation of land claims that exist in perpetuity. These pre-existing regimes are not easily reformed or eliminated.

My case study about discrimination against the Roma peoples' nomadism reveals an identical pattern. Ancient discrimination regimes were implemented by the states of Europe in an effort to contain, expel, or marginalise the Roma peoples. This not only resulted in the segregation of the Roma peoples within European states, but also Balkanised states that worked to contain the Roma. For example, Great Britain's planning laws contain discriminatory provisions for the expulsion of the Roma caravan settlements through to the current day. Furthermore, discriminatory practices by states against the Roma, including torture, extra-judicial execution, pogroms, and other forms of violence, served to segregate the Roma long before the existence of the minority regime. The cases demonstrate that, but for the establishment of human rights and the minority regime, the Roma lack a legal remedy to change their situation.

Discriminatory regimes tend to remain entangled within states establishing patterns of tradition, custom, and social mores that are perpetuated through intergenerational transmission long after the elimination of the regimes' biased provisions. The minority regime does not foster Balkanisation but, instead, offers new terms for group integration into the state based upon respect for human rights. The normative claim that minority protections result in Balkanised, tribal, ghetto-ised, or illiberal parochial groups who have survived centuries of subjugation and persecution, is a mistaken one. Such assumptions merely provide a theoretical foundation for the continuation of regimes that violate human rights, because they undermine the application of minority protections. The minority regime restores national unity and common citizenship by permitting historically segregated groups just terms upon which they can base their re-integration into the civic life of the nation-state.

As an example, the sovereignty claims of indigenous minority groups such as Aboriginals in Canada demonstrate that these groups prefer to maintain national unity, rather than to secede and become independent states. As I discussed in section 4.11, Canada's Aboriginal nations, similar to indigenous minorities in other states, have exercised claims for autonomy within Canada while pursuing their struggles for self-determination. This is illustrated by the Tungavik Federation of Nunavut's land claim agreement finalised in 1991 resulting in a tripartite agreement between Canada, the Government of the Northwest Territories and the Inuits' Tungavik Federation of Nunavut leading to the creation of Canada's *Nunavut territory* and government established on 1 April 1999. It has jurisdictional powers and governance institutions similar to those of the Northwest Territories.[21] Ever-increasing numbers of domestic constitutions now recognise self-government for minority groups, some going so far as to guarantee the right to secession for qualified nations. State constitutions incorporating these new provisions include Fiji, Papua New Guinea, the Philippines, Spain and Ethiopia.[22] Modern states use a range of instruments such as multilateral treaty, bi-lateral agreements, UN Security Council decrees, local legislation, devolution schemes, and home-rule initiatives to provide autonomous arrangements for internal minority groups.

Examples include Great Britain's Westminster Parliament devolution schemes for Wales, Scotland and Northern Ireland; Denmark's Accession Treaty for the Faeroe Islands as well as passage of The Home Rule Act recognising Greenland; Finland's Accession Treaty for the Aland Islands; the Nordic Council of Ministers' initiative on Sami autonomy; the Republic of Moldova's law granting special status to Gagauzia (Gaguaz Yer); the Spanish parliament legislation granting self-government to the northeastern region of Catalonia; Italy and Austria's framework treaty granting autonomy to Trentino-South Tyrol; Panama's grant deeds awarded to the indigenous Shuara's communities' territories; constitutional provisions in Argentina, Bolivia, Brazil, Ecuador, Guatemala, Mexico, Nicaragua, Panama and Peru recognising indigenous peoples; and the Israel-PLO agreement to establish Palestinian Authority autonomy on the West Bank and Gaza Strip *statu nascendi*.[23]

The minority regime also contains Rousseauian obligations from minority groups toward their respective states. Minority regimes, starting with the League of Nations' minority protection treaty system, through to the current UN regime, include requirements for minority group responsibility to the state's territorial unity, national loyalty and solidarity, guarantees against irredentism, and citizenship obligations.

---

[21] Wherrett, Jill. *Aboriginal Self-Government* (Ottawa, Library of Parliament, 1999), 12.

[22] Zelim A. Skurbaty, ed., *Beyond A One-Dimensional State: An Emerging Right to Autonomy?* (Leiden, Martinus Nijhoff Publishers, 2005), 14.

[23] *Ibid.*, 248, 300, 431, 500, 509, 532, 525,535. Meaning that Palestinian autonomy is at the beginning of a process that is leading to statehood.

By itself, the minority regime contains no obstacle to the state's citizenship requirements for language proficiency, military conscription, jury-duty, voting, taxation, civic education, and citizenship training. On this question, it works more as a shield than a sword, in that its objective is to prevent state-building campaigns from engaging in coercive assimilation or other violent practices that target members of minority groups.

6.1b. *Human Rights and the Minority Regime*

The second challenge posed to the minority regime that it provides state authority for the illiberal acts of religious groups is characterised by similar problems. In section 1.3b, I provide legal authority explaining the administration of the UN's minority regime. Protections for minority groups are required to comply with all other human rights. Article 27 (minority rights) of the *ICCPR* incorporates minority protection as an integral component of the Covenant. The basis for the minority regime is found in the *Universal Declaration of Human Rights, 1948*[24] (UDHR), whose articles that prohibit discrimination (Article 2), and guarantee nationality (Article 15), freedom of religion (Article 18), association (Article 20) and, most importantly, the enjoyment of cultural life (Article 27). The UDHR is based upon the idea that such rights are designed to promote the development of friendly relations between nations as well as a protection against regimes based upon tyranny and oppression.

Because the minority regime is incorporated into the UN's human rights' covenant, cultural rights, as with other social, civil, and political aspects of the right, must comply with one another. All rights are capable of similar conflicts, and of being exploited to justify illiberal practices. The political and civil rights to the freedom of speech are frequently used as a defense for all types of activity that conflict with other important protections, as well as with social obligations. These include conflicts between free speech rights with laws prohibiting child pornography, slander and liable, hate speech, as well as yelling "fire" into a crowded theatre. Similarly, cultural rights may be abused by majority and minority groups alike. Majority religious groups in western societies are as capable of illiberal acts as are minority religious groups. Witness the westernised religious practices of male circumcision, so-called serial divorce, and prohibitions against women and married men in the priesthood. Under the minority regime, cultural groups are no more entitled to violate non-derogable human rights than are states.[25]

[24] *Universal Declaration of Human Rights*, 1948, U.N. doc. A/811.

[25] *How to Resolve Conflicts Between Individual and Collective Rights?* By Martin Scheinin, Scheinin, Martin and Toivanen, Reetta ed., *Rethinking Nondiscrimination and Minority Rights* (Turku/Abo, Abo Akademi University Institute for Human Rights and German Institute for Human Rights, 2004). From a paper given at the European University Institute/Nordic Colloquium on Cultural Rights, Florence, Italy, July 2005.

The HRC cases I discuss in section 4.7, that is, *Lovelace v. Canada*[26] and *Kitok v. Sweden*,[27] demonstrated the manner in which the HRC interprets conflicts between cultural rights and other Covenant protections. In both cases, the HRC, acting under authority provided by the minority regime, overturned domestic rules authorising discriminatory practices by indigenous minority groups including marital (Lovelace) and professional (Kitok) restrictions. The HRC decision demonstrates that both minority groups, as much as state authorities, may not engage in arbitrary practices that deprive individuals of their human rights under the Covenant, particularly as they affect the rights of women. The approach interpreted by the HRC in these cases provides a clear boundary for states, as well as minority groups, to manage their affairs in a manner compatible with human rights.

6.1c. *Final Comments*

The minority legal tradition offers a structure for normative speculation and empirical research. Legal scholarship is not primarily concerned with theories of the state, systems of inter and intra governmental relations, nor theoretical concepts upon which international and intra state-group relations are founded. Instead, jurists tend to discuss the legal mechanisms for the implementation of human rights. There is a necessity for both normative as well as empirical scholarship to examine these subjects within a framework that recognises the minority legal tradition. Some scholars are already engaged in such projects.[28] There is no requirement for a gap to exist between legal scholarship and political theory on the subject of multiculturalism.

My aim in this research is to lower the intensity of normative discussions on whether or not the minority regime constitutes group-based versus individual rights, equal by contrast to differential treatment, as well as parochial interests over the national good. The USA's civil rights leader, the late Reverend Martin Luther King, Jr., explained that it is not necessary to change the philosophical foundations of the USA Constitution to pass civil rights legislation. Neither is it necessary to alter the theoretical basis of society to recognise the minority legal tradition. It is enough to understand that the cultural contributions of human groups are a valuable aspect of our existence; further,

---

[26] *Lovelace, supra*, note 122, at 95.

[27] *Ivan Kitok v. Sweden*, Communications No. 197/1985, CCPR/C/33/D/197/1985 (1988).

[28] *See* Shachar, Ayelet. *Multicultural Jurisdictions, Cultural Differences and Women's Rights* (Cambridge, Cambridge University Press, 2001), 2, 5, 10, 12–13, 15, 133, 151–160. On p. 133, Shachar describes the *Malaysian Islamic Family Act*, 1984. The law adopts the Islamic doctrine of *harta sepencarian* which guarantees women receive equal or one-half distribution of assets in court-awarded divorce decrees. Also, on p. 160, *The German Basic Law* mandates religious education in public schools while challenging illiberal policies of religious leaders as a condition for public access.

that this is a value worth protecting. The minority regime provides necessary instruments for minority groups to achieve simple justice. The Reverend Martin Luther King Jr. said that to resolve conflicts in racial relations, "peace is not merely the absence of tension, but it is the presence of justice."[29] The world's sovereign states are brought closer to a vibrant peace when they recognise the just aspirations of minority groups to access and enjoy their culture.

[29] Reverend Martin Luther King Jr., "A Realistic Look At the Question of Progress in the Area of Race Relations", Address at Freedom Rally, St. Louis, Missouri, 10 April 1957.

Bibliography

United Nations Documents

United Nations, Economic and Social Council, Commission on Human Rights, Sub-Commission on the Prevention of Discrimination and the Protection of Minorities, First Session, *Report Submitted to the Commission on Human Rights* (New York, United Nations, 23 March 1948)

United Nations, Economic and Social Council, Commission on Human Rights, Seventh Session, *Study on the Legal Validity of the Undertakings Concerning Minorities, Memorandum by the Secretary-General* (New York, United Nations, 27 March 1951) Doc. No. E/CN.4/367/Add.1

United Nations General Assembly, 35/169. *Question of Palestine* (New York, United Nations, 15 Dec 1980) Doc No. A/RES/35/169 (A-E)

United Nations, Economic and Social Council, Commission on Human Rights, *Study of the Problem of Discrimination Against Indigenous Populations* (New York, United Nations, 1982) Doc. No. E/CN.4/Sub.2/1982/2/Add.1

United Nations General Assembly, Thirty-seventh session, *Question of Palestine, The Situation in the Middle East, Report of the Special Committee to Investigate Israeli Practices affecting the Human Rights of the Population of the Occupied Territories* (New York, United Nations, 12 October 1982)

United Nations, Economic and Social Council, Commission on Human Rights, *Study of the Problem of Discrimination Against Indigenous Populations* (New York, United Nations, 14 July 1983) Doc. No. E/CN.4/Sub.2/1983/21/Add.4

United Nations, *Initial reports of States parties due in 1977, Addendum, Canada* (New York, United Nations, 15 Sept 1983) Doc. No. CCPR/C/1/Add.62

United Nations, Economic and Social Council, Commission on Human Rights, Forty-third Session, *Compilation of proposals concerning the definition of the term "minority"* (New York, United Nations, 14 Nov 1986) Doc. No. E/CN.4/1987/WG.5/WP.1

United Nations, Human Rights Committee, *Second periodic reports of States parties due in 1988, Addendum, Canada* (New York, United Nations, 3 Nov 1989) Doc. No. CCPR/C/51/Add.1

United Nations, Centre for Human Rights, *Elimination of all forms of intolerance and discrimination based on religion or belief* by Elizabeth Odio Benito (New York, United Nations, 1989)

United Nations, Human Rights Committee, *Third periodic reports of States parties due in 1990, Addendum, Canada* (New York, United Nations, 4 Sept. 1990) Doc. No. CCPR/C/64/Add.1

United Nations, Centre for Human Rights, *Study on the Rights of Persons belonging to Ethnic, Religious and Linguistic Minorities by Francesco Capotorti* (Geneva, United Nations, 1991)

United Nations, Centre for Human Rights, *Status of the Individual and Contemporary International Law: Promotion, Protection and Restoration of Human Rights at National, Regional and International Levels* by Erica-Irene A. Daes (Geneva, United Nations, 1992)

United Nations, Economic and Social Council, Commission on Human Rights, Protection of Minorities, *Possible ways and means of facilitating the peaceful and constructive solution of problems involving minorities, Final report submitted by Mr. Asbjorn Eide* (Geneva, United Nations, 3 Aug 1993) Doc. No. E/CN.4/Sub. 2/1993/34/Add. 3

United Nations, *International Human Rights Instruments* (New York, United Nations, 12 May 2004) Doc. No. HRI/GEN/1/Rev.7

United Nations, Human Rights Committee, *Core document forming part of the reports of States Parties: United States of America.* 17/08/94 (Geneva, United Nations, 17 Aug 1994) Doc. No. HRI/CORE/1/Add.49

United Nations, Human Rights Committee, *Initial reports of States parties due in 1993: United States of America. 24/08/94* (Geneva, United Nations, 24 Aug 1994) Doc. No. CCPR/C/81/Add.4

United Nations, Human Rights Committee, *Summary record of the 1401st meeting: United States of America. 17/04/95* (New York, United Nations, 17 April 1995) Doc. No. CCPR/C/Sr.1401

United Nations, Economic and Social Council, Commission on Human Rights, *Second interim report on human rights and extreme poverty prepared by the Special Rapporteur, Mr. Leandro Despouy* (New York, United Nations, 5 July 1995) Doc. No. E/CN.4/Sub.2/1995/15

United Nations, Human Rights Committee, *Concluding Observations of the Human Rights Committee: United States of America. 03/10/95* (New York, United Nations, 3 October 1995) Doc. No. CCPR/C/79/Add.50; A/50/40, paras. 266–304

United Nations, Human Rights Committee, *Summary record of the 1405th meeting: United States of America 24/04/95* (New York, United Nations, 24 April 1995) Doc. No. CCPR/C/SR.1405

United Nations, Economic and Social Council, Commission on Human Rights, *Extrajudicial, summary or arbitrary executions, Report by the Special Rapporteur, Mr. Bacre Waly Ndiaye, submitted pursuant to Economic and Social Council, Commission on Human Rights resolution 1995/73* (New York, United Nations, 25 Jan 1996) Doc. No. E/CN/1996/4

United Nations, Committee On The Elimination of Racial Discrimination, *Fourteenth periodic report of States parties due in 1996, Addendum, Republic of Bulgaria* (New York, United Nations, 5 Aug 1996) Doc. No. CERD/C/299/Add.7

United Nations, Economic and Social Council, Commission on Human Rights, *Extrajudicial, summary or arbitrary executions* (New York, United Nations, 24 Dec 1996) Doc. No. E/CN.4/ 1997/60

United Nations, Economic and Social Council, Commission on Human Rights, Fifty-third Session, *Rights of Persons Belonging to National or Ethnic, Religious and Linguistic Minorities, Report of the Secretary-General* (New York, United Nations, 8 Jan 1997) Doc. No. E/CN.4/1997/82

United Nations, Committee on the Elimination of Racial Discrimination, Fiftieth Session, *Concluding observations of the Committee on the Elimination of Racial Discrimination, Bulgaria* (New York, United Nations, 23 April 1997) Doc. No CERD/C/304/Add. 29

United Nations, Human Rights Committee, *Fourth periodic reports of States parties due in 1995, Addendum, Canada* (New York, United Nations, 15 Oct 1997) Doc. No. CCPR/C/103/ Add.5)

United Nations, Economic and Social Council, Commission on Human Rights, Fifty-fourth Session, *Question of the Realization in all Countries of the Economic, Social and Cultural Rights Contained in the Universal Declaration of Human Rights and in the International Covenant on Economic, Social and Cultural Rights and Study of Special Problems Which the Developing Countries Face in Their Efforts to Achieve These Human Rights* (New York, United Nations, 22 Dec 1997) Doc. No. E/CN.4/1998/25

United Nations, *Core document forming part of the reports of States Parties: Canada. 12/01/98* (New York, United Nations,12 Jan 1998) Doc. No. HRI/CORE/1/Add.91

United Nations, Economic and Social Council, Commission on Human Rights, Fifty-fourth Session, *Racism, Racial Discrimination, Xenophobia and Related Intolerance* (New York, United Nations, 1 April 1998) Doc. No. E/CN.4/1998/NGO/98

United Nations, Economic and Social Council, Committee on Economic, Social and Cultural Rights, *Concluding observations of the Committee on Economic, Social and Cultural Rights: Canada. 10/12/98* (New York, United Nations, 10 Dec 1998) Doc. No. E/C.12/1/Add.31

United Nations, Human Rights Committee, *Summary Record of the 1738th Meeting* (New York, United Nations, 7 March 1999) Doc. No. CCPR/C/SR. 1738

United Nations, Human Rights Committee, Sixty-fifth Session, *Concluding observations of the Human Rights Committee: Canada. 07/04/99* (New York, United Nations, 7 April 1999) Doc. No. CCPR/C/79/Add.105

United Nations, Economic and Social Council, Commission on Human Rights, *Written statement submitted by North-South XXI, a non-governmental organisation in special consultative status* (New York, United Nations, 28 June 1999) Doc. No. E/CN.4/Sub.2/1999/NGO/11

United Nations, Economic and Social Council, Commission on Human Rights, *The concept and practice of affirmative action* (New York, United Nations, 19 June 2000) Doc. No. E/CN.4/ Sub.2/2000/11

United Nations, Economic and Social Council, Commission on Human Rights, Sub-Commission on the Promotion and Protection of Human Rights, Fifty-second Session, *Working paper on the relationship and distinction between the rights of persons belonging to minorities and those of indigenous peoples by Ms. Erika-Irene Daes and Mr. Asbjorn Eide* (New York, United Nations, 12 July 2000) E/CN.4/Sub.2/2000/10

United Nations, Economic and Social Council, Commission on Human Rights, *Comprehensive Examination of Thematic Issues Relating to Racial Discrimination* (New York, United Nations, 19 June 2000) Doc. No. E/CN.4/Sub.2/S000/11

United Nations, Economic and Social Council, Commission on Human Rights, *The human rights problems and protections of the Roma* (New York, United Nations, 23 June 2000) Doc. No. E/CN.4/ Sub.2/2000/28

United Nations, Economic and Social Council, Commission on Human Rights, *Commentary by Asbjorn Eide, Chairperson of the Working Group on Minorities* (New York, United Nations, 2001) Doc. No. E/CN.4/Sub.2/AC.5/2001/2

United Nations, Commission for Human Rights, Harvard WorldMUN, Belo Horizonte 2002, *Themes and Developments in the Discourse on Human Rights* (New York, United Nations, 2002)

United Nations, Commission of the High Commissioner for Human Rights, *Special Procedures of the Economic and Social Council, Commission on Human Rights* (New York, United Nations 03/10/2003)

United Nations, *Annotation to the Provisional Agenda, A Note by the Secretary-General* (New York, United Nations, 25 March 2003) Doc. No. E/CN.4/Sub.2/A.C.5/2003/1/Add.1

United Nations, Economic and Social Council, Commission on Human Rights, Ninth Session, *Regional Seminar on Minority Rights: Cultural Diversity and Development in Southeast Asia* (New York, United Nations, 5 May 2003) Doc. No. E/CN.4/Sub2/AC.5/2003/WP.14

United Nations, Economic and Social Council, Commission on Human Rights, Ninth Session, *The Rom in the Americas* (New York, United Nations, 5 May 2003) Doc. No. E/CN.4/Sub.2/ AC.5/2003/WP.17

United Nations, Economic and Social Council, Commission on Human Rights, Fifty-fifth Session, *Annotations to the Provisional Agenda* (New York, United Nations, 25 March 2003) Doc. No. E/CN.4/Sub.2/AC.5/2003/1/Add.1

United Nations, Economic and Social Council, Commission on Human Rights, Ninth Session of the Working Group on Minorities, *Conclusions and Recommendations of the Sub-Regional Seminar on Minority Rights: Cultural Diversity and Development in South-East Asia* (New York, United Nations, 25 April 2003) Doc. No. E/CN.4/Sub.2/AC.5/2003/2

United Nations, Economic and Social Council, Commission on Human Rights, Fifty-fifth Session, *Possible New United Nations Mechanisms for the Protection and Promotion of the Rights of Minorities* (New York, United Nations, 5 May 2003) Doc. No. E/CN.4/Sub.2/AC.5/2003/WP.3

United Nations, Economic and Social Council, *Human Rights* (Geneva, United Nations, 25 June 2002) Doc. No. E/2003/73

United Nations, Office of the High Commissioner for Human Rights, *Regional Workshop for the Adoption and Implementation of Affirmative-Action Policies for People of African Descent in Latin America and the Caribbean* (Geneva, United Nations, 9 May 2003)

United Nations, Office of the High Commission for Human Rights, *Minorities* (Geneva, United Nations, 2003)

United Nations, General Assembly, Fifty-eighth Session, *Effective promotion of the Declaration on the Rights of Minorities, Report of the Secretary-General* (New York, United Nations, 7 Aug 2003) Doc. No. A/58/255

United Nations, Office of the high Commissioner for Human Rights, *Fact Sheet No. 18 (Rev.1), Minority Rights* (Geneva, United Nations, 16/10/2003)

United Nations, General Assembly, *Status of the International Covenant on Economic, Social and Cultural Rights, the ICCPRand the Optional Protocols to the International Covenant on Civil and Political Rights, Report of the Secretary-General* (New York, United Nations, 22 Aug 2003) UN Doc. No. A/58/307

United Nations General Assembly, Official Records, Fifty-eighth Session, Office of High Commissioner for Human Rights, *Report of the United Nations High Commissioner for Human Rights* (New York, United Nations, 2003)

United Nations, Economic and Social Council, Fifty-fifth Session, *Annotations to the Provisional Agenda* (New York, United Nations, 25 March 2003) Doc. No. E/CN.4/Sub.2/AC.5/2003/1/Add.1

United Nations, Economic and Social Council, Commission on Human Rights, Working Group on Minorities, *Possible New United Nations Mechanisms for the Protection and Promotion of the Rights of Minorities* (New York, United Nations, 16 May 2003)

United Nations, General Assembly, Fifty-eighth Session, *The fight against racism, racial discrimination, xenophobia, and related intolerance and the comprehensive implementation of and follow up to the Durban Declaration and Programme of Action* (New York, United Nations, 22 Aug 2003) Doc. No. A/58/313

United Nations, *Compilation of General Comments and General Recommendations Adopted by Human Rights Treaty Bodies* (New York, United Nations, 2004) Doc. No. HRI/GEN/1/Rev.7

United Nations, Economic and Social Council, Commission on Human Rights, Sixtieth Session, *Question of the Violation of Human Rights in the Occupied Territories, Including Palestine* (New York, United Nations, 8 Sept 2003) Doc. No. E/CN.4/2004/6

United Nations, Economic and Social Council, Commission on Human Rights, Sixtieth Session, *Specific Groups and Individuals: Minorities, Report of the High Commissioner* (New York, United Nations, 24 Feb 2004) Doc. No.E/CN.4/2004/75

United Nations, *Compilation of General Comments and General Recommendations Adopted by Human Rights Treaty Bodies* (Geneva, United Nations, 12 May 2004) Doc. No. HRI/GEN/1/Rev.7

United Nations, Human Rights Committee, *Consideration of Reports Submitted by States Parties Under Article 40 of the Covenant, Fifth Periodic report, Canada* (New York, United Nations, 18 Nov 2004) Doc. No. CCPR/C/CAN/2004/5

United Nations, Office of the United Nations High Commissioner for Human Rights, *Selected Decisions of the Human Rights Committee under the Optional Protocol*, vol.5 (Geneva, United Nations, 2005) Doc. No. CCPR/C/OP/5

United Nations, Economic and Social Council, *General Comment N. 16 (2005), Article 3: the equal right of men and women to the enjoyment of all economic, social and cultural rights* (Geneva, United Nations, 13 May 2005) Doc. No. E/C.12/2005/3

United Nations, Committee on the Rights of the Child – Thirty-ninth Session, General Comment No.6 (2005), *Treatment of unaccompanied and separated children outside their country of origin* (Geneva, United Nations, 3 June 2005) Doc. No. CRC/GC/2005/6

United Nations General Assembly Resolutions

United Nations, General Assembly-Fifteenth Session, General Assembly Resolution 1514, *Declaration on the granting of independence to colonial countries and peoples* (New York, United Nations, 14 Oct 1960)

United Nations, Office of the High Commission for Human Rights, *General Assembly Resolution 2106 of 21 Dec 1965* (New York, United Nations, 21 Dec 1965)

United Nations, General Assembly-Twenty Fifth Session, General Assembly Resolution 2621, *Programme of action for the full implementation of the Declaration on the Granting of Independence to Colonial Peoples* (New York, United Nations, 12 Oct 1970)

United Nations, General Assembly-Twenty Fifth Session, General Assembly Resolution 2625, *Declaration on Principles of International Law concerning Friendly Relations and Co-operation among States in accordance with the Charter of the United Nations* (New York, United Nations, 24 Oct 1970)

United Nations, General Assembly- Twenty Fifth Session, General Assembly Resolution 2708, *Implementation of the Declaration on the Granting of Independence to Colonial Countries and Peoples* (New York, United Nations, 14 Dec 1970)

United Nations, General Assembly- Twenty Fifth Session, General Assembly Resolution 2734, *the Declaration on Strengthening of International Security* (New York, United Nations, 16 Dec 1970)

United Nations, Office of the High Commission for Human Rights, *General Assembly Resolution 2106 of 30 Nov 1973* (New York, United Nations, 30 Nov 1973)

United Nations General Assembly Declarations

United Nations, General Assembly, *Universal Declaration of Human Rights, 1948* (New York, United Nations, 16 Dec 1948) Doc. No. A/811

United Nations, General Assembly, *Declaration on the Granting of Independence to Colonial Countries, and Peoples*, GA Res. 1514, UN GAOR, fifteenth Session, Supp. No. 16, p. 67, Doc. No. A/L.323 and Add. 1–6 (1960)

United Nations, General Assembly, *Convention against Discrimination in Education* (Geneva, United Nations, 14 Dec 1960)

United Nations, *UNESCO Declaration of the Principles of International Cultural Co-operation (1966)*

United Nations, *General Assembly, Declaration on Principles of International Law Concerning Friendly Relations and Co-operation among States in Accordance with the Charter of the United Nations*, 24 Cot 1970, UNGA Res. 2625 (XXV), UN GAOP, twenty-fifth Session, Supp. No. 28

United Nations, General Assembly, *Declaration on Race and Racial Prejudice* (Geneva, United Nations, 27 Nov 1978)

United Nations, *UNESCO Declaration on Race and Racial Prejudice, 1978*

United Nations, General Assembly, *Declaration on the Elimination of all Forms of Intolerance and of Discrimination Based on Religion of Belief, 1981* (New York, United Nations, 25 Nov 1981)Doc. No. A/36/684

United Nations, General Assembly, *Declaration on the Rights of Minorities, 1992* (New York, United Nations, 18 Dec 1992) Doc. No. A/Res/47/135

United Nations, General Assembly, *Draft Declaration on the Rights of Indigenous Peoples* (New York, United Nations, 1994) Doc. No. E/CN.4/Sub

United Nations, *UNESCO Declaration on Cultural Diversity (2001)*

United Nations Publications

United Nations, *The Right to Self-Determination, Historical and Current Development on the Basis of United Nations Instruments* by Aureliu Cristescu (New York, United Nations, 1981) Doc. No. E/CN.4/Sub.2/404/Rev.1

United Nations, Dept. of Public Information, *UN Briefing Papers, Human Rights Today, A United Nations Priority* (New York, United Nations, 1998)

United Nations, Secretariat of the Working Group on Minorities, *Pamphlet No 1–4 of the UN Guide for Minorities* (Geneva, United Nations, undated)

Council of Europe

Parliamentary Assembly, "Recommendation 1557 (2002), The legal situation of Roma in Europe" (Strasbourg, Council of Europe, 2002)

Parliamentary Assembly, "Legal situation of the Roma in Europe, Doc 9397 revised" (Strasbourg, Council of Europe, 19 April 2002)

Organisation for Security and Co-operation in Europe

Max van der Stoel, "Report on the situation of Roma and Sinti in the OSCE Area" (The Hague, Netherlands, Organisation for Security and Co-operation in Europe, High Commissioner on National Minorities, 10 March 2000)

Office for Democratic Institutions and Human Rights (ODIHR), "OSCE Supplementary Human Dimension Meeting on Roma and Sinti Report" (Washington D.C., The International Bank for Reconstruction and Development, The World Bank, 11 April 2003)

Organisation for Security and Cooperation in Europe, 497th Plenary Meeting, "Decision No. 566, Action Plan on Improving the Situation of Roma and Sinti Within the OSCE Area" (The Hague, Neatherlands, Organisation for Security and Co-operation in Europe, 27 Nov 2003)

Jurisprudence

Permanent Court of International Justice (PCIJ)

Statute of the Permanent Court of International Justice, 19 Dec 1920 6 LNTS 309

Question of the Greco-Bulgarian Communities (Advisory Opinion), 31 July 1930, PCIJ Rep Series E No 7

Minority Schools in Albania (Advisory Opinion), 6 April 1935, PCIJ Rep Series E No 11

Effects of the Advisory Opinion of 6 April 1935, Minority Schools in Albania, PCIJ Rep Series E No 12

Consistency of Certain Danzig Legislative Decrees with the Constitution of the Free City (Advisory Opinion), 4 Dec 1935 PCIJ Rep Series E No 12

International Court of Justice (ICJ)

Western Sahara (Advisory Opinion), 16 Oct 1975 <http:www.icj-cij.org/icjwww/idecisions/isummaries/isasummary751016.htm> accessed 08/08/2005

South West Africa Cases, 1966 ICJ Rep. 6

International Criminal Tribunal for the Former Yugoslavia

Prosecutor v. Dusko Tadic (Decision on Motion for Review) IT-94-1-R (30 July 2002)

United Nations Human Rights Committee (UNHRC)

Lovelace v. Canada, Communication No. R.6/24, UN Doc. Supp. No. 40 (a/36/40) at 166 (1981)

L.S.N. v. Canada, Communication No. 94/1981

Ivan Kitok v. Sweden, Communication No. 197/1985, CCPR/C/33/D/197/1985 (1988)

Dominique Guesdon v. France, Communication No. 219/1986, Doc. No. CCPR/C/39/D/219/1986 (1990)

T.K. v. France, Communication No. 220/1987, CCPR/C/37/D/220/1987

M.K. v. France, Communication No. 222/1987, CCPR/C/37/D/222/1987

Ballantyne, Davidson and McIntyre v. Canada, Communications Nos. 359/1989 and 385/1989, 31 March 1993, CCPR/C/47/D/359/1989 and 385/1989/Rev.1

Lubicon Lake Band v. Canada, Communication No. 167/1984 (26 March 1990) UN Doc. Supp. No. 40 (A/45/40) at 1 (1990)

Sara et al. v. Finland, Communication No.431/1990, UN Doc. CCPR/C/50/D/431/1990 (1994)

Lansman et al. v. Finland, Communication No. 511/1992, 26 October 1994, UN Doc. CCPR/C/52/D511/1992

Mahuika et al. v. New Zealand, Communication No. 547/1993, 27 Oct 2000, CCPR/C/70/D/547/1993

Lansman et al. v. Finland, Communication No. 671/1995, 30 October 1996, UN Doc. CCPR/C/58D/671/1995

Diergaardt et al. v. Namibia, Communication No. 760/1997, 25 July 2000, CCPR/C/69/D/760/1996

Aarela and Nakkalajarvi v. Finland, Communication No. 779/1997, 24 October 2001, CCPR/C/73/D/779/1997

Lansman et al. v. Finland, Communication No. 1023/2001, 17 March 2005, CPPR/C/83/D/1023/2001

European Court of Human Rights

Belgian Linguistics Case, 1 EHRR 252 (1968)

Abdulaziz, Cabales and Balkandali v. United Kingdom (App nos 9214/80, 9473/81) 7 EHRR 471 (1985)

In the Case of Billi v. Italy (App no 13/1992/358/432) ECHR 2 Feb 1993

In the Case of Buckley v. the United Kingdom (App no 23/1995/529/615) ECHR 26 Aug 1996

Case of Asenov and Others v. Bulgaria (App no 90/1997/874/1086) ECHR 28 Oct 1998

Case of Velikova v. Bulgaria (App no 41488/98) ECHR 18 May 2000

Thlimmenos v. Greece (App no 34369/97) ECHR 06/04/2000

Case of Mattoccia v. Italy (App no 23969/94) 25 July 2000

Case of Varey v. the United Kingdom (App no 26662/95) ECHR 21 Dec 2000

Case of Beard v. the United Kingdom (App no 24882/94) ECHR 18 Jan 2001

Case of Chapman v. the United Kingdom (App no 27238/95) ECHR 18 Jan 2001

Case of Coster v. the United Kingdom (App no 24876/94) ECHR 18 Jan 2001

Case of Jane Smith v. the United Kingdom (App no 25154/94) ECHR 18 Jan 2001

Case of Lee v. the United Kingdom (App no 25289/94) ECHR 18 Jan 2001

Case of Conka v. Belgium (App no 51564/99) ECHR 5 Feb 2002

Case of Anguelova v. Bulgaria (App no 38361/97) ECHR 13 June 2002
Slivenko v. Latvia (App no 48321/99) ECHR 09/10/2003
Chamber Judgement in the Case of Hirst v. The United Kingdom (No.2) (App no 74025/01) ECHR 30/03/2004
Case of Balogh v. Hungary (App no 47940/99) ECHR 20 July 2004
Case of Sidjimov v. Bulgaria (App no 55057/00) ECHR 27/04/2005
Case of Molnar v. Hungary (App no 22592/02) ECHR 05/01/2005
Case of Nachova and Others v. Bulgaria (App no 43577/98 and 43579/98) 26 Feb 2004, 6 July 2005
Case of Moldovan and Others v. Romania (App nos 41138/98 and 64320/01) ECHR 12 July 2005
Case of Bekos and Koutropoulos v. Greece (App no 15250/02) ECHR 13 Dec 2005

Canada

The Royal Proclamation of 7 October 1763, by the King. George R.
St. Catherines Milling & Lumber Co. v. The Queen (1888) 14 Cas. 46 (J.C.P.C.)
Attorney-General of Canada v. Lavell [1974] S.C.R. 1349
Nowegijick v. The Queen et al. [1983] C.T.C. 20
Guerin v. The Queen [1984] 2 S.C.R. 335
James Matthew Simon v. Her Majesty The Queen [1985] 2 S.C.R. 387
Andrews v. Law Society of British Columbia [1989] 1 S.C.R. 143
Ronald Edward Sparrow v. Her Majesty the Queen [1990] 1 S.C.R. 1075
Bert Horseman v. Her Majesty the Queen [1990] 1 S.C.R. 901
Dorothy Marie Van der Peet v. Her Majesty the Queen [1996] 2 S.C.R. 507
Degamuukw v. British Columbia [1997] 3 S.C.R. 1010
Reference re Secession of Quebec [1998] 2 S.C.R. 217
Law v.Canada [1999] 1 SCR 497
Corbiere v. Canada (Minister of Indian and Northern Affairs) [1999] 2 S.C.R. 203
Sawbridge Band v. Canada [2002] 2 F.C. 346

Royal Commission

Canada, Department of Indian and Northern Affairs, Royal Commission on Aboriginal Peoples, Report of the Royal Commission on Aboriginal Peoples, vol.1–5, Dussault, Rene; Erasmus, Georges, Co-Chairs; Chartrand, Paul L.A.H.; Meekison, J. Peter; Robinson, Viola; Sillett, Mary; and Wilson, Bertha, Commissioners (Ottawa, Canada, 1996)
Canada, Department of Indian and Northern Affairs, Royal Commission on Aboriginal Peoples, Aboriginal Self-Government Legal and Constitutional Issues by Patrick Macklem et al. (Ottawa, Canada Communication Group-Publishing, 1995)

USA

Johnson and Graham's v. William M'Intosh, 21 U.S. 543 (1832)
The Cherokee Nation v. The State of Georgia, 30 U.S. 1 (1831)
Samuel A. Worcester v. The State of Georgia, 31 U.S. 515 (1832)
Korematsu v. United States, 323 U.S. 214 (1944)
Dennis v. U.S. 339 U.S. 162 (1950)
Brown v. Board of Education, 347 U.S. 483 (1954)

Sherbert v. Verner et al., Members of South Carolina Employment Security Commission, et al. 374 U.S. 398
Griggs v. Duke Power Co., 401 U.S. 229 (1970)
Palmer v. Thompson, 403 U.S. 217 (1971)
Furman v. Georgia, 408 U.S. 238 (1972)
Gregg v. Georgia, 428 U.S. 153 (1976)
Washington v. Davis, 426 U.S. 229 (1976)
Lockett v. Ohio, 438 U.S. 586 (1978)
Santa Clara Pueblo v. Julia Marinez 436 U.S. 49 (1978)
Regents of the University of California v. Bakke, 438 U.S. 265 (1978)
Adarand Constructors, Inc. v. Pena, 515 U.S. 200 (1995)
U.S. v. Virginia 518 US 515 (1996)
Gratz v. Bollinger et al., 123 S. Ct. 2411, 2325 (2003)

Australia

Gerhardy v. Brown (1985) 57 ALR 472

India

Balaji v. State of Mysore, 439 AIR 1965 SC 648
State of Kerala v. N.M. Thomas, AIR 1976 S.C. 493
Indra Sawhney v. Union of India, AIR 1993 SC 477
Indra Sawhney v. Union of India, AIR 2000 SC 498

Books

Acton, John Emerich Edward Dalberg. *The History of Freedom and Other Essays, ed. John Neville Figgis* (New York, Books for Libraries Press, 1907)
Acton, Thomas ed., *Gypsy Politics and Traveller Identity* (Hertfordshire, University of Hertfordshire Press, 1991)
Aiko, Pekka *et al.* eds., *Operationalising the Right of Indigenous People to Self-Determination* (Saarijarvo, Gummerus Printing, 2000)
Akermark, Spiliopoulou Athanasia. *Justifications of Minority Protection In International Law* (The Hague, Kluwer Law International, 1997)
Akzin, Benjamin. *State and Nation* (London, Hutchinson University Library, 1964)
Alfredson, Gudmundur *et al. Minority Rights: A Guide to United Nations Procedures and Institutions* (Sweden, Minority Rights Group and Raoul Wallenberg Institute of Human Rights, 1998)
Anaya, S. James. *Indigenous Peoples In International Law*, Second Edition (Oxford, OUP, 2000)
Anderson, Benedict. *Imagined Communities, Reflections on the Origin and Spread of Nationalism* (London, Verso, 1983)
Anderson, Carol. *Eyes Off the Prize, The United Nations and the African-American Struggle for Human Rights*, 1944–1955 (Cambridge, CUP, 2003)
Azcarate, P. De. *The League of Nations and National Minorities, An Experiment*, Trans. Eileen E. Brooke (Washington D.C., Carnegie Endowment for Peace, 1945)
Bailey, Thomas A. *Woodrow Wilson and the Lost Peace* (Chicago, Quadrangle Paperbacks, 1944)

Barros, James. *The League of Nations and the Great Powers, the Greek-Bulgarian Incident, 1925* (Oxford, Clarendon Press, 1970)
Barry, Brian. *Culture and Equality* (Oxford, Blackwell Publishers Ltd., 2002)
Batstone, David. *From Conquest to Struggle, Jesus of Nazareth In Latin America* (Albany, State University of New York Press, 1991)
Bellman, Harold. *Architects of the New Age, Bright, Kossuth, Lincoln, Mazzini & Tolstoy* (London, Sampson Low, Marston & Co., Ltd., 1929)
Benhabib, Seyla. *Situating the Self, Gender, Community, and Postmodernism in Contemporary Ethics* (Oxford, Blackwell Publishers, 1992)
Berdahl, Clarence A. *The United States and The League of Nations* (Geneva, Librairiekendig, 1932)
Berlin, Isaiah. *Four Essays On Liberty* (London, OUP, 1969)
Bodin, Jean. *On Sovereignty* (Cambridge, CUP, 1992)
Boot, Michteld. *Genocide, Crimes Against Humanity, War Crimes: Nullum Crimen Sine Lege and the Subject Matter Jurisdiction of the International Criminal Court* (Antwerpen, Intersentia, 2002)
Borrows, John. *Recovering Canada, The Resurgence of Indigenous Law* (Toronto, University of Toronto, 2002)
Bossuyt, Marc J. *Guide to the "Travaux Preparatorires" of the ICCPR*(Dordrecht, Martinus Nijhoff Publishers, 1987)
Bourchier, J.D. *The Bulgarian Peace Treaty, Speeches Delivered in the British Parliament* (London, Christophers, 1922)
Brookes, Edgar H. *What is Wrong With The League of Nations, A Constructive Criticism of The League of Nations in Working, With Certain Practical Suggestions* (London, Leonard & Virginia Woolf At The Hogarth Press, 1928)
Brownlie, Ian and Goodwin-Gill, Guy S. eds., *Basic Documents on Human Rights*, Fourth Edition (Oxford, OUP, 2002)
Brierly, J.L. *The Covenant and The Charter* (Cambridge, CUP, 1947)
Burleigh, Michael. *The Third Reich, A New History* (Oxford, Pan Books, 2000)
Burleigh, Michael *et al. The Racial State, Germany 1933–1945* (Cambridge, CUP, 1991)
Bumstead, J.M. *The Peoples of Canada, A Post-Confederation History*, Second Edition (Oxford, OUP, 2004)
Buzan, Barry. *People, States, and Fear* (Sussex, Wheatsheaf Books Ltd., 1983)
Campbell, Scott Duncan. *The Administration of Indian Affairs in Canada* (Hangchow, The Canadian Institute of International Affairs, 1931)
Canovan, Margaret. *Nationalism and Political Theory* (Cheltenham, Edward Elgar, 1996)
Cardinal, Harold. *The Unjust Society, The Tragedy of Canada's Indians* (Edmonton, M.G. Hurtig Ltd., 1969)
Carens, Joseph H. *Culture, Citizenship, and Community, A Contextual Exploration of Justice as Evenhandedness* (Oxford, OUP, 20000)
Carr, Edward Hallett. *Nationalism and After* (London, MacMillian & Co. Ltd., 1945)
Castles, Stephen *et al. Citizenship and Migration, Globalization and Politics of Belonging* (London, MacMillan Press Ltd., 2000)
Cavanagh, Matt. *Against Equality of Opportunity* (Oxford, OUP, 2002)
Centre for the Study of Public Policy (VCIOM). *Russians in the Baltics: a 1991 Survey* (Glasgow, University of Strathclyde, 1997)
Chadwick, H Munro. *The Nationalities of Europe and The Growth of National Ideologies* (Cambridge, CUP, 1945)
Cicero, Marcus Tillius. *De Legibus* (I, 15)
Claude, Inis L. *National Minorities An International Problem* (Cambridge, Harvard University Press, 1955)

Clebert, Jean-Paul. *The Gypsies*, Trans. Charles Duff (London, Vista Books, 1963)
Clements, Kendrick A. *et al. Woodrow Wilson, American Presidents Series* (Washington D.C., CQ Press, 2003)
Clogg, Richard ed., *The Greek Diaspora in the Twentieth Century* (New York, St. Martins Press, Inc., 1999)
Cole, Douglas and Ira Chaikin. *An Iron Hand Upon The People, The Law Against the Potlatch on the Northwest Coast* (Seattle, University of Washington Press, 1990)
Dardian, Vahakn N. *The History of Armenian Genocide, Ethnic Conflict from the Balkans to Anatoli to Causasus* (Providence, Berghan Books, 1997)
Darwin, Charles. *On the Origin of Species by Means of Natural Selection, or the Preservation of Favoured Races in the Struggle of Life* (London, 1959)
Dawson, Michael C. *Black Visions, The Roots of Contemporary African American Political Ideologies* (2001, The University of Chicago Press, Chicago)
Devans, Neal *et al.*, eds. *Redefining Equality* (Oxford, OUP, 1998)
de Tocqueville, Alexis. *Democracy in America*, Trans Harvey C. Mansfield and Delba Winthrop (Chicago, Chicago University Press, 2000)
DeVattel, Monsieur. *The Law of Nations; or Principles of the Law of Nature Applied to The Conduct and Affairs of Nations and Sovereigns*, ed., Joseph Chitty (London, Law Booksellars & Publishers, 1834)
Dinstein, Yoram *et al.* eds., *International Law at a Time of Perplexity, Essays in Honour of Shabtai Rosenne* (Dordrecht, Martinus Nijhoff Publishers, 1989)
Drago, Edmund L., *Black Politicians and Reconstruction In Georgia, A Splendid Failure* (Georgia, University of Georgia Press, 1992)
Drzewicki, Krzystof. *Human Rights and the Rights of Minorities in the OSCE and the Council of Europe* (Turku, Abo Akedemi, Institute for Human Rights, 2005)
Dudziak, Mary. *Cold War, Civil Rights, Race and the Image of American Democracy* (Princeton, Princeton University Press, 2000)
Dworkin, Ronald. *Sovereign Virtue, The Theory and Practice of Equality* (Cambridge, Harvard University Press, 2000)
Eagleton, Terry. *The Idea of Culture* (Oxford, Blackwell Publishers Ltd., 2000)
Etzioni, Amitai. *The Common Good* (Malden, Polity Press Ltd., 2004)
Etzioni, Amitai ed., *The Communitarian Reader, Beyond the Essentials* (Lanham, Rowman & Littlefield Publishers Inc., 2004)
Fabre, Cecile. *Social Rights Under the Constitution* (Oxford, Clarendon Press, 2000)
Flanagan, Tom. *First Nations? Second Thoughts* (Mortreal & Kingston, McGill-Queen's University Press, 2000)
Fonseca, Isabel. *Bury Me Standing, The Gypsies and Their Journey* (London, Vintage, 1996)
Gellner, Ernest. *Nations and Nationalism* (Oxford, Blackwell Publishers Ltd., 1993)
Ghanea, Nazila *et al.* eds., *Minorities, Peoples and Self-Determination, Essays in Honour of Patrick Thornberry* (Leiden, Martinus Nijhoff Publishers, 2005)
Green, Thomas Hill. *Lectures on the Principles of Political Obligation* (London, Longmans, Green, and Co., 1921)
Green, Thomas Hill. *Lectures on the Principles of Political Obligation*, ed. Dario Bagnoli (Uxbridge, Cambridge Scholars Press, 2002)
Gutman, Amy. *Multiculturalism* (Princeton, University of Princeton Press, 1964)
Hannum, Hurst. *Autonomy, Sovereignty, and Self-Determination, The Accommodation of Conflicting Rights* (Philadelphia, University of Pennsylvania Press, 1990)
Hart, H.L.A. *The Concept of Law*, Second Edition (Oxford, OUP, 1961)
Hechter, Michael. *Containing Nationalism* (New York, OUP, 2000)
Henkin, Louis. *Constitutionalism, Democracy and Foreign Affairs* (New York, Columbia University Press, 1990)

Henkin, Louis ed., *The International Bill of Rights, The Covenant on Civil and Political Rights* (New York, Columbia University Press, 1981)
Henrard, Kristin. *Devising an Adequate System of Minority Protection, Individual Human Rights, Minority Rights and the Right to Self-Determination* (London, Martinus Nijhoff Publishers, 2000)
Heraclides, Alexis. *The Self-Determination of Minorities In International Politics* (UK, Frank Cass & Co. Ltd., 1991)
Hertzberg, Arthur ed. *The Zionist Idea, A Historical Analysis and Reader* (New York, Harper and Row, 1959)
Hill, Robert E. *Marcus Garvey and The Universal Negro Improvement Association Papers*, Vol. II, 27 Aug 1919–1931 (Los Angeles, University of California Press, 1983)
Hinkley, Edyth. *Mazzini, The Story of a Great Italian* (London, George Allen & Unwin Ltd., 1924)
Hinsley, *F.H. Sovereignty*, Second Edition (Cambridge, CUP, 1986
Hirschon, Renee. *Heirs of the Greek Catastrophe, The Social Life of Asia Minor Refugees in Piraeus* (Oxford, OUP, 1989)
Hitler, Adolf. *Mein Kampf*, First Published as *My Struggle* (London, Radius Book/Hutchinson & Co. Ltd., 1936)
Hobbs, Thomas. *Leviathan*, Ed. Richard Tuck (Cambridge, CUP, 1991)
Hobhouse, L.T. *The Elements of Social Justice* (London, Routledge/Thoemmes Press, 1933)
Hobhouse, L.T. *Liberalism* (Oxford, OUP, 1964)
Hobsbawm, E.J. *Nations and Nationalism Since 1780, Programme, Myth, Reality* (Cambridge, CUP, 1900)
Hoover, Herbert. *The Ordeal of Woodrow Wilson* (London, Museum Press Ltd., 1958)
Ishii, Viscount Kikujiro. *Diplomatic Commentaries*, Trans. William R. Langdon (Baltimore, The John Hopkins Press, 1936)
Jawowsky, Oscar. *The Jews and Minority Rights 1898–1919* (New York, Columbia University Press, 1933)
Jawowsky, Oscar *et al. International Aspects of German Racial Policies* (Oxford, OUP, 1937)
Jervis, Alice De Rosen Trans. *Mazzini's Letters* (London, J.M. Dent & Sons Ltd., 1930)
Joseph, Sara, *et al. The International Covenant on Civil and Political Rights, Cases, Materials, and Commentary* (Oxford, OUP, 2000)
Karatnycky, Adrian *et al.*, eds. *Freedom In The World, The Annual Survey of Political Rights & Civil Liberties, 2003* (New York, Freedom House, Rowman & Littlefield Publishers, Inc., 2003)
Kayali, Hasan. *Arabs and Young Turks: The Ottoman Empire 1908–1918* (Berkeley, University of California Press, 1997)
Kedourie, Elie. *Naionalism,* Fourth Expanded Edition (Oxford, Blackwell Publishers Ltd., 1960)
Kelly, Paul ed., *Multiculturalism Reconsidered* (Oxford, Blackwell Publishers Ltd., 2002)
Kendrick, Donald ed., *Gypsies in the Ottoman Empire, A Contribution to the History of the Balkans* Trans Olga Apostolova (Hertfordshire, Centre de recherches tsiganes, University of Hertfordshire Press, 2000)
Kendrick, Donald *et al.*, *The Destiny of Europe's Gypsies* (London, Cox & Wyman Ltd., 1972)
King, Desmond. *Actively Seeking Work, The Politics of Unemployment and Welfare Policy in the United States and Great Britain* (Chicago, The University of Chicago Press, 1995)
King, Desmond. *Making Americans, Immigration, Race, and the Origins of the Diverse Democracy* (Cambridge, Harvard University Press, 2000)
King, Desmond. *The Liberty of Strangers* (Oxford, OUP, 2005)
King, Gary *et al. Designing Social Inquiry, Scientific Inference in Qualitative Research* (New Jersey, Princeton University Press, 1994)

Knock, Thomas J. *To End All Wars, Woodrow Wilson and the Quest for a New World Order* (New Jersey, Princeton University Press, 1995)

Knox, T.M. Trans. *Hegel's Philosophy of Right* (London, OUP, 1952)

Knudsen, Erik Lance. *Great Britain, Constantinople, and the Turkish Peace Treaty 1919–1922* (London, Garland Publishing, Inc., 1987)

Kohn, Hans. *The Age of Nationalism, The First Era of Global History* (New York, Harper & Bros., 1962)

Kohn, Hans. *Nationalism, Its Meaning and History* (Princeton, D. Van Nostrand Company, Inc., 1955)

Kondis, Basil *et al.*, eds. *The Greek Minority In Albania, A Documentary Record (1921–1993)* (Thessaloniki, Institute for Balkan Studies, 1994)

Kukathas, Chandran. *The Liberal Archipelago, A Theory of Diversity and Freedom* (Oxford, OUP, 2003)

Kymlicka, Will. *Multicultural Citizenship* (Oxford, OUP, 1995)

Kymlicka, Will. *Finding Our Way, Rethinking Ethnocultural Relations in Canada* (Ontario, OUP, 1998)

Kymlicka, Will *et al.*, eds., *Can Liberal Pluralism be Exported? Western Political Theory and Ethnic Relations in Eastern Europe* (Oxford, OUP, 2001)

Kymlicka, Will *et al.*, eds., *Citizenship In Culturally Diverse Societies: Issues, Contexts, Concepts* (Oxford, OUP, 2000)

Kymlicka, Will. *Contemporary Political Philosophy: An Introduction*, Second Edition (Oxford, OUP, 2002)

Kymlicka, Will. *Politics In the Vernacular, Nationalism, Multiculturalism and Citizenship* (Oxford, OUP, 2001)

Kymlicka, Will *et al.*, eds., *Language Rights and Political Theory* (Oxford, OUP, 2003)

Kymlicka, Will. *Multicultural Odysseys, Navigating the New International Politics of Diversity* (New York, OUP, 2007)

Ladis, Stephen P. *The Exchange of Minorities Bulgaria, Greece and Turkey* (New York, The MacMillian Company, 1932)

Lansing, Robert. *The Peace Negotiations, A Personal Narrative* (Port Washington, Kennikat Press, 1921)

Laski, Harold J. *Studies In The Problem of Sovereignty* (New Haven, Yale University Press, 1917)

La Torre, Massimo. *Citizenship and Social Rights, A European Perspective* (San Domenico, Italy, European University Institute, 1998)

Lemkin, Raphael. *Axis Rule In Occupied Europe, Laws of Occupation, Analysis of Government, Proposals for Redress* (Washington D.C., Carnegie Endowment for International Peace, Division of International Law, 1944)

Levy, Guenter. *The Nazi Persecution of the Gypsies* (Oxford, OUP, 2000)

Levy, Jacob. *The Multiculturalism of Fear* (Oxford, OUP, 2000)

Liegeois, Jean-Pierre. *Gypsies An Illustrated History* (London, Al Saqi Books, 1986)

Liegeois, Jean-Pierre. *School Provision for Ethnic Minorities: The Gypsy Paradigm* (Hertfordshire, Gypsy Research Centre, University Hertfordshire Press, 1987)

Liegeois, Jean-Pierre. *Roma, Gypsies, Travellers* (Strasbourg, Council of Europe Publishing and Documentation Service, 1994)

Liegeois, Jean-Pierre, *et al. Roma/Gypsies: A European Minority* (London, Minority Rights Group, 1995)

Lippert, Owen ed., *Beyond The Nass Valley, National Implications of The Supreme Court's Delgamuukw Decision* (Vancouver, The Fraser Institute, 2000)

Lodge, Henry Cabot. *The Senate and the League of Nations* (New York, Charles Scribner's Sons, 1925)

Macartney, C.A. *National States and National Minorities* (London, OUP, 1934)
Macklem, Patrick. *Indigenous Difference and the Constitution of Canada* (Toronto, University of Toronto Press, 2001)
Mail, Hugh, ed. *Minority Rights In Europe, The Scope for a Transnational Regime* (London, Royal Institute of International Affairs, 1994)
Mair, L.P. *The Protection of Minorities, the Working and Scope of the Minorities Treaties, Under the League of Nations* (London, Christophers, 1928)
Mandel, Michael. *The Charter of Rights and the Legalisation of Politics in Canada* (Toronto, Thomas Educational Publishers, Inc., 1994)
Marcuse, Herbert. *Reason and Revolution* (London, Routledge, 2000)
Marshall, T.H. *Citizenship and Social Class and Other Essays* (London, CUP, 1950)
Marushiakova, Elena and Popov, Vesselin. *Gypsies in the Ottoman Empire, A Contribution to the history of the Balkans*, Ed. Donald Kenrick, Trans. Olga Apostolova (Hertfordshire, University of Hertfordshire Press, 2001)
Mayall, David. *English Gypsies and State Policies* (Hertfordshire, University of Herfordshire Press, 1995)
McRoberts, Kenneth *et al.*, *The Charlottetown Accord, the Referendum, and the Future of Canada* (Toronto, University of Toronto Press, 1993)
Metcalfe, Eric, "Are Cultural Rights Human Rights? A Cosmopolitan Conception of Cultural Rights," diss. University of Oxford, 2000.
Meron, Theodore. *Human Rights Law Making In the United Nations, A Critique of Instruments and Process* (Oxford, Clarendon Press, 1986)
Mill, John Stuart. *On Liberty and Other Essays* (Oxford, OUP, 1998)
Miller, David. *Citizenship and National Identity* (Malden, Blackwell Publishers Ltd., 2000)
Miller, David. *On Nationality* (New York, OUP, 1995)
Miller, David Hunter. *The Drafting of the Covenant, Vols. 1 & II* (New York, G.P. Putnam's Sons, 1928)
Miller, J.R. *et al.*, *Bounty and Benevolence, A History of Saskatchewan Treaties* (Montreal & Kingston, McGill – Queen's University Press, 2000)
Miller, J.R. *Canada and the Aboriginal Peoples, 1867–1927* (Ottawa, The Canada Historical Association, 1997)
Miller, J.R. *Shingwauk's Vision, A History of Native Residential Schools* (Toronto, University of Toronto Press, 1996)
Miller, J.R. *Skyscapers Hide the Heavens, A History of Indian-White Relations in Canada* (Toronto, University of Toronto Press, 1989)
Miller, J.R. ed., *Sweet Promises, A Reader on Indian-White Relations in Canada* (Toronto, University of Toronto Press, 1991)
Milloy, John S. *A National Crime, The Canadian Government and the Residential School System, 1879–1986* (Winnipeg, The University of Manitoba Press, 1999)
Ministry of Interior, Department of Refugees. *The League of Nations and the Greeks and Armenians in Turkey* (Constantinople, Ministry of Interior, 1921)
Modeen, Tore. *The International Protection of National Minorities in Europe* (Turku, Abo Akademi, 1969)
Moses, Wilson Jeremiah. *The Golden Age of Black Nationalism, 1850–1925* (Connecticut, Archon Books, 1978)
Mulhall, Stephen and Swift, Adam. *Liberals and Communitarians* (Oxford, Blackwell Publishers, 1992)

Musgrove, Thomas D. *Self-Determination and National Minorities* (Oxford, Clarendon Press, 1977)
Nowak, Manfred. *CCPR Commentary, UN Covenant on Civil and Political Rights* (Arlington, N.P. Engel, 1993)
Okely, Judith. *The Traveller-Gypsies* (London, CUP, 1983)
O'Mahony. *Bulgaria and the Powers* (Sofia, St. Patrick's Orphanage, 1925)
Oppenheim, L, ed., *International Law and Diplomacy* (New York, Longmans, Green & Co., 1919)
Orlin, Theodore S. *et al.*, eds., *The Jurisprudence of Human Rights Law: A Comparative Interpretive Approach* (Turku, Institute for Human Rights, Abo Akademi, 2000)
Osiander, Andreas. *The States System of Europe 1640–1990 Peacemaking and Condition International Stability* (Oxford, Clarendon Press, 1994)
Pentassuglia, Gaetano. *Minorities in International Law, An Introductory Study* (London, Council of Europe Publishing, 2002)
Polish Ministry of Information. *The German Fifth Column In Poland.* (London, Hutchinson & Co. Ltd., 1942)
Phillips, Alan and Rosas, Allan eds., *Universal Minority Rights* (Turku, Institute For Human Rights, 1995)
Pilkington, Doris. *Rabbit Proof Fence* (New York, Miramaz Books, Hyperion, 1996)
Pollack, Sir Frederick. *League of Nations* (London, Stevens & Sons, Ltd., 1922)
Power, Samantha. *A Problem From Hell, America and the Age of Genocide* (New York, Basic Books, 2002)
Preece, Jennifer Jackson. *National Minorities and the European Nation-States System* (Oxford, Clarendon Press, 1998)
Putnam, Robert G., ed. *Universal Human Rights* (New York, St. Martin's Press, Inc., 2000)
Radcliffe, Lord of Werneth. *The Problem of Power* (London, Secker & Warburg, 1952)
Ratner, Steven R. *et al.*, *Accountability for Human Rights Atrocities In International Law, Beyond the Nuremberg Legacy* (Oxford, Clarendon Press, 1997)
Raz, Joseph. *Ethnics In The Public Domain, Essays In The Morality of Law and Politics* (Oxford, Clarendon Press, 1995)
Raz, Joseph. *The Morality of Freedom* (Oxford, Clarendon Press, 1986)
Rehfisch, Farnham ed., *Gypsies, Tinkers and other Travellers* (London, Academic Press, 1975)
Robinson, Jacob, *et al. Were the Minorities Treaties a Failure?* (New York, Institute of Jewish Affairs of the American Jewish Congress and World Jewish Congress, 1943)
Robinson, Nehemiah. *The Genocide Convention, Its Origins and Interpretation* (New York City, Institute of Jewish Affairs, World Jewish Congress, 1949)
Rousseau, Jean-Jacques. *The Social Contract and other later political writings*, Trans. Victor Gourevitch (Cambridge, CUP, 1997)
Salzberger, Ronald P. *et al.*, eds. *Reparations for Slavery, A Reader* (Maryland, Rowman & Littlefield Publishers, 2004)
Schabas, William. *Genocide in International Law, the Crime of Crimes* (Cambridge, CUP, 2000)
Scheinin, Martin *et al.*, eds. *Rethinking Non-Discrimination and Minority Rights* (Turku, Abo Akademi, 2004)
Sellars, Kirsten. *The Rise and Rise of Human Rights* (Gloucestershire, Sutton Publishing Limited, 2002)
Shachar, Ayelet. *Multicultural Jurisdictions, Cultural Differences and Women's Rights* (Cambridge, CUP, 2001)
Shaney, Yuval. *The Competing Jurisdictions of International Courts and Tribunals* (Oxford, OUP, 2003)

Shaw, Albert ed. *The Messages and Papers of Woodrow Wilson, Vol. I* (New York, The Review of Reviews Corp., 1924)
Shaw, M.N., *International Law*, Third Edition (Cambridge, CUP, 1994)
Silman, J. ed., *Enough is Enough: Aboriginal Women Speak Out* (Toronto, The Women's Press, 1987)
Simpson, A.W. Brian. *Human Rights and the End of Empire* (Oxford, OUP, 2001)
Skurbaty, Zelim A. ed., *Beyond a One-Dimensional State: An Emerging Right to Autonomy?* (Leiden, Martinus Nijhoff Publishers, 2005)
Smith, Anthony. *National Identity* (Reno, University of Nevada Press, 1991)
Smith, Anthony D.S. *Nationalism In The Twentieth Century* (Oxford, Martin Robertson & Co., 1979)
Smith, Anthony. *Nations and Nationalism In A Global Era* (Cambridge, Polity Press, 1995)
Smith, Jeremy. *The Bolsheviks and the National Question, 1917–1923* (New York, St. Martin's Press, Inc., 1999)
Stallybrass, W.T.S. *A Society of States or Sovereignty, Independence, and Equality in a League of Nations* (London, George Routledge & Sons, Ltd., 1918)
Stead, Alfred. *The Truth About Bulgaria* (London, J. Miles & Co. Ltd., n/d)
Sweet, Alec Stone. *The Judicial Construction of Europe* (Oxford, OUP, 2004)
Stone, Julius. *International Guarantees of Minority Rights, Procedure of the Council of The League of Nations in Theory and Practice* (London, Oxford University Press, 1932)
Stone, Julius. *Regional Guarantees of Minority Rights, A Study of Minorities Procedure in Upper Silesia* (New York, The MacMillan Company, 1933)
Suksi, Mark ed., *Autonomy: Applications and Implications* (The Hague, Kluwer Law International, 1998)
Tamir, Yael. *Liberal Nationalism* (New Jersey, Princeton University Press, 1993)
Taylor, Charles. *Reconciling The Solitudes. Essays on Canadian Federalism and Nationalism.* (Montreal, McGill Queens University Press, 1993)
Thornberry, Patrick. *Indigenous Peoples and Human Rights* (Manchester, Manchester University Press, 2002)
Thornberry, Patrick. *International Law and the Rights of Minorities* (Oxford, Clarendon Press, 1991)
Thornberry, Patrick *et al.*, *Minority Rights In Europe, A Review of the Work and Standards of The Council of Europe* (Strasbourg, Council of Europe Publishing, 2004)
Varouxakis, Georgios. *Mill on Nationality* (London, Routledge, 2002)
Walters, F.P. *A History of the League of Nations, Vol. I* (London, OUP, 1952)
Weaver, Sally M. *Making Canadian Indian Policy, The Hidden Agenda, 1968–1970* (Toronto, University of Toronto Press, 1981)
Wells, H.G. *Playing at Peace* (London, National Council for the Prevention of War, 1927)
Wight, Martin. *System of States* (New Jersey, Leicester University Press, 1977)
World Peace Foundation. *League of Nations, Vol I. 1917–1918 Vol.II. 1919* (Boston, World Peace Foundation, 1919)
Wright, Richard. *Black Power* (London, Dobson Books, Ltd., 1954)
Young, Iris Marion. *Justice and the Politics of Difference* (Princeton, Princeton University Press, 1990)

Articles

Allen, Edward, "Out Treaty, Our Inherent Right to Self-Government: An Overview of the Nisga'a Final Agreement," International Journal on Minority and Group Rights 11 (2004): 233–249
Alfredsson, Gudmundur *et al.*, "Minority Rights: A Guide to United Nations Procedures and Institutions" (London, Minority Rights Group International, 1998)

American Bar Association, House of Delegates, Reports and Recommendations of the Section of International and Comparative Law on the Human Right Covenant and the Genocide Convention to the House of Delegates of the American Bar Association and Resolutions Adopted by the House of Delegates (House of Delegates, American Bar Association, 8 Sept., 1949)

Andrew Drzemczewski, "The Prevention of Human Rights Violations: Monitoring Mechanisms of the Council of Europe," Colloquy on The Prevention of Human Rights Violations, Panteion University, Athens Greece, 24–25 May 1999

Assefa, Getachew, "Protection of Minority rights in Federal systems: The Case of Ethiopia," (Ethiopia, Addis Ababa University, 2005)

Besant, Annie and Miller, Frederick, "Socialism vs. Individualism," Chair, S.G. Johnson, Esq., The Mechanics Hall, Nottingham, UK 25 October 1890.

Barker, P.J., "The Doctrine of Legal Equality of States," The British Yearbook of International Law (1924) : 1–20

Browne, Jude and Stears, Marc, "Capabilities, resources and systematic injustice: a case of gender inequality" Politics, Philosophy and Economics 4 (2005): 355–373

Buruma, Ian, "The Hague vs. Belgrade, The Hague might not be the ideal place to try Slobodan Milosevic, but it's a better option than Belgrade," The Guardian Unlimited 19 February 2002

Clements, Luke *et al.*, "Patrin, The Rights of Minorities: a Romany Perspective," OSCE Office for Democratic Institutions and Human Rights Bulletin 4(4) (1996).

Clements, Luke *et al.*, "The Traveller Law Reform Bill, A Brief Guide" (Cardiff, Cardiff Law School, The Traveller Law Research Unit, 2001) 1–22

Cohen, Marshall, "Groups and the Equal Protection Clause," Philosophy and Public Affairs 5 (2) (1976): 107–177

Committee on Foreign Relations, United States Senate, Ninety-seventh Congress, The Genocide Convention Hearings Before the Committee on Foreign Relations (Washington D.C., U.S. Government Printing Office, 1982)

Chenier, Nancy Miller, "Suicide Among Aboriginal People: Royal Commission Report," Library of Parliament (Ottawa, Library of Parliament, Research Branch, 23 Feb 1995) 1–6

Chretien, Jean, "Statement of the Government of Canada on Indian Policy" (Ottawa, Office of the Minister of Indian Affairs and Northern Development, 1969)

Crenshaw, Kimberle Williams, "Race, Reform, and Retrenchment: Transformation and Legitimation in Anti-Discrimination Law," Harvard Law Review 161 (5) (1988): 1331–87

Davis, John Lang-Don, "Fifth Column," (London, John Murray, 1939–1941)

Department of Multiculturalism and Citizenship, "Multiculturalism: What is it Really About?" (Ottawa, Ministry of Supply and Services Canada, 1991)

Eide, Asbjorn, "Final Text of the Commentary to the United Nations Declaration on the Rights of Persons Belonging to National or Ethnic, Religious and Linguistic Minorities" (Geneva, UN Centre for Human Rights, 2001)

Fawcett, James, "The International Protection of Minorities" (London, Minority Rights Group, n/d)

Fein, Helen, "Denying Genocide: From Armenia to Bosnia," A Lecture Delivered to the London School of Economics and Political Science, University of London, 22 Jan 2001.

Fraser, Nicholas, "Opinions of difference," Financial Times 17 April 2004

Freedman, Sandra, "Discrimination," eds. Peter Cane and Mark Tushnet, The Oxford Handbook of Legal Studies (2003): 202–225

Furi, Megan and Wherrett, Jill "Indian Status and Band Membership Issues" (Ottawa, Library of Parliament, Parliamentary Research Branch, 1996) 1–19

Gurr, Ted and Harff, Barbara, "Toward Empirical Theory of Genocides and Politicides: Identification and Measurement of Cases Since 1945" International Studies Quarterly 32(3) (Sept. 1988): 359–371

Hilling, Carol and Venne, Janique, "Proposal for an Agreement-In-Principle With the First Nations of Mamuitun and Nuitashkuan," (Ottawa, Library of Parliament, Parlimentary Research Branch, 2003)

Hogan, Miles, "The Nisga'a Final Agreement and International Norms," International Journal on Minority and Group Rights 11 (2004): 299–325

Hurley, Mary *et al.*, "Aboriginal Self-Government," (Ottawa, Parliamentary Research Branch, Library of Parliament, 27 Sept 1999)

Judt, Tony, "Israel: The Alternative," New York Review 25 Sept 2003

"Justice for Hawaiians," The New York Times, ed. International Herald Tribune, 7 June 2006, 08/06/2006 <http:www.iht.com/bin/print_ipub.php?file=/articles/2006/06/07/opinion/edhawaii.php>

Kaiser Commission on Medicaid and the Uninsured, "Uninsured in America, Key Facts (Washington D.C., The Henry J. Kaiser Family Foundation, March 2000)

King, Desmond and Waldren, Jeremy, "Citizenship, Social Citizenship and The Defence of Welfare Provision," B.J. POL.S 18: 415–443

Kondis, Basil, "The Greeks of Northern Epirus and Greek-Albanian Relations," Historical Review 1 (1897–1918), 2 (1919–1921): 7–57

Kunz, Josef. L, "The Present Status of the International Law for the Protection of Minorities," The American Journal of International Law 48 (2) (1954): 282–287

Leslie, John, *et al.* eds., "The Historical Development of the Indian Act" (Ottawa, Department of Indian Affairs and Northern Development, Treaties and Historical Research Centre, P.R.E. Group, Aug 1978)

Library of Parliament, "Canadian Multiculturalism" (Ottawa, Library of Parliament, 1994) 1–13

Magin, Janis, "Senate denies Hawaiians special status," International Herald Tribune 12 June 2006, 13/06/2006 <http:www.iht.com/bin/print_ipub?file=/articles/2006/06/11/news/Hawaii.php>

Makkonen, Timo, "Multiple, Compound and Intersectional Discrimination: Bringing the Experiences of the Most Marginalised to the Fore" (Turku, Institute for Human Rights, April 2002) 1–59

Martin Luther King, Jr., "Letter from a Birmingham Jail," 16 April 1963 letter to Bishop C.C.J. Carpenter, Bishop Joseph A. Durick, Rabbi Milton L. Grafman, Bishop Paul Hardin, Bishop Holan B. Harmon, the Reverend George M. Murray, the Reverent Edward V. Ramage and the Reverend Earl Stallings.

Martin Luther King, Jr., "A Realistic Look At the Question of Progress in the Area of Race Relations," Address at Freedom Rally, St. Louis Missouri, 10 April 1957

McGoldrick, Dominic. The Human Rights Committee, Its Role in the Development of the ICCPR(Oxford, Clarendon Press, 1991)

McHugh, James, "The Myth of the Sacred: The Charter, the Courts, and the Politics of the Constitution in Canada," American Review of Canadian Studies 3 (22 Sept 2003): 442(3)

McLean, Renwick, "Autonomy passes for Catalonia," International Herald Tribune, 31 March 2006, 08/06/2006<http://www.iht.com/articles/2006/03/30/news/spain.php

Niemi, Heli, "National Implementation of Findings by United Nations Human Rights Treaty Bodies, A Comparative Study" (Turku, Institute for Human Rights, Dec 2003)

Office of the High Commissioner on National Minorities, The Oslo Recommendations regarding the Linguistic Rights of National Minorities & Explanatory Note (The Hague, Office of the High Commissioner on National Minorities, 1998)

Orlin, Theodore S., "No Longer at the Whim of the Sovereign.", Conference on Human Rights in the Age of Globalisation, University of Dayton, Dayton, 19–21 Nov 2004

Peach, Ceri, "London and New York: Contrasts in British and American Models of Segregation," International Journal of Population Geography 5 (1999): 319–346

Petrova, Dimitrinia, "The Human Rights Situation of Roma in Europe," (Warsaw, OSCE Implementation Meeting on? Human Dimension Issues, 6 Nov 1998)

Pentassuglia, Gaetano, "Minorities Issues Handbook, Minorities in International Law" (Strasbourg, Council of Europe, n/d)

Pohl, Otto, "Eastern Europe's Roma borrow tools of U.S. black activists," International Herald Tribune 7 May 2006, 07/05/2006 www.iht.com/bin/print_ipub.php?file=/articles/2006/5/07/news/gypsy.php

Puxon, Grattan, "Roma: Europe's Gypsies, The Minority Group Report No. 14" (London, Minority Rights Group Ltd., 1987)

Report of the Nunavik Commission, "Amiqqaaluta, Let US Share, Mapping the Road Toward a Government for Nunavik," (Nunavik, Nunavik Commission Report, 2001)

Ringold, Dena *et al.*, "Roma in an Expanding Europe: Breaking the Poverty Cycle," Conference Edition of A World Bank Study (Washington D.C., The International Bank for Reconstruction and Development, 2003)

Sacerdoti, Giorgio, "New Developments In Group Consciousness and The International Protection of The Rights of Minorities" Israeli Yearbook on Human Rights 13 (1983): 116–144

Schabas, William, "Preventing Genocide and Mass Killing: The Challenge for the United Nations" (London, Minority Rights Group International, 2006)

Schabas, William, "The Genocide Convention at Fifty," spec. report of United States Institute of Peace 41 (7 Jan 1999)

Schabas, William, "The Rwandan Courts in Quest of Accountability, Genocide Trials and Gacaca Courts", Journal of International Criminal Justice 3 (2005) 879–895

Schwelb, Egon, "Civil and Political Rights: The International Measures of Implementation," American Journal of International Law 62(3) (1968): 828–868

Scott, Duncan Campbell, "The Administration of Indian Affairs in Canada" (Hangchow, The Canadian Institute of International Affairs, 1931)

"Serbia and Montenegro pave separate roads," Reuters, The Associated Press, ed. International Herald Tribune, 4 June 2006, 08/06/2006 <http:www.iht.com/articles/2006/06/04/news/balk.php>

Shapiro, Peter, "The Citizenship Dilemma," Standford Law Review 51 (1988): 597–639

Stears, Marc, "The Vocation of Political Theory, Principles, Empirical inquiry and the Politics of Opportunity," European Journal of Political Theory 4 (2005): 325–350

Taylor, Christine, "Building a Business Case of Valuing Ethnocultural Diversity," The Conference Board of Canada 143–95 (1991): 1–20

Urban Institute, "Millions Still Face Homelessness in a Booming Economy"(Washington D.C., The Urban Institute, 2005)

Westeen, Peter, "The Empty Idea of Equality," Harvard Law Review 95 (1981): 537–596

Wherrett, Jill, "Aboriginal Self-Government," (Ottawa, Library of Parliament, Parliamentary Research Branch, 17 June 1999) 1–16

Appendix

The Persecution Regime of the Roma Peoples by England, France, and Spain (1530–1900)

England's Persecution Regime (1530–1914)[1]

Authority	Legislative Decree	Punishment
22 Henry VIII, c.10 1530	An Acte concernynge outlandish People, callynge themselves Egyptians	Recital of the frauds of certain outlandish people called Egyptians. Such people shall be punished by imprisonment and loss of goods. Proclamation of departure of all Egytians. Goods shall be restored to the parties robbed, or forfeiture. to the party of double the value. One moiety of goods seized given to the seizor.
22 Henry VIII, c.12 1530–1	An Acte concnyng punysshement of Beggers and Vacabundle	Recital of the increase of beggars and vagabonds, and evils resulting thereform. An act for the punishment of vagrants, those practicing the "crafty sciences", and people feigning knowledge in palmistry. Punishments included the pillory, whipping, and having an ear cut off.
1 Edw VI, c.3 1547	An Acte for the punyshment of vacaboundes and relief of the Poore and Impotent	A statute against vagabondism, directed at wandering persons and those not seeking work. Punishments included enslavement, branding and chains.
3 & 4 Edw VI, c.16 1549–50	An Acte towching the punyshment of vacabonde and other Ydle persons.	A further Act against vagabonds, extended to include other idle persons.

[1] Mayall, David. *English Gypsies and State Policies* (Hertfordshire, University of Hertfordshire, 1995) 23–26

England's Persecution Regime (1530–1914)

Authority	Legislative Decree	Punishment
5 & 6 Edw VI, c.21 1551–2	An Acte against Tynkars and Pedlars	Forbade tinkers, pedlars and such like vagrants persons, "who are more hurtful than necessary", to travel from place to place to place without licence from the justices, under penalty of 14 days imprisonment.
1& 2 Philip & Mary, c.4 1554	An Act for the punishement of certayne Persons calling themselves Egyptians.	Gypsies forbidden to enter the country. Persons bringing them in were liable to a fine of 40s. Egyptians so brought in and remaining one month were declared felons. No trial per Medietatum Linguae. Present Gypsies remaining 20 days forfeited their goods. Such Egyptians not returning in 40 days were declared felons and liable to the death penalty. Proviso for Egyptians going into service.
5 Eliz., c. 20 1562	An Act for further Punishment of Vagabondes, calling themselves Egyptians.	Extended penalties of 22 Henry VIII, c.10 and 1& 2 Philip & Mary, c.4. Punishments permitted in 1554 legislation extended to persons found in the company of Egyptians. All persons found disguised in company of vagabond Egyptians for one month were declared felons without clergy. Proviso for infants under 14. Persons born in the realm were not compelled to quit.
14 Eliz, c.5 1572	An Acte for the punishment of vagabonds and for the relief of the Poor	Against vagabonds, rogues, sturdy beggars, pedlars and tynkers. The first appearance of 'rogues' in the statute books.
39 Eliz, c.4 1597–8	An Acte for punishment of Rogues Vagabonds and Sturdy Beggars	Declared as rogues and vagabonds "…all tynkers wandering abroade…and all such p'sons, not being Fellons, wandering and p'tendting themselves to be Egipcans or wandering in the habite Forme or Attyre of counterfayte Egipcians."

(*Continued*)

England's Persecution Regime (1530–1914) (*Cont.*)

Authority	Legislative Decree	Punishment
13 /geo II, c.24 1739–40	Vagrant Act	An Act against vagrancy which makes the distinction between idle and disorderly persons, rogues and vagabonds, and incorrigible rogues.
17 Geo II, c.15 1743	Justices Commitment Act	"…all persons pretending to be Gypsies, or wandering in the habit and form of Egyptians, or pertending to have skill in palmistry, or pretending to tell fortunes were to dealt with as rogues and vagabonds and punished accordingly."
23 Geo III, c.83 1783	Rogues and Vagabonds Act	Extended provisions dealing with rogues and vagabonds.
50 Geo III, c.41 1810	Hawkers and Peddlers Act	Necessitated the purchase of a license for hawkers and pedlars.
3 Geo IV, c.41 1822	Vagrancy Act	Simplified pervious laws relating to vagrants, rogues and vagabonds, & c., and consolidated them into one Act. Repealed former Acts But re-enacted most of their provisions.
3 Geo IV, c.126, s.121 1822	Turnpike Road Act	Any Gypsy encamping on the side of a turnpike road was liable to a fine of 40s.
5 Geo IV, c.83, 1824	Vagrancy Act	Penalties of 3 months imprisonment for any one pretending to tell fortunes by palmistry, or otherwise to deceive; any one wandering abroad and lodging under any tent or cart, not having any visible means of subsistence, and not giving a good account of himself.
5&6 Will IV, c.50, s.72, 76 1835	Highways Act	Penalties for Gypsies and others camping on the highway. Liable to a fine of 40s.
34 & 35 Vict, c.96 1871	Pedlars Act	Extension of 50 Geo III, c.41

England's Persecution Regime (1530–1914)

Authority	**Legislative Decree**	**Punishment**
38 & 40 Vict, c.56 1876	Commons Act	Empowered local authorities to make bye laws effectively closing Commons to Gypsies. (s.29).
44&45 Vict, c.45 1881	Pedlars Act	Extension of 34 & 35 Vict, c.96
48 & 49 Vict, c.72, 1885	Housing of the Working Classes Act	Applied provisions of 38 & 39 Vict, c.59 to nuisances in tents, vans, &c. District Councils empowered to make bye laws in this Respect (s.9).
51&52 Vict, c.33 1888	Hawkers Act	Extended pervious provisions re hawkers.
52&53 Vict, c.72 1889	Infectious Diseases (Notification) Act	Provisions of Act apply to moveable dwellings just as it applies to houses.
52&53 Vict, c.50, 1889	Local Government Act	Allowed County Councils to make bye laws for the prevention of vagrancy (s.57).
54 & 55 Vict, c.76, 1891	Public Health (London) Act	Sanitary regulations re vans, tents,&c (s.95).
56&57 Vict, c.73, 1894	Local Government Act	Parish councils empowered to regulate village greens and open spaces.
62 & 63 Vict, c.30, 1899	Commons (Inclosure) Act	District Council can apply to Board of Agriculture to make Bye laws for the regulation of Commons.
8 Edw VII, c.67, 1908	Children's Act	Enforced compulsory education. for children of travellers (s.118).

France's Persecution Regime 1504–1803[2]

Authority	Roma Prohibition	Punishment	Repeated Offence or non-compliance
1504 Louis XII	Residence	Banishment	
1510 Grand Council	Residence	Banishment	Hanging
1539 Frances I	Residence	Banishment	Corporal punishment
1561 Charles IX	Residence	Banishment	Men: gallays and corporal punishment. Men, women Men, women and children: head shaved
1606 Henry IV	Gathering (max. 3 or 4)	Punishment as 'vagabonds and evil-doers'	
1647 Louis XIV regency	Being a 'Bohemian'	Galleys	
1660 Louis XIV	Residence	Banishment	Galleys or corporal punishment
1666 Louis XIV	Being a 'Bohemian'	Men: galleys. Women and girls: flogging, branding and banishment	
1673 Louis XIV	Residence	Banishment	Galleys
1682 Louis XIV	Being a 'Bohemian'	Men: galleys for life. Women: head shaved. Children: sent to poor house	Women: branded and banished
1700–16 1720/21/22 Lorraine	Begging, vagabondage in general	Banishment	Iron collars, branding and banishment
1719 and other Years		Sentencing to the galleys is altered to deportation	

[2] Liegeoise, Jean-Pierre. *Gypsies An Illustrated History* (London, Al Saqi Books, 1986) 95–109.

France's Persecution Regime 1504–1803

Authority	Roma Prohibition	Punishment	Repeated Offence or non-compliance
1723 Lorraine	Residence, gathering in the Woods or main roads	Banishment: communities should gather, 'march in Formation and open fire on them'	
1724 Louis XV Vagabonds and vagrants	Residence, nomadism, gathering of more than 4 adults	Adult men: galleys (5 years). Others: flogging and poor house	
1764 Vagabonds and vagrants	Residence, nomadism	Adult men: galleys (3 years). Others: confinement in poor house (3 years), then choice of domicile and trade	Galleys (9 years) and, for further repetition, in perpetuity; confinement (9 years) or in perpetuity
Year II	Giving or seeking Alms	Fine to the value of two days' work, incarceration	
1802 Basque Country	Residence, being a 'Bohemian'	Deportation failure	
1803 Bonaparte		Children, women, aged: to the poor house Young men: navy, army. Adult men: forced labour	
19th Century Various local and regional measures	Residence, being a 'Bohemian'	Removal, banishment, prison	

Spain's Persecution Regime (1499–1783)

Year	Order	Punishment
1499	Find a trade and master, cease travelling together, within 60 days	100 lashes and banishment. For repeat offenders: amputation of ears, 60 days in chains, and banishment. Third time offenders to become slaves of those who captured them.
1525/28/34	Same order reiterated	Same punishment
1539	Same order, within three months. Travelling In groups of more than 3 forbidden.	6 years in the galleys.
1560 and others	Same. Travelling in groups of more than 2 forbidden. 'Dress and clothing' of Gitanos banned.	Up to 18 years in the galleys for those over 14. Later altered: for nomads, death; for Settled people, the galleys.
Early 17th Century	Identical measures by parliament or the king each year. Horse-dealing forbidden.	The populace may form armed groups to Pursue Gypsies.
1611	Gypsy occupations must be connected with working the land.	
1619	Banishment of all Gitanos from the kingdom within 6 months or settlement in a locality with over 1000 inhabitants. Dress, name, and language of the Gitanos banned.	
1633	Same. Public and Private meetings banned. Gitanos must merge with the rest of the population, undistinguished in any way. The name Gitano and Gypsy dress forbidden.	Men: 200 lashes and 6 years in the galleys. Women: banishment; 2 years exile, fine of 50,000 maravedis.
		A Gitano found outside the assigned locality becomes a slave to the apprehending person. If discovered with a firearm: 8 years in the galleys.

Spain's Persecution Regime (1499–1783)

Year	Order	Punishment
1695	Census of all Gypsies within 30 days; they must declare their trade, way of life, weapons, mounts, etc., then 30 more days to leave the kingdom or settle in a locality of over 200 inhabitants. Horse forbidden. Fairs and markets forbidden. Dress and language forbidden.	Men: 6–8 years in the galleys. Women: 100 lashes and banishment.
		Men aged 17 to 60: 6 years in the galleys. Men aged 14 to 17: imprisonment. Women: 100 lashes and banishment. Nobles: fine of 6000 ducats and half of legal expenses. Others: 10 years in the galleys.
1717	Same. Places of residence are set out: list of 41 localities	
1726	Same. Gypsies forbidden to appeal against sentences of courts.	
1731	Frequent surprise visits to Gypsies' houses to check compliance with all articles. Trade with Gypsies forbidden.	Fine of 200 ducats
1745	Settlement in assigned places within two weeks.	Execution: 'It is legal to fire upon them and take their Life.' Churches no longer asylums. Armed troops to comb the countryside.
1746	Reference to 1717/27/31/38 Settlement in 41 localities, and 35 new ones added. Families must be dispersed: 1 for each 100 inhabitants, and only 1 percent.	

(*Continued*)

Spain's Persecution Regime (1499–1783) (*Cont.*)

Year	Order	Punishment
1749	Great round-up and various decrees. Separation of 'bad and the good' through inquires and witnesses' reports.	For the 'bad': public works; escapees to be hanged. Motherless girls sent to the poor houses or into service for hones people. Older girls and wives of sentenced men with children under 7 to be 'educated in Christian doctrine and the holy fear of God' and sent to factories.
1783	Reiteration of previous orders: dress, way of life, and language forbidden, settlement compulsory, within 90 days. The name Gitano forbidden, to be removed from all documents. Restrictions on trade and place of residence lifted.	Branding. For repeat offenders: 'death, with no appeal'.

Index

Index of Cases

About the Author

William Kurt Barth was awarded his Doctorate of Philosophy in Politics from the University of Oxford, United Kingdom on 14 July 2007. He is an alumnus of St Antony's College, Oxford, where he also served as a Fellow of the University's Rothermere American Institute. Dr. Barth formerly worked in Washington DC and California as a career-service lawyer and manager for the US Department of Housing and Urban Development during the Administration of President Bill Clinton. He also holds a Master's Degree in Public Administration from Harvard University's John F. Kennedy School of Government, Cambridge, Massachusetts, a Juris Doctorate from Loyola University School of Law, Los Angeles, California and Bachelor of Arts Degree (Magna Cum Laude) in Political Science from the University of California at Los Angeles (UCLA). Dr. Barth is an active member in good standing of the State Bar of California.

www.ingramcontent.com/pod-product-compliance
Lightning Source LLC
LaVergne TN
LVHW080848300926
849162LV00003B/372

* 9 7 8 9 0 0 4 1 6 8 4 2 8 *